Contemporary Political Ideologies

ontemporary Political Ideologies

Movements and Regimes

Fourth Edition

Roy C. Macridis

Brandeis University

Scott, Foresman/Little, Brown Series in Political Science
SCOTT, FORESMAN AND COMPANY
Glenview, Illinois   Boston   London

LIBRARY OF CONGRESS
Library of Congress Cataloging-in-Publication Data

Macridis, Roy C.
  Contemporary political ideologies: movements and regimes/Roy C.
Macridis. — 4th ed.
      p.   cm.
  Includes bibliographies and index.
  ISBN 0-673-39839-0
  1. Political science — History.   2. Comparative government.
I. Title.
JA81.M316 1989
320.5'09 — dc19   88-11616
                                                                        CIP

1 2 3 4 5 6 7 8 9 10 — MVN — 94 93 92 91 90 89 88

Printed in the United States of America

CREDIT

Excerpt from "The Soldier," from *The Collected Poems of Rupert Brooke*. Copyright
1915, Dodd, Mead & Company. Copyright © renewed 1943, 1971 by Edward
Marsh. Used by permission of Dodd, Mead & Company.

This book is dedicated to the memory of my late son, Peter.

Preface

This fourth edition of the book that first came out in 1979 is an indication of the vitality of political ideologies and the interest they hold for students. Without ideology we are almost without a conscience, without law and order, without an anchor and a port. Without ideology we can have no vision of other worlds we want to sail to. Ideologies fashion our motivations, our attitudes, and the political regimes under which we live. They not only shape and consolidate values but they also command change and movement.

This new edition is in response to a number of suggestions and comments I have received over the last few years, and I am grateful to all those who took the trouble to write to me. I have expanded my references to the American scene, especially American conservatism, to include the religious right and the extreme right, and I have introduced some direct references to the American "capitalist" ideology. I have noted some of the changes in communist ideology—or at least the intimation of change—and some of the challenges communism as an ideology seems to be confronting, for they appear to be just as serious as those faced by liberal democracies. I have also added, in response to a number of solicitations from colleagues, a note on Christian Democracy and the renewed concerns of the Catholic Church with social and economic questions.

The most important addition, however, is a new chapter on feminism, which I include with great trepidation. I have raised questions that I hope will not offend anybody! Is it an ideology? Or is it a movement that may be interpreted as an extension of the universalistic ethic of liberalism?

The number of colleagues who read the whole or parts of the manuscript at various stages and various occasions continues to grow, as does my gratitude to each and all of them. They include, for the previous editions: Professor Fred von der Mahden of Rice University, Professor George J. Graham of Vanderbilt University, Professor Robert McHenry of Montgomery College, Professor John Gunnell of the State University of New York at Albany, and Professor Eric Nordlinger of Brown University. The manuscript for this fourth edition was read by: Professor Richard Kraus of Oregon University, Professor Merlin Gustafson of Kansas State University, Professor William Nelson of James Madison University, and Professor David Prindle of the University of Texas (Austin). Special thanks go to Professor David E. Schmitt of Northeastern University, who reviewed this manuscript, as well as all previous editions — his comments never missing the mark. Professor Kenneth C. Farmer of Marquette University and Professor Andrew Milnor of the State University of New York at Binghamton read the last draft of this edition and offered sound suggestions for some reorganization. Professor David O'Brien of the College of Holy Cross read the parts that deal with Christian Democracy and Liberation Theology, and Professor Barbara Lewis of Rutgers University gave a much appreciated nod to my chapter on Feminism. I thank each and all of them.

A number of colleagues wrote to me with comments and ideas as well as pointing out errors they had found. I am particularly thankful to Professor John George of Oklahoma State University, Professor Donald W. Brandon of the University of California at San Francisco, and Professor Frank C. Darling of Principia College.

As in the past, I was helped by some of my students: Elizabeth Windrove, a graduate student at Brandeis, did most of the spade work on my chapter on feminism, and Leagh Peake, also a graduate student, helped me with the section on liberation theology and Christian Democracy. Alan Minski, a graduating senior, did a good part of the research for my section on the religious right and the extreme right in the United States. I learned a great deal from all three of them. And again, as previously, my warmest thanks to Geraldyn Spaulding for typing the new manuscript in various versions — always in readable form.

Finally my thanks to my editor, John Covell, for all the help he gave me and to Billie Ingram of Scott, Foresman and Rose Sklare of Editorial Services of New England for supervising the copy editing and production of the book.

This book is dedicated to my late son, Peter, who turned out to have been the only "ideologue" in the family. He drowned in the Columbia River on March 11, 1978, while trying to realize a youthful dream with his friend, Tim Black — crossing the United States from West to East by canoe.

Roy C. Macridis
Waltham, Mass.

June 1, 1988

Contents

Contemporary Political Ideologies

One person with a belief is a social power
equal to ninety-nine who have only interests.

JOHN STUART MILL

1 | *Political Ideologies: Introduction*

Every . . . state is a species of association, and . . . all associations are instituted for the purpose of attaining some good. . . . We may therefore hold . . . that the particular association [the State] which . . . includes all the rest will pursue this aim most. . . .
                                        ARISTOTLE   Politics

. . . Aspirations, passion, hope, volition and choice . . . belong inalienably to the life of mind and the spirit. Without them . . . we languish, we perish. We must not allow ourselves to be paralyzed by thought; rather we must use it. We dare not forever stand and wait. It is late and there is a world at stake.
                                HENRY AIKEN   Ideology— A Debate

Whether we know it or not, all of us have an ideology, even those who claim openly that they do not. We all believe in certain things. We all value something—property, friends, the law, freedom, or authority. We all have prejudices, even those who claim to be free of them. We all look at the world in one way or another—we have "ideas" about it—and we try to make sense out of what is going on in it. Also, we are attracted to those with similar values and ideas, who like the same things we do, who have prejudices similar to ours, and who, in general, view the world in the same way we do. We talk of "like-minded" people, individuals who share certain beliefs and we tend to congregate with them—in clubs, churches, political parties and movements, various associations, and so on. Moreover, no matter how independent we claim to be, we all are influenced by ideas. We are sensitive to appeals made to us—to our honor, patriotism, family, religion, pocketbook, race, or class—and we can all be manipulated and aroused. We are creators and creatures of ideas—of ideologies—and through them we manipulate others or are ourselves manipulated.

1

Ideologies are very much a part of our lives; they are not dead and they are not on the decline anywhere, as some authors have argued.

Ah, but a man's reach should exceed his grasp,
Or what's a Heaven for?

wrote Browning in 1885. Almost a century later, a strong upsurge in ideological and utopian movements made powerful governments totter as many sought their own vision of heaven on earth. "Be rational; think of the impossible" was one of the slogans of intellectuals and students in the late 1960s.

Not only are ideologies surviving, their all-embracing importance is again being recognized. "Neo-Marxists" now agree that a drastic revolutionary overhaul of the society, if there is to be one, must be above all a moral and intellectual revolution: a revolution in the *ideology* of society. It must create its own "counterconsciousness," its own "counterculture"—a new set of beliefs and values and a new style of life that will eat, like a worm, into the core of prevailing liberal-capitalist orthodoxy. Only with its ideological core gone can the old society be changed and replaced. The socialization of the means of production, economic planning, communism, and the abolition of income inequalities—none of these can have a chance of success until and unless the ideas that people have about society and about their relations with each other change.

What Is an Ideology?

Ideology has been defined as "a set of closely related beliefs, or ideas, or even attitudes, characteristic of a group or community."[1] Similarly a *political* ideology is "a set of ideas and beliefs" that people hold about their political regime and its institutions and about their own position and role in it. Political ideology accordingly appears synonymous with "political culture" or "political tradition." The British or the Americans or the French or the Russians pattern their political life on the basis of different sets of interrelated ideas, beliefs, and attitudes.

Various groups, however, within one and the same political community may, and often do, at given times and under given conditions, challenge the prevailing ideology. Interests, classes, and various political and religious associations may develop a "counterideology" that questions the status quo and attempts to modify it. They advocate change rather than order; they criticize or reject the political regime and the existing social and economic arrangements; they advance schemes for the restructuring and reordering of the society; and they spawn political movements in order to gain enough power so as to bring about the changes they advocate. In this sense, a political ideology moves people into action. It motivates them to demand changes in their way of life and to modify the existing political,

1. Plamenatz, *Ideology*, p. 15.

social, and economic relations. In discussing ideologies—all ideologies—
we must always bear in mind these two all-important characteristics: a
given political ideology rationalizes the status quo, whereas other, competing ideologies and movements challenge it.

Philosophy, Theory, and Ideology

A distinction should be made between philosophy or theory on the one
hand, and ideology on the other. "Philosophy" means literally love of
wisdom—the detached and often solitary contemplation and search for
truth. In the strictest meaning of the term, "theory" is the formulation of
propositions that causally link variables to account for or explain a phenomenon, and such linkages should be empirically verifiable, as they are in
the natural sciences. However, in the social sciences it is very difficult to
come up with empirical verifications. What separates theory or philosophy
from ideology is that while the first two involve contemplation, organization of ideas, and whenever possible, demonstration, ideology shapes beliefs that incite people into action. Men and women organize to *impose*
certain philosophies or theories and to realize them in a given society.
Ideology thus involves action and collective effort. Even when they origi-
nate (as they often do) in philosophy or theory, ideologies are inevitably
highly simplified, and even distorted, versions of the original doctrines. It
is always interesting to know the philosophy or the theory from which an
ideology originates. But it is just as important to understand ideology as a
distinct and separate entity to be studied in terms of its own logic and
dynamics rather than in terms of the theory from which it stems or of how
closely it resembles that theory.

It is difficult to understand when and under what circumstances a
theory or a philosophy becomes transformed into an ideology—that is,
into an action-oriented movement. Important theories and philosophic
doctrines remain unnoticed and untouched for generations before they
are "discovered." History may be compared to a freezer where ideas and
theories are stored for use at a later time. Different works of Plato, for
example, have been at various times the origin of different ideological
movements. Similarly, whereas a powerful ideological movement developed from the major works of Karl Marx, it is his early works today—the
"early Marx" or the "young Marx"—that have been adapted to suit some
contemporary movements and tastes. There is a dialectic between ideas, as
such, and social needs, but both are needed in order to have an ideology.
Heartfelt demands arising from the social body may fail for the lack of
ideas; and ideas may go begging for a long time for the lack of relevance to
social needs.

Philosophy and Political Ideology: Major Themes

The debt most political ideologies owe to political speculation and philosophy is quite obvious when we look at some of the major themes that political ideologies address: (1) the role and the nature of the individual (human nature); (2) the nature of truth and how it can be discovered; (3) the relationship between the individual and the group, be it the tribe, the small city-state, or the contemporary state as we know it; (4) the characteristics of political authority — its source and its limits, if any; (5) the goals and the mechanics of economic organization; and (6) the much-debated issue of material and economic equality as it relates to individual freedom. Normative judgments about each of the themes mentioned above and many more are the very "stuff" of contemporary political ideologies. Some have been hotly debated over many centuries and will continue to be debated.

The Individual

Political ideologies are addressed to each one of us; they all begin with one preconception or another about us — about human nature. Some believe that we are the creatures of history and the environment, that our nature and characteristics are interwoven with the material conditions of life and ultimately shaped by them. Human nature is plastic and everchanging and with the proper "social engineering" — another word for education — it can be shaped into a pattern. Many ideologies assume that with the proper changes in our environment and the proper inculcation of new values, "new" men and women can be created. There is nothing sacrosanct, therefore, in our present institutions and values; on the contrary, many of them are downright bad. On the other hand, many well-known philosophers, especially those in the period of the Enlightenment and in the nineteenth century, have presented a different notion of human nature. People have some innate characteristics: we are born with traits of sociability, goodness, and rationality. We are also endowed with rights, such as life, liberty, and property. Institutions are but a reflection of these human traits and rights, and a political organization must respect them; indeed, it must provide the best means for protecting them. Therefore, the State that protects these rights cannot invade them — the State is limited. Finally, other political philosophers have argued that human nature is "greedy," "selfish," and "bellicose" and that it is the duty of the State to curb our ignoble drives. Political power and coercion are what make social life possible and safe.

The Nature of Truth

Is there one truth that can be imposed? Or is truth progressively discovered as many ideas and points of view compete with each other — every generation adding something to it? The notion that there is one truth revealed only to some or perceived authoritatively by them requires us to

Plato (c. 427–347 B.C.)

Plato was a Greek philosopher, a disciple of Socrates, and the
founder of philosophic idealism, according to which ideas
exist in themselves and by themselves, forming a perfect and
harmonious universe. As a political philosopher, Plato wrote
The Republic, an ideal state with a strict class structure ruled by
philosopher-kings who divested themselves of property and
family ties in order to rule for the common good. Plato's description of a more practical state can be found in his *Laws*.

submit to it. We must hew as closely as possible to what is given, and obey those who speak for it. Human beings are thus deprived of the freedom to seek truth, to experiment with new ideas, to confront each other with different points of view, and to live in a system that tolerates different ways.

On the other hand, there are those for whom a constant exploration of the universe by human beings and a constant inquiry into the foundations and conditions of life is the only way to discover truth. "Such is the nature of the understanding that it cannot be compelled to the belief of anything by outside force," wrote John Locke. People who hold this view favor competition of ideas, advocate tolerance for all points of view, and want to assure the conditions of freedom that are indispensable for ongoing inquiry. This is what we call pluralism. If one Absolute Truth did exist, pluralists would be the last to impose it for fear that it would deprive human beings of the challenge of discovering it!

The Individual and Society

For some social scientists there is no such entity as an "individual." The individuals are perceived as part of a herd or a group whose protection and survival require cooperation. The individual is considered helpless outside the group or the State. The group or the State then makes the rules of conduct and establishes the relationship between rulers and ruled. The individual is a "social being" — first and last!

The other point of view stresses the opposite — the primacy of individuals. They are perceived as having originally lived in the state of nature and endowed with reason and natural rights. To protect themselves and their belongings, these individuals contrive to create a political society that protects their lives and their property. The political system — the State — is made up of individuals, by the individuals, and for the individuals. It is the result of a contract — freely entered upon.

As with theories about human nature, our view of the relationship between the individual and the society often determines our political ideology. Those who give primacy to the group show an inclination to emphasize the "organic" nature of society and the political system: it is a whole, like our body, and the individuals are like the cells of our organism. They are only parts that fit into the whole; they have no freedoms and rights. The "organic" theory puts the accent on the whole and the close interdependence of the parts that is required to make it function. This theory does not make room for *change*, since any change unbalances the existing relationships among the parts and hence endangers the whole — the society. It is also totalitarian in the name of society's overriding purpose to which all parts and individuals remain subservient.

Those who assume the primacy of the individual reach diametrically opposite conclusions. *The individual is all that counts.* Individuals make the political society in which they live, and they can change it. Political life is an act of will and political authority is based on consent. The society consists of a maze of overlapping, cooperating, or conflicting wills and units—both individuals and groups—participating in the political system.

Political Authority

Basic divisions on the nature and organization of political authority derive from theories discussed above about the nature of truth and about the relationship between the individual and the group. Belief in one overriding truth leads almost always to an authoritarian position. It is *elitist*. It assumes that a small group "knows" and is capable of governing on the basis of certain qualities. For Plato these qualities were *intellectual:* the philosopher-king; for some they are *prescriptive:* based on inheritance. The qualities deemed necessary for governing could also be *charismatic:* appeal and personality, or *class*—either the property owners or the working class—having a historical mission of ruling or transforming the society.

On the other hand, those who postulate that political authority derives from the will of individuals favor limiting political authority in order to allow for participation and open deliberation. They advocate freedom of thought and expression, respect for individual freedoms, and freedom from associations, political parties, and all other organizations. *No claims to rule based on birth, heredity, wealth, intellectual superiority, or prescriptive titles are accepted.* No "monopoly of truth" is conceded—to anybody.

Equality and Property

Many of the most important political ideologies can be distinguished in terms of the answers they try to provide to the following questions: *Who produces and what is produced? Who gets what and how much?* The answers are very complex and all the more so since the very concepts and questions, let alone the answers, are laden with emotions and values; they are steeped in ideology.

The central issue remains that of equality. For the early liberals, equality was interpreted narrowly to mean equality before the law, or equality of all to vote and participate in the choice of political leaders. Yet, unless people have equal access to education and material living standards (even if minimal), equality before the law is a fiction. Throughout the twentieth century, as we shall see, those who advocated political or legal equality above all clashed with the proponents of material equality. There is a constant tension between material and economic equality on the one hand and formal legal and political equality on the other.

Liberal democracies have emphasized freedoms and property rights—even when they have been forced to qualify them for the sake of greater material equality. Socialism and communism on the other hand have tended to stress material equality. But throughout the twentieth century virtually all political regimes and all political ideologies have come to terms with the need for providing greater material opportunities and equality. As a result, there has been a corresponding change in our concepts of property and of property relations.

Property is no longer defined only in terms of land or the real estate one owns or even in terms of liquid wealth and high salaries, although these assets are still important. For most people in most societies, "property" has now become "public" in the sense that it consists of claims against the State that individuals have for services and benefits to which they are entitled. Education, health, housing, transportation, old age pensions, unemployment benefits, and special assistance programs have become rights—"entitlements"—and they are just as important as property rights. Whatever the justification or the adequacy of such entitlements, they have significantly changed the distribution of material benefits and the nature of property in most all societies. For many people, such services and benefits have provided a cushion just as important as ownership, and they ensure at least some degree of material equality.

Notions about human nature, truth, political authority, freedom, property and equality, and the production and the distribution of goods and services are present in each and every ideology we shall study. They are the major building blocks of all contemporary ideologies and movements. Men and women organize behind their respective visions of a just and better world or barricade themselves to defend their own visions of justice—in their own world. Political philosophy gives us all a chance to contemplate these notions in a detached and objective way; political ideologies and movements often transform them into a battle cry.

The Uses of Political Ideology

An ideology, then, is a set of ideas and beliefs held by a number of people. It spells out what is valued and what is not, what must be maintained and what must be changed, and it shapes accordingly the attitudes of those who share it. In contrast to philosophy and theory, which are concerned with knowledge and understanding, ideologies relate to social and political behavior and action. They incite people to political action and provide the basic framework for political action.

Legitimization

As pointed out earlier, one of the most important functions of a political ideology is to give value to a political regime and its institutions. It shapes the "operative ideas" that make a political regime work. It provides the basic categories by which the people know the political regime, abide by the rules, and participate in it. To perform this all-important role, a political ideology must have a *coherent set of rules* and it must set them forth as clearly as possible. Although a constitution is a political document that embodies these rules, it cannot function well unless it is valued by the people. A political ideology shapes these values and beliefs about the constitution and lets the people know their role and position within their own political regime.

Solidarity and Mobilization

A common sharing of ideas integrates individuals into the community, a group, a party, or a movement. Commonly held ideas define the things that are acceptable and the tasks to be accomplished, excluding all others. Ideologies play the same role that totems and taboos play in primitive tribes, defining what is common to the members and what is alien. The Soviet Communist ideology, for instance, unifies those who adhere to it by branding the outside world of capitalism as the enemy. All ideologies perform this function of unifying, integrating, and giving a sense of identity to those who share it, but they do so with varying degrees of success. Nationalism as an ideology, for instance, has provided the unifying and integrating force that has made it possible for nation-states to emerge and retain their positions. The greater the integration sought and the stronger the solidarity to be maintained, the greater the emphasis on unifying symbolisms.

Leadership and Manipulation

Although ideologies incite people to action, what kind of action and for what purpose, depends very much on the content and substance of an ideology. Manipulation of ideas, a special case, often involves the conscious and deliberate formulation of propositions that incite people to action for ends that are clearly perceived only by those in power or attempting to get political power. They may promise peace in order to make war, freedom in order to establish an authoritarian system, socialism in order to consolidate the position and privileges of the property holders, and so on.

Ideology can often be used as a powerful instrument of manipulation. Usually in times of social distress and anxiety, or when society seems divided into warring groups and frustration warps daily life, simple propositions and promises on how to remove the evils besetting society fall upon receptive ears and minds. The demagogue, the leader, the self-professed savior is lurking somewhere in all societies in such times to spread his or her message and to manipulate those who seem to have nowhere else to turn.

Communication

A coherent set of ideas — an ideology — shared by a given number of people makes communication among them much easier. It provides a *common, highly simplified special language,* like shorthand. Words have special meaning — "the Reds," "the bleeding-heart liberals," "the pigs," "the Establishment," "fat cats," "the power elite," "the chosen people," or "communist conspiracy." These are terms easily understood by those who belong to a given group, and they help others to place them within a given ideological family. They are, of course, very crude terms, and ideologies usually provide more sophisticated ones. "The last stage of capitalism," "neocolonialism," "avant-garde of the working class," "democratic centralism," "democratic pluralism," "human rights," and "gradual change" are commonly understood by those who use them in their own respective political group or party. These terms can help the outsider to identify the ideological family to which the speaker belongs. A common ideology simplifies communication and makes common effort easier for all those who accept it.

Communication is also made easier because people with a common ideology look upon the outside world with the same preconceptions. They all have the same binoculars! People receive messages from the world outside and have to put these messages into some kind of order—into concepts. These concepts, in terms of which messages for the outside world are sorted out, depend on ideology. For some, the condition of the poor calls for study and concern; for others, it is a bore—the situation of the poor is attributed to innate laziness. This, however, is an extreme case. More frequent are cases of interpretation or evaluation, where the same event is seen from a different viewpoint—a different ideological perspective. The assassination of a political leader is applauded by some and regretted by others. Any Soviet move anywhere in the world is an indication of the Communist expansionist conspiracy for some; for others, it is an inevitable reaction to American provocation! People may also reject messages because of their ideology. A mystic is blind to the world outside; for a scientist, the world is a constant source of wonder to be studied and explained.

Expression

Ideology provides a vehicle to express our wants, our interests, and our hopes, and even our personal drives and anxieties. Some have argued that the primary function of an ideology is to rationalize and protect material interests or to provide for a powerful medium for their fulfillment. Thus, liberal democracy has been viewed as the rationalization of the interests of the rich and the relatively well-to-do, while revolutionary Marxism is an instrument for the satisfaction of the demands of the propertyless, the workers, and the poor.

But it is not only interest that spawns an ideology. Emotional drives and personality traits are expressed through different ideologies. It has been argued, for instance, that there is a distinct "authoritarian personality" which finds expression and fulfillment through being subject to rank and authority. In this manner, any ideology can provide a form of expression, and usually brings like-minded people together. The Anti-Vivisection League, environmentalists, anti- and proabortionists, proponents or opponents of the Equal Rights Amendment, as well as Democrats, Communists, and Fascists, all may give vent to their personality, interests, and emotions through their particular ideology.

Ideology, then, provides for *emotional fulfillment.* People are proud of their ideas and proud of each other and all those who share them. They belong to the group that espouses them just as people belong to their families. They relate to it, and help each other in a common search of realization. A person who has an ideology that is shared within a group of people is likely to be happy and secure: basking in the togetherness of the common endeavor. Identifying with it, he or she is never alone.

Criticism and Utopia

Ideologies often embody *social criticism.* Criticism confronts existing beliefs and attempts through argument and persuasion to challenge and change them. Critical examination of social and political beliefs has also played an important role in the development of new ideologies and the rejection of others. Many beliefs have yielded to it, to be replaced by others. Institutions like slavery, property, hereditary monarchy, bureaucratic centralization, and many others have been critically challenged and accordingly abandoned or qualified.

In certain instances, criticism may be pushed to extremes. Certain ideologies are like a *dream,* an impossible and unrealizable quest. An "ideological" person is one who criticizes and rejects the existing order of things while dreaming of other and better worlds: world government, perfect equality, abundance for all, elimination of force, and abolition of war. Many political ideologies have something of this quality, but those that have it in an exaggerated form are called *utopias,* a word derived from the Greek for "nowhere." If we give this particular meaning to the term, we are implying that an "ideologue" is either naive or dangerous or a little bit crazy, ignoring Shakespeare's pithy remark that dreams are the stuff that life is made of!

Ideology and Political Action

Above all, ideology *moves* people into concerted action. Sometimes it moves a whole nation; sometimes it is a group, a class or a political party that unites behind certain principles to express their interests, demands, and beliefs. In France, socialism is still for many the vindication of a longstanding quest for equality — material equality. In the United States, on the other hand, it is political and economic liberalism — the freedom to produce, consume, think, and worship — that seem to be the major rallying point for many political movements. An example of a single-issue organization motivated by ideology to take political action is the "environmentalists," who, both in the United States and elsewhere, seek to put an end to the despoliation of our physical environment; they share many of the same objectives with the various "No Nuke" organizations. Other powerful single groups want to reintroduce religious teaching and prayers in the schools, while still others mount a fierce campaign against abortion. "Welfare liberals" continue to reconcile freedoms with state intervention and welfare legislation to mitigate the harshness of economic competition. Communism—whether adopted by a nation, a movement, or a party that challenges the existing political order—is an ideology that projects a vision of abundance, equality, and peace. Most of the Communist movements view the Soviet Union as the legitimate advocate of a new social order that will replace the existing one.

The dynamics of politics, therefore, lie in the ideas people develop. But the same is true with political institutions, movements, social groups, and political parties. We have to focus on the ideologies they represent, and the beliefs they propagate and legitimize. The same is true for political attitudes. They, too, are fashioned by political ideologies. It is in terms of different constellations of attitudes that major political movements and ideologies can be identified and described. Liberals share common attitudes with regard to race relations, economic policy, prayers in the school, the United Nations, taxes, the draft, nuclear weapons, food stamps, social security, and so on. Conservatives can be identified in terms of a set of different attitudes with regard to some of the same issues; so can Socialists or Communists.

In studying political ideologies, we are studying the dynamics of political systems—the type of political regime, its constitution and institutions—the degree to which the regime is accepted, the existing conflicts within the regime, and the manner in which conflicts can be resolved. Compatibility of ideological outlooks makes for stability and acceptance; incompatibility always presages conflict, instabilities, and possibly revolutions.

Types of Political Ideologies

Political ideologies address themselves to values: the quality of life, the distribution of goods and services, freedom and equality. If there were agreement on each and all there would be one single ideology shared by all. But there is no agreement within any society nor, needless to say, among the various political societies of the world. People hold different views; nations project different values and beliefs.

It is precisely here that we see the role of political ideologies: they mobilize men and women into action in favor of one point of view or another, and in favor of one movement or party or another. Their aim is invariably either the preservation of a given point of view or the overhaul of the existing state of things, including the political system itself. The British squire who defended his privilege and his property; the workers who formed trade unions or parties to defend their interests; the American conservatives—all have had a common set of ideas that united them into a common posture. The same is true for the small terrorist bands who seize planes. They want to destroy what they despise most — the complacency of an orderly society interested in material satisfaction.

We can divide political ideologies into three broad categories.

1. Those that defend and rationalize the existing economic, social, and political order at any given time in any given society, which we call *status quo* ideologies.
2. Ideologies that advocate far-reaching changes in the existing social, economic, and political order, which we call *radical* or *revolutionary* ideologies.
3. In between there is, of course, a large gray area favoring gradual changes. We may call these the *reformist* ideologies.

One way to state the difference between *status quo, reformist,* and *revolutionary* ideologies is to think of maps and mapmaking. Someone who diligently learns to read a map and to travel by following given routes and signals may be considered to represent a status quo mentality or ideology: he or she simply follows the rules and the signs and is guided by them. On the other hand, a person who attempts to trace his or her own route and to change the signals, but not the destination, is a reformist. There is an agreement that the means must change, not the end. *But a revolutionary changes both the map and the destination.*

This classification is merely a formal one because ideologies shift and change not only in content but also in the particular functions and roles they perform. A revolutionary ideology, for instance, may become transformed into one of status quo when it succeeds in imposing its own values and beliefs. Similarly, the same ideology may be a status quo ideology, protecting the existing order of things in a given place at a given time, and a revolutionary one in a different place or at a different time. Communism in the Soviet Union is a status quo political ideology, while in other countries communism is considered to be a revolutionary one. While workers in the nineteenth century were rising in the name of socialism against western European liberalism which had become a status quo ideology, liberalism was very much a revolutionary ideology in the eyes of many in central Europe and in Russia.

Status quo, reformist, and revolutionary ideologies can also be distinguished by the tactics they use to realize their goals. They relate to persuasion, organization, and force. Few, if any, ideologies rely exclusively on one to the exclusion of the others. Most use, in different proportions, all three. The more fundamental and comprehensive the goals are and the more an ideology and a political movement challenge the status quo, the greater the chances that it will resort to organized force, without, of course, neglecting organization and persuasion. A political ideology, on the other hand, that has limited and incremental goals, as is the case with reformist ideologies, is more likely to resort to political organization and persuasion, but without excluding the use of force.

In general, political ideologies and movements that challenge the status quo are more likely to use force at the time when they confront it.

This was the case with liberalism before it overthrew the aristocratic and monarchical regimes in the eighteenth century and after, and with the Communist and other revolutionary movements first in Russia and later in other countries. Yet, when such political ideologies succeed — when they have been transformed into political regimes and have implemented their major goals and consolidated their position — persuasion and organization are likely to take the place of force.

There is one qualification to these generalizations. According to some analysts there are some political ideologies for which force is a necessary and permanent characteristic. And there are others for which persuasion and political organization, rather than force, is an inherent characteristic. Some authoritarian systems — and communist regimes are included — institutionalize the use of force in order to bring about and maintain compliance. On the other hand, liberal and democratic regimes, committed to political competition and pluralism, eschew the use of force. If it is to be used, it is only as a last resort.

The Major Political Ideologies: Criteria of Choice

If we look at the spread of contemporary political ideological movements, we have a rich choice of subjects: liberalism, capitalism, democratic socialism, socialism, communism, national communism, consociationalism, corporatism, Eurocommunism, anarchism, Gaullism, Stalinism and post-Stalinism, communalism, self-determination in industry, Titoism, Maoism, welfarism, to say nothing of variations that come from the Third World under various labels. Which ones shall we discuss, and why? We obviously need some criteria to help, and I suggest four: *coherence, pervasiveness, extensiveness,* and *intensiveness.*

Coherence   By coherence I have in mind the overall scope of an ideology, along with its internal logic and structure. Is it complete? Does it spell clearly a set of goals and the means to bring them about? Do its various propositions about social, economic, and political life hang together? Is there an organization — a movement or a party — to promote the means of action envisaged? Are the goals varied and many, or is there a single overriding goal?

Pervasiveness   Pervasiveness refers to the length of time that an ideology has been "operative." Some ideologies may show decline over a period of time, only to reappear. Others have been operative over a long period, despite variations and qualifications. Whatever the case, the basic test is the length of time during which an ideology has been shared by people, affected their lives, and shaped their attitudes and actions.

Extensiveness   This refers simply to a crude numerical test. How many people share a given ideology? One can draw a crude "ideological map" showing the number of people sharing common political ideologies. The larger the "population space" of a given ideology, the greater its extensiveness. How many people are influenced today by communism? By liberalism? By socialism? By anarchism? An estimate of numbers will answer the question of extensiveness.

Intensiveness   Finally, by intensiveness I mean the degree and the intensity of the appeal of an ideology — irrespective of whether it satisfies any of the other three criteria. Does it evoke a spirit of total loyalty and action? "Interest is sluggish," wrote John Stuart Mill. Ideas are not! They are like weapons that in the hands of even a small minority may have a far greater impact on society than widely shared interests. Intensiveness implies emotional commitment, total loyalty, and unequivocal determination to act even at the risk of one's life. It was this kind of intensiveness that Lenin managed to impart to his Bolsheviks, to the Communist party.

Ideally, we should choose among various ideologies only those that satisfy *all* the criteria set forth here — coherence, pervasiveness, extensiveness, and intensiveness. However, this would fail to do justice to some ideologies that have played or are playing an important role in political life, even though they may satisfy only one or two of these criteria, and I intend to take some such movements into account.

For each ideology to be discussed, I shall begin by examining the basic theoretical formulations to which it owes a major debt, and describe its transformation into a political movement and, in some cases, into a political regime. We should never lose sight of the fact that we are dealing with ideas that become political movements and lead people to political action; that their "influence" can be assessed in terms of the strength of the movements and parties through which ideas become readied and armed for a struggle for supremacy. Ideologies are not disembodied entities; they are not abstractions. They exist because men and women share them and adopt them as part of their own lives. Ideologies are weapons when men and women make them so; but they are also havens that produce companionship, cooperation, and fulfillment.

Value Judgment   One last remark is in order. If there are so many ideologies and if all of us share different ideologies to help us "know" the outside world and prompt us to act in one way or another, which one of them is "correct"? If all ideologies provide us with different views and perceptions of the world, how do we know what the world is really like? How can we describe the landscape if we use different binoculars? This is the nagging question throughout the book — the question of the validity of a given ideology. When it comes to political ideologies there is really no authoritative test to produce definitive proof of validity. We can only present the various political ideologies in terms of their internal logic, their coherence, and their relevance to the outside world.

This book does not ask, therefore, which ideologies are "true" and which are "false," even if it criticizes and passes judgment on them. Rather, our approach will be expository: Where does an ideology come from? What does it posit? What does it purport to achieve? What have been its accomplishments or failures?

	Major Political Ideologies			
	COHERENCE	PERVASIVENESS	EXTENSIVENESS	INTENSIVENESS
Democratic Liberalism }	Strong	Long	Wide	Mediocre
Democratic Socialism }	Weak	Long	Wide	Weak
Utopian Socialism }	Weak	Sporadic	Limited	High
Communism	Strong	Long	Wide	High
Conservatism	Weak	Long	Wide	Weak
Facism/ Nazism }	Weak	Sporadic	Uncertain	High
Nationalism	Weak	Long	Wide	High
Anarchism	Weak	Sporadic	Limited	High

Bibliography

Abercrombie, N. et al. *The Dominant Ideology Thesis*. London: Allen and Unwin, 1980.

Apter, David (ed.). *Ideology and Its Discontents*. Englewood Cliffs, N.J.: Prentice-Hall, 1964.

Aristotle. *Politics*. Translated by Ernest Barker. New York: Oxford U.P., 1962.

Aron, Raymond. *The Opium of the Intellectuals*. New York: Norton, 1962.

Bell, Daniel. *The End of Ideology*. Rev. ed. New York: Free Press, 1965.

———. *The End of Ideology—On the Exhaustion of Political Ideas in the Fifties*. New York: Free Press of Glencoe, 1960.

Bluhm, William T. *Ideologies and Attitudes: Modern Political Culture*. Englewood Cliffs, N.J.: Prentice-Hall, 1974.

Bracher, Karl D. *The Age of Ideologies: A History of Political Thought in the Twentieth Century*. London: Weidenfeld and Nicolson, 1982.

Brown, L. B. *Ideology*. New York: Penguin, 1973.

Cox, Richard H. *Ideology, Politics and Political Theory*. Belmont, Calif.: Wadsworth, 1968.

Feuer, L. *Ideology and the Ideologists*. Oxford: Blackwell, 1975.

Grimes, Alan and Horowitz, Robert (eds.). *Modern Political Ideologies*. New York: Oxford U.P., 1959.

Habermas, J. *Legitimation Crisis*. London: Heinemann, 1976.

Hartz, Louis. *The Liberal Tradition in America*. New York: Harcourt, Brace, 1955.

Jenkins, Thomas. *The Study of Political Theory*. New York: Random House, 1955.

Kramnick, I. and Watkins, Frederick. *The Age of Ideology—Political Thought 1950 to the Present.* Englewood Cliffs, N.J.: Prentice-Hall, 1964.

Lerner, Max. *Ideas Are Weapons: The History and Uses of Ideas.* New York: Viking, 1939.

Lichtheim, George. *The Concept of Ideology and Other Essays.* New York: Random House, 1967.

Mannheim, Karl. *Ideology and Utopia.* New York: Harcourt Brace and World, 1955.

McLellan, D. *Marxism after Marx.* London: Macmillan, 1980.

———. *Ideology.* Minneapolis: University of Minnesota Press, 1986.

Minogue, K. *Alien Powers: The Pure Theory of Ideology.* London: Weidenfeld and Nicolson, 1985.

Oakeshott, Michael. *The Social and Political Doctrines of Contemporary Europe.* New York: Cambridge U.P., 1942.

Plamenatz, John. *Ideology.* New York: Praeger, 1970.

Rude, George. *Ideology and Popular Protest.* London: Lawrence and Wishart, 1980.

Shklar, Judith N. *Political Theory and Ideology.* New York: Macmillan, 1966.

Thompson, J. *Studies in the Theory of Ideology.* Cambridge: Polity Press, 1984.

Watkins, Frederick. *The Age of Ideology: Political Thought from 1750 to the Present.* Englewood Cliffs, N.J.: Prentice-Hall, 1964.

Wolin, Sheldon. *Politics and Vision.* Boston: Little, Brown, 1960.

Part One

Democracy: Many Roots and Families

Our constitution is called a democracy because power is in the hands not of the few but of the many.

THUCYDIDES   Funeral Oration of Pericles

Democracy literally means "the government of the people." It comes from the Greek word *demos*, people, and *kratos*, government or power. The concept developed first in the small Greek city-states, and the Athenian democracy (roughly between 450 B.C. and 350 B.C.) is what we always go back to as the principal early example. Pericles, the great Athenian statesman, speaking in 431 B.C., defined it in the following terms:

> Our constitution is named a democracy, because it is in the hands not of the few but of the many. But our laws secure equal justice for all in their private disputes and our public opinion welcomes and honors talent in every branch of achievement . . . on grounds of excellence alone. . . . Our citizens attend both to public and private duties and do not allow absorption in their various affairs to interfere with their knowledge of the city's. . . . We decide or debate, carefully and in person all matters of policy, holding . . . that acts are foredoomed to failure when undertaken undiscussed.[1]

In this classic formulation Pericles identifies the following characteristics of a democracy:

1. Thucydides, *The History of the Peloponnesian War*. Edited and translated by Sir Richard Livingston. New York: Oxford U.P., "The World's Classics," 1951, pp. 111–113.

1. Government by the people with the full and direct participation of the people.
2. Equality before the law.
3. Pluralism—that is, respect for all talents, pursuits, and viewpoints.
4. Respect for a separate and private (as opposed to public) domain for fulfillment and expression of an individual's personality.

Participation, equality before the law, pluralism and individualism for everyone (except for women and also the many slaves): these were the cornerstones of early democracy, before it disappeared from Greece and the then known world after a relatively short, and unsuccessful, revival in Rome.

Contemporary Democracy: Major Phases

Contemporary democratic thought goes back to the sixteenth century and earlier. It has many roots: feudal practices and institutions, theories about natural law and natural rights, the religious wars and the demand for toleration, the assertion of property rights and freedom to pursue individual economic ventures, the notion of limitations upon political authority—to name only some of them. The basic landmark is provided by the English philosopher John Locke who, writing in the latter part of the seventeenth century, developed in some detail four of the cardinal concepts of democracy: *equality, individual freedom, government based upon consent of the governed,* and *limitations upon the State.* Locke's theories led to the development of representative and parliamentary government.

The second historical landmark—the emergence of economic liberalism—came with the works of Adam Smith, especially his *Wealth of Nations* (1776), and of a new school of radical philosophers known as the "utilitarians." In the first half of the nineteenth century they developed the theory of the "economic man," driven by the twin impulse to satisfy pleasure and avoid pain. In line with Adam Smith, they constructed theoretically a limited State that would allow individuals freedom to pursue their own interests. The utilitarians became the exponents of economic individualism—that is, capitalism.

Throughout the nineteenth century Locke's theory of consent and representative government was broadened, but economic liberalism and economic individualism came constantly under scrutiny and criticism. The works of the French philosopher Jean Jacques Rousseau, especially his *Social Contract* (1762), were used to broaden the theory of participation so as to include everybody. The role of the State was reassessed to favor more intervention in economic and social matters for the better protection of the poor, the unemployed, the old, the young, and many disadvantaged groups. For the first time the notion of a *Positive State*—one that acts to provide social services and to guarantee economic rights—appeared. Finally, beginning in the twentieth century and extending well into the present, socialists and a growing number of democrats have begun to broaden the notion of a Positive State. They ask for sweeping reforms of the economic system so that the State assumes the obligation of providing an ever-increasing number of services. This is the *Welfare State*.

Socialists question economic individualism and want to replace it with a system in which productive resources are owned and managed by the State itself. The economy is to be run by the State, no longer for the purpose of profit, but to further social and community needs. Many of the Socialist parties have been committed to this, and they represent a synthesis that combines democratic political and individual rights with massive state intervention in the economy and socialization of major units of production.

Thus, in discussing democracy as an ideology, we are dealing with a very rich and comprehensive body of thought and action—one that has undergone shifts and changes in the past three centuries and has produced a great variety of political movements. We shall look at the liberal phase of democracy often referred to as capitalism first, then its growing welfarist, socialist, or collectivist orientation, and finally at the conservative ideologies that remain within the framework of democracy.

2 | *Democracy and Liberalism*

Give me the liberty to know, to utter, and to argue
freely according to conscience. . . .

JOHN MILTON

Laissez-faire, laissez-passer

The individual — his or her experiences and interests — is the basic concept associated with the origin and growth of liberalism and liberal societies. Knowledge and truth are derived from the judgment of the individual, which in turn is formed by the associations his or her senses make of the outside world — from experience. There is no established truth, nor any transcendental values. Individual experience becomes the supreme value in itself, and the joining of many individual experiences in deliberation is the best possible way for a community to make decisions.

In its earliest phase, individualism is cast in terms of natural rights — freedom and equality. It is steeped in moral and religious thought, but already the first signs of a psychology that considers material interests and their satisfaction to be important in the motivation of the individual appear. In its second phase it is based on a psychological theory according to which the realization of interest is the major force that motivates individuals. In its third phase it becomes "economic liberalism" — generally referred to as capitalism.

Interest, in turn, is related to satisfaction of pleasure. Liberalism is anchored on this simple proposition: men and women strive to maximize pleasure and minimize pain. But it is not up to the collectivity to impose it; it is not up to a philosopher or a political party to determine it. On the contrary, it is up to individuals to pursue it and in so doing fulfill themselves. Knowledge that stems from experience and education will presumably set limits beyond which pleasure-maximization will not be pushed.

The propositions of early liberalism were directed against eighteenth-century absolutism and the many feudal practices that lingered on.

22

Absolutism, supported by a landed aristocracy, stifled human activity while maintaining the feudal privileges of the nobility at a time when the growth of manufacturing and commerce (even if ever so gradual) had begun to open up new vistas of individual effort, exploration, wealth, and change. Yet nations were divided internally into many jurisdictions with different laws, different standards, different tariffs, different regulations, and different weights and measures, all of which impeded communication, trade, and individual freedoms. The famous expression *laissez-faire, laissez-passer* was the battle cry of the burghers, the tradesmen, the moneylenders, the small manufacturers. "Let us do; let us pass" was the motto of the new middle classes. This liberalism was a challenge to the existing order, because laissez-faire capitalism, as we still call it, was the ideology that expressed the interests of the middle class; it stood against absolutism, and especially against political and economic constraints.

Liberals proclaimed individualism and individual freedoms—especially freedom of movement and trade; they borrowed from the past to develop what gradually became a comprehensive theory of individual rights to challenge and to limit absolute political power; they appealed to and represented the rising new classes and the new forms of wealth that began to appear in western Europe. They also received the support of the peasants, against the landed aristocracy, and the workingmen, who became attracted by the promise of freedoms and equality. As a political ideology, liberalism appealed to large sectors of the society, while being opposed by the monarchy, the landed aristocracy, and the Church.

The Three Cores of Liberalism

Liberalism consists of three cores. One is *moral,* the second is *political*, and the third is *economic*. The moral core contains an affirmation of basic values and rights attributable to the "nature" of a human being—freedom, dignity, and life—subordinating everything else to their implementation. The political core includes primarily political rights—the right to vote, to participate, to decide what kind of government to elect, and what kind of policies to follow. It is associated with representative democracy. The economic core has to do with economic and property rights. It is still referred to as "economic individualism," the "free enterprise system," or "capitalism," and pertains to the rights and freedoms of individuals to produce and to consume, to enter into contractual relations, to buy and sell through a market economy, to satisfy their wants in their own way, and to dispose of their own property and labor as they decide. Its cornerstones have been private property and a market economy that is free from State controls and regulations.

The Moral Core

Long before Christianity, the notion had developed that the individual human being has innate qualities and potentialities commanding the highest respect. With a spark of divine will or reason, each and every individual should be protected, respected, and given freedom to seek fulfillment.

The Stoics and the Epicureans put individuals — their freedom, their detachment, their personal life — above all considerations of social utility or political expediency. Early Christians went a step further to proclaim that all individuals are the children of God, that we are all brothers and sisters, that our first duty is to God, and that salvation is the ultimate fulfillment. Temporal powers cannot impinge on this, but even if they did (in order, for example, to collect taxes or to maintain order) there were still many things that belonged *only* to God.

A number of inferences stem from this notion of the moral and rational nature of the individual. Many of them have been institutionalized in the practice of liberalism and continue to be essential to it. Recent proclamations supporting human rights in the United Nations and elsewhere represent one of the oldest battle cries of liberalism.

Personal Liberty   Personal liberty consists of all those rights guaranteeing the individual protection against government. It is the requirement that men and women live under a known law with known procedures. Locke wrote: "Freedom is . . . to have a standing rule to live by, common to everyone of that society and made by the legislative power erected in it."[1] Such a law protects all and restrains the rulers. It corresponds to individual "freedoms" — freedom to think, talk, and worship. No policeman will enter one's home at night without due authority; no individual, even the poorest or lowest, will be thrown into prison without a chance to hear the charges and argue before a judge; nobody will have to discover one Sunday morning that his or her church is closed, or that their son or daughter has disappeared, and so forth. To American students such freedoms appear self-evident and naturally due. Unfortunately this is not quite so; in fact, they are in constant jeopardy everywhere.

Civil Liberty   While personal liberties in general define a set of protections, civil liberties indicate the free and positive channels and areas of human activity and participation. In liberal ideology and practice, they are equally valued. Basic to the liberal faith is the concept of freedom of thought. The only way to define this positively is to state it as the right of individuals to think their own thoughts and learn in their own ways from experience with nobody impeding the process. Freedom of thought is closely associated with freedom of expression, freedom of speech, freedom to write, freedom to publish and disseminate one's thoughts, freedom to discuss things with others, and freedom to associate with others in the

1. Locke, *Second Treatise on Civil Government,* Chapter 4.

peaceful expression of ideas. We find these freedoms enshrined in the First Amendment of the United States Constitution, and also in many solemn documents in British and European political history—the Bill of Rights, the Petition of Rights, the Declaration of the Rights of Man, and so on.

The achievement and implementation of full civil liberties in the societies of western Europe and the United States took time. Until the end of the nineteenth century, there were countries where people were excluded from political participation because of their ideas—religious or other. Censoring of books, pamphlets, and the press was a common practice long after Milton wrote his famous pamphlet against censorship, *The Areopagitica,* in 1644. Freedom of the press had a particularly shaky existence until the end of the nineteenth century, and freedom of association—to form clubs, groups of like-minded people, political parties, trade unions, and religious sects—was hedged and qualified until almost the same time.

What is more, at no time could civil liberties be taken for granted. There were and still are constant exceptions and setbacks. There is always an inclination on the part of certain groups to deny to others what they do not like, and there is a pervasive suspicion on the part of political authorities of nonconformist and dissenting groups.

Social Liberty   Freedom of thought and expression, protections against government in the form of personal and civil rights, have little value if the individuals are not given a proper recognition so that they can work and live in accordance with their talents and capabilities. Social liberty corresponds to what we refer to today as opportunities for advancement or social mobility. It is the right of all individuals, irrespective of race and creed and irrespective of the position of their parents, to be given every opportunity to attain a position in society commensurate with their capabilities. Personal liberties may become an empty or purely formal prescription if they impose discrimination. There is little hope in the life of a Mexican peon, or a black, or the poor, if they know that they and their children will always remain tied down to the same occupation, status, education, and income. Only when equal opportunities are seen to be provided for all can all forms of discrimination be abolished.

The Economic Core

As already pointed out, liberalism was the ideology of the middle classes rising to replace the old landed aristocracy. Their purpose was to liberate individual economic activity, to establish large trading areas that corresponded to the nation-state and if possible the world, and to do away with all obstacles to the transportation and the trading of goods. It was their aim to reorganize the economy, to introduce new methods (the market), and to invest capital in factories and machines.

Economic liberties, and in general the economic core of liberalism, assumed at least as great an importance as what we have called the moral core. The right to property, the right of inheritance, the right to accumulate wealth and capital, freedom to produce, sell, and buy—all contractual freedoms—became an essential part of the new social order. Emphasis was put on the voluntary character of the relations between various economic factors, whether the employer, the worker, the lender, the producer, or the consumer. Freedom of contract was more valued than freedom of speech. The pattern of social life, according to which people were born and belonged in certain social categories and groups, was shattered, and the individuals became free to shape their own situation by voluntary acts and contractual relations with others. One great British historian, Sir Henry Maine, claimed that the essence of liberalism lay precisely in this transition from "status" (fixed group relations) to "contract" (individual self-determination).

The meeting point of various individual wills, where contractual relations were made, is the market. Here the individual—the famous "economic man"—propelled by self-interest, buys and sells, hires laborers, borrows or loans money, invests in joint-stock companies or maritime ventures, and finds employment. The market reflects the supply and demand for goods, and this in turn determines their prices. The market is the best barometer to register economic activity, because demand obviously pushes prices up, and hence incites production until the demand is met and prices begin to level off. Since the market does not sanction the incompetent and the inefficient, goods produced that do not meet a demand or are not widely desirable fall in price, until the producer is driven out of business, and replaced by a shrewder one.

Thousands of individual entrepreneurs face not only millions of consumers, who compare quality and prices, but also each other. If a given product sells well and fast, other manufacturers will produce it, increasing the supply and thus bringing prices down. The system is supposed to be both sensitive to consumer demand as well as entirely open, allowing for entry of new competitors and the exit of unsuccessful ones. Prices faithfully register the volume of demand and supply adjusted to it.

It is a system that at least in theory favors the consumer: prices cannot be fixed, the volume of production cannot be controlled, competition makes monopolies or cartels impossible. But the gains for the producers are also great; they can take advantage of the same law of supply and demand in hiring or dismissing workers, in settling on the wages to be paid, and in setting the prices of new products. It is a system that provides the best mechanism for production and the satisfaction of wants, and its classic formulation was provided by Adam Smith.

Adam Smith and *The Wealth of Nations* The bible of liberal economic theory was, and still remains, Adam Smith's *The Wealth of Nations*. Smith's purpose was to open the channels of free individual economic effort and to defend the free market economy as the best instrument for the growth of wealth—individual, national, and worldwide. Each person, he assumes, is the best judge of his or her actions and interests. If people are allowed a free hand to pursue these interests they will, and by so doing will improve the wealth of the society and the nation as a whole. What counts above all is to

Adam Smith (1723–1790)

Adam Smith was a social philosopher and political economist, best known for his major work, *An Inquiry into the Nature and Causes of the Wealth of Nations* (1776), in which he developed his theories of economic liberalism, competition, and free trade. His major plea was to release human activity from all State administrative and economic controls, allowing the individuals to seek individual profit and the satisfaction of wants. Adam Smith claimed that there were fundamental economic laws, such as the law of supply and demand, that provided for the self-regulation of the economy. He is the father of economic liberalism.

give free rein to individual action and limit the role of the State to the simple maintenance of order and defense.

Adam Smith rose against every conceivable state intervention in commerce, agriculture, and manufacturing. He was against not only tariffs, trade associations and combinations, labor unions and state regulations, but also monopolies and almost any form of public enterprise. He favored free contractual relations. The State had to keep its hands and agents off.

Though Adam Smith spoke of the "Divine Hand of Providence" bringing order and wealth out of the myriads of individual wills and interests that compete with each other in trying to satisfy their respective interests, his faith was not in divine providence. Rather he believed that a social and economic harmony would result from the free competition and interplay of economic interests and forces. In his words, natural order would be promoted in every country by the natural inclinations of the individuals if political institutions had never thwarted those natural inclinations. If all systems of restraint were completely taken away, natural liberty would establish itself. Or as one of Smith's followers put the matter even more succinctly:

> As soon as a need becomes the object of public service the individual loses part of his freedom, becomes less progressive and less man. He becomes prone to moral inertia which spreads out to all citizens.[2]

Jeremy Bentham and Utilitarianism　But the real father of liberalism was Jeremy Bentham. His philosophy, followed also by James Mill and John Stuart Mill, is known as *utilitarianism,* from the term utility. Its basic elements can be summarized as follows:

1. Every object has a utility—that is, every object can satisfy a want.
2. Utility, as the attribute of an object, is subjective. It is what we like or do not like. It is amenable only to some crude quantifiable criteria that relate to the duration, the intensity, and the proximity of the pleasure that a given object can provide. There are no qualitative criteria that can be established by anybody but the user. For some a poem has a greater "utility" than a hot dog. For others the hot dog comes first. The market ultimately registers utility as it reflects the volume of goods in demand.
3. The purpose of our lives is to satisfy pleasure (that is, to use goods that have utility for each one of us) and to avoid pain. This is the *hedonistic* or the *felicific calculus* that applies not just in economic life but also in any other aspect of an individual's existence.

In order to work, this utilitarian model must be allowed to operate freely. If every man and woman were free to maximize pleasure and avoid

---

2. Cited by Harold Laski, *The Rise of European Liberalism*, p. 203.

THE BETTMANN ARCHIVE. INC.

Jeremy Bentham (1748–1831)

Jeremy Bentham was the founder of the Utilitarian School, according to which pleasure-maximizing, pain-avoiding (the so-called *felicific calculus*) is the source of human motivation. His various works, such as *Fragment on Government* and *Defense of Usury,* and most particularly his *Introduction to the Principles of Morals and Legislation*, expounded the theories of individualism and economic freedom. Benthamite liberals were extremely influential through the nineteenth century in England in pushing for administrative, criminal law, taxation, and economic reforms.

pain, "the greatest happiness for the greatest number" would result. More people would be happy than unhappy!

The concept of utility and the utilitarian ethic is not restricted to the economy. It applies to everything. Social institutions, artistic works, education, philosophy—all must meet the test of utility and provide pleasure, in varying degrees, to some, or conversely result in pain if they are absent. *Utility* as a criterion of social, political, and economic life replaces moral and natural *rights.*

Thus millions of individuals armed with small calculators, so to speak, constantly sift the pleasurable in a given society from the painful, maximizing the first and minimizing the second. The calculations are always directly related to self-interest, but they are not necessarily simple. The individual will have to balance a number of requirements—for example, the immediate utility an object may have compared to the far greater utility it may represent in five or ten years; the possibility of suffering deprivation and even pain *now* in order to enjoy pleasure later on; the pain that may be suffered in order to derive pleasure from protecting loved ones; the intensity of a given pleasure as opposed to its duration; and finally, overall considerations of peace and tranquility at home and national defense against outside enemies. They too represent a utility, no matter what the immediate pain of providing for them may be.

These considerations show that while self-interest and the pleasure-maximizing calculations are the motivating force for all of us, a point comes when considerations other than the pure and immediate satisfaction of interest enter into the equation of social, political, and economic life. Self-interest gives way to *enlightened* self-interest.

John Stuart Mill and Enlightened Self-Interest Enlightened self-interest becomes an important criterion to guide the individual. For instance, someone who forgoes an immediate pleasure in order to derive a greater one later on shows enlightenment. Accepting a lesser pleasure in order to maintain a *fairly* pleasurable existence, rather than insisting on the maximum pleasure possible and in the process risking the loss of everything, is also "enlightenment." The same criteria apply to groups or classes of people. If they act in terms of enlightened self-interest, they may consider concessions to other social groups or classes rather than risk the loss of all they have.

John Stuart Mill came to grips with this problem by redefining utility. He introduces qualitative standards and establishes a hierarchy of pleasures on the basis of criteria that are *not* subjective. Some pleasures are better than others because of their intrinsic quality, not because of the particular pleasure they give to an individual. A poem has more utility than a hot dog!

There is therefore a necessary gradation in the utility of different goods. Some have a higher value even if they give pleasure to only few; others may, in the long run, prove to be painful even if they give pleasure to many. What then? Shall we introduce a dictator or a philosopher-king who will impose his hierarchy of pleasures upon society and make it produce goods and services that correspond to it? Or should we expect individuals to make the right choice?

The last question is not speculative. It is right before us. Driving a car is pleasurable, but by depleting our energy resources American drivers weaken the country to the point where it may be unable to defend many of the values that are equally pleasurable to us—our freedoms, for instance. A comprehensive scheme of public transportation would be preferable to

John Stuart Mill (1806–1873)

John Stuart Mill was an English philosopher, who had studied under the strict tutelage of his father, a foremost utilitarian, James Mill. John Stuart Mill considerably modified utilitarian thought to abandon the simple pleasure-maximizing, pain-avoiding formula and to seek qualitative criteria to evaluate human behavior and motivation. In his essay *On Liberty* (1859) he developed the theory of moral (as opposed simply to economic) individualism and linked it to requirements of education and enlightenment. He was forced to introduce collective and social considerations and thus had to allow, contrary to what he seemed to profess, for state intervention. Many consider Mill, because of this, to be one of the precursors of socialism. However he is known primarily for *On Liberty*, in which he strongly advocates individualism.

private ownership of cars. But how can the people be led to make the right decision?

The utilitarians, and particularly John Stuart Mill, put their hopes in education, and in the wisdom and self-restraint of the middle classes. It was the obligation of the State to establish education, and it was the function of education to *enlighten* self-interest in terms of collective, group, social, and national interests and considerations. Education would transform an essentially hedonistic society into a body of civic-minded citizens—who in the last analysis would choose public transportation! They would put the general good above their own particular pleasure.

The Political Core

Four basic principles make up the political core of liberalism: *individual consent, representation and representative government, constitutionalism*, and *popular sovereignty*.

Individual Consent   As we have already noted, "status" had been giving place to "contract." Contractual theories became the basis of political authority. Men and women simply consent to bind themselves in a political system and to accept its decisions. The Mayflower Compact of 1629, when the Pilgrims wrote a "constitution," is the best illustration.

It was John Locke who developed the theory of consent in detail. Men and women, he pointed out, live in the state of nature with certain natural rights: life, liberty, and property. At a given time they discover that it is difficult to safeguard these rights without a common authority committed to them and to their protection. They agree to set up a political society consisting of a common legislature, a common judge, and a common executive. The first will interpret and safeguard the natural rights, the second will adjudicate conflicts about these rights, and the third will provide for enforcement. The contract is made by all individuals, and those who do not agree are not bound by it. They can leave! *The source of political authority and the powers of the State over those who stay is their consent.* The purpose of the State is the better preservation of the natural rights of life, liberty, and property.

Representation   But who can make decisions within this system? According to Locke it is the legislature elected by the people (at the time, to be sure, on a very limited franchise). However, the legislature must accept certain restraints, all of them implicit or explicit in the original contract setting up the political system. It cannot deprive individuals of their natural rights, cannot abolish their freedom, and cannot do away with their lives or take away their property. The political authority—the legislature—is restrained by the very nature of the compact that originally established it.

RADIO TIMES HULTON PICTURE LIBRARY

John Locke (1632–1704)

John Locke was an English philosopher generally considered
one of the founders of empiricism. His principal works include
Letters on Toleration (1689–1692), *Essay Concerning Human Understanding* (1690), and *Thoughts on Education* (1693). As a political
philosopher Locke developed in his *Two Treatises on Government* the contract theory of the State, according to which the
State is the custodian of natural rights and is founded upon the
consent of the government in order to protect these rights —
specifically, the rights of life, liberty, and property. It led to the
elaboration of institutions of a limited State and a limited
government.

Locke's idea of representative government, then, is based on the notion that political authority derives from people. But moral, civil, and economic or property individual rights cannot be transgressed. The majority and its elected representatives can make all and any decisions, but the original contract and the good sense of the people who made it, as well as of their representatives, restrain it from violating the people's natural rights. Thus, the British tradition establishes parliamentary sovereignty and majority rule, rather than the checks and balances and judicial review, as in the United States.

It should be noted, however, that while Locke gave to the legislature the right to make decisions without any limitations, his theory of representation and representative government applied only to a small number—those who held property. They represented the middle classes and the landed aristocracy. It was only much later, when the franchise was expanded to most citizens (and ultimately to all) that the problem of how to limit the majority—that might decide to take away the property of the few—assumed particular importance.

Theories of representation and representative government also stemmed directly from utilitarian premises that led ultimately to the "one man, one vote" principle. At first the utilitarians attacked the vested interests, the aristocracy, the landowners, the Church, and the well-to-do, and discarded the notion that these groups, more than others, had a special stake in the country and hence had a special right to represent the community and govern it. Mill argued that the best individual protection was to allow each and all to select their representatives. "Human beings," he pointed out, "are only secure from evil at the hands of others in proportion to their ability to protect themselves,"[3] and he believed that representation was the best protection.

However, John Stuart Mill did not quite accept the notion of the supremacy of the representatives—the legislature—and with it the right of the majority to govern. He and many other liberals feared that if all the people were given the right to vote and to elect their own representatives, and if decisions in the representative assembly were to be made by majority vote, then the poor would use their numerical strength to take care of *their* interests at the expense of the middle classes and all others. There were, therefore, a number of direct and indirect restraints. One was the proposition that representative government could function well only when the educational level of the voters had improved. Citizens should learn to think of the "general prosperity and the general good" rather than their own immediate interest; in other words, the system could work well only when people as a whole acted according to their enlightened interest. Mill wrote:

> The positive evils and dangers of representative government
> can be reduced to two: general ignorance and incapacity, and

---

3. J. S. Mill, "Considerations on Representative Government," in *Utilitarianism*, Chapter 3, p. 43.

the danger of its being under the influence of interests not identical with the general welfare of the community.[4]

He mentioned specifically the "body of unskilled laborers" who were ignorant and likely to act at the expense of the general welfare.

Mill also had an aversion to the development of large national political parties which could mobilize the vote and capture a majority through the organization and discipline of its members. Moreover, he was in favor of property and age qualifications. He favored these at least for the candidates for election, who in this way would come from the middle classes and would have the proper level of maturity and moderation. He also favored giving a great weight — more votes — to people with education. Finally, he was in favor of a second chamber, the House of Lords, representing "personal merit" and acting as a "moral center of resistance" against the decisions of a popularly elected assembly — that is, against the majority.

Despite their insistence on representation and elections, the liberals hedged and hemmed at the power of the legislature and the right of the majority to decide. They did not have enough confidence in the people. Yet, notwithstanding their fears of the poor, the ignorant, and "the many," the utilitarian premises led gradually to universal suffrage. Representation and representative government gradually spread, and with it majoritarianism, the right of the majority to form a government and make decisions for all, gained legitimacy.

Constitutionalism   The notion of restraints on political authority, as proposed by Locke, influenced the framers of the United States Constitution. They feared arbitrary and absolute power so much that they rejected a concentration of power in the hands of any one body, whether it be the legislature, or even the majority of the people. While stressing the idea of natural rights, individual freedoms, and the derivation of authority from the people, they wanted to find a way to make it impossible for any single organ or government to become truly sovereign and overwhelm the others. Their emphasis was more on how to restrain political power, even when it was based on the will of the people, than on how to make it effective.

The answer was a written Constitution which limits power, sets explicit restraints (including the ten amendments) on the national government and the individual states, and which institutionalizes the separation of powers in such a manner that one power checks another. At no time would it be possible for one branch — executive, legislative, or judicial — to overwhelm and subordinate the others. Having accepted the idea of fully representative government through periodic elections, the founders of the American Constitution put heavy restraints upon it.

This is essentially what we mean by constitutionalism. Constitutionalism provides solid guarantees for the individual by explicitly limiting

4. Ibid., Chapter 6, p. 86.

government; it also provides clear procedures for the implementation of the government's functions. In many cases it establishes a watchdog, in the form of a judicial body, to safeguard the Constitution and all the restraints written into it. In addition, it provides procedures through which the responsibility of the governors to the governed is maintained by periodic elections. The government is both *limited* and *responsible*. But the idea of limitations is far more important than that of popular sovereignty. The United States Constitution established a republic, not a democracy.

Popular Sovereignty It was Jean-Jacques Rousseau who set up the model of a popular democracy before the French Revolution of 1789. He too found the source of political authority in the people. They were sovereign, and their sovereignty was "inalienable, infallible, and indestructible."[5] In contrast to those who favored representation and representative government, Rousseau believed in direct government by the people. There were to be no restraints on the popular will. He called it "the general will" and claimed that under certain conditions it was always right and that representation would only distort it. In the last analysis, he argued, nobody could really represent anybody else. Something like town meetings in small communities would be the only appropriate instruments for the expression of the general will.

Rousseau's affirmation of the absolute power of the general will, that many interpreted to be the will of the people, had revolutionary implications. It pitted an extreme doctrine of popular sovereignty against absolutism, which was current in France and many other continental countries in the eighteenth century. But it also antagonized liberals who believed in representative government with restraints and were particularly reluctant to see all the people participate directly or indirectly in decisions.

Consent, representation, popular sovereignty leading to majority rule, and constitutional restraints on the state and its government (even on a majority) obviously emphasize different forms of liberal thought and put the accent on different values. They inevitably lead to different political institutions. Emphasis on constitutional restraints and the protection of individual and minority rights — economic rights at first — led to the type of liberalism, still very much in evidence in the United States, that restricts the majority and allows the judiciary to act as the supreme umpire. On the other hand, emphasis on the Rousseauian idea of popular sovereignty leads to unrestricted majority rule, either directly by the people or by their representatives. In between these two extremes liberals and liberal institutions attempted, not always successfully, to find a solution that reconciled the idea of majoritarianism with the notion of restraints. Limitation on representative assemblies, various voting qualifications, a bicameral legislature in which one chamber is not directly elected by the people but represents wealth or birth or some other attribute of "moderation," and

5. Rousseau, *The Social Contract*, Book 2.

THE BETTMANN ARCHIVE, INC.

Jean-Jacques Rousseau (1712–1778)

Jean-Jacques Rousseau was a French philosopher who, in contrast to the rationalism of the French eighteenth-century philosophers (the Encyclopedists), stressed the role of sentiments and emotions, thus becoming the precursor of many nineteenth-century romantics. He wrote widely on a number of subjects, but his two most important works are on education (*Emile*, 1762) and on politics (*The Social Contract*, 1762). In the latter he argued for the sovereignty of the people, claiming that the "general will" emanating from them is absolute and infallible. It was the combination of this theory of general will and his emphasis on feeling and emotion that led him to glorify nationalism as an all-embracing myth that creates unity and solidarity among a people. The best exposition of his theory of nationalism can be found in his *Considerations on the Government of Poland*, written in 1770.

the veto of the monarch or a president were the devices most often used to deny a numerical majority the power to make decisions.

Throughout the nineteenth century the main stresses within the political core of liberalism lay in the conflict between those who, in line with Locke and some of the utilitarians, advocated restraints on the legislature and the majority, and those who, in line with Rousseau's theory of popular sovereignty, pressed for uninhibited majority rule.

The State and the Individual

Liberalism was an anti-State philosophy and remains one in the sense that, all other things being more or less equal, it values the individual and his or her initiative more than the State and its intervention. Nowhere has this position been better set forth than in John Stuart Mill's essay *On Liberty,* published in 1859. To approach it, let us set forth two models, the totalitarian and the liberal. According to the first, the individual and the civil society (i.e., the family, economic organizations, school and universities, and so on) are controlled by the State. It is therefore the State that shapes the social institutions on the basis of a predetermined scheme of values. The State exacts conformity and obedience.

The liberal model presents an entirely different order of things. Individuals and their social institutions are separate from the State. Strictly speaking, they constitute two different spheres of life and action. But when the two spheres do intersect, the intersection should cover only a limited and recognized area. Spontaneity, creativity, experimentation, and the search for truth are within the domain of individuals and their social institutions. It is at best and at most the function of the State to maintain order, to see that nobody in his or her relations with others uses force, to protect civil liberties and personal freedom, and at the same time to maintain the economic freedom of the individual. In other words, the role of the State is to protect the individual.

In his essay *On Liberty* Mill summarizes this by asserting:

1. That every restraint imposed by the State is bad.
2. That even if the individual cannot do certain things well, the State should not do them for fear that it might undermine the individual's independence and initiative.
3. That any increase in the powers of the State is automatically bad and prejudicial to individual freedoms: it decreases individual freedom.

Thus Mill views the State on the one hand, and society and the individual on the other, in a mechanical and antithetical kind of relationship. The increase of the powers of the State necessarily involves the decrease of powers of individual correspondingly, people must be extremely vigilant not to allow an increase in the power of the State.

The most crucial problem for liberal thought has been the identification of exactly where the lines separating the State, on the one hand, and society and individuals, on the other, intersect. One might develop an elastic concept, allowing a fairly wide area within the intersecting lines, in which the State can intervene (numbers 2 and 3 in Figure 2-1). Or, in line with the thinking of early liberals, one might allow for the minimum area of intersection in which the State can intervene (number 1 in Figure 2-1). Here the intersection would encompass only order and protection. In this latter case, the State becomes something like a police officer or a "night watchman" making sure that the factory does not burn down and no thieves break in and otherwise allowing full autonomy within the factory, or the university, or the home, or the school. The smaller the area included

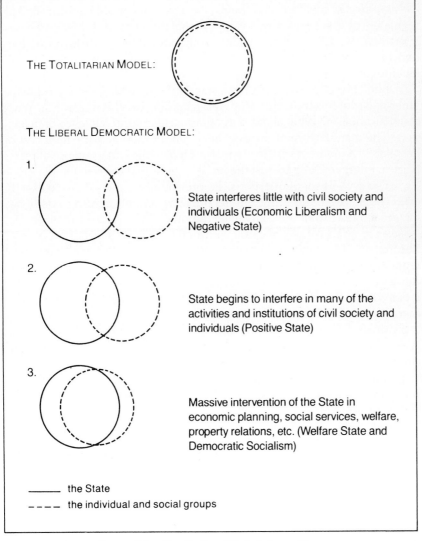

FIGURE 2-1   The limits of State intervention.

within the intersecting lines of Figure 2-1 the closer we are to laissez-faire liberalism: the larger the area the more we move in the direction of the *Positive State* or the *Welfare State*, perhaps even getting close to socialism.

Self-regarding and Other-regarding Acts

Different periods in the history of liberalism tell us where the lines have been drawn. War, for example, necessitates State intervention. But this was considered to be an exception, since there is an understanding that with the passing of such a national emergency the situation would revert to the original liberal model. John Stuart Mill provided us with a criterion for drawing the lines. To Mill, all individual acts that affect the individual — *self-regarding acts,* as he called them — are acts that cannot be controlled or regulated by the State. However, acts that concern and affect others — *other-regarding acts* — can and should come under the control and regulation of the State. Thus, the area within our intersecting circles should include the other-regarding acts.

But "affect" provides no clean standard. Is smoking self-regarding or other-regarding? Is the use of drugs self-regarding or other-regarding? What about alcoholism? What about pornographic literature? Violence on television? The manufacture of drugs? The administration and the high cost of hospitals? The additives put in our foods? Ownership and use of private cars? Nuclear energy? These are just the first questions that come to mind.

The second set of questions is more complex, and relates to exactly *when* the State should bring into its purview other-regarding acts (if we have managed to define exactly what they are). Can it do so only *after* an act is *shown* to affect others, or can it control it because it *might* affect others? The first would provide a very strict and limiting criterion. The State could regulate the manufacturing of drugs only when it is shown that they have caused cancer. The second interpretation, however, provides a very generous criterion whereby the State can intervene. It would do so every time there is some doubt about the consequences certain drugs can have upon individuals. Drugs that *might* cause cancer should be taken off the market. Whenever certain acts or goods *might* affect others, they should be regulated and controlled.

Mill did not have to answer these questions explicitly, because of the way he defined self-regarding and other-regarding acts. *All individual acts, he claimed, are self-regarding except those that cause harm to others. The criterion in terms of which other-regarding acts are defined is that of harm. Only if harm is done can the State intervene.* Commerce, production, consumption are self-regarding.[6] The State should not intervene. But so, of course, are freedom of thought and expression and freedom of association. The State should not intervene here either. So, in the last analysis, the individual has the

---

6. J. S. Mill, "Of the Limits of the Authority of Society over the Individual," in *Utilitarianism,* Chapter 4.

right to get drunk and to use drugs. However, your actions become other-regarding, and hence invite State intervention, when they cause harm to others. You can stay in your attic drinking beer as long as you want; you are free to indulge in this self-regarding act. But if you start throwing the empty cans out of a window and you endanger passersby, then the act becomes other-regarding.

However, the moment we give a more relaxed definition of what is other-regarding, and introduce the concept of *effect* or *influence* rather than *harm*, then we move in the opposite direction to favor State intervention and regulation. The police officer may try to save you from too much beer or drugs, even if you have not harmed anybody!

Pluralism   The liberal ethic and the liberal ideology are intensely individualistic. However, liberalism is used also to refer to the rights and freedoms not only of individuals but also of groups and associations. Replace the individual with the group or an association to which he or she belongs and you have pluralism. Groups demand and expect the same treatment in regard to tolerance, representation, and participation that the individuals have. With the breakdown of rigid class and religious or ethnic solidarities in many modern systems, thousands of groups have mushroomed. Groups organize; they make their demands. Public policy, it is expected, will then be made in response to their demands. As Professor Apter writes, "The notion of individual competitions is replaced [under pluralism] by a network of organizational competition, influence, accountability and information in which groups can organize and, by exercising rights, realize interests to affect policy outcomes."[7]

But groups may make claims that go beyond the mere satisfaction of interest. They may claim the same autonomy that the individuals claim. These are claims for ethnic, racial, local, functional, occupational, and economic autonomy. Their implementation requires a great deal of decentralization of the democratic State. Very often demands on the part of certain groups even go beyond decentralization to assert separation and independence from the State. Sometimes pluralism is used to justify economic democracy — that is, the rights of certain groups and organizations to decide by themselves on the economic activities in which they are engaged without any intervention from the State.

As long as there is a basic agreement in the political society on the rules that determine political competition, pluralism and liberalism can coexist. But the moment a group or a combination of groups subordinate others, they will dominate the society and coerce the individual. This may clearly be the case with industrial corporations, trade unions, other economic groups, ethnic groups, and even religious sects. The early liberal theorists feared group dominance and tried in one way or another to make it difficult for groups to develop and to supplant the individuals. They

---

7. Apter, *Introduction to Political Analysis*. Cambridge, Mass.: Winthrop, 1978, pp. 314–315.

argued that a group is not a moral entity like the individual. It overshadows the individuals and subordinates them to the imperative of group solidarity. As a result, groups pose the danger of subverting individual freedoms.

Liberalism and Capitalism in America

The doctrine of economic liberalism—emphasizing the market economy and competition, exalting the profit motive and private entrepreneurship, and building on the premises of self-interest in its pursuit of a world of social harmony and progress—was constantly contested in England, where it originated, and on the continent of Europe, where it never managed to gain a firm foothold. It provoked a strong reaction from intellectuals, Socialists, Christian reformers, liberal and traditional Catholic intellectuals as well as the Catholic hierarchy and was looked upon with strong repugnance by monarchists and the aristocracy. Liberals, buffeted from their right and their left, had to qualify economic liberalism by allowing for restraints and regulation of the market economy.

In contrast, economic liberalism or rather capitalism, as it is commonly referred to, flourished in the United States. It began to reflect the remarkable industrial growth which the country enjoyed after the Civil War and which continued until the Great Depression of 1929.

Andrew Carnegie (1835–1919) considered the search for and accumulation of wealth to be the central goal of our civilization, and found in the market and competition the best arena to test the caliber of men—their abilities and industry. As with the earlier Protestant ethic, Carnegie believed that wealth was an indication of divine grace and that it was bestowed only on industrious and frugal men. But he also believed that, commensurate with their station in society, the wealthy had a special duty to help the less fortunate through charity and other humanitarian endeavors.

In contrast to Carnegie's paternalistic capitalism, William Graham Sumner (1840–1910) suggested a pure individualistic ethic. Competition was to be the rule and success or failure would be determined in the marketplace. It would provide a selective mechanism to sort out the industrious from the lazy, the virtuous from the wicked. He contended that the search for equality, espoused by the Socialists, would bring only disaster. For Sumner, equality meant that the "worst would become the standard" and that it would pull down the rest to the lowest common denominator of competence, work, production, and wealth. Only through conflict, competition, and struggle could the best impose themselves and thus attain wealth for themselves and the society as a whole. As with Carnegie, the market became the best instrumentality for the "survival of the most able," just as nature had been for the "survival of the fittest" in Charles Darwin's theory of evolution. Capitalism, therefore, was the precondition of human progress.

THE BETTMANN ARCHIVE

Andrew Carnegie (1835–1919)

Andrew Carnegie epitomized the puritan ethic of individual effort and success—in the form of amassing wealth. His family came from Scotland to the United States when he was thirteen to settled in Allegheny, Pennsylvania. After working in various jobs he served in the Pennsylvania railroad system and in the transportation office of the War Department during the Civil War, just before the industrial boom and the expansion of the railroads in the country. He formed his own steel company and consolidated his many holdings into the Carnegie Steel Corporation that he sold to the U.S. Steel Corporation in 1901. He then retired to devote his time and immense wealth to philanthropy, in line with the principles laid down in his article *Wealth* published in the North American Review (June, 1889), according to which the successful (i.e., the wealthy) must use their wealth for the "public good" as they see it.

Today capitalism in the United States continues to be portrayed in highly simplified terms. The basic tenets are as follows:

1. The major actor in society — indeed the primary actor — is the individual who, using his reason, is best suited to satisfy his needs and interests. The maximization of individual well-being (material wealth and profit) is the driving force of the economy. Consumer demand determines the supply of goods and the inventive entrepreneur provides them.
2. The free market is the most reliable and flexible mechanism for regulating supply and demand through the price mechanism.
3. Change (often used synonymously with progress) can be brought about through the dynamics of individual effort, competition, and entrepreneurship.
4. The individual, however, is not only an "economic man" to be left free to act according to his interests; he is also a moral man with a conscience, volition, and reason. To curb the economic efforts of individuals would be to seriously undermine their other freedoms and, most important of all, to deprive them of their right to pursue their own lives according to their individual best judgment.
5. The State must remain out of the market.

These prescriptions were not easily reconcilable with the kind of majoritarian democracy that developed in Europe where the majority could, and in fact did, pass legislation to regulate the economy — for example, fixing prices and wages, setting hours of work, and taking other actions that had a direct effect on the economy. But in America the U.S. Constitution did not endorse majoritarianism. On the contrary, it provided for a series of safeguards *against* majority rule by putting a number of rights and especially property rights beyond its reach. The American judiciary upheld the laissez-faire ideology by striking down legislative measures that attempted to regulate the free market and impose limitations on contractual freedoms. Time after time, state laws regulating child labor, working conditions, hours of work, and minimum wages were struck down by federal courts and the Supreme Court.

The majority of the American judiciary endorsed the prevailing ideology of capitalism, and for a long time the courts both sustained and promoted it. It was only with the advent of the New Deal in 1933 that the first serious efforts to qualify the freedom of the market and the tenets of capitalism were made through state regulation and welfare policies. But the "new" liberals of the 1970s, and more especially in the last decade, have revived the ideology of capitalism. Free enterprise and a free market, competition and profit, continue to be widely accepted. The American political agenda remains cast within the framework of capitalism.

Achievements:
The Expansion of Liberalism

If we take a fairly thick brush and paint onto the canvas of the nineteenth century all the liberal achievements in the realm of economic rights, civil liberties, and political rights, the picture that emerges is breathtaking. The liberals and the liberal movements and parties changed the economic, social, and political structure of Europe, and drastically modified the international community as well. Some of the major achievements are listed here.

Slavery was outlawed. In the United States it continued until the Civil War, but the importation of slaves after 1808 had been declared illegal. In England the slave trade was banned in 1807, and slavery was abolished in the British Empire in 1833. France followed in 1848; the Netherlands in 1869; Argentina in 1853; Portugal in 1858; Brazil in 1888. Serfdom was abolished in Russia in 1861.

Gradually *religious disabilities* against holding political or other offices were abandoned virtually everywhere. Catholics, Protestants, Jews, Quakers, and nonconformist religious minorities were allowed full participation by the end of the nineteenth century.

After bitter controversies, *toleration* was granted and the Church and the State were separated in many countries. Religious affiliations and worship became a personal right.

Freedom of press, speech, and association were granted. By the end of the nineteenth century, in western Europe, Britain and its dominions, and the United States, rare were the cases where people could not express their views or were penalized for the views they did express, no matter how heretical or subversive.

The State began to provide *education* and to require children to attend school up the age of ten, twelve, or fourteen.

The vote was gradually extended to all males first, and to women only after World War I. There was universal suffrage in England by 1884; in France in 1848; in Italy by the end of the century; in Russia in 1905 (but not for long); and in Germany and the Scandinavian countries in varying degrees by the end of the century. In the United States, male universal suffrage (limited to whites) was established in the 1820s. Property qualifications for voters and candidates were eliminated, but some other qualifications — literacy, age, or residence — remained. All in all, the prediction of Lord Macaulay that "universal suffrage is utterly incompatible with the existence of civilization" proved quite wrong!

Nothing illustrates the force of liberalism better than the reforms undertaken in France after the revolution of 1830. The second chamber was changed from a hereditary one to one in which members sat for life; the electorate was broadened by lowering the age qualifications to twenty-five instead of thirty; property qualifications were reduced from three hundred francs to two hundred. Candidates for office were to be thirty years old instead of forty, censorship was abolished, extraordinary tribunals were eliminated, schools were set up in every commune by the State and the control of the Church over them was put to an end. These reforms were modest; indeed, they stopped far short of what democrats wanted to accomplish. But they were moving in the direction of democracy. It took, for example, just eighteen years (after another revolution) before universal suffrage was introduced to France, in 1848.

Similarly, the liberal Reform Act of 1832 in England provided for a property qualification of ten pounds a year, thus excluding the poor and the workers from voting but allowing the middle classes to do so. The act increased the electorate to about 750,000 out of a total population of about 13.5 million. Further extensions in 1867 and 1884 followed, bringing the workers in the political system.

Constitutions, constitution-making, and constitutionalism were everywhere in the air. Even where a constitution had only symbolic character it still echoed the aspiration of citizens to limit government and establish the rules that made the holders of power responsible to the people or their representatives.

In Russia a movement for a constitution which would limit the powers of the tsar emerged in 1824; in Greece liberal constitutions were promulgated in 1827 and again in 1843; in Germany a liberal constitution was prepared by a convention that met in Frankfurt in 1848; in France liberal constitutions were promulgated (after the failure of the ones established during the French Revolution) in 1830, 1848, and 1871. In Spain, Portugal, Italy, and in many Latin American republics, constitutional documents came into force by the end of the nineteenth century and often earlier. Even Poland, the Austro-Hungarian Empire, and the Turkish Empire experienced liberal reforms that were embodied in constitutional documents or charters.

These reforms were not granted easily; occasionally they were granted only to be withdrawn. Frequently liberal political movements were repressed, but the overall impact was the same—broadening and safeguarding civil liberties, and extending political participation to an ever-growing number of people in every political system. Above all, they imposed responsibility and restraints, no matter how fragile and temporary, upon the holders of political power. This in itself helped to erode the claims of absolutism.

Representative government became increasingly accepted throughout Europe and in the English-speaking countries. With the exception of Russia (with a notable interval between 1905 and 1914), there was hardly a political system in the nineteenth century which did not introduce representative assemblies and did not give them some (often considerable) power over decisions. In many cases, the assembly was given the power to censure the government and force it out of office. Representative assemblies participated in the formulation of laws and decided on taxation and expenditures. Within limits (and sometimes without any restriction) debate was free and representatives were not liable for their words and actions in the legislature.

As the suffrage expanded to new groups, *political parties* began to emerge, seeking the vote in order to govern on the basis of pledges they offered to the electorate. They became transmission belts between the people and the government, making the latter increasingly responsive to popular demands and aspirations, and helping translate demands and wants into policy and action. Parties emerged, at first in the United States where male universal suffrage was introduced as early as 1824, with platforms, leadership, organization, and ideological loyalties. In England they gradually evolved from factions and cliques, manipulated and controlled by the king and the landed gentry, into national organizations representing the new towns and the middle classes. The Liberals and Conservatives, the two large parties, established national headquarters, designated candidates, prepared their platforms, solicited membership, and vied for office against each other after the middle of the nineteenth century. The Conservatives followed the logic of liberalism and enacted legislation enfranchising new groups by lowering property qualifications. Their leader, Disraeli, spoke of the union between "the cottage and the throne," an expression that symbolized the reconciliation of the aristocracy with the principles of democracy and the needs of the common man.

In France the nobility continued to influence the vote and political parties were numerous, badly organized, regional rather than national, and without clear-cut platforms. Until 1880 their differences were about the political regime: some favoring the republic, others a return to the monarchy, and still others aspiring to Bonapartism. It was only by the very end of the nineteenth century that the socialists became unified into one party; the centrist groups — republican, anticlerical, and liberal — formed the Radical-Socialist party.

In Germany the powerful Social Democratic party had the best organization and the largest membership and became revisionist and reformist rather than a revolutionary party. It was opposed by the Center party (liberal but appealing to Catholic groups), the Liberals (a middle-class party), and the Conservatives.

Almost everywhere the development of political parties strengthened the liberal-democratic principles and institutions. It allowed the people to opt directly for candidates and policies and brought the governments that emerged from elections closer to their control.

Liberalism had, of course, a profound impact on *economic life.* Freedom of movement (a simple right in our eyes) became a reality for the first time. A journeyman, a merchant, a manufacturer, or a farmer could move not only their produce and goods but themselves without any prior restraint and prior permission. They could dispose of their property and do as they pleased with it. Individuals became free to change professions just as easily as they could change their domiciles; they could enter into partnership or agree to provide their services on the basis of mutually binding agreements. Not only their home but also their property became a "castle" against intervention, regulation, and confiscation by an arbitrary ruler.

There was (though not everywhere) a *trend against all forms of tariffs* and all indirect restrictions on the movement of goods—first, against internal tariffs that allowed cities, municipalities, or regional authorities to tax goods at the point of their entry or exit. But even more, a great movement got under way, spearheaded by British industrial and trading groups, to reduce and even to eliminate all external tariffs that taxed goods coming into or moving out of a state. It favored worldwide free trade. As one of Adam Smith's disciples wrote in 1846:

> There is no human event that has happened in the world more calculated to promote the enduring interests of humanity than the establishment of the principle of free trade.[8]

Despite their aversion to state intervention in social and economic matters, liberals were forced to consider *limited interventions.* "Poor laws" were introduced to keep the destitute from starvation. As unemployment assumed menacing proportions in the 1840s, public workshops were established in France and at one time they employed as many as a quarter of a million people. Child labor legislation gradually began to prohibit the employment of children under certain ages, and required them to go to school. A ten-hour working day was decreed in England in 1846. Factory laws began to provide for the safety of workers. They were to receive compensation for accidents caused in their work. By the end of the century many of these measures had been expanded to provide added protection, including the first steps in the direction of health insurance.

In the name of liberalism a vast movement in favor of *national self-determination* and national independence spread all over Europe. It culminated in the Wilsonian principles of self-determination. Throughout the nineteenth century, dynasties disintegrated and new nations came into being. Greece (1827), Norway (1830), and Belgium (1830) became independent. A Polish liberal national uprising in favor of independence took place in 1831. Italy became a unified national state in 1870, and Germany followed in 1871. The Ottoman Empire, encompassing the Balkans, Turkey, and the Middle East, cracked wide open, allowing for the emergence of a number of independent states, some late in the nineteenth century and the beginning of the twentieth. Bulgaria, Rumania, part of Yugoslavia, and Alabania became new national states. The Austro-Hungarian Empire evolved into Hungary, Serbia, and ultimately Czechoslovakia. Powerful liberal independence movements manifested themselves within the Tsarist Empire. Most of these new states undertook constitutional reforms providing for individual rights, election and popular participation, and restraints on the government.

8. Cited by Donald Read, *Cobden and Bright.* London: St. Martin's Press, 1968, p. 65.

Conclusion

In overall terms, nineteenth-century liberalism shows a remarkable record in bringing forth and institutionalizing civil rights, political rights, and economic freedoms. It was equally potent in causing a profound reconsideration of the position of the aristocracy, the Church, and many unreconstructed traditionalists. But the century was also remarkable for the growth and the unprecedented development of technology and production. This, despite the many miseries that continued to afflict the workers, gave credence to some of the assertions of Adam Smith and the utilitarians. Economies grew; world population began a rapid climb; water and rail communications were established, bringing people closer together in their national community as well as in the world; new cities developed rapidly while many old ones were literally torn apart and rebuilt; currency in gold or paper money and new banking practices facilitated exchange while savings were channeled into new investments. Nations mushroomed in the name of self-determination. The best eulogy on the spirit of the innovation and the modernity that bourgeois liberalism exemplified was given by its greatest critic, Karl Marx, in the *Communist Manifesto.*

> Constant revolutionizing of production, uninterrupted disturbance of all social relations, everlasting uncertainty and agitation, distinguish the bourgeois epoch from all earlier times. All fixed, fast-frozen relationships, with their train of venerable ideas and opinions, are swept away, all new-formed ones become obsolete before they can ossify. All that is solid melts into air, all that is holy is profaned. . . .

At the end of the century a new factor was injected into the liberal philosophy—social justice. It was needed to support individuals in one form or another when their self-reliance and initiative could no longer provide them with protection, or when the market did not show the flexibility or the sensitivity it was supposed to show in satisfying basic wants. A new spirit of mutual aid, cooperation, and service began to develop. It became stronger with the coming of the twentieth century.

Bibliography

Bentham, Jeremy. *An Introduction to the Principles of Morals and Legislation.* New York: Harper & Brothers, 1952.

Berlin, Isaiah. *Four Essays on Liberty.* New York: Oxford University Press, 1969.

Black, Eugene (ed.). *Posture of Europe, 1815–1940.* Homewood, Ill.: The Dorsey Press, 1964.

——.*Victorians: Culture and Society.* New York: Harper & Row, 1973.

Briggs, Asa. *The Age of Improvement.* London: Longmans, 1959.

Clark, G. Kitson. *An Expanding Society: Britain 1830–1900.* New York: Cambridge U.P., 1967.

Dahl, Robert A. *A Preface to Democratic Theory.* Chicago: University of Chicago Press, 1956.

"Declaration of the Rights of Man and of the Citizen." In Paul H. Beik, *The French Revolution.* New York: Harper & Row, 1970.

Dicey, A. V. *Lectures on the Relationship Between Law and Public Opinion in England During the 19th Century.* NewYork: Macmillan, 1952.

Friedman, Milton. *Capitalism and Freedom.* Chicago: University of Chicago Press, 1963.

Gray, John. *Liberalism.* Minneapolis: University of Minnesota Press, 1986.

Halevy, E. *The Growth of Philosophic Radicalism.* London: Faber, 1952.

Hallowell, John H. *The Moral Foundations of Democracy.* Chicago: University of Chicago Press, 1954.

Hamilton, Alexander, Madison, James, and Jay, John. *The Federalist Papers.* New York: New American Library, 1961.

Hartz, Louis. *The Liberal Tradition in America.* New York: Harcourt, Brace and World, 1962.

Hayek, Friedrich A. *The Road to Serfdom.* Chicago: University of Chicago Press, 1944.

Hobhouse, L. T. *Liberalism.* New York: Oxford U.P., 1964.

Jefferson, Thomas. *Drafts of the Declaration of Independence.* Washington, D.C.: Acropolis, 1963.

Laski, Harold J. *The Rise of European Liberalism.* Atlantic Highlands, N.J.: Humanities Press, 1962.

Levine, Andrew. *Liberal Democracy: A Critique of Its Theory.* New York: Columbia U.P., 1981.

Lively, Jack. *Democracy.* Oxford, England: Basil Blackwell, 1975.

Locke, John. *Two Treatises on Government.* Edited by Peter Laslett. New York: New American Library, 1965.

MacPherson, C. B. *The Political Theory of Possessive Individualism.* Oxford, England: Hobbes and Locke, 1962.

———. *The Real World of Democracy.* Oxford, England: Clarendon Press, 1966.

———. *Democratic Theory: Essays in Retrieval.* Oxford, England: Clarendon Press, 1973.

———. *The Life and Times of Liberal Democracy.* New York: Oxford University Press, 1977.

McIlwain, Charles H. *Constitutionalism: Ancient and Modern.* Ithaca, N.Y.: Cornell U.P., 1958.

Mill, John Stuart. *Consideration on Representative Government.* New York: Bobbs-Merrill, Library of Liberal Arts, 1958.

———. *On Liberty.* 1956.

———. *Utilitarianism.* 1957.

Palmer, R. R. *The Age of the Democratic Revolution.* 2 volumes. Princeton, N.J.: Princeton U.P., 1959.

Palmer, R. R. and Colton, Joel. *A History of the Modern World Since 1815.* New York: Knopf, 1971.

Revel, Jean-Francois. *Without Marx and Jesus: The New American Revolution has Begun.* New York: Doubleday, 1971.

Rousseau, Jean-Jacques. *The Social Contract and Discourse on Inequality.* New York: Washington Square Press, 1967.

Rugiero, E. *The History of European Liberalism.* Boston: Beacon Press, 1959.

Sartori, Giovanni. *Democratic Theory.* New York: Praeger, 1965.

Sidorsky, David. *The Liberal Tradition in European Thought.* New York: G. P. Putnam's Sons, 1970.

Smith, Adam. *The Wealth of Nations: Representative Selections.* New York: Bobbs-Merrill, 1961.

Tawney, R. H. *Religion and the Rise of Capitalism.* New York: New American Library, 1954.

Thomson, David. *Europe Since 1815.* 2nd rev. ed. New York: Knopf, 1957.

————. *Democracy in France Since 1870.* 4th ed. New York: Oxford U.P., 1964.

Thurman, Arnold. *The Folklore of Capitalism.* New Haven, Conn.: Yale University Press, 1937.

Weber, Max. *The Protestant Ethic and the Spirit of Capitalism.* New York: Charles Scribner's Sons, 1958.

3 | *Radical Democracy, Socialism, and the Welfare State*

> *But man in society not only lives his individual life: he also modifies the form of social institutions in the direction indicated by reason — in such a manner . . . that will render them more efficient for securing freedom. . . .*
>
> SYDNEY OLIVER   The Fabian Essays in Socialism

The year 1848 represents the watershed of European liberalism. From it powerful and divergent currents began to flow. From Paris to Palermo, from Frankfurt and London to Budapest, Vienna, and Madrid, the poor, the workers, and the peasants, who had left the countryside for the urban centers, rose to take power away from the propertied classes in the name of *radical democracy* and *socialism*. Writing in the same year, John Stuart Mill commented on the industrial and technological achievements of the period and pointed out that they had improved the living standard of the middle classes only. "They have not as yet," he added, "begun to effect those great changes in human destiny, which it is their nature . . . to accomplish."[1]

The middle classes found themselves wavering. Some sided with radical democrats and the socialists and joined forces with them in an alliance that could not last. Others backed conservative groups — the nobility, the Church, the landowners — that had resisted liberalism.

Using the three basic cores of the liberal democratic ideology as a guide, it is relatively easy to map out its evolution and to assess its present position.

1. Cited by Asa Briggs, *The Age of Improvement.* London: Longmans, 1959, p. 303.

Radical Democrats

Radical democrats accepted the moral core of liberalism — civil rights, individual freedoms, freedom of press, religion, and association (though they insisted on the secularization of many of the functions that the Church provided, such as education, and favored outright expropriation of its landed domains). They also supported the political core but interpreted it in Rousseauian terms: all political power should come directly from the people and a majority could make all decisions directly or through sovereign representative assemblies. They were against all voting qualifications and against any restraints on the exercise of popular will. They also began to express fundamental reservations about the economic core.

Radical Democrats in England and France

A strong radical democratic movement developed in England roughly between 1830 and 1850. This was *Chartism,* a movement of middle-class reformers with working-class support. Their program (the Charter) seemed to be primarily political, calling for universal manhood franchise, equal electorate districts, "one man, one vote," annual parliaments, elimination of all property qualifications, and the secret ballot. The leaders, Feargus O'Connor, Francis Place, and William Lovett, attempted time after time to pressure Parliament into passing legislation in accordance with Charter, but without success.

But in addition to political reform, a strong group among the Chartists urged for social and economic reform. Sometimes they came close to the socialist ideas that were circulating in England and the Continent at the time. They demanded the regulation of hours of work and wages, and the need for social benefits for the workers.

> Eight hours to work; eight hours to play
> Eight hours to sleep; eight bob [shillings] a day

was one among many Chartist slogans. Some of the Chartist leaders openly advocated socialist measures:

> It is the duty of the Government to appropriate its present surplus revenue, and the proceeds of national and public property, to the purchasing of lands, and the location thereon of the unemployed poor. . . .

> The gradual resumption by the State . . . of its ancient, undoubted, inalienable domain, and sole proprietorship over all the lands, mines, tributaries, fisheries, &c., of the United Kingdom and our Colonies; for the same to be held by the State, as trustee in perpetuity, for the entire people. . . .

It is the recognized duty of the State to support all those of its subjects, who, from incapacity or misfortune, are unable to procure their own subsistence.[2]

In France during the same period, radical democracy took a more extreme form. Louis Blanqui, one of the early social reformers, moved very close to revolutionary socialism and led a number of armed uprisings against the governmental authorities. Louis Blanc, another social reformer, came closer to the Chartist position. He believed political reforms were essential, but it was the duty of the State to safeguard the "right to work." He urged the government to set up national workshops to employ workers, and he believed that such workshops would compete successfully with privately owned firms. As time went on radical democracy in France increasingly moved in the direction of economic and social reforms—especially after 1848 when universal manhood suffrage, one of the major demands, was adopted. It raised the electorate overnight from a quarter million to nine million voters.

Thus, many radical democrats parted company with liberals on the definition of the economic core. They questioned the laissez-faire model of capitalism as it had been portrayed by Adam Smith. They were in favor of using the State in order to correct some of the evils and the uncertainties of the market, but they went beyond the mere search for corrective measures. They emphasized the importance of social and collective goals that could best be implemented by collective (i.e., State) action. They favored extensive State regulation not simply through legislation but through direct action and performance. Not just laws regulating child labor, but inspection and enforcement was demanded; not only poor laws providing for relief, but the actual operation of State workshops to provide employment to the poor. They demanded that the provision of social services be implemented directly by the public authorities.

Most radical democrats, however, did not advocate socialism. Their position was that the State should act and intervene where major social services and needs were involved without reaching out to expropriate property or to directly take over economic activities such as production and trade. They favored wide regulations and occasional direct controls but not the socialization of the means of production.

If we situate the radical democrats in terms of our basic cores of liberalism, we shall find them strong on the political core (leaning all the way to majoritarianism and popular sovereignty), strong on the moral core, but faithful to only a few of the basic principles defined as the economic core of early liberalism. In 1869, the French politician Jules Gambetta summed up the *political* program of radical democrats everywhere in his Belleville Manifesto, and intimated at the same time the need for economic reform:

2. Cited in G. D. H. Cole and A. W. Filson, *Working Class Movements: Selected Documents.* New York: St. Martin's Press, 1965, p. 79.

... I think that there is no other sovereign but the people and that universal suffrage, the instrument of this sovereignty, has no value and basis unless it be radically free.

He asked for:

... the most radical application of universal suffrage; ... individual liberty to be ... protected by law; ... trial by jury for every kind of political offense; complete freedom of the Press; ... freedom of meeting ... with liberty to discuss all religious, philosophical, political, and social affairs; ... complete freedom of association ... separation of church and state; free, compulsory, secular primary education; ... suppression of standing armies; ... abolition of privileges and monopolies.[3]

Liberal and Radical Democrats: Reconciliation

With the exception of a few who remained attached to the economic philosophy of Adam Smith, most liberals, and what we have called radical democrats, gradually came to terms. Liberals have accepted the full logic of democracy. The franchise has been extended to cover all citizens, male and female, above eighteen. All of the many qualifications for voting based on literacy, age, residence, income, and so on, have been eliminated. Restraints on representative assemblies have been virtually lifted except in cases where the chief executive is also elected directly by the people. In all existing constitutional monarchies the monarch has become a mere figurehead.

The people were mobilized in large mass parties and these parties, in many countries, exercise a controlling influence over their representatives. In some instances provisions for referenda give the people an additional measure of direct democracy. Popular democracy and majority rule expressed through direct elections for or against the members and candidates of large national political parties have been accepted by all liberals and democrats to be the major source of policymaking. At the same time the moral core of liberalism in the form of individual and minority rights has been reaffirmed.

There has also been a similar reconciliation between radical democrats and liberals with regard to economic matters. Liberal, as well as many other parties, even when they call themselves conservative, have found themselves increasingly in agreement. State intervention to support economic activities in the form of price and other controls is deemed acceptable; State intervention through direct or indirect means to stimulate economic activity is again deemed desirable; State regulation of a growing number of economic activities is viewed as indispensable; State direct involvement in providing for unemployment assistance and State indirect

3. Cited in David Thomson, *Democracy in France Since 1870*, 5th ed. New York: Oxford U.P., 1969, pp. 315–316.

and direct action to provide for employment is now taken for granted in most democracies. Thus, the functions of the State are viewed not only as supportive or regulatory; they have actually become complementary to the private sector.

The Socialist Impulse

Socialism as a philosophy of life and as a scheme for the organization of society is as old as (perhaps older than) democracy or any other form of social, economic, or political organization. Some consider it, in fact, to have been prevalent among primitive societies where it has been suggested that land was collectively owned.

Socialism also represents an ethic diametrically opposed to that of private ownership and private profit and the inequalities that these systems may lead to. It is an ethic of an egalitarian and free society, from which the words "mine" and "yours" are eliminated.

Utopian Socialism

Utopian socialists, beginning with Thomas More (1478–1535), through Francis Bacon (1561–1621), and Tommaso Campanella (1568–1639), down to some of the most important French and British utopian socialists of the nineteenth century, shared a set of common ideas.

1. They had an aversion to private property and the exploitation of the poor by those who owned the wealth, whether landed, commercial, or industrial. "Property is theft" was the curt aphorism of the French socialist Proudhon. The Romantic poet Shelley voiced these early nineteenth- century socialist beliefs:

> The seed ye sow, another reaps,
> The wealth ye find, another keeps,
> The robes ye weave, another wears,
> The arms ye forge, another bears.

2. A passionate commitment to collectivism — the common ownership of wealth — was partly based on notions about primitive communism, and partly on ideas of mutual cooperation and social solidarity. Thus, socialism was seen as the way to extirpate strife, antagonisms, and selfishness. Utopian socialists shared the nostalgic vision of the Roman poet Virgil about bygone happy ages:

> No fences parted fields, nor marks nor bounds
> Divided acres of litigious grounds,
> But all was common.

In a famous passage, Rousseau expressed similar thoughts:

The first man, who after enclosing a piece of ground, took it into his head to say, *this is mine,* and found people simple enough to believe him, was the real founder of civil society. How many crimes, how many wars, how many murders, how many misfortunes and horrors, would that man have saved the human species, who pulling up the stakes or filling up the ditches should have cried to his fellows: Beware of listening to this impostor; you are lost, if you forget that the fruits of the earth belong equally to us all, and the earth itself to nobody![4]

3. A passionate belief in what might be called "social collectivism" emphasized the interdependence and solidarity of social life — the "social nature" of men and women, as opposed to the individualistic or utilitarian ethic. Communitarianism was the supreme value; individualism, competition, and self-interest were detested.

4. There were many divergences among the early utopian socialists on *how* to bring socialism about. Some believed in violence and revolution, but did not spell out any details; others believed in persuasion and example. For instance, the British socialist Robert Owen (1771–1856) set up a model textile factory in East Lanark, Scotland, where such features as the good working conditions and wages, and the participation of the workers in some of the profits were to become a model to convince other businessmen that it was in their own interests to follow the same pattern. Most utopian socialists, however, believed in education. If men and women were properly educated they would opt for socialism, and it was the task of the intellectuals to provide this kind of education.

5. Many, especially among the French utopian socialists, were what we would call today social engineers. Society would be controlled and manipulated so that under proper conditions and with the proper social organization, human beings could attain perfection — both moral and material.

Most of the utopian socialists were not democrats. They paid lip service to the moral core of liberalism but argued that liberal political and economic principles and practices could not bring it about. A "new ideology" had to be imposed first, or inculcated through education. They never managed to form a party or even a political movement, but their writings had a profound influence on the development of socialist thought.

Democratic Socialism

We have already noted that by the end of the nineteenth century there developed a gradual reconciliation between the proponents of liberalism and the radical democrats in the form of political democracy. A similar reconciliation was also beginning to take place — one that developed

---

4. Rousseau, *The Social Contract and Discourse on the Origins of Inequality,* Book 1.

throughout the twentieth century, and accounts for what today is generally called democratic socialism.

Nineteenth-century democrats endorsed popular sovereignty and majoritarianism while accepting the individual and civil rights that we have discussed as the moral core of liberalism. This set the tone for state intervention to regulate the market, to correct malfunctioning, and to provide social service. But socialism, as first propounded by Marx and some utopian socialists, rejected the political core of liberalism. Thus, even if for a short period of time, socialism appeared to be directly opposed to basic democratic principles and practices.

However, revolutionary Marxism gave place by the end of the nineteenth century to "revisionism." In France, in Germany, especially in England, but also in Belgium, Holland, and the Scandinavian countries, socialist parties began increasingly to accept the logic and the techniques of democracy. Their goal was modified to bringing about social change through peaceful political means and established democratic procedures, and they became attached to the moral core of liberalism and its stress on individual and civil rights. Socialists began to consider these ideals as ends in themselves rather than as means to be used for the conquest of power. They became increasingly attracted to electoral politics, especially when socialist candidates won appreciable numbers of votes at the polls. They began to see the proper instrument for change in democracy and realized that they could substitute democratic process for revolution and force.

The Fabians   In England at this time a number of intellectuals were expounding on socialism. Most important were the Fabians (who took their name from the Roman general Fabius, whose defensive "wait and see" tactics gradually weakened Hannibal's invading forces until they were defeated). The Fabians and the Fabian Society, which they established in 1884, relied on three forces: *time,* which meant that socialism would come about gradually; *education,* to persuade the elites and the people that socialism was a superior system, morally and economically, to capitalism; and *political action* in the context of democratic and parliamentary institutions. This meant the formation of a Socialist party that would present its socialist doctrine to the people for their approval. There was not even a mention of the use of force, and nothing about revolution: in fact, many of their socialist principles were inspired by the Bible. British socialism was steeped in moral, egalitarian, and humanistic values, seeking human dignity and freedom in a society from which profit and selfishness had been removed.

The philosophic foundations of Fabian socialism were set forth in *The Fabian Essays,* published in 1889. George Bernard Shaw, one of the movement's leaders, wrote:

> It was in 1885, that the Fabian Society ... set ... two definite tasks; first, to provide a parliamentary program for a Prime

Minister converted to Socialism . . . and second, to make it as easy and matter-of-course for the ordinary respectable Englishman to be a Socialist. . . .[5]

THE BETTMANN ARCHIVE, INC.

Sidney and Beatrice Webb

Sidney Webb (1859–1947), an Englishman of petit bourgeois background, spent over ten years in the service of the Colonial Office. In 1885, the year he joined the bar, he also joined the Fabian Society, a group of British socialists dedicated to the education of the British people in socialist principles. In 1889, Webb, along with other notable Fabians such as George Bernard Shaw and Graham Wallas, issued *The Fabian Essay in Socialism*, a book which was to become a classic of non-Marxist socialist thought. In 1887, Sidney Webb was married to Beatrice Potter (1858–1943), a woman of similar views. Both were heavily involved with social issues, and they were active in the formation of the British Labour Party. Sidney drafted its manifesto—*Labour and the New Social Order*—which served as the party's platform in the elections of 1918, 1922, and 1924.

5. Shaw (ed.), *The Fabian Essays in Socialism.* London: Allen & Unwin, 1958, p. 33 (1st ed. 1889).

TABLE 3-1   The Rise of the Labour Party Vote

GENERAL ELECTION	SEATS CONTESTED	MEMBERS RETURNED	LABOUR VOTE
1900	15	2	62,698
1906	50	29	323,195
1910 (Jan.)	78	40	505,690
1910 (Dec.)	56	42	370,802
1918	361	57	2,244,945
1922	414	142	4,236,733
1923	427	191	4,348,379
1924	514	151	5,487,620
1945	**640**	**393**	**11,632,891**

The Fabians favored socialization of the means of production, state controls, and broad welfare measures to bring about as much social equality as possible. They had no regard whatsoever for the economic core of liberalism and advocated drastic overhaul of the economy; in doing so they went way beyond the simple regulation of social legislation advocated by radical democrats (and increasingly acquiesced in by liberals). They favored the abolition of property and of the free enterprise system. Socialism was declared, however, to be an advanced form of individualism: "Socialism is merely individualism rationalised, organised, clothed, and in its right mind."[6]

At the beginning of this century, in 1901, the Fabians and the leaders of the major British trade unions formed the Labour party, and by 1906 were running their own independent candidates for election. They won 323,195 votes and secured twenty-nine seats in the House of Commons. Socialism began to gain the respectability that the Fabians wanted to give it (Table 3-1).

In 1918, Fabian intellectuals provided a definitive platform for the Labour Party. The party declared the need for

> ... the gradual building up of a new social order based, not on internecine conflict, inequality of riches, and dominion over subject classes, subject races, or a subject sex, but on the deliberately planned cooperation in production and distribution, the sympathetic approach to a healthy equality, the widest possible participation in power, both economic and political, and the general consciousness of consent which characterise a true democracy.[7]

Socialism was explicitly and proudly endorsed by the Labour party, in order

6. Ibid., p. 99.
7. Cited in G. D. H. Cole, *A History of the Labour Party Since 1914*. London: Routledge and Kegan Paul, 1948, p. 65.

to secure for the producers by hand or by brain the full fruits of their industry, and the most equitable distribution thereof that may be possible, *upon the basis of the common ownership of the means of production* and the best obtainable system of popular administration and control of each industry and service.[788] [Emphasis added.]

European Revisionism   In western Europe it was revolutionary Marxism that remained the dominant intellectual force and inspiration of working-class socialist movements, but in the latter part of the nineteenth century, democratic socialism (in the name of "revisionism") began to gain the upper hand.

Revisionism became a distinct ideological movement, based on the works of Eduard Bernstein, a German socialist who produced the most comprehensive criticism of Marx and Marxism. He pointed out that:

1. The liberal capitalist system was not about to collapse, as Marx had anticipated.

2. The number of capitalists and property owners was increasing absolutely rather than decreasing, as Marxist theory stipulated it would. Thanks to the corporations and the stock exchange, a greater number of people began to "own" property in the form of stocks.

3. The capitalistic economy was generating an ever-increasing number of jobs as production became more specialized. The middle classes were, in fact, growing in number and changing in character. They no longer consisted of people who owned property, as in the past, but of new salaried personnel: technicians, engineers, white-collar workers, service personnel, civil servants, those in the liberal professions, teachers, and so on. Thus, instead of a pyramid with a huge base and sharp apex, the changing class structure under liberal capitalism was beginning to resemble a stepped pyramid in which blocks of decreasing width were superimposed upon each other.

According to Bernstein, class structure could be schematized, as shown on the left in Figure 3-1, as a stepped pyramid made up of many intermediate layers. This was contrary to Marx's view (to the right), which represents society as a smooth-sided pyramid, with the capitalist class at the apex.

4. As societies democratized, allowing for equal and universal franchise, associational freedoms, and the formation of political parties, strong working-class parties would be able to assume political power against the capitalist class and use the State as an instrument for their own protection and to secure a better allocation of goods and services. This would be accomplished through legislation and nationalizations. Bernstein felt that Marx had seriously underestimated the capabilities of the democratic state to intervene in favor of the workers and the underprivileged.

8. Ibid., p. 72.

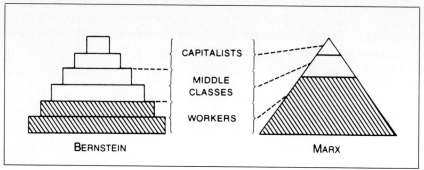

FIGURE 3-1   Bernstein's schematization of capitalist society (left)
compared to Marx's (right).

In the light of these observations, Bernstein concluded that *Evolutionary Socialism* (the title of his book, published in 1899 — ten years after *The Fabian Essays* were published) and not revolutionary socialism was to gain ascendancy. It was step-by-step and stage-by-stage development of socialism that would gradually replace capitalism.

Bernstein's analysis was prophetic. Revisionism was gradually adopted by the socialist parties, and revolutionary socialism and its tactics were abandoned. Socialism became synonymous with *democratic socialism*. It accepted parliamentary government and elections and emphasized, almost exclusively, political activity within the framework of bourgeois legality and democracy. It signified the abandonment of revolutionary class struggle. The workers were to devote themselves to improving their working conditions, their pension benefits, and their wages within the capitalistic economy, and to see to it that a larger share of the national wealth went to them and their families. The trade unions and democratic political action were to become the instruments for the realization of such tasks.

The socialist movements and parties in Europe began to move, therefore, close to the position of the British Labour party. They, too, accepted the logic of democracy and began to rely more and more on elections, votes, and the conquest of political power through elections. In so doing, they endorsed fully both the moral and the political cores of liberalism but remained hostile to private property and the market economy, promising to socialize the means of production when they achieved full power. But, as with the British Labour party, their approach became gradualistic, even eclectic and pragmatic. Socialists on the Continent and the Labour party in England began to propose only specific and selective measures, dealing primarily with the major industries. Small shopkeepers, manufacturers, farmers, and also many large industrial firms and groups would be allowed to operate on their own.

What revisionism accomplished was to mobilize a strong percentage of the workers in favor of democratic change and to convince them (not always completely) that they could promote and defend their interests within the democratic political institutions. Socialism, as such, remained the ultimate end, and strong socialist parties, supported by the vote of the workers, were expected to press for or undertake comprehensive measures for the welfare and well-being of the workers. Even if socialist parties did not gain a majority, they could still carry great weight within representative assemblies and could directly influence governments to adopt measures favoring the working class. Broad educational reforms, health, accident, and unemployment insurance, retirement benefits, paid holidays, the reduction of work hours, paid vacations, collective bargaining, welfare measures for the poor and the incapacitated, public works, reform in tax policies favoring low income groups, and progressively increasing taxes on middle and higher incomes—these were essential and beneficial measures to ameliorate the conditions of the workers within the broad framework of both capitalism and democracy. The dismantling of capitalism, in the form of widespread nationalizations, could wait or be selectively undertaken under propitious political and economic circumstances.

The Great Synthesis: Democratic Socialism and the Welfare State

Ultimately, this was the general posture assumed by European socialist parties (and the Socialist party of the United States) at the end of World War I. Ever since, socialist parties have been advocating the cause of socialism in a democratic setting with full respect for democratic institutions. In so doing, they have been extending the pact between liberals and radical democrats further into what, in effect, has become a liberal-radical and democratic-socialist synthesis or, better, *democratic socialism.*

The concept of the triple core of liberalism will again help us identify the consensus that has evolved over the last fifty years. Democrats *and* socialists now fully accept *both* the moral core and the political core. In fact, the political and moral cores have expanded. Freedoms have been maintained and extended—for workers, the underprivileged, and minorities. It is not only political parties but, even more so, the various interest groups and associations that make their demands known and that participate in policymaking.

Differences continue to exist when it comes to the economic core but they are no longer sharp or irreconcilable. In many cases agreement on the content of policies to be pursued by far overshadows ideological or policy differences. Reconsideration by democrats of the validity and the efficacy of laissez-faire economics and equally significant, second thoughts on the part of socialists on the efficacy and wisdom of nationalizations and state controls, have helped bridge and reconcile differences.

The premise of a free market and a price mechanism reflecting the law of supply and demand gave way gradually — even if only so gradually in the United States — to regulation. Overriding questions of health, education, unemployment, and poverty required regulatory legislation. Wild fluctuations in prices in the market called for controls, especially when they affected the prices of essential commodities like food and housing. Monopolies, which gave private owners control over needed commodities and hence freedom to adjust prices to satisfy the insatiable profit motive, had to be dealt with. Gradually, and especially in the twentieth century, the classic model of economic liberalism became an abstraction.

Keynesian Economics Reliance on the automatic performance of the market — for the adjustment of prices, savings, and employment — came under serious reconsideration thanks to the theoretical insights of the English economist John Maynard Keynes (1883–1946). According to Keynes, the market by itself could not provide a full utilization of resources, and the state should move into the picture with indirect controls.

By increasing the flow of money and decreasing the interest rates, there could be renewed investments, which would snowball into the creation of new jobs and hence more revenue to stimulate further demand. Thus unemployment would be absorbed and resources fully utilized. In the process, inflationary pressures would be avoided with appropriate tax measures. In this manner, capitalism would be both reformed and salvaged. The public authorities would become its guardian angel, and no structural modifications involving property rights, entrepreneurial freedoms and incentives, or state planning in the allocation of resources or in price-fixing would be required. "Keynesianism" resulted in policies adopted in a number of countries ever since the 1930s, including Nazi Germany and the United States, especially through the development of public works projects, public spending, and more generally through fiscal policy — including deficit financing. Today when we talk about "capitalism," we virtually always have in mind reformed capitalism, in which the public authorities, through fiscal policy and spending, play a determining role in the market.

The Welfare State The major instrument for ensuring social and economic rights became the welfare state — the complex of public services and payments that correspond to "entitlements." The very magnitude of entitlements is staggering. In the late 1970s, total government payments to individuals in various forms and through various services amounted to from 18.7 percent of the gross national product in the United States to as much as 40–50 percent in countries such as France or Sweden. In the United States about half of the total for medical expenses came from public funds. In Germany and Holland it was about 70 percent, while in Sweden, France, and Britain it amounted to over 90 percent.

To provide for social services and maintain incomes above the poverty level, the State simply extracts, through taxation, a growing percentage of the gross national product (goods and services produced) and redistributes a sizable portion of it in the form of services and cash payments.

In all contemporary democracies the growth of social and economic rights calls for a series of choices, and this is what public policy is all about. Which services should be provided for everybody? What groups merit special attention? What are the limits below which poverty exists and should be prevented? The list is long, but by and large most democratic regimes have followed a similar route in establishing similar priority choices. Children and education came first with minimal educational services, but with ever-expanding requirements for schooling, a free college education was added in some countries, the United States being the first to do so.

The aged came next, with emphasis on pensions. In many countries the age limit for retirement is set at sixty for women and sixty-two for men.

The third step came with legislation requiring the State to provide for employment or to cover the unemployed through special benefits (unemployment insurance). It is presently financed through compulsory contributions and public funds, and public subsidies have steadily grown. In Europe after World War II, a comprehensive scheme was developed, which provided for uniform payments and minimum income levels. In the United States, since the Social Security Act of 1935, an ever-expanding number of employees have been included, contributions have been raised steadily, and benefits have increased.

Health care was the fourth step. Originally undertaken by private and religious organizations, it has been increasingly assumed by government agencies either through insurance programs or through direct payments and services. Germany was the first country to develop a nation-wide health program even before the turn of the century. England followed after the turn of the century, and in 1948 it introduced a most comprehensive medical care program: it nationalized all health services and hospitals and incorporated almost all the doctors into the National Health Service. Health care became free, a matter of right. In Sweden a health insurance plan is mandatory and every citizen receives health care free of charge. In France medical expenses are covered through a system that combines insurance paid for by individuals with direct payments by the employer and the State. In the United States it is only after age sixty-five that citizens become directly covered through the Medicare programs.

Although education, health, retirement, and unemployment coverage do provide some safeguards against unaffordable costs, the so-called safety net is full of holes. Despite this supplementary income, there are millions who find themselves without adequate income—they are the poor.

It is to plug these holes and support the poor that the income maintenance and public assistance programs have been developed. They are aimed at raising minimal income levels to tolerable ones. Minimum wages become a matter of public policy and most democratic regimes have set a minimum floor below which wages cannot fall. But with a family to support, a minimum wage is often inadequate.

Various income maintenance programs are used to raise the family income. Tax exemptions, special benefits in the form of cash payments, rent allowances, food subsidies, special allowances for children, day care centers for working mothers, school luncheons, maternity benefits, and all sorts of other free services are calculated to do so.

Public assistance programs and related special treatment and payments are afforded to special categories of the public. Although these programs also vary from one country to another, they are almost always available, at least for a given time. However, their purpose is to provide a family with a minimum income, not to equalize income, even if they lessen the distance between the rich and the poor. Security and often a small cushion of adequacy are all that can be expected.

Democracy and Socialism: Current Trends

Democracy, liberalism, radical democracy, democratic socialism, the welfare state—in successive waves through the nineteenth century and into the twentieth—have shaped the "great synthesis." Its major feature is the reconciliation of individual and political rights and freedoms with massive State intervention in the economy, an intervention that in some countries has included the socialization of some key sectors of industrial production. It is a synthesis that in varying degrees can be found in most contemporary democracies.

Where do we stand today? Early liberalism stressed personal rights and civil rights—the moral core. This was retained by democracy, which also expanded the political core of liberalism by institutionalizing majoritarianism, organizing political parties, eliminating voter qualifications, and minimizing restraints on the power of the representative assemblies. It also urged the regulation and control of economic life. Socialism maintained respect for individual and civil rights (the moral core), accepted the political core, and squarely introduced the question of comprehensive economic controls and welfare measures. It favored collectivization of the means of production gradually and selectively, with many qualifications and hesitations, over the last two decades.

Liberals, democrats, and socialists find themselves in agreement on many policy issues confronting modern democracies, or at least their disagreements appear to divide them less. There is an ideological convergence and a synthesis of points of view—indicating an attachment to the principles of democracy, and only secondary differences with regard to the running of the economy. This is true despite the recent trends in many western democracies toward deregulating the economy, reducing taxes and the expenditures that the welfare state entails, and putting the emphasis once more on entrepreneurship and production—the supply side rather than stimulating the economy through spending. Yet "Reaganomics" in the United States or "Thatcherism" in England, and most recently deregulation in France, continue to allow for vast expenditures by the State. More than 42 percent of the total spending in most industrialized democracies in Europe comes from the government and as much as 32 percent in the United States. In other words, free enterprise and the market economy operate within the context of powerful economic supports provided by the State. The Divine Hand of Providence has often been replaced by the not so godly—according to many—hand of the State.

Democracy: Crisis and Prospects

Today, looking at the map of the world, we find democracy and democratic institutions implanted in the whole of western Europe, North America, Australia, and New Zealand. It seems to have gained some roots in India and even more so in Japan. Democracy has become "operational" for more than a billion people if India is counted. Many of them have a standard of living that ranks among the highest, and they live under conditions of "modernity." Indeed, if we were to exclude India, we can say that they represent the countries with the highest per capita income in the world.

It would be downright silly, however, to assume or to pretend that the synthesis we have outlined is complete and that it has been successful and widely accepted everywhere. Not more than forty countries in our world today have a democratic regime. Democratic systems and ideologies have not gained new recruits, especially in the Third World nations where the label is often used but it has a very different meaning. Finally, all contemporary democracies—liberal or socialist—face some immediate and urgent challenges. There are many strains and stresses. Some people, in fact, talk of a "crisis of democracy."[9]

9. M. J. Crozier, S. P. Huntington, and J. Watanuki, *The Crisis of Democracy*. New York: New York U.P., 1975. I have summarized some of the arguments of the authors.

The crisis of democracy everywhere lies in its lack of a transcendental ideology. There are no absolutes associated with it, except the moral autonomy of the individual. Democracy consists of a set of procedures to preserve and to promote this profoundly individualist ethic. But otherwise as an ideology—to use Marx's phrase—democracy does not "grip the masses." It offers no easy solution to many of our predicaments and it promises no blue horizons except the ones that we open up through our own exertions. It is not geared to a scheme of history which tells us that a democratic development is inevitable and just. On the contrary, it tells us that we make our history and that in the process we may make mistakes. It sets no unifying themes. It tells us that we are all different from each other and that we rightfully should follow our own drummer; we are not meant to "march in step." In short, there is no vision to guide us. There are no "true believers" among real democrats—only skeptics!

How do democracies define the "public good"? It is not ordained by divine word; it is not decreed by a ruling governing body; it is not identified with that of a class—though the bourgeoisie claimed to be its spokesman for a long time. The public good is the sum total of the thousands of interests that compete with each other (although some may argue that it is not even that). It lies in the existence of procedures that allow for competition. It is the procedures, then, that have value in themselves—the Constitution, parliamentary government, party and economic competition, and so on. Procedures, however, are only forms—ways of doing things; they are not easily converted to substantive values to which people become passionately attached. Democracy provides the means, the instruments, and the processes of political life; it does not, like so many ideologies, tell us what life is all about. We are free to find out—or to give up and have somebody tell us!

The Crisis of Rising Expectations

Everybody is familiar with the term "the revolution of rising expectations." It is common not only among poor nations which have recently gained their independence and are underdeveloped, but also among the peoples of the rich countries in western Europe and the United States. The most characteristic manifestation of the "revolution" is that all people want *more of everything*—more wealth, a higher standard of living, better education, greater security, better health care, more participation in decision making, more leisure, and greater equality. The speed with which these expectations have escalated and have converged has created serious problems.

The crisis of modern democratic regimes is primarily caused by the disparity between ideology and institutional capabilities. Ideology conjures up a world of plenty and immediate fulfillment. It shapes the new moral imperatives of equality and of equal sharing in opportunities and benefits. However, institutions are slow to respond to the pressure, and as a result, democratic regimes are faced with the prospect of instability.

It is simply difficult to meet all the rising demands, not only because resources are limited, but because structural and institutional changes are needed in order to meet them. New services are required and new institutional mechanisms must be put in place. Even the most open and responsive systems experience a time lag between demands being made and registered and developing new mechanisms to respond to them — let alone satisfy them.

The intensity and number of demands from minorities, professional organizations, trade unions, student groups, cultural associations, and so on (many couched in sharp ideological terms) threaten to overwhelm the existing democratic institutions. This is a *revolutionary prospect*, because it is likely to cause upheavals in the institutional framework of democratic societies. But it is also conceivable that democratic elites may have to resort to repressive measures in order to curb demands and stifle the rising expectations. This is the *authoritarian prospect*. There is, of course, the possibility that some democratic societies may "muddle through" by adjusting their institutions to meet the new demands, constantly experiencing temporary dislocations but capable of reforms.

The Crisis of Institutions

Representative institutions, either in parliamentary or presidential systems, face a double crisis in performance and legitimacy. Gone are the days when the radical democrats believed that universal manhood suffrage and representative government would solve all social and economic evils. Only a small number now believe that representative assemblies really represent the people. Few think that, out of the welter of interests represented in the representative assemblies, a common purpose and common policies for society as a whole can evolve. There is a crisis of democratic representative institutions.

If the representative assemblies are no longer viewed as being truly representative, new institutions must be sought to safeguard the interests of the people at large. One such proposal is direct participation. This is the demand for a direct say in decision making by all those who are affected. The corollary is decentralization of the decision-making mechanism; the virtual dismantling of the bureaucratic apparatus of the States into small and manageable units such as the city, the locality, the particular administrative services, the neighborhood. Thus the citizen can participate, and the recipients or beneficiaries of services may have a direct say and direct supervision of them. Questions about urban renewal or new housing construction should be decided by those living in the particular areas concerned, and welfare service should be decentralized in a manner to allow for the recipients' direct control and management. The accent is put on "community control," on "neighborhood city halls," and "direct democracy" in the economy. Parochial and local "nationalisms" are beginning to develop. Small towns, localities, and neighborhoods are beginning to claim precedence over national representative organs.

The Crisis of Authority

Institutional weakness, real or imaginary, seems to parallel a profound moral crisis — a crisis of the authority of the democratic State. It is translated into a widespread decline in the consensus democracies enjoyed in the past. Many of the traditional authority structures have weakened: for instance, the Church, the family, the social elites, and more recently the trade unions. Similarly, highly valued organizations like the army or the university have declined in importance. None of them play the role they played in the past, serving to structure demands, to slow down the urge for immediate fulfillment, and to inculcate respect for existing institutions. These agencies no longer play the role of intermediary between the State and the public at large to sustain its authority and to secure agreement on its decisions. On the contrary, particularisms have begun to assert their primacy — special interests, particular ethnic groups, special localities, different religious bodies; they all assert their virtual autonomy. This further undermines consensus for a democratic policy and makes compliance with the decisions of the democratic State uncertain.

The Crisis of Legitimacy

These are the words of a noted sociologist:

> Democracy, as the sorry history of Europe has shown, is a fragile system . . . [it may collapse] when political parties or social movements can successfully establish "private armies" whose resort to violence — street fighting, bombings, the breakup of their opponent's meetings or simply intimidation — cannot be controlled by the elected authorities, and whose use of violence is justified or made legitimate by the respectable elements in society.[10]

Daniel Bell is, of course, referring here to the Nazi and Fascist movements and their counterparts in central Europe that we shall discuss in Chapter 9, but today both the legacy of guerrilla war and the growth of terrorism pose the same dangers for contemporary democracies.

Guerrilla warfare occurred widely after World War II as the various colonies attempted to oust the colonial power. It took the form of both political organization and military confrontation. At first, small detachments with makeshift arms would begin to harass the colonial administration and the forces allied to it. At the same time a large network of political

---

10. Daniel Bell (ed.), *The Radical Right.* New York: Doubleday, 1963, p. 33.

support was being built to support the guerrillas. Under a leadership and a party, the indigenous population was organized to give its total support to the fighting forces.

Guerrilla warfare and terrorism in advanced democracies, in the form of urban guerrillas such as Italy's Red Brigades, or Germany's Baader-Meinhof group, have been responsible for the assassinations of top political leaders. Here and in other democratic societies, extremist groups advocating revolution, separatism, or anarchism approximate the model of guerrilla warfare. A prerequisite to this activity is the organization of a group of faithful supporters who will support the terrorists, urban guerrillas, and revolutionaries. How can democracy defend itself?

The most pressing danger is that democratic societies, faced with dissent and acts of violence by terrorist organizations, may seek counter-revolutionary policies which will force them to jettison democratic principles and practices. Repressive measures, serious qualifications of political and individual freedoms, special forms of control and police surveillance may be introduced, indeed *have* been introduced, in the name of counter-terrorism. Democracy remains fragile indeed, and never more so than when multiple and conflicting ideological movements begin to undermine the support it needs.

Socialism:
Crisis and Prospects

Socialism, as an ideology and movement, offered suggestions about social and economic organization and the role of the State and also advocated measures to end inequalities in opportunities and income. Socialist governments, with adequate support to implement their ideology and programs, have been relatively few in the post-World War II period. One example, however, is the Labour party in English government from 1945–1951, 1964–1970, and again from 1974–1979. In Germany, the Social Democratic party—only in coalition with the Liberals—was in office between 1973 and 1982. In Sweden, Socialists have been in government for about half a century with two short interruptions. In Austria, they have had an uninterrupted rule since the end of World War II.

Both the British Labour party and the German Social Democrats had to qualify considerably one of the major tenets of socialism—the nationalization of the economy. After the first nationalization effort of the Labour party (1945–1951) during which coal mines, railroads, electricity, gas, iron, and steel were nationalized, the emphasis was put on welfare legislation, an equitable incomes policy, and efforts to meet the demands of the trade unions and to arrest inflation. Reconstruction of the economy, in order to maintain Great Britain's competitive position in the world economy, became a primary target. In 1979 the Labour government gave place to the Conservatives who seemed determined to restrict the role of the State in economic matters, and the conservatives again won election in June 1987.

Today, the Labour party is badly divided, with some left-wing socialists moving in a doctrinaire fashion once again toward comprehensive nationalizations and the imposition of State controls. But the moderates have seceded from the Labour party, and have formed a reformist Social Democratic party that cooperates closely with the Liberals. Together they have established a potentially strong third party—the "Alliance."

In Germany the Social Democrats, in effect, abandoned their commitment to socialization as early as 1959 in the Bad Godesberg Congress with the slogan "the State whenever necessary; freedom whenever possible." In office the German Social Democrats undertook no major structural reforms of the economy. However, they introduced welfare legislation and maintained a wage policy that favored the workers—something that was made possible by the remarkable strength and competitiveness of the German industry. But they lost the election both in 1983 and in 1987 and, like the Labour party in England, have faced internal splits with some of the left-wing groups advocating a different foreign policy and drastic economic and structural reforms.

It is only in Sweden and in Austria that "socialism" has fared well, but again, with some serious qualifications. Sweden, during a long Socialist party rule, did not undertake nationalizations of the economy. The private sector is stronger by far than the public one. There are institutions that provide for bargaining and compromise between the State, the strong cooperatives, the trade unions, and the private sector. The State is, in effect, a redistributive agency that attempts to equalize incomes through welfare legislation and public services. In Sweden the Socialist party was defeated in 1976 in the face of rising demands for greater economic and social freedoms. It was returned to office in 1982, however, and has introduced some tentative measures favoring workers' ownership of a small fraction of industrial capital.

The disarray of the Labour party, the difficulties of the Socialists in Sweden, and the virtual complete acceptance of free enterprise by the German Social Democrats all seemed to spell the decline of socialism. Social democratic and reformist policies meant greater tolerance for a free economy and private incentive rather than socialism. Many nationalizations, in fact, involved bankrupt industries and monopolies. The State took them over at the expense of the taxpayer. Their management was not superior to that of the private sector. In fact in some countries—notably in Italy—the bureaucratization of the economy because of nationalizations resulted in low productivity and inefficiency at high cost to the consumer. Many political leaders, even those from the left, have since urged that management again be returned to the private sector.

In England, Germany, and other countries, socialism had been supported by a strong working class organized in powerful trade unions, and the Socialist parties had been its spokesmen. But Karl Kautsky, one of the fathers of the German social democracy, had noted that as Socialist parties became transformed from parties of the working class to "parties of the people," their militancy and ideology underwent profound changes. Socialist parties and governments had to represent the nation; they became the representatives of many socioeconomic groups — especially the new white-collar workers and the new middle classes. The Socialist parties had to compromise and use the State to arbitrate rather than to impose a given point of view or follow a given economic or social blueprint. Their ideology became more comprehensive and more diffuse. Socialist parties became like all other parties, and as the magic of nationalizations began to wane, socialists, too, came to terms with capitalist structures and practices — notably the market. Their commitment to democracy made it impossible for them to *impose* their program, as the Marxists would have done, and as they had in fact done in the Soviet Union and in eastern Europe.

Perhaps nothing better illustrates the predicament of socialism than the rise and fall of French socialism. The French Socialist party came to power in May 1981 — with the election of a Socialist president and a Socialist majority in the National Assembly. It proceeded with speed and great ideological commitment to the realization of the Socialist blueprint: the nationalization of all banks and the major industrial sectors and the strengthening of the welfare programs. Health, retirement, and unemployment benefits were increased; paid vacations for the workers were extended to five weeks; early retirement provisions were made and wages were raised. The intention of these reforms was to achieve what virtually all other European Socialist parties, including the British Labour party, had foresaken. However, by 1983 the French Socialists likewise abandoned their plan in the face of growing unemployment, high budget deficits, a growing trade deficit, a high rate of inflation, and negative public opinion. They began to turn to the private sector and to gradually privatize the firms they had nationalized, many of which showed deficits. From public management they moved to private entrepreneurship. But the damage had been done, and in the election of March 1986 it was the Conservative and Liberal political parties that gained a majority in the National Assembly. In the election of 1988 the Socialist Party was unable to gain a majority in the National Assembly, even though Francois Mitterrand — a self-styled Socialist — was returned to the Presidency.

Even if they return to power once more, the French Socialists will do so on a radically modified agenda that will resemble increasingly that of the German Social Democrats. They will remain committed to the welfare state but gradually will abandon nationalizations in favor of the private sector and the market economy.

By the end of the twentieth century it appeared that socialism had run its course. It had served well the working classes, the underprivileged, and society as a whole: the need of economic equality became increasingly accepted; it had "legitimized" the State even in the eyes of the workers and had shown them that it was no instrument of a class, as the Marxists had argued, but an institution capable of arbitrating among groups and classes to provide for service on the basis of need; it had developed a body of legislation that in effect mitigated the hardships of economic conflict and poverty in the form of programs in health insurance, retirement policies, family care, housing, full employment, and free education. On the other hand, socialism had not provided a solution to economic growth, higher productivity, and economic well-being. Above all it had not managed to reconcile the principle of individual freedom with that of equality. Too much individualism led to inequalities; but too much emphasis on equality appeared to be an invasion of individual freedoms—a steamroller that wiped out initiative, thwarted experimentation, and discouraged effort. Lastly, socialism had not even attempted to give an answer to international problems. The building of a transnational and supranational community of free peoples remained out of reach and sight. In fact, socialism, like communism elsewhere, continued to be associated with nationalism.

Christian Democracy*

Christian democracy is an ideology and a political movement that rightfully belongs to our discussion of democracy in this part of our book. It is both a reaction to the radical democratic movements of the nineteenth century and more particularly to the growth of socialism and communism. It is also a positive affirmation of a doctrine developed by the Catholic Church, a doctrine which accepted democracy and vigorously advocated social reform to meet the social unrest and the plight of the working classes that was brought about by the industrial revolution.

By the end of the nineteenth century "Liberal Catholicism" succeeded in gaining the pope's acceptance of democracy. "Social Catholicism" had for some time attempted to address the social problems resulting from the industrial revolution by way of social and economic reforms. The positions of the two, however, were not always easy to reconcile. Many liberal Catholics were concerned more about democracy (the right to vote, political participation, and individual freedoms) than social reform; on the other hand, many social Catholics, who favored social reforms, rejected democracy—some of them, in fact, especially in France, were outright monarchists. "Christian democracy" is the movement that brought the two together.

The origins of Christian democracy can be traced back to the beginning of the nineteenth century, as early as the French Revolution. A French priest, Félicité de Lamennais (1782–1854), may well be considered its founder. He defended *both* democracy and social reform, argued for the separation of Church and State, extolled liberties in the State and even within the Church, espoused the cause of the working men and women, favored the formation of workers' associations, argued for social and economic equality, and defended freedom of conscience, freedom of association, and freedom of the press. He proposed welfare measures, claiming that the State had the obligation to provide employment and guarantee workers' wages.

---

*As indicated in my preface Leigh Peake, a graduate student at Brandeis, did a great deal of the spade work in the form of notes and drafts for the writing of this section.

THE BETTMAN ARCHIVE

Félicité de Lamennais (1782–1854)

Félicité de Lamennais may well be considered the founder of Christian Democracy. An ardent advocate of theocracy at first he shifted to a reformist, democratic and even revolutionary position to argue in favor of political and individual freedoms and freedom of conscience that were condemned by the pope in his encyclical *Mirari Vos* (1832). He abandoned the church and wrote his best known book *Paroles d'Un Croyant* (1834) expounding political democracy and at times socialism.

Gradually Christian democrats grew in numbers throughout Europe; they continued to agitate within and outside the Church for workers' cooperatives and associations, public works to provide for employment, better wages and working conditions, and shorter working hours. They began to actively participate in political life. Catholic parties developed not only to protect the interests of the Church but also to infuse political life with a Christian and social doctrine that could promote social legislation. In Germany the Catholic "center" group received 17 percent of the vote in the election of 1871. In Switzerland the Swiss Center Party was formed in

1845, and during the mid-nineteenth century Catholic parties began to spring up in Belgium, Holland, and Austria.

The consolidation of Christian democracy, however, stems from one of the most monumental papal encyclicals on social and economic matters, *Rerum Novarum* ("The Condition of the Working Class"), which was issued on May 15, 1891. Pope Leo XIII sought to bring the Church back into the mainstream of social thinking and reform. He acknowledged that the ruthless exploitation of the workers prevented the spiritual development of the masses and that the economy should provide for material well-being without which spiritual life could not be nourished. Wages, he insisted, should be determined not by economic considerations alone, but by taking into account the basic needs of the individual. Property too must be subject to social and moral restraints. He maintained that while all people had the right to own property, they did not have the right to use property to the detriment of their neighbors and their community.

He issued a compelling call for the end of the misery of the worker:

> . . . there can be no question whatever, that some remedy must
> be found, and quickly found, for the misery and wretchedness
> which press so heavily at this moment on the large majority of
> the very poor. . . . Working men have been given over, isolated
> and defenseless, to the callousness of employers and the greed
> of unrestrained competition.[11]

Pope Leo XIII asserted that the Church had an obligation to seek a solution to these problems: "The Church, as an institution, has an obligation to care for the temporal needs of its children." But to attain social justice, "not only the Church, but all human means must conspire." This invites the State.

"The first duty of the rulers of the State should be to make sure that the laws and institutions, the general character and administration of the commonwealth, shall be such as to produce public well-being. . . ." More importantly,

> It would be irrational to neglect one portion of the citizens and
> to favor another; and therefore the public administration must
> duly and solicitously provide for the welfare and the comfort of
> the working people.

This is particularly the case for the poor and the helpless. They have "a claim to special consideration," and should be "specially cared for and protected by the commonwealth."

The encyclical concluded with a call for "Workmen's Rights": the cessation of work on Sundays and festivals, restrictions on the number of work hours, and regulation of labor by children and women, as well as "just wages." But wages cannot be determined solely through bargaining, for

---

11. For the text see *Seven Great Encyclicals.* Glen Rock, N.J.: The Paulist Press, 1963, pp. 1–36.

. . . there is a dictate of nature more imperious and more ancient
than any bargain between man and man, that the remuneration
must be enough to support the wage-earner in reasonable and
frugal comfort.

Rather than have the State control wages, Pope Leo XIII advocated the
establishment of "Societies or Boards" (comprised of workers and employers) and the formation of Catholic workers' associations through which the
worker and employer will play a role in the remedy of the current problems. Forty years later, in 1931, another pope, Pius XI, reiterated the principles enunciated in *Rerum Novarum* and broadened them in his encyclical,
Quadragissimo Anno.[12] The pope acknowledged the worldwide spread of
capitalism in words that, curiously enough, are reminiscent of those used
by Karl Marx in the *Communist Manifesto,*

> . . . with the diffusion of modern industry thoughout the world,
> the "capitalist" economic regime has spread. . . . everywhere.
> . . . Not only is wealth concentrated in our times but an immense
> power and despotic economic dictatorship is consolidated in
> the hands of a few, who often are not owners but
> only the trustees and managing directors of invested funds
> which they administer according to their own arbitrary will and
> pleasure.

Concentration of power and unlimited competition, he noted, "lets only
the strongest survive."

He noted with satisfaction the changes in socialism and distinguished
democratic socialism from revolutionary communism: socialism not only
professes the rejection of violence, but modifies and tempers to some degree, if it does not reject entirely, the class struggle and the abolition of
private ownership. He saw socialism as moving away from communism
back toward the fundamentals of the Christian tradition, "for it cannot be
denied that its demands at times come very near those that Christian
reformers of society justly insist upon."

The work contract, he stated, must be modified to become a sort of
"partnership contract" so that "workers and other employees . . . become
sharers in ownership or management or participate in some fashion in the
profits received." He also lashed out against the evils of free competition.

> . . . . Free competition, while justified and certainly useful pro-
> vided it is kept within certain limits, clearly cannot direct eco-
> nomic life—a truth which the outcome of the application in
> practice of the tenets of this evil individualistic spirit has more
> than sufficiently demonstrated.

Accordingly, the Church must become the shield of the oppressed
workers and the tutor of the capitalist classes, uniting them into a common

---

12. For the text see ibid., 124–176.

enterprise, into associations (corporations) that bring them together for the common goals of production and distribution of goods in which self-ishness will be curbed and the human dignity of all will be safeguarded and promoted.

> The Corporations are composed of representatives of the unions . . . of workingmen and employers of the same trade and profession and as genuine and exclusive instruments and institutions of the State they direct and coordinate the activities of the syndicates in all matters of common interest. Strikes and lockouts are forbidden. . . . Little reflection is required to perceive the advantages in the institution thus summarily described: peaceful collaboration of the classes, repression of socialist organization and efforts, the moderating authority of a special ministry.

This is a comprehensive statement of the doctrine of corporatism — already sketched out in *Rerum Novarum*.

Christian Democratic Parties

Christian democratic parties reemerged with renewed strength after the liberation of Europe in 1945: in Germany, France, Belgium, Austria, Holland, and Italy and in the 1970s in Portugal and Spain and beyond in Latin America. Their renewed strength was due precisely to the synthesis they provided between *social Catholicism*, which was committed to social reform, and *liberal* or *democratic Catholicism*, which was committed to democracy.

Christian democratic movements had opposed fascism and participated in great number in the various resistance movements against the Nazi or Fascist regimes or the puppet regimes they established. The MRP in France ("Popular Republicans") became the largest single party in the year immediately after the liberation. In the election of June 2, 1946, the MRP won 28.1 percent of the vote, and its leaders held key positions in the cabinets formed thereafter. In Italy, Christian democracy emerged as the largest single party after the liberation and, despite losses, has held this position ever since. Christian Democrats in the Federal Republic of Germany — replacing the old Catholic "center" party — have continued strong ever since the end of World War II, heading the governing coalition for twenty-eight out of the last thirty-six years. In Switzerland, Norway, Austria, Holland, and Belgium Christian democratic parties have continued to command the vote of 20 to 30 percent of the electorate. In the 1970s and 1980s Catholic parties in Spain and Portugal reappeared and gained momentum. Beyond Europe, Christian democracy also developed, especially in Latin America. In Chile, Christian Democrats won the presidency in 1964 and commanded 31 percent of the vote in the election of 1973. They have opposed both military dictatorship and communism.

While they defend the interests and moral tenets of the Church with regard to legislation concerning the subsidies, immunities, and freedoms for the Church and the clergy, as well as legislation regarding primary education, divorce and abortion, Christian democratic parties are no longer "confessional parties." They appeal to all citizens, irrespective of their religion, and they get the vote of many non-Catholics.

Ever since the end of World War II, Christian democratic parties have strongly favored policies promoting international and regional organizations. For instance, the European Common Market, established in 1958, was the outcome of the common efforts of Christian democratic leaders in the Federal Republic of Germany, Italy, and France with the full support of their counterparts in Belgium and Holland.

They have become "interclass" parties; that is, they appeal to voters among all classes. In fact, they correspond to early papal pronouncements against class divisions and class struggle with their themes of social justice and harmony among workers, farmers, professionals, business groups, and other segments of society. In this respect, they differ from traditional liberal parties, who appealed to the middle classes; from peasant parties, who appealed to farmers; and from Socialist and Communist parties, who appealed directly to trade unions and the working class.

The Call to Action

The 1960s was the decade during which the Church moved with great energy toward fulfilling its worldly mission of mobilizing the faithful to strive directly for the betterment of social, political, and economic conditions. Drastic changes had taken place that called for the reconsideration of the role of the Church and in issuing a call for a Vatican Council (Vatican II) on December 25, 1961 — a special meeting in the Vatican of the Bishops of the Catholic Church — Pope John XXIII noted the changes:

> Today the Church is witnessing a crisis under way within society. While humanity is on the edge of a new era, tasks of immense gravity and amplitude await the Church, as in the most tragic periods of its history. . . . It is a question in fact of bringing the modern world into contact with the vivifying and perennial energies of the gospel.[13]

It was the purpose of the Council to address itself to the "crisis" and instruct the subordinate clergy and, through it, the Catholic laity. However, the movement included all of "humanity," — not just Catholics. The Council set the tone by addressing its message to "all Men" and all nations rather than only Catholics.

The Council identified "two issues of special urgency": "peace between peoples" and "social justice," and the pronouncements that flowed from it became, so to speak, the new charter of an embattled Church trying to

---

13. This was in essence the message of a third major encyclical that resulted from Vatican II. Entitled *Gaudium et Spes* ("The Church in the Modern World"), it was issued in 1965.

reach every corner of the world and keeping very much in mind its brethren in the Third World.

The Church "can and should indeed initiate activities on behalf of all men. . . ." The Council proclaimed that the Church should become a player in history, a force in action — *praxis* — directly concerned with "this world" while never losing sight of the "other." It urged all Christians to become involved and take action on international problems that affect war and peace, nuclear weapons, the plight of the poor everywhere, the tragic imbalances in the economies of the nations that comprise our world, working conditions and just wages, political repression, and the corruption of public officials. It urged the bishops to speak on particular issues in their respective countries and to inspire the flock to follow them.

The Bishops Speak   And the bishops did speak and on a great many occasions, both in the western world and in the Third World (see Chapter 13). The French and German bishops addressed themselves to the issue of nuclear weapons in 1984 and so did the American Bishops in 1983. The National Conference of American Bishops also issued a statement on "Economic and Social Problems in the United States" in 1986.[14] Despite important differences in emphasis, all the bishops condemned nuclear war in the most unequivocal terms.

Dealing with the American economy, the American bishops addressed themselves to the "bread and butter" issues of American society and suggested sweeping reforms. "Our economic activity," they proclaimed, "in factory, field, office or shop feeds our families — or feeds our anxieties. It exercises our talents — or wastes them. It raises our hopes — or crushes them. It bring us into cooperation with others — or sets us at odds."

They forcefully restated the Catholic doctrine: "Every economic decision and institution must be judged in light of whether it protects or undermines the dignity of the human person"; that "all people have a right to participate in the economic life of society"; and that "all members of society have a special obligation to the poor and vulnerable."

The American bishops then proceeded, and this is the novelty of their statement, with *specific* policy suggestions:

On employment: The American bishops considered employment to be a basic human right which must be protected. They particularly noted women's disadvantaged position due to a lack of adequate day care centers. They recommended that the fiscal and monetary policies of the nation, such as federal spending, taxes, and interest rate policies, should be coordinated so as to achieve the goal of full employment. They suggested . . . "expansion of job-training and apprenticeship programs in the private sector administered and supported jointly by business, labor unions, and

14. "Out of Justice, Peace," joint pastoral letter of West German bishops; "Winning the Peace," joint pastoral letter of French bishops, edited with an introduction by James Schall, S.J., Ignatius Press, San Francisco, 1984; "The Challenge of Peace. God's Promise and Our Response," National Conference of (U.S.) Catholic Bishops (1983); pastoral letter on "Catholic Social Teaching and the U.S. Economy" (1986).

government." They endorsed affirmative action and stipulated that men and women should receive equal pay.

On poverty: The bishops noted that poverty poses an "urgent moral and human challenge": it undermines human dignity and individual development. To alleviate poverty, they no longer appealed to the generosity of the rich; instead they suggested "fundamental changes in social and economic structures. . . ." They advocated changes in the tax system to benefit the poor, and suggested that *all* policies should be designed to foster the stability of the family. "A thorough reform of the nation's welfare and income-support programs" is needed, including:

1. Programs designed toward self-sufficiency
2. Adequate levels of support to cover basic needs
3. National levels (rather than state levels) of eligibility for aid as well as minimum benefit levels
4. Welfare for two-parent as well as single-parent families

The Developing Nations: As with previous papal encyclicals, the American bishops called for an international authority to oversee the distribution of the world's wealth. They felt that since the United States had such vast economic power it should assume certain responsibilities and take immediate steps to help emerging nations through:

1. Development assistance
2. Preferential option for the poor
3. Resolution of the debt crisis facing the Third World by offering long payment terms, lower interest rates, and cancellation of debts where possible

Never before had such a detailed statement on social and economic matters been issued by any church. It went into specific recommendations way beyond any of the papal encyclicals that preceded it. For the first time, the American Catholic Church was proposing a comprehensive social and economic program—a new "New Deal"—with specifics on how it should be implemented. It was more of a political platform than a sermon from the pulpit! And it was the kind of platform that many social democratic parties would proudly endorse.

Thus the Catholic Church has moved from its earlier position of aloofness and noninvolvement to become an active champion of both democracy and social reform. In the spirit of the Christian democracy that sprang forth at the turn of the nineteenth century, it appeals to all men and women and to all secular institutions. It promotes tolerance and reform with a voice that has grown increasingly urgent. Both the pope—as his recent encyclical issued on February 18, 1988, on the "Social Concerns of the Church" shows—and the bishops speak with a voice that transcends national concerns and barriers. Their criticism is directed against both the Communist ideology that enslaves the individual and the liberal capitalist ideology that degrades the individual and fosters competition instead of cooperation and harmony. The division of the world into "eastern" and "western" blocs is now unacceptable to the Chruch because it subjugates the poor and underdeveloped nations to the designs of the two superpowers. It took almost a century, but the voice of Christian democracy has grown into a powerful force in the never-ending struggle for individual liberation, spiritual fulfillment, economic security, and freedom.

Bibliography

Ambler, John S. (ed.). *The French Socialist Experiment.* Philadelphia: Institute for the Study of Human Issues, 1985.

Beer, Samuel H. *British Politics in the Collectivist Age.* New York: Vintage, 1969. Reedited under the title *Modern British Politics,* 1982.

Bell, Daniel and Kristol, Irving (eds.). *Capitalism Today.* New York: New American Library, 1971.

Bernstein, Eduard. *Evolutionary Socialism.* New York: Charles Scribner's Sons, 1961.

Brus, Wlodzimierz. *The Economics and Politics of Socialism.* London: Routledge & Kegan Paul, 1974.

Buber, Martin. *Paths in Utopia.* Boston: Beacon Press, 1958.

Carens, Joseph H. *Equality, Moral Incentives, and the Market: An Essay in Utopian Politico-Economic Thinking.* Chicago: University of Chicago Press, 1981.

Cerny, Philip G. and Schain, Martin A. (eds.). *Socialism, the State and Public Policy in France.* New York: Methuen, 1985.

Cole, G. D. H. *A History of Socialist Thought.* (6 volumes) London: Macmillan, 1953–60.

Colton, Joel. *Leon Blum: Humanist in Politics.* Cambridge, Mass.: M.I.T. Press, 1974.

Crossman, R. H. S. (ed.). *The New Fabian Essays.* New York: Praeger, 1952.

———. *The Politics of Socialism.* New York: Atheneum, 1965.

Cyr, Arthur I. *Liberal Party Politics in Britain.* New Brunswick, N.J.: Transaction Books, 1977.

Dahl, Robert A. *Democracy in the United States.* 3rd ed. Chicago: Rand McNally, 1976.

Desfosses, Helen and Levesque, Jacques (eds.). *Socialism in the Third World.* New York: Praeger, 1975.

Engels, Friedrich. "Socialism: Utopian and Scientific." In Robert C. Tucker, *The Marx-Engels Reader.* 2nd ed. New York: Norton, 1978, pp. 683–717.

Galbraith, John Kenneth. *American Capitalism: The Concept of Countervailing Power.* Rev. ed. Boston: Houghton Mifflin, 1956.

———. *The New Industrial State.* Boston: Houghton Mifflin, 1967.

Gay, Peter. *The Dilemma of Democratic Socialism.* New York: Columbia U. P., 1952.

Girvetz, H. K. *From Wealth to Welfare: The Evolution of Liberalism.* Stanford, Calif.: Stanford U. P., 1950.

Goldberg, Harvey. *The Life of Jean Jaurés.* Madison: University of Wisconsin Press, 1962.

Halévy, Elie. *The Growth of Philosophic Radicalism.* Boston: Beacon Press, 1955.

Hancock, Donald M. and Sjoberg, Gideon (eds.). *Politics in the Post-Welfare State.* New York: Columbia U. P., 1972.

Harrington, Michael. *Socialism.* New York: Bantam Books, 1972.

Heilbroner, Robert L. *The Limits of American Capitalism.* New York: Harper & Row, 1967.

Huntington, Samuel et al. *The Crisis of Democracy,* New York: New York U. P., 1975.

Joll, James. *The Second International, 1889–1914.* New York: Praeger, 1956.

Jordan, Bill. *Freedom and the Welfare State.* London: Routledge & Kegan Paul, 1978.

Lowi, Theodore J. *The End of Liberalism.* New York: Norton, 1969.

Manuel, Frank. *Utopian Thought in the Western World.* Cambridge, Mass.: Harvard U.P., 1979.

Markovic, M. *Democratic Socialism: Theory and Practice.* New York: St Martin's Press, 1982.

Mills, C. Wright. *The Power Elite.* New York: Oxford U. P., 1956.

Novak, Michael. *The American Vision: An Essay on the Future of Democratic Capitalism.* Washington, D.C.: American Enterprise Institute for Public Policy Research, 1978.

Paterson, William E. and Thomas, Alastair. *The Future of Social Democracy in Western Europe.* New York: Oxford U. P., 1986.

Rawls, John. *A Theory of Justice.* Oxford, England: Clarendon Press, 1972.

———. *A Theory of Justice.* Cambridge, Mass.: Harvard U. P., 1971.

Research Institute on International Change. *The Relevance of Liberalism.* Boulder, Colo.: Westview Press, 1977.

Sandel, Michael J. *Liberalism and the Limits of Justice.* Cambridge: Cambridge U. P., 1982.

Sartori, Giovanni. *Democratic Theory.* New York: Praeger, 1965.

Schlesinger, Arthur, Jr. *The Age of Roosevelt,* vols. 1 and 2. Boston: Houghton Mifflin, 1957.

Schumpeter, Joseph A. *Capitalism, Socialism and Democracy.* New York: Harper & Row, 1950.

Shaw, George Bernard (ed.). *The Fabian Essays in Socialism.* London: Allen & Unwin, 1958. (Reprint of 1889 Edition)

Walzer, Michael. *Radical Principles: Reflections of an Unreconstructed Democrat.* New York: Basic Books, 1980.

On Christian Democracy

Abbott, Walter M. (ed.). *The Documents of Vatican II.* N.Y.: Herder & Herder Association Press, 1966.

Freemantle, Anne. *The Papal Encyclicals in Their Historical Context.* New York: G. P. Putnam & Sons, 1956.

———. *The Social Teachings of the Church.* New York: New American Library, 1963.

Fogerty, Michael P. *Christian Democracy in Western Europe 1820–1953.* Notre Dame, Ind.: University of Notre Dame Press, 1957.

Hales, E. E. Y. *The Catholic Church in the Modern World.* Garden City, N.Y.: Doubleday, 1958.

Hanson, Eric. *The Catholic Church and World Politics.* Princeton: Princeton University Press, 1987.

Hollis, Christopher. *The Achievements of Vatican II.* New York: Hawthorn Books, 1967.

Hughes, Philip. *The Church in Crisis: A History of the General Councils, 325–1870.* Garden City, N.Y.: Doubleday, 1961.

Laski, Harold. *Authority in the Modern State.* New Haven, Conn. Yale University Press, 1919.

O'Brien, David J. and Shannon, Thomas A. *Renewing the Earth.* Garden City, N.Y.: Doubleday, 1977.

Wallace, Lillian Parker. *Leo XIII and the Rise of Socialism.* Durham, N.C.: Duke University Press, 1966.

4 Democracy and Conservatism: England and the U.S.A.

The good citizen is a law-abiding traditionalist.
RUSSELL KIRK   What Is Conservatism?

It could be said that conservatism is more a state of mind than a political ideology. In order to be conservative one must have something to conserve—property, status, power, a way of life. Conservatives are therefore likely to be those who have power or wealth or status and who simply want to keep things the way they are. Also, a significant number of people—mostly among rural groups, those who live in small towns, the old and the uneducated—cannot imagine something different, or are afraid of change. They too want to keep their way of life the way it is.

However, even if we were to define conservatism simply as the defense of the status quo and the rationalization and the legitimization of a given order of things—in other words as a "situational ideology"—we would find that conservative ideology has its own logic.[1] Conservative movements always and everywhere borrow from some of the same principles, irrespective of the particular situation they face at a particular time. They are the following:

1. Individual liberties are more important to conservatives than "equality."
2. They have a pronounced allergy for political power—and are against its concentration in the hands of anybody, especially the people.

1. In a penetrating article, Samuel Huntington indicates that conservatism can be viewed as (1) an ideology that emanated from the aristocracy as it rationalized its position and interests against the French Revolution of 1789—*aristocratic conservatism;* (2) an ideology that contains substantive prescriptions about the organization of social and political life—*autonomous conservatism;* (3) an ideology arising from a given situation in which the status quo is threatened by the prophets and the activists of change—*a situational ideology.* Conservatism is ". . . the articulate, systematic, theoretical resistance to change. It is primarily an ideology that defends the status quo." (In *American Political Science Review,* v.LI, June 1957, no. 2, pp. 454–473)

3. They insist on an organic theory of the society involving a hierarchy of groups and classes and a cooperation among them—the community and its interests are always above the individual.
4. They have a respect for tradition and "inheritance"—that which is bequeathed to us from our ancestors.
5. Religion, with its reverence for authority, is dear to the conservatives.
6. They distrust "reason" and the propriety of using it as a solution for social problems.
7. Almost all conservative ideologies are elitist. Some people are better equipped than others; some are superior, while some (generally the many) are inferior.

These principles were invoked throughout the nineteenth century as certain groups fought to maintain their position against the egalitarian and reformist principles of democracy, liberalism, and, later on, socialism and Marxism.

A final note: the terms "conservative" and "reactionary" should not be confused as they so often are. A conservative doesn't want change—but will acquiesce to it—at least to gradual change. A "reactionary," on the other hand, is often one who wants to change things radically in order to reestablish the past. A conservative is against rapid change; a reactionary is one who doesn't accept the change that has already taken place! Nor should conservatism be confused with authoritarianism. The latter favors a concentration of political power in the hands of a leader or a group, is against individual and political freedoms, rejects popular participation in almost any form, and accepts repression and the use of force.

Classic Conservatism: The British Model

The best formulation of conservative ideology was given by Edmund Burke, in the latter part of the eighteenth century. The best implementation of it has been, through the nineteenth century and until today, that of the British Conservative party.[2] Variants of the British model could be found in Germany under Bismarck, in France during the so-called Orleanist period (1830–1848) and in some of its offshoots during the period of the Third French Republic (1871 – 1940), and in Gaullism. But almost nowhere on the Continent did an alliance of the aristocracy and the upper classes, the Church, the monarchy, and the army lead to the "classic" form of conservatism tied to constitutional democracy that prevailed in England.

European conservatives often chose to reject constitutional democracy and representative government. In the United States there have been many variants of a conservative ideology, but the absence of a nobility and

2. An excellent discussion of the evolution of conservative ideology can be found in the relevant parts of Samuel H. Beer, *British Politics in the Collectivist Age.* New York: Vintage, 1949.

the success of the egalitarian ethic and liberalism account for the virtual absence of any genuine conservative movement or ideology that has had any impact.

Classic conservatism is characterized by certain basic propositions that relate to political authority, to a conception of society and the nature of the individual, and to the relationship between the national economy and the State.

The Political Society

Society, according to early British conservative thought, is organic and hierarchical. Classes and social groups fit together in the same way as do the various organs of our bodies. One is indispensable to the others; it cannot function without them. Relations between them must be harmonious and balanced, and each group and each class performs the functions that are necessary to the others for the good health of the whole. Society is not like a machine, say a clock, in which the motions are eternally identical and where each part has no idea of what the other parts are doing. Rather, it is a combination of many parts, each one of which understands its role and perceives society as a whole. Unlike the machine, society knows it has a purpose; unlike a clock it grows and changes. "The whole," wrote Edmund Burke, ". . . is never old, middle-aged, or young." It "moves on through . . . perpetual decay, fall, renovation, and progression."[3]

Society thus consists of interdependent parts — and all the parts are equally conscious of the interdependence. Each one does its own work, but what it does makes sense only when the whole is understood and valued. Farmers grow crops; soldiers keep order and give protection; priests improve our minds and souls; the leaders govern and balance the various parts. The parts working together almost lose the sense of their separateness. Society is not a "mixture" of various roles, groups, qualities, and activities. It is, as Aristotle said, much more of a "compound" in which the parts blend with each other to become something different from what they are individually. They become a society.

Different functions and roles inevitably suggest a hierarchical organization and social inequality. Some of society's roles are more important than others, and some people do more important things than others. This means that there must be a subordination of some individuals to others. Persons endowed by nature with certain qualities that others do not have should play the most important roles. Equality and freedom, as abstract propositions, are not acceptable to the conservative ideology. Rather, it emphasizes *rights* and *liberties.* These derive not from rational principles or from natural law but from specific institutional and legal arrangements, and from history and tradition. They give to individuals and to groups specific benefits, protections, and claims that are commensurate with their

3. Burke, *Reflections on the French Revolution,* p. 162.

functions and roles. Nor is the idea of material equality for all seriously entertained. Material benefits should correspond to the talent shown and the work done.

The "whole" — this society that consists of the harmonious interdependence of many parts — is formalized in the Constitution. This is not a written document, and in fact there is no way, according to conservative thinkers, a constitution can be set down. The Constitution is a set of customs, understandings, rules, and especially traditions, that define political power and set limits upon its exercise. Power thus enshrined by habit, custom, and tradition becomes authority; that is, it is accepted and respected. In this way, it is the Constitution that binds the whole of the citizenry to its rulers and the rulers to the citizenry within the nation. Conservatives, however, are not necessarily nationalists. To them the nation-state is a social and historical reality, the product of many centuries of common life and togetherness. But it is not a supreme moral value unless it has managed to embody justice and order. "To make us love our country, our country must be lovely" was the pithy comment of Burke.

Political Authority

In contrast to those who establish the foundations of political authority on contract and consent, conservatives find it in tradition, custom, and in what they call inheritance and prescription. Society as a living whole is the result of natural evolution. The Constitution of England and its various parts — the monarchy, the House of Lords and the nobility, the House of Commons, individual rights, the judiciary — are an "entailed inheritance." One accepts it, and lives on it, but cannot waste it. In a famous passage, Burke sees in the State something like a mystery: its parts and its majesty cannot be dissected, analyzed, and put back together in the same or in a different way. *The State cannot be made.* He wrote:

> The state ought . . . to be looked upon with . . . reverence. . . . It is a partnership in all science; a partnership in all art; a partnership in all perfection . . . between those who are living, those who are dead and those who are to be born. . . . Each contract is but a clause in the great primeval contract of eternal society, linking the lower with the higher natures, connecting the visible with the invisible world, according to a fixed compact sanctioned by the inviolable oath which holds all physical and all moral natures, each in their appointed place.[4]

Conservatives, therefore, have no use for the "contract" theory of the State propounded by the early liberals. The idea runs counter to the organic theory of society and to the role history and tradition play in the formation of a state. Burke insisted that even if there were a contract it was

4. Ibid., p. 139–140.

Edmund Burke (1729–1797)

Edmund Burke was the most eloquent expounder of British conservative ideology. Originally, Burke appeared to be a liberal arguing not only against the prerogatives of the crown and in favor of parliament, but also for the autonomy of the colonies in North America. These views were expressed in *Thoughts on the Causes of the Present Discontents* (1770). It was the French Revolution and its excesses that accounted for his masterpiece *Reflections on the French Revolution* (1790), in which he presented arguments favoring tradition and prescription, and the sanctity of law and authority, while cautioning against anything but the most gradual expansion of popular participation in affairs of the State.

shaped by history and tradition, and once made "it attaches upon every individual of that society, without any formal action of his own." We are born into political society like our father and forefathers; we do not make it.

Change

Given the emphasis on tradition, conservative thought is generally opposed to change unless it is gradual. Our "partnership with the dead" should not be broken, for fear that this would undermine the living and those still to be born. Modifications become necessary, but on balance the past carries more weight than the present. As for the future, there are many would-be reformers and social engineers, and conservatives distrust them. Innovation is suspect, and Burke claimed it was prompted by "selfish temper and confined views." As a result, the conservatives fall back upon the existing and widely shared values that have kept the society together. Religion is one of the most important; so is common law and even prejudices. As Edmund Burke put it, "wise prejudice," consecrated by long usage, is "better than thoughts untried and untested."

Religion, tradition, the common law, and prejudice—all give the individual shelter and solace; they provide stability that in the last analysis is a higher value than change. All these things, together with the State and its organs, must be strengthened with the proper pomp and ritual that appeal to the common people. The crown itself is a symbol that, through ritual, secures support and obedience. More than fifty years after Burke, another British conservative, Walter Bagehot (1826–1877) spoke of the "symbolic" or "ceremonial" part of the Constitution—the monarch—providing for the attachment of the common people and unifying political society. The cabinet, the prime minister, and parliament were the "efficient part"—the government, though this was understood only by the elite and hardly appreciated by the common people.[5]

If change is to come, however, it must be natural and slow—one and the same thing for conservatives. Conservatives may even favor change in order to preserve. Change must reflect new needs and be the result of cautious adjustment with past practices. The British conservatives *allowed* for changes in the Constitution, which they venerated; thus came about the gradual extension of the franchise, the ascendancy of the popularly elected House of Commons over the hereditary House of Lords, and the development of a civil service based on merit, as well as economic and social reforms. But they did so often under pressure, and with the aim of preserving what they valued most. In their efforts to slow down reform, however, British conservatives remained firmly attached to the basic democratic principles of representative government, elections, and the rule of law.

5. Bagehot, *The English Constitution.* New York: Oxford U.P., 1936.

The purpose of the State and its leaders is to balance the whole and to create unity and commonality of purpose out of diversity. Government leadership and decision making should be entrusted to "natural leaders" — men or women of talent, high birth, and property, who have a stake in the interests of the country and in its fortunes. As late as the middle of the nineteenth century many argued in England that noblemen could own, outfit, and command whole regiments in the army and the explanation given was simple — they cared more about England's welfare than did the common people. They had a greater stake in the defense of the country.

As a conservative put it recently, "Government is instituted to secure justice and order . . . and . . . the first principle of good government allows the more energetic natures among a people to fulfill their promise while ensuring that these persons shall not tyrannize over the mass of men."[6] Quality and not election should therefore be the source of leadership. Conservatives fought against the rapid extension of the franchise, acquiescing to it reluctantly, and did not accept the full logic of majority rule until very recently. The principle of one man–one vote was unacceptable, and the notion that decisions could be made by simple arithmetic majority could be entertained only when that majority, by long habits of obedience, had become self-disciplined. That would be when the majority had accepted the restraints that law and tradition had inculcated so as to act in accordance with the fundamental rules of the past.

The natural leaders hold the interests of the country in trust. They act on behalf of the people and the society. The trust, however, is almost a complete and blanket grant of power — it is not a delegation.

Another way of explaining the same conservative notion of trusteeship is to refer to it as the theory of *virtual representation*. Today we agree that representatives represent their constituency, those who elect them, and the country in general, but their capacity to make decisions for us stems directly from elections and from the *mandate* they receive from their constituency or the electorate at large. Virtual representation, on the other hand, is the capacity to represent and make decisions by virtue of qualities other than mere election. Conservative thinking returns to the idea of birth and wealth. Persons who have one or both can represent the people and the nation by virtue of their position better than elected representatives. They are what in medieval times were called the *valentior pars* (the better part) of the community. This again shows the reluctance by conservatives to extend the franchise and accept majoritarianism.

Thus the natural leaders should govern and the many should follow. This reflects the typical British conservative attitude, which still is evident today. Many of the members and leaders of the Conservative party still think that they are endowed with capabilities with which they can govern better than any other party and its leadership. They still believe that they

---

6. Russell Kirk, "Prescription, Authority and Ordered Freedom," in F. S. Meyer (ed.), *What Is Conservatism?*, p. 33.

can hold the interest of the country in trust better than all others. They also think that the government has autonomous and independent powers to govern and that, once elected, it is free to exercise them. It is a government that once elected cannot be given instructions or be delegated to do some things and not others. So, there is an element of authoritarianism and elitism still lurking in the hearts of all good conservatives, together with a certain distrust for the "common people" or the "mass."

Paternalism

While conservatives believe that the propertied classes and the landed aristocracy have special privileges, they also agree that such privileges and their exercise have corresponding social obligations. Here there is a strong element of paternalism, whereby the natural leaders have to cater to the well-being of the common people by providing them with relief when out of work and at other times improving their living conditions. Because of their organic theory of the society, conservatives tended to subordinate economic interests to the overall interest of the collectivity. Social solidarity and social cooperation are given precedence over particular interests. Finally, the purpose of "the whole" goes beyond simple material considerations. The State is an all-encompassing agency for providing justice and order. It has a moral purpose to which particularisms and economic interests must yield.

For all these reasons conservatives reject the utilitarian philosophy of economic liberalism. Self-interest, unrestrained competition, individualism, and the very notion that the society is held together by competing claims and antagonisms — such ideas are repugnant to them. They reject laissez-faire economics, or at best tolerate it on condition that individual effort and competition not be allowed to tear apart the fabric of the society. They accept economic individualism if it allows everybody to show his or her worth and capabilities; they reject it if it leads to sharp inequalities and social strife that would upset the balance of the whole. British conservatives have favored State intervention and welfare measures, unlike other conservative parties on the Continent and elsewhere.

Constitutional Government and Democracy

The British conservatives and their Conservative party became strong advocates of constitutional and representative government. In contrast to the European conservatives they did not waver in their support of democracy and parliamentary institutions. Authoritarian and totalitarian solutions appealed to only a negligible number of their leaders and followers. In this way conservatism, while representing the status quo groups, recognized the realities of social change and the necessity of guiding it and reducing its speed rather than arresting it altogether. Classic conservatives appear something like a well-controlled dam and not a bulwark against the forces of change.

After the nineteenth century, Conservatives not only accepted major economic changes, such as the establishment of Britain's welfare state and the nationalization of its industries, but they themselves also *introduced* social and economic reforms. In 1951, when the Conservatives replaced the Labour government, they assumed the direction and the management of the nationalized industries and the welfare system Labour had built. The Conservative party did not reject Labour's social economic and welfare legislation; it tried to slow their pace of reform until it judged society as a whole had time to adjust to it. Thus, conservatives reconciled themselves to a new social and economic order.

The Conservative party remains staunchly committed to democratic principles. While the authority of the leader of the party is given greater scope than in the case of other parties, notably Labour, the Conservative party developed into a mass party with three to four million members. It holds annual conferences, allows its various organs considerable autonomy, holds free debates in which policy resolutions come from the floor, and can be endorsed despite the opposition of the leadership. It now recruits its candidates for the House of Commons without consideration of their personal wealth and ability to contribute to their own campaign or to the party. In general, despite its affinities with the upper status groups and wealthier segments of the population, it has managed to appeal to and get support from many of the voters who belong to the working or lower middle classes. The marriage between the cottage and the throne that the great Tory leader of the Victorian period, Disraeli, had suggested, developed into strong ties between the people and the Conservative party leadership. As a result the party has survived as one of the two major political groups in England. Since 1945 it has held the reins of government for about twenty-five years.

To sum up some of the basic characteristics of classic conservative thought: there is a belief that society is like an organism; that its parts are hierarchically arranged; that authority should be entrusted to natural leaders. There is a rejection of individualism and egalitarianism; a strong belief in custom and tradition and an aversion to change; emphasis on religious and ritualistic symbolisms to solidify the union of the whole. Yet at the same time there is a strong commitment to a government under law guaranteeing individual rights, an acceptance of representative government, and with it an acknowledgment of the increased participation of all the people, an implementation of the Welfare State, and above all, a rejection of authoritarian solutions. Conservatism has thus legitimized itself as an ideology consistent with democracy.

People who like change and innovation, and find themselves at odds with the conservative ideology, should not be particularly hasty in rejecting it. Classic conservatism, as portrayed here, was and remains a brake to rapid change. But it channeled the well-to-do and, more important, millions of voters, into accepting gradual and peaceful change. Conservatives have been distrustful of human reason and majoritarianism. But they never attempted to control the first or to outlaw the second. They (like the

British Socialists) presented their position and policies in the context of democracy. The conservative ideology—in a sense the creature of the British ruling groups—tamed the class that formulated it, disciplined its followers to act within the logic of individual and associational freedoms, and accepted free political competition without which democracy cannot exist. By creating an ideology that taught the British ruling classes how to bend in order not to break, they legitimized not only gradual change but all change, if and when the electorate demanded it, and they prepared their followers to accept change, if not always with grace, at least without countering it with force.

Conservatives in the U.S.A.

There are three strands in American conservatism. One follows the Burkian tradition; a second is in essence a rediscovery of classic economic liberalism, i.e., capitalism, and both the terms neoliberalism and conservatism are used to denote it; the third is an affirmation of traditional religious values, which is fundamentalist.

American Conservatives and the British Model

As we saw in our discussion of British conservative ideology, conservatives admire and try to preserve the past; they are elitist in that they believe in natural leaders; they accept only gradual and incremental change; they admire a well-balanced and hierarchically structured society, and they emphasize the need for authority. "Civilized man lives by authority," according to a (British-born) American conservative.[7] Conservatives believe that societies develop norms—that is, enduring standards of behavior—and that we obey them because of habit and tradition. "The sanction to norms," writes the same author, "must come from a source other than private advantage or rationality"—the two basic propositions used by liberals to explain our obedience to the State. The real source of authority and obedience "is tradition." For conservatives, "the good citizen is a law-abiding traditionalist."[8]

To most Americans these propositions are alien. "Man is created equal"; all of us are "endowed" with liberty. The American dream has been that change, through the manipulation of the environment in order to get more out of it, is equated with progress toward a better future, and a person's worth lies in achievement, not birth, inheritance, or status. As for society, it has no meaning and reality outside of the individuals who make it and can remake it. There is no hierarchy and no organic quality about it; there is no fixed subordination of some to others, and no structure of deference. The self-made person is still the symbol of Americanism, and of the

---

7. Russell Kirk, "Prescription, Authority and Ordered Freedom," in F. S. Meyer (ed.), *What Is Conservatism?*, p. 23.
8. Ibid., p. 31.

constant restlessness, mobility, and change of Americans and American society. Law is but a convenient external standard that we set up and change to accommodate our domestic conflicts—hardly a norm maturing and gaining strength and respect with time until obedience to it becomes a tradition.

As noted earlier, economic liberalism became the dominant American political creed, and virtually all social thinkers called themselves liberals. Few dared called themselves conservatives until very recently. There was little to conserve and a lot to change and to conquer: more wealth to amass and greater material benefits to realize for all. Outside of individual effort and achievement neither norms nor "tradition" nor "wise prejudice," as Burke had put it, restrained the myth of material success and self-improvement that was the heart of the beliefs of Americans. When the labor leader Samuel Gompers was asked in the latter part of the nineteenth century what it was that American labor wanted, he gave the answer that all Americans understood: "More!" In a society holding such an ideal, genuine conservatives were likely to find themselves out of place or, what amounts to the same thing, there was no place for them.

The American political tradition therefore has few conservative authors or leaders in any way comparable to the British ones: Henry Adams, John Calhoun, Herman Melville, Brooks Adams, Irving Babbitt, and Walter Lippmann are among the best known. Calhoun, without any doubt, had a profound influence in the years until the Civil War. But his impact has not been a more lasting one than that of the others. The real classic conservatives—the "humanistic value preservers"—who venerate tradition, order, and natural law, have been very few indeed. The reason is that the American system and the American society were made in the name of human reason and individual rights, not tradition. Real conservatives in the United States must either go directly to the British sources for inspiration, which they often do, or try to find the particular institutions and ideas that best correspond to the conservative ideology in the American experience, which they have tried to do. The only conservative ideology they claim to find is in the Constitution and in the thinking of the framers that produced it and, of course, in the political philosophy of some of them as it was expounded in the Federalist Papers.

American conservatives have tried to draw their inspiration from the Constitution because of its limitations on direct democracy and because of its emphasis on law. The American republic is "a government of law and not men." It is a republic and not a democracy—a state in which separation and the balance of powers make it impossible for any single branch of government to gain enough power to endanger the rights of the people. It is a system carefully engineered to make it impossible for a numerical majority to control all branches of government, at one and the same time, and to establish a tyranny—one that is considered just as bad as the tyranny of a minority or a group of men or of one man. Restraints are built into the system not only against the governmental organs, federal and state, but against the people as well. It is in this that American conservatives find the "wisdom of the framers."

Similarly, in the Federalist Papers that provide for a defense of the Constitution and embody the philosophy of the framers, notably Madison and Hamilton, references are made and institutions are defended in terms that are close to British conservative ideas and vocabulary. Thus, the "electoral college," that was supposed to be free, once chosen, to elect the president, is viewed and defended as a body of wise men who are considered more reliable to make the proper choice than the people directly. The early mode of election for the Senate, by the state legislatures, again provided for an indirect mode of election whose purpose was to filter the popular choice. It is significant, however, that the electoral college has ceased to play the independent role it was supposed to play, and that the Senate is now elected directly by the people of the various states. Emphasis on law — a government of law and not men — remains an important ingredient of a conservative ideology, yet only a careful examination of the jurisprudence of the Supreme Court, the ultimate custodian of the Constitution, can answer to what extent. Furthermore, it should be remembered that nowhere did the Constitution grant power to the Supreme Court to declare acts of Congress unconstitutional and to set them aside.

This interpretation of the Constitution and the intentions of its framers as being essentially conservative and a reflection of a conservative ideology must be considered seriously. The framers were afraid of "the people," the majority, and they looked for "natural leaders." Many had a profound respect for tradition, but this hardly makes them and the Constitution, as it developed, conservative. Conservatives in England believed in the wise exercise of power and extolled established authority; they put politics and political wisdom above everything else except religion and divine or natural law; they thought, as we have seen, that a political society was a living organism to which material and functional interests were subordinated. Wise leadership kept this organism together.

The framers of the United States Constitution, on the other hand, feared political power. It could be abused and might be abused by anybody and everybody — even by "wise rulers." They were skeptical about the possibility of legitimizing power and creating a strong political authority. Their solution was to weaken authority as much as possible by fragmenting it and dividing it. The solution was a mechanical one — it reflected no belief in tradition, custom, or in natural leaders. Like the Newtonian physics which influenced the framers, the intent was to establish an equilibrium of forces and governmental organs.

This philosophy was fully consistent with the climate of opinion of the times. By downgrading the powers of the government and by providing for checks and balances for each and all its organs, the framers hoped to liberate society (i.e., the individual, the economy, voluntary associations, the churches, and so on) from the State and from political domination. The best government was the one that governed the least and left individuals free to pursue their material interest in the best utilitarian manner, and to maximize their pleasure and avoid pain as they saw fit. The "do-it-yourself man" of Benjamin Franklin was to emerge not only unfettered by political power, free of tradition and prescription, but also free from the wisdom of political elites and their natural leaders! This was, and remains, the very opposite of classic conservatism.

The Conservative Neoliberals

Despite the foregoing, the term conservative has gained respectability during the last twenty-five years. The conservative ideology has gained many followers, and there are many who proudly claim to be conservative. What is the meaning of the term? And who are these new conservatives?

To begin with, conservatives in the United States today are very different from British conservatives. In fact, they are liberals who subscribe by and large to the tenets of nineteenth-century capitalism and want to return to what, in their opinion, worked so well for this country. They believe in economic individualism, competition, and the free enterprise system. They are against State intervention.*

What do these conservatives stand for? First and foremost, for individual initiative and freedoms. But they narrowly interpret both to mean *economic freedom* — freedom of enterprise, freedom to work irrespective of whether or not one belongs to a union, freedom of contract, a free market economy. One of the most sophisticated of the neoconservatives, William F. Buckley, points this out:

> Conservatives have failed to alert the community to the interconnection between economic freedom and — freedom. . . . It is a part of the conservative intuition that economic freedom is the most precious temporal freedom, for the reason that it alone gives to each one of us, in our comings and goings in our complex society, sovereignty — and over that part of existence in which by far the most choices have in fact to be made, and in which it is possible to make choices, involving oneself, without damage to other people. And for the further reason that without economic freedom, political and other freedoms are likely to be taken from us.[9]

Thus the new conservatives ask that the federal government (and often the state governments) move out of the economy; that if and when welfare measures are needed they should be undertaken at the state and local levels and not the federal one; that the federal budget and federal expenditures be sharply reduced; that income taxes and many other federal and state taxes be sharply curtailed. In effect, conservatives ask for the dismantling of much of the New Deal legislation and the Welfare State.

Many arguments favor the position of the conservatives, and we are already familiar with some of them: bureaucracy leads to inefficiency; state controls and regulations stifle competition and are wasteful because they

9. William F. Buckley, Jr., *Up From Liberalism.* New York: McDonnell, Oblensky, 1959, p. 166.
* In the last decade British conservatism, under Margaret Thatcher, has been moving in the same direction.

increase the cost of production. State controls lead to increasing deprivation of moral freedoms, and, most important, of the freedom to make our
own choices and to assume our own responsibilities. We become dependent upon bureaucratic, impersonal services for which nobody is responsible. In 1946 Friedrich von Hayek, a professor of economics at the University of Chicago, wrote *The Road to Serfdom,* in which he sounded the alarm
and set the tone for the neoconservatives. State intervention and economic
planning, he argued, and the end of individual economic freedoms, would
result in moral degradation for all of us and the ultimate loss of our political
freedoms as well. The bureaucratic state would make choices for us — what
to produce and what to consume, where to work and where to live, what
income to make, and so on. The same theme is repeated by Buckley:

> What all conservatives in this country fear, and have plenty of
> reason to fear, is the loss of freedom by attrition. It is therefore
> for the most realistic reasons, as well as those of principle, that
> we must resist every single accretion of power by the State. . . .[10]

What do conservatives propose? Buckley provides a list of particulars:

> . . . to maintain and wherever possible enhance the freedom of
> the individual to acquire property and dispose of that property
> in ways that he decides on. To deal with unemployment by
> eliminating monopoly unionism, featherbedding, and inflexi-
> bilities in the labor market, and be prepared, where residual
> unemployment persists, to cope with it locally, placing the po-
> litical and humanitarian responsibility on the lowest feasible
> political unit. . . .[11]

We can identify the conservatives, then, in terms of a cluster of issues.
Less taxation, reduction of the federal budget, withdrawal of the State
from economic regulation and control, reduction of public expenditures
(federal and state), sharp reduction in welfare services and in the size of the
bureaucracies, and more initiative and freedom to local government bodies are some of the issues. Yet conservatives, irrespective of the positions
they take regarding social and economic matters, have remained within
the framework of constitutional democracy. At no time do they envisage
the use of force or repressive tactics, in or out of government. They believe
in political competition and political freedoms, and use the political process
to gain support.

Conservatives have been gaining strength. Increased taxation in the
1970s, coupled with inflation and unemployment, turned the public away
from the Welfare State. The middle classes felt threatened. The disillusionment with the welfare liberalism may well have accounted for Ronald
Reagan's victory in the presidential elections of 1980 and 1984. He favored
lower taxes; reduction in welfare spending; reduction in the scope of the

10. Ibid., p. 179.
11. Ibid., p. 202.

federal government and in its place a "new federalism" that would return many welfare services to the states; and a promise to give more freedom to the private sector of the economy and the market.

Conservatives in the United States today echo the liberal voices of the nineteenth century. They stress the economic core of liberalism and remain attached to the moral and political core. Their growing strength derives from the disenchantment of many people, particularly the middle classes, with what now seem to be the deficiencies in State controls, public spending, high taxes, and centralized decision making through an ever-growing bureaucracy. But there is also the argument that public spending and public controls undermine the moral initiative of individuals and dull their incentives and inventiveness so that, in the last analysis, productivity and economic growth are undermined. The myth of "rugged individualism," so central to nineteenth-century American liberalism, remains remarkably strong. So too is the notion that the character and moral fiber of a person can be tested only through competition and individual effort—whereby only the best survive.

In the last few years, nobody has better expressed the position of the conservatives than Nobel Prize winner and economist Milton I. Friedman. His book[12] (written with his wife Rose) popularized the basic arguments against State intervention in the economy and the belief that such intervention will inevitably lead to controls that will undermine the moral autonomy of the individuals and erode their political freedoms.

The Religious Right*

Conservatives, as noted, yearn for stability. They feel at home with old habits and surroundings; they cherish the norms and values passed on to them. In short, it is aversion to any change in lifestyles, work habits, and mores that characterizes conservatives. Such an aversion often correlates directly with an attachment to religious values shaped over a long period of time. This is the case with American fundamentalism—a movement committed to the preservation of fundamental religious values; values that are true because they are revealed by God and therefore beyond critical inquiry. They can be found in God's word as stated in the Bible.

In the last two decades, fundamentalism, or the "religious right," as it is loosely referred to, has gained strength. In the United States, the most dynamic and mobile society in the world, where the only truth accepted is the freedom to question it, fundamentalism is a movement attempting to find a permanent shelter—an anchor that will hold the individual back from critical inquiry and experimentation. And the greater and faster the changes in a society, the greater becomes the longing for stability and certainty. As a result, both the depth and pace of change have forced many

12. Milton and Rose Friedman, *Free to Choose.*
*As indicated in my Preface Alain Minsk, a graduating senior, did a great deal of the spade work in the form of notes and drafts for the writing of this section.

fundamentalists to come out and fight in order to protect what they feel is being threatened. As society has become more modern and "scientific," fundamentalists have seen their traditional beliefs challenged. They have become activists not only to preserve the values they cherish but also to restore them. They have moved from defense to offense in order to defeat the critics and enemies of their way of life. They have entered politics and their theology has been transformed into a political movement designed to enact or change legislation to promote their conservative views. They have moved "from the Pew to the Precinct," in the words of Jerry Falwell, one of their leaders.

It is not easy to clearly distinguish the theology of the various sects that comprise the religious conservative movement: Baptists and Southern Baptists, Pentacostals, and Southern Lutherans are among the most prominent. The greatest number of believers are situated in the so-called Bible Belt and beyond: Tennessee, Virginia, Georgia, Florida, Arkansas, Louisiana, Mississippi, Texas, North and South Carolina, and Alabama. (A Gallup Poll indicated that 50 percent of all evangelicals are from the South.) But they are also strong in Michigan, Missouri, Ohio, and in a number of western states, and tens of millions throughout the country have been mobilized by fundamentalists. In fact, one-third of the American population proclaims itself as "Born-Again Christians," according to a Gallup Poll.

While religious themes continue to prevail, it is the way they have been shaped into a political program and the way believers have been organized into political action that counts. A common political philosophy emerges even when there are theological disputes among sects, as there are, particularly between fundamentalists and evangelicals. This common political ideology has been shaped by a number of prominent religious leaders—Rousas J. Rashdoony, Tim Lattaye, Gary North, Jerry Falwell, George Marsden, Pat Robertson, and others. Through newly established theological seminaries, foundations and universities, newspapers and journals, radio and television, the themes that organize the political battle lines, often in close cooperation with conservative organizations like the Conservative Caucus, the National Conservative Political Action Committee and others, have become clear.

The shortest distance between the Pew and the Precinct, one might add, is radio and television. Through the Christian Broadcasting Network (CBN), the third largest cable network in the country, more than 30 million people are reached daily. If one were to add various affiliated stations, the figure is close to 50 million. The evangelicals have become increasingly "televangelicals."

Both general and specific themes have been developed by ministers and theologians and espoused by others for political purposes. The "political ministers" have tried to create a mass movement that cuts across religious lines to include Protestants, Catholics, Jews, blacks, whites, farmers, businessmen, and housewives. This is the "Moral Majority," which was formed "to combat the legalization of immorality," under the leadership, until October 1987, of Jerry Falwell. The movement directly confronts some of the critical issues that concern Americans: abortion, pornography, the use of drugs, the breakdown of the family, homosexuality, and other "moral cancers" to which AIDS has most recently been added.

Political Action and Organization The fundamentalists who have spearheaded the Moral Majority movement pride themselves on their strong organization, which is defined and described in terms appropriate to a paramilitary organization: commitment of the individual and readiness to sacrifice "even life itself" for the sake of the "company of the faithful"; absolute discipline in the willingness of all to obey the commands of the leadership; evangelical zeal — to spread the gospel and convert people; absolutism — the acceptance of God's word as the absolute truth; and, finally, fanaticism.

Fundamentalists have little patience with dialogue, argument, and self-criticism. But in building the Moral Majority, efforts have been made to allow for internal debate and pluralism, and present a common political front on those basic moral and political positions that unite the greatest number possible. The battle against pornography, drugs, and abortion are likely to receive the most widespread support. So is national defense, though there are differences as to how much defense is needed. A blanket anti-Communist stance (often anti-Soviet) is also widely supported by nationalists and those who fear atheism. School prayer is also overwhelmingly endorsed. However, the reintroduction of religious education (even if indirectly) in the school curriculum divides the followers. There are also potential tensions between blacks and whites within the movement. The black fundamentalists overwhelmingly accept the moral code: profamily, antiabortion, and pro-school prayer, but they do not agree with the movement's opposition to welfare legislation.

The scope of the movement's political activities has been comprehensive and many-faceted. Voters have been so well mobilized to register that millions of previously indifferent citizens have now joined the voting public. (In the 1980 election the Moral Majority claimed responsibility for the registration of 2.5 million voters.) Large amounts of money have been raised to support candidates, but each candidate is carefully screened to determine his or her stand on the critical moral issues. Pamphlets, letters, and radio and television messages have been used to support or reject candidates. There has also been lobbying of congressmen and senators in Washington and in state legislatures as well as federal and state officials. Above all, a constant stream of educational and political materials keep coming out of religious study and research centers to reach out to the believers.

The embattled ministers of God have entered politics in earnest. In the process, their emphasis on traditionalism, their rejection of critical inquiry, and their goal of imposing their own moral and religious values upon all Americans suggest a potential move away from the basic norms of democracy. However, they do not challenge the Constitution; they simply wish to align it to their moral and religious imperatives.

In general, the fundamentalists are beginning to weigh heavily on the political agenda of the country. "Moral-social" issues are now dominating the political debate and increasingly affecting the position of the candidates, while critical issues relating to the economy, foreign policy, education, and defense are not given the high priority and the public debate they deserve. In other words, the fundamentalists and evangelicals are reshaping the political horizon and one of their most active leaders, Pat Robertson, showed remarkable strength within the Republican party in his bid to be nominated for the presidency in 1988.

Reaganism and the Conservatives   Conservatives by and large supported Ronald Reagan. Both as a candidate and as a president, Reagan endorsed most of the conservative propositions. He was a fundamentalist on most social-moral questions (abortion, pornography, school prayer, etc.); he disavowed a "permissive" society by advocating greater police powers against suspected criminals; he opposed the ERA; he appointed conservative justices on the federal courts; and he strengthened national defense against the Soviets—he was the president who called the Soviet Union an "Evil Empire." Reagan emerged as the champion of economic liberalism, favoring deregulation, reduction in taxes and welfare spending, and a return to the market and free-enterprise economy. It is difficult to imagine a president who could be closer to the conservative positions while at the same time appealing to the center.

The conservative support began to wane, however, as Reagan had to compromise with the center of his party and with many of the Democrats who held a majority in the House of Representatives and in both houses of Congress in the last two years of his term in office. He was unable to sustain an interventionist policy in Nicaragua, and he began to shift his position on the Soviet Union by considering and ultimately singing agreements on nuclear arms in December 1987. Conservatives became impatient with the lack of decisive measures for dismantling the welfare state and reducing government spending, and they fought for a constitutional amendment to set a limit on the federal deficit.

The Gorbachev visit to Washington in December 1987, the signing of a treaty on missiles in Europe, and Reagan's visit to the Soviet Union in May 1988 were blows to the conservatives. Many of them turned against Reagan, and Richard Viguerie, one of their influential leaders, could no longer "recognize the man he had supported." Conservatives organized a nationwide movement against "appeasement" and remained confident that they could influence the political agenda for the future.

Bibliography

Banfield, Edward C. *The Unheavenly City.* Boston: Little, Brown, 1970.

Bellah, Robert N., Madsen, Richard, et al. *Habits of the Heart: Individualism and Commitment in American Life.* Berkeley, Calif.: University of California, 1985.

Buckley, William F., Jr. *Up From Liberalism.* New York: McDonnell, Oblensky, 1959.

———. *Did You Ever See a Dream Walking? American Conservative Thought in the 20th Century.* Indianapolis: Bobbs-Merrill, 1970.

Burke, Edmund. *Reflections on the Revolution in France.* New York: Bobbs-Merrill, Library of Liberal Arts, 1955.

Calhoun, John C. *A Disquisition on Government.* Indianapolis: Bobbs-Merrill, 1958.

Cecil, Lord Hugh Richard. *Conservatism.* London: Williams and Nurgate, 1912.

Cole, Steward Grant. *History of Fundamentalism.* Hamden, Conn.: Archon Books, 1963.

Conway, Flo, and Siegelman, Jim. *Holy Terror.* Garden City, N.Y.: Doubleday, 1982.

Diggins, John P. *Up From Communism: A Conservative's Odyssey in American Intellectual History.* New York: Harper & Row, 1976.

Fackre, Gabriel. *The Religious Right and Christian Faith.* Grand Rapids, Mich.: William B. Eerdmans, 1982.

Falwell, Jerry. *The Fundamentalist Phenomenon.* Garden City, N.Y.: Doubleday, 1981.

Flake, Carol. *Redemptorama.* Garden City, N.Y.: Anchor-Doubleday, 1984.

Friedman, Milton, and Friedman, Rose. *Free to Choose.* New York: Harcourt Brace Jovanovich, 1980.

Gasper, Louis. *The Fundamentalist Movement.* Paris: Tenn. Mouton & Co., 1963.

Hadden, Jeffrey, and Shupe, Anson. *Televangelism, Power and Politics.* Boston: Beacon Press, 1988.

Hayek, Frederick A. *The Constitution of Liberty.* London: Routledge and Kegan Paul, 1960.

———. *The Road to Serfdom.* Chicago: University of Chicago Press, 1946.

Hearnshaw, F. J. C. *Conservatism in England.* London: Macmillan, 1933.

Holden, Mathew, Jr. *Varieties of Political Conservatism.* Beverly Hills, Calif.: Sage Publications, 1974.

Jorsted, Erlig. *Politics of Doomsday.* Nashville, Tenn.: Abington Press, 1970.

Kater, John. *Christians on the Right: The Moral Majority in Perspective.* New York: Seabury Press, 1982.

Kirk, Russell. *The Conservative Mind,* rev. ed. Chicago: Henry Regnery, 1960.

——— (ed.). *The Portable Conservative Reader.* New York: Penguin Books, 1982.

Marsden, George M. *Fundamentalism and American Culture.* New York: Oxford U.P., 1980.

Meyer, Frank S. (ed.). *What Is Conservatism?* New York: Holt, Rinehart and Winston, 1964.

Nash, George H. *The Conservative Intellectual Movement in America.* New York: Basic Books, 1976.

Nisbet, Robert A. *The Quest for Community.* New York: Oxford U.P., 1953.

———. *Conservatism.* Minneapolis: University of Minnesota Press, 1986.

Rogger, Hans, and Weber, Eugen (eds.). *The European Right: A Historical Profile.* Berkeley, Calif.: University of California Press, 1981.

Rossiter, Clinton. *Conservatism in America.* 2d rev. ed. New York: Knopf, 1966.

Schuettinger, R. L. (ed.). *The Conservative Tradition in European Thought.* New York: Capricorn Books, 1969.

Sigler, Jay A. *The Conservative Tradition in American Thought.* New York: Capricorn Books, 1969.

Steinfels, Peter. *The Neoconservatives: The Men Who Are Changing American Politics.* New York: Simon and Schuster, 1979.

Viereck, Peter. *Conservatism: From John Adams to Churchill.* Princeton, N.J.: Van Nostrand, 1956.

Wald, Kenneth. *Religion and Politics in the U.S.A.* New York: St. Martin's Press, 1987.

Part Two

Communism: from One to Many

In place of the old bourgeois society . . . we shall have an association in which the free development of each is the condition for the free development of all.

KARL MARX AND FRIEDRICH ENGELS
The Communist Manifesto

The socialist and conservative political ideologies, as outlined in Chapters 3 and 4, remain solidly within the democratic tradition. They are fully compatible with individual freedoms, political liberties, political competition, representative assemblies, and constitutionalism. This is not the case with communism. It rejects individual and associational freedoms; uses force as an instrument of governance; and relies on a single party, excluding all political competition among parties and groups. Representative assemblies are but a rubber stamp unanimously accepting the policies formulated by the leadership. Elections are controlled by the State apparatus and by party officials. Communism is in essence — no matter what it promises for the future — a totalitarian ideology:

1. The ideology is official, that is, espoused by the leadership to the exclusion of all other ideologies. It is total and comprehensive and everything becomes subordinate to it. Society is to be restructured in terms of the posited ideological goals.
2. The purpose of the single party is to control, intimidate, and govern. It is the major vehicle of political mobilization and recruitment. No political competition is tolerated.
3. All associations, all groups, and all individuals are subordinate to the party, the State, and the leader. There is no cultural pluralism. Education, literature, art, music, architecture — all must yield and conform to the overriding objectives and goals of the political ideology. Groups and

individuals, family life, social and recreational activities, the schools, and the economy must all be synchronized with the political regime. All must "march in step" with it.

4. The use of violence is institutionalized through the police and other specialized instruments of coercion and intimidation.

5. The party directly, or through the State, has a monopolistic control of mass communications and overall economic activities.

Needless to say, these characteristics represent extreme or "ideal" types, helpful for the purpose of analysis. None of them are likely to be found in their pure form. Even in portrayals of the most extreme of totalitarian systems, like Huxley's *Brave New World* or Orwell's *1984*, the total conformity of the society and the individual to the ideology and leader are shown to be elusive. Dissent and nonconformity can never be eliminated entirely. Furthermore, in the communist doctrine, totalitarian controls are supposed to be temporary — they represent a historical phase after which individual freedoms will return. The "dictatorship of the proletariat" paves the way to the disappearance of the State; the socialization of the means of production destroys the class structure of the society and makes the use of force unnecessary; production is not geared to profit but to need. A true communist system not only will become increasingly egalitarian but also will become more open and free. Finally, nations and national wars will give place to a fraternal and egalitarian international community. However, there is no assurance that the professed goals of communism will ever be realized. There is no clear evidence that they are being implemented in any communist regime, and especially in the Soviet Union. Stalinism represented, as we shall see, a political movement that remained very remote from the professed doctrinal goals of communism. There is also no indication that communist regimes are immune either to war or nationalism. The appeal to past or newly fabricated nationalist myths, in an effort to integrate the people, characterizes communist movements and regimes, just as it does right-wing totalitarian ones. Conflict seems to be very much in evidence today, pitting some communist regimes against each other while the prospect of expansion or domination of others is ever-present.

5 | *Marxism and Communism*

Marx was a genius; we others were at best talented.
Without him the theory would not be by far what it is
today. It, therefore, rightly bears his name.

FRIEDRICH ENGELS

Communism is literally the economic and social system whereby all the means of production are concentrated in the hands of the community or the State, and in which the production and allocation of goods and services is decided upon by the community and the State. Generally, however, communism has meant much more. It has been "an ideal, a political movement, a method of analysis and a way of life."[1] As an ideal, it promises an egalitarian society with production geared to need — a society in which the dream of abundance will be realized. As a political movement it represents the organization of men and women striving to attain freedom; as a method of analysis it sets forth propositions that explain the past and point to the future development of our societies; finally, as a way of life it portrays a new type of citizen for whom the communitarian and social attributes of human nature will gain ascendancy over egotism and private interest.

Whether taken singly, or all together as they usually are, the trends represent what communism has been — one of the most powerful myths and ideologies in history. It takes the form of a moral imperative — how to create a collective and social ethic that will override self-interest and do away with the demons of profit and private property, which are seen as the cause of subjugation of the many to the few.

Ever since antiquity, the theme of the *moral* superiority of communal ownership, in contrast to private property, interest, and individualistic aspirations, has been kept alive. It is defended in Plato's *Republic,* where no private property is allowed the rulers, the Guardians, in order that they can give their full attention to communitarian values and govern in the

1. Alfred Meyer, *Marxism,* p. 1.

109

interest of the whole. The myth of communism appears and reappears in many religious writings in which property is viewed as the result of "man's fall." It is part of secular law and does not exist through "divine" or "natural" law. The theme reemerges with particular force in the writings of many utopian socialists in the decades after the French Revolution and well into the nineteenth century. After the industrial revolution, the dream of favoring collective ownership and eliminating all income inequalities and poverty has been particularly potent.

Not until the middle of the nineteenth century, however, did the ideal become transformed into a political movement, and not until the end of the century did the ideology take on flesh and blood with the formation of political parties. In 1920, communism gained ascendancy in one country, the Soviet Union, and spread thereafter with renewed vigor all over Europe. By World War II the ideology had crystallized firmly into the Soviet political system, and after the war it established itself in other countries—in eastern Europe and China, with noticeable spillovers elsewhere. But at about the same time, under the impact of a number of forces, communism began to splinter into various sects (national or ideological) to such an extent that today a discussion of the movement has to specify *what kind* of communism we are talking about. Even more, the early fraternal cooperation among communist states has given place to rivalries.

Today communism plays two quite separate roles. In a number of countries it sustains a political system, which is the official, or, as we called it, the *status quo* ideology. This is clearly the case in the Soviet Union, eastern Europe, and some of the Balkan countries. In Asia, such countries as China, North Korea, Laos, Vietnam, and Cambodia have communist regimes. In parts of Africa and the Middle East, such as Angola, Ethiopia, Mozambique, and South Yemen, communism has gained a foothold. Even in the North American sphere of influence, there is, despite the vigilance of the United States, one fully established communist regime, Cuba and a fledgling one in Nicaragua. Today, at least 30 percent of all peoples of the world live under communist regimes and the communist ideology.

In virtually all other countries communist ideologies and movements play *a revolutionary role*, seeking political power and domination through various means. There are strong communist parties in France, Italy, Portugal, Spain, and Greece, and in countries of the Third World.

Almost a century and a half ago, in 1848, Marx wrote *The Communist Manifesto;* it transformed communism from only a theory into a strong political movement. In his opening sentence he spoke of "a specter" that haunted Europe—"the specter of communism." Today it is a reality. Communism, either in the form of established political regimes or as a powerful political revolutionary movement, inspires, mobilizes, and organizes for political action a greater number of people than any other political ideology. But what kind of communism is it?

As with other ideologies, communism can be viewed in two different ways. First, as a body of theory and philosophy it requires us to examine

HISTORICAL PICTURES SERVICE, INC., CHICAGO

Karl Marx (1818–1883)

Born in Germany, where he studied law, philosophy, and history, Karl Marx and his family settled in London when he was thirty years old. There he began a lifelong cooperation with Engels to develop a communist ideology and to translate it into political action. In 1848 they produced *The Communist Manifesto,* urging the workers to rise and take over the means of production from the exploiting capitalist class. In 1864 he founded the First International whose purpose was to unite the workers everywhere in a revolutionary struggle. A prodigious worker, a committed man, and also one of the most learned and creative minds of the nineteenth century, Marx, like Freud half a century later in psychology, suggested a new way of looking at social life and history. Accordingly, material and economic conditions are responsible for the shaping of our values, morality, attitudes, and political institutions. Marx singled out property relations to be the key element and the exploitation of "have-nots" by the "haves" to be at the heart of liberal capitalism. It was, at the same time, the reason for a working-class revolution, and the vindication of communism. He wrote voluminously, but his major work is the analysis of the capitalist economy in *Capital,* the first volume of which was published in 1867 and the second and third posthumously, by Engels, in 1885 and 1894.

and analyze it with one question in mind: How valid is its theory and underlying philosophic assumptions? Second, as a political ideology and movement it requires us to examine the way in which its basic philosophic and theoretical propositions have been translated into an action-oriented movement (i.e., an ideology). While the first level of analysis is important, we shall emphasize communism here as a political ideology and a movement for political action, and stress some of its contemporary characteristics.

The Legacy of Marx

It was Karl Marx and his associate Friedrich Engels who provided us, through their writings and their political activities, with the foundations of contemporary communism. Of the two, Marx was the dominant intellectual figure. He published major theoretical works on economics and philosophy and produced a series of pamphlets on various aspects of political tactics. After his death in 1883, Engels synthesized, some might say simplified, some of his ideas. When we speak of Marxism, however, we are referring to the combined work of Marx and Engels.

Marx and Engels provide us with a comprehensive philosophy of economic, social, and political life, that includes the rejection of capitalist society, the dynamics of a communist revolution, and the promise of a new society.

The Sources That Inspired Marx

Four sources combined to produce the overall synthesis that constitutes Marxism. They are:

1. Hegel's philosophy, especially his philosophy of history
2. The works of the British economists, notably, Ricardo, Adam Smith, Malthus, and others
3. The French utopian socialists, even though they were criticized sharply by Marx and Engels
4. The social and economic reality of the mid-nineteenth century, particularly in England

The first gave Marx a dynamic and evolutionary theory of history based on conflict; the second provided him with a new objective analysis of economic phenomena in which all economic factors were viewed in abstract terms as commodities, or variables, relating to each other on the basis of demonstrable and quantifiable laws; the third provided hints on the construction of the future society.

As for the reality of British industrial society in the middle of the nineteenth century, it had a profound impact on both Marx and Engels. Working conditions were dismal, hours of work long, children and women were employed at starvation wages for twelve, fourteen, and sometimes

HISTORICAL PICTURES SERVICE, INC., CHICAGO

Friedrich Engels (1820–1895)

Friedrich Engels was Karl Marx's companion, associate, and collaborator. Born in Germany, he lived most of his life in England. He collaborated with Marx on many publications including *The Communist Manifesto,* and edited the second and third volumes of *Capital* after Marx's death. While he played an important role in the formulation of the communist doctrine, Engels himself admitted that the real theoretical inspiration came from Marx. Engels himself wrote *The Origins of the Family; The Condition of the Working Class in England in 1844; Socialism: Utopian and Scientific* (1892); *Anti-Dühring* (1877–78) and a number of other less important essays. He took part in the founding of the First International in 1864 and the Second International in 1889.

sixteen hours a day, living conditions were abominable, and life expectancy low. The miseries of the workers contrasted sharply with the well-being of those who had land, property, and money (i.e., capital), and could employ others. Conditions like these provoked not only moral indignation but also widespread protest. Workers rebelled and wrecked the new machines for fear they would deprive them of work; regimentation in the factory under the new industrial order was deeply resented, and workers attempted to use their numbers against the employers who, in turn, made use of the instruments of coercion available to them.

But this movement of protest against the early conditions of industrialization and capitalism was unorganized and diffuse. Marx and Engels provided a theory that gave an order and a direction to it.

The Rejection of Capitalism

For Marx, the rejection of capitalism is *not* based on moral or humanitarian considerations. It derives from what he considered to be the empirical reality of the capitalist economy. It obeys certain laws. Understanding them and studying them leads to the unavoidable conclusion that capitalism is doomed. Marx's anatomy of capitalism is also its autopsy!

The key to the understanding of capitalism and its inevitable demise is the notion of value, surplus value, and profit. The student can easily follow the Marxist critique of the capitalist economy by following Marx's own steps:

1. Only labor creates value.
2. Machines, land, and all other factors of production create no new value. They pass on to the product a value equivalent to the portion of their value used as they depreciate during the process of production.
3. The capitalist (the entrepreneur) pays the worker only a subsistence wage.
4. The worker produces a value that is twice as much (generally speaking) as what he or she gets in wages.
5. The difference between what the capitalist pays the worker and what the worker produces is the *surplus value* pocketed by the capitalist.
6. All profits derive from the surplus value, though the actual profit does not correspond to the amount of surplus value extracted by a given capitalist.
7. In the market there is a fierce competition among capitalists. Each tries to sell more; a large volume of goods sold, even at lower prices, will bring added income.
8. This incites the capitalist to modernize and mass-produce, to introduce better machines, and to increase the productivity of labor.
9. A modern firm manages with fewer workers to produce and hence sell more. As a result more and more workers are laid off.
10. Thus the modern firm can reduce prices by lowering its profit *per unit.*

11. Many firms that fail to modernize are gradually driven out of business. They employ more workers and they pay out more in wages, and thus cannot compete with the lower prices the modernized firms set.
12. As a result, many firms have to close down. Capital becomes increasingly concentrated into fewer and fewer hands and in larger and more modern firms, in which more machinery and modern technology is introduced.
13. Capitalism reaches a point where a small number of highly modernized large firms can produce goods efficiently and cheaply. However, with a great number of people out of work there are not enough buyers for the products, so firms can no longer make a profit. Production becomes restricted.
14. Profit and private property, the great incentives of the industrial revolution, now become obstacles to the plentiful production of goods.
15. The legal forms of capitalism (private profit and private property) come into conflict with the means of production (efficiency, high productivity, and potential abundance).

This is the Marxist scheme in a nutshell. Some explanations must be added.

The heart of capitalism and capitalist production is to be found in private property and profit. Capitalism emerged when landed property began to give place to capital and to the manufacturing of goods in the factory. The purpose of production is profit — that is, how the capitalist can get from the market a value for the product that is higher than all he spent to produce it, including the use of land, the cost of machines as they are amortized over the years, and, of course, wages paid. The difference between what the entrepreneurs spend to produce and what they receive for the product is the *profit* — one of the most dynamic incentives for capitalist production and growth.

Marx develops an ingenious theory to explain profit. It is *the theory of surplus value.* The worker is paid wages that are determined by the market through the law of supply and demand. The daily wage corresponds to the price of goods the worker and his family need and consume in one day. During the same day, however, the worker has produced goods that have a much higher value. The difference between value produced (owned and sold by the entrepreneur) and what is paid out in wages is the *surplus value.* Marx contends that generally wages tend to correspond to not more than half of the value the worker produces. So, the other half goes to the entrepreneur — to the capitalist. This is Marx's argument.

There are, of course, qualifications. For instance, the increased growth of mechanization in the plant (what we call today technological advances) gives to some capitalists and firms the possibility of producing more with very few workers. Consider automation, for instance, and computers. The firms that make technological advances and invest in machines make the highest profit. Where does it come from? Marx answers by making a distinction between what he calls *constant capital* (technology, machines, and so on) and *variable capital* (workers employed). Since only workers produce value, the greater their number, the greater their surplus value, and hence the profit.

Yet the truth seems to be precisely the other way around. The more modern the firm, the more advanced its machines and technology, the fewer the workers, the higher the profit. The reason for this apparent contradiction is quite simple: competition among industrialists in the market is ferocious; the one who manages to improve the productivity of the worker through the use of machines, increasing the units the worker can produce every hour, manages to produce in the same given period of time twice as many goods as his competitors and is therefore able to sell the same product at a lower price. By selling twice as much, he will thus take in more than his competitors, even if his profit *per unit* is smaller. Industrialists are thus able to derive a profit from the surplus value their competitors make, compete with them successfully, and, by selling cheaper, drive them out of the market. The margin of profit begins to fall on each item but as productivity goes up, the fall is compensated by the volume of sales.

The Law of Capitalist Accumulation

The distinction between *constant capital* and *variable capital,* and the fact that the technologically advanced firms with the newest machines make profit at the expense of the backward ones, who rely upon a higher percentage of variable capital (workers), accounts for the trend toward technology and modernization. Many firms go bankrupt but the survivors accumulate in their hands an ever greater part of the capital. Fewer and fewer capitalists own the means of production, while more and more small firms disappear. The whole social structure becomes lopsided with a tiny minority controlling production for the purpose of making profit, while the vast majority of the people have nothing but their labor to sell, exactly when it becomes less needed!

However, the capitalists who survive become the victims of their success. Having established firm control over the means of production, the capitalist class now finds it difficult to find enough buyers for their products. This is implicit in the law of capitalist accumulation, or rather, it is the other side of the coin of the same law—the law of pauperization.

The Law of Pauperization

More and more people are dispossessed of the means to produce. More and more fall into the category of proletariat. Thus, as the firms develop more sophisticated machinery, a greater number of people find themselves living in a state of misery. Many cannot find work. Many become "marginals" moving from one place to another without a role, without skills, and in a state of constant deprivation and humiliation. They are the *lumpenproletariat*—the army of the unemployed and also unemployable, people from the countryside or those recently demoted from the middle or low middle classes. They become a permanent fixture of capitalist societies.

Unemployment, however, also affects the qualified, skilled, and semiskilled workers. It becomes permanent. Therefore, capitalism inevitably reaches a point at which it cannot utilize all resources and satisfy all needs, even basic ones. In fact, a point comes when a given percentage of the population may not be part of the economic system — they do not work in it and they cannot buy and enjoy what it produces. Millions of human beings become "surplus labor," unwanted and useless.

To conclude: the profit motive — a driving and dynamic motive in the early stages of capitalism — becomes a drag and an impediment in its most advanced stage. It has pushed the capitalists to modernize and to accumulate capital and industrial equipment; it has indeed made production easier and much more efficient; *objectively speaking* it has made it possible for human beings in a society to supply all their wants and more. Capitalism thus achieves a most remarkable breakthrough by creating all the material conditions for the good life. Marx is full of praise for the bourgeoisie and for capitalism when he views its historical role.

> The bourgeoisie . . . has been the first to show what man's activity can bring about. It has accomplished wonders far surpassing the Egyptian pyramids, Roman aqueducts, the Gothic cathedrals; it has conducted expeditions that put in the shade all former Exoduses and crusades. . . .

> The bourgeoisie has through its exploitation of the world market given a cosmopolitan character to production and consumption in every country. In place of the old wants, satisfied by the production of the country, we find new wants, requiring for their satisfaction the products of distant lands and climes. In place of the old local and national seclusion and self-sufficiency, we have intercourse in every direction, universal interdependence of nations. And as in material, so also in intellectual production. The intellectual creations of individual nations become common property. National onesidedness and narrow-mindedness become more and more impossible, and from the numerous national and local literatures there arises a world literature.

> The bourgeoisie, by the rapid improvement of all instruments of production, by the immensely facilitated means of communication, draws all, even the most barbarian, nations into civilization. . . .

> The bourgeoisie has created enormous cities, has greatly increased the urban population as compared with the rural, and has thus rescued a considerable part of the population from the idiocy of rural life. . . . [2]

2. In *The Communist Manifesto*. See Tucker (ed.), *The Marx-Engels Reader*, pp. 469–500.

Yet it is precisely at this point that the capitalistic economy can no longer provide for profits. By pressing heavily upon the middle class, and by creating a chronic state of unemployment among the independent artisans and the small farmers, which reduces them gradually to the ranks of the poor and the dispossessed, many are being deprived of the means to buy things and meet their needs. Demand goes down and with it comes lower profit. To keep the rate of profit the capitalist is now forced to produce less, to control prices, to develop monopolies in order to avoid competition, and to form cartels to keep prices up. Whereas profit was a positive incentive to industrial growth and production, now it becomes a shackle. This is the point when capitalism has outlived its purpose — it can produce plenty but there is no incentive to do so. It is at this point that Marx pronounces its death sentence!

The student will note that thus far there has not been a single note of moral approbation or disapprobation. Marx gives us a "scientific" account, that is, a description of what he sees happening, a description which fits his basic laws of the capitalist economy. As capitalist production and the capitalist economy develop they begin to show contradictions that *inevitably*, that is to say, for reasons inherent in the system itself, will be self-destructive. The major contradiction which ultimately unfolds itself is the discrepancy between the productive capacities that the system has developed and the legal forms of production (i.e., private property and profit). Capitalism will collapse because private property and profit become *dysfunctional* — they are no longer adequate incentives for production.

The analysis of the laws accounting for the demise of capitalism, however, do not amount to a "rejection" of capitalism. People must become aware of something, become dissatisfied with something, and move actively against something in order for there to be a rejection. Rejection is a subjective phenomenon associated with a collective desire and consciousness and with concerted action. *This is the revolutionary side of Marxism.*

The Dynamics of the Communist Revolution

In contrast to his economic analysis, in which Marx set up theories and hypotheses and sought their confirmation in the empirical world of the capitalist economy, his whole notion of a revolution is the culminating point of philosophic speculation and is not amenable to the same rules of scientific inquiry. It includes: (a) a philosophy of history, (b) a theory of class struggles, (c) a theory of the State, (d) the historical act of "revolution," and (e) the utopian world to follow. We shall discuss each of them.

A Philosophy of History

History has been defined as a set of tricks that the living play upon the dead. For Marx, there are no such tricks! For him, the living constantly interact with the dead. Men and women are both the product of history, bound by the conditions it creates, and also the makers of history in reacting to those conditions and changing them. But this is only within the limits that history itself allows.

We can look at history in evolutionary terms: gradual changes occur not only in our material world but also in human knowledge and the way we think. The individual gets better and better control of his or her environment. In this sense there is progress. Another method is to look at history without any notion of direction at all—just as all a matter of chance. We can conquer war and misery but they can defeat us too! The third view is that we move in circles with periods of great achievement, material well-being, and knowledge, alternating with periods of decay and ignorance. Our task in this case is like that of Sisyphus (cursed by the gods to carry a rock to the top of the mountain and to see it tumble down the moment he reached the peak) but with the destiny of humankind, so to speak, on our backs. We rise and then crash down into the ravine, only to start again and again and again. This is the cyclical theory.

All these theories are interesting but none of them answers the question of why there is "history" at all, why there is change and movement. Why do we change our ways? Why do we find out about germs? Why did we move from the Stone Age? Why did we invent a new language called mathematics and find out about regularities in the universe which surrounds us? Is it out of "love"? Is it because human beings are "rational"? Is it the divine will that pushes us? Marx answers this crucial question by using the works of the German philosopher G. W. F. Hegel (1770–1831) to develop a theory of history and change.

According to Hegel,[3] history moves through conflict—a conflict of ideas. He believes that there is something like a divine will, an Absolute, destined to finally unfold itself fully in the universe, but the process of unfolding is not evolutionary. It takes place through struggle between opposing ideas. The idea of beauty has opposing it the idea of ugliness, the idea of truth that of falsehood, the idea of liberty that of slavery, and so on. Throughout history and its various stages there is a constant and Homeric battle between opposing ideas, called by Hegel *dialectic idealism.* It goes something like this: each phase in history corresponds to the manifestation of certain ideas or an idea. It is called the *thesis.* However, it includes its opposite, its *antithesis.* Thesis and antithesis struggle with each other until the antithesis manages to absorb the thesis or to combine with it in one form or another. This combination is called a *synthesis,* representing a new stage in history. Every synthesis in turn becomes a thesis that suggests automatically its antithesis which comes into conflict with it to lead to a new synthesis and so forth. . . . A point comes *when history will have exhausted itself—the best possible synthesis will have occurred.* God or the Spirit will have fully unfolded itself in the universe!

---

3. Hegel, *The Philosophy of History.* New York: The Colonial Press, 1900.

This sounds abstruse and it is. But the important thing to retain is that Hegel makes conflict the mother, the father, and the midwife of history. He is not an evolutionary, he does not believe in cyclical movements, he traces all change to conflict between ideas.

Marx maintains the dialectic (the notion of conflicting opposites); he maintains the whole scheme of historical movement in terms of thesis-antithesis-synthesis. However, he is clearly not an idealist. Writing in his preface to *Capital,* Marx tells us himself how he changed the very foundations of Hegel's philosophy of history while maintaining the basic structure.

> My dialectic method is not only different from the Hegelian, but its direct opposite. To Hegel, the life-process of the brain, i.e., the process of thinking, which under the name of "the Idea," he even transforms into an independent subject, is the demiurgos (creator) of the real world, and the real world is only the external, phenomenal form of "the idea." With me on the contrary the idea is nothing else than the material world reflected by the human mind, and translated into forms of thought ... With Hegel (the dialectic) ... is standing on its head. It must be turned rightside up again. . . .[4]

In other words, Marx found, in the material world of our senses and our working conditions, the source of ideas and the source of conflict and change and not the other way around, as Hegel had done.

Dialectic Materialism   This is what, in contrast to "dialectic idealism," has become known as *dialectic materialism.* The stages of historical development, the specific contents of a thesis, an antithesis, and a synthesis are not to be found in the not-so-easily observable world of ideas but in the empirical world — in our society. It is a momentous shift. It makes Marx a social scientist, an empiricist, and one concerned with observable phenomena. The Hegelian abstraction now becomes a theory leading to hypotheses about human and social life that can be observed and tested.

Types of Conflict   What is the conflict that generates movement and change and accounts for history? There are two types of conflict according to Marx, the first between the human being as a social being (society) and the environment (the outside world). The second is between social groups.

Man Against Nature   Every social group, from the primitive tribe on, attempts to carve, out of its environment and out of nature, as much as it can in order to live and meet its needs. It is a basic struggle and human beings are affected deeply by it; their thoughts, their social institutions, their law and values are influenced by this interaction between themselves and the world in which they live. They depend on it in part; they are its creatures and even its slaves. Yet they try to overcome it and survive in it;

---

4. Marx, Preface to *Capital.*

they try to change it and emancipate themselves from its mastery. Real freedom will come when they have fully conquered it. Marx believes that one day they will succeed. The whole of humanity will be free. It will conquer nature and use it to its own ends.

Class Conflict

The second conflict is that among individuals and groups in one and the same society. It is not an indiscriminate conflict haphazardly pitting individual against individual; it is highly structured. The conflict is between classes; it is a *class struggle.*

But what is a class? The word has been used to define nobility, riches, education, intellect, and other characteristics of certain groups. Marx, however, gives a very precise definition to the term. *A class is defined in terms of the relationship individuals have to the means of production.* Very simply, there are two classes, consisting of those who own property and those who do not. This has been the reality of social life and the basic source of conflict and change. Class struggle is the motor force of dialectic materialism.

Yet property has taken many forms. To each form corresponds a different "class." For each class there has been an "antithesis" corresponding to the emerging new class. The antithesis "devours" the thesis, borrowing from it what was most useful and discarding what was useless. In every case it is conflict—a revolution—that brings the antithesis—the emerging class—to power.

Each historical phase corresponded to new and different forms of private property. Landed property was the characteristic of the feudal period and the landed aristocracy; but within it money, gold, and commerce made their appearance. Artisans, small manufacturers, and merchants emerged, with them commercial capital, and finally manufacturing and industry. They were destined to become a new class, an antithesis, the *bourgeoisie.* The French Revolution of 1789 epitomized, in a way, the end of the landed aristocracy and the coming of the middle class to power, emphasizing new types of property and new productive forces. But the moment the capitalists and the various groups allied to them emerged, the antithesis was already present. It was *the working class*—a small cloud on the blue horizon of bourgeois capitalism. With no property of its own, with nothing to sell but its labor, and subject to the laws of capitalistic economy, the cloud of the working class grew bigger and bigger. The class struggle was on, presaging the storm and the inevitable revolutionary conflict between the workers and the bourgeoisie.

Infrastructure and Superstructure   In the constant interaction between society and environment, and in the constant class struggle that corresponds to various historical stages, human beings not only develop particular forms of property, they also change them. For each phase there is a particular set of ideas and norms, and these correspond to and are fashioned by the interests of the property-owning class. They rationalize and legitimize (i.e., make acceptable to all) the dominance of the ruling and property-owning class. This theory, which traces and attributes moral ideas and norms directly or indirectly to economic factors, is called *economic determinism:* it states that how and where we live and work fashion our ideas about the world. Capitalists have a set of ideas about society and the world that correspond to their interests and to their dominance. The workers begin to develop theirs to express their needs and interests.

In the Marxist vocabulary the totality of factors that determine a person's relations to private property and work constitute the *infrastructure:* they are the material and objective social conditions. On the other hand, the way we look upon society—the ideas we have about it, in a word our ideology—is the *superstructure.* This superstructure includes religion, law, education, literature, even the State. It is an ideology fashioned by the dominant class, the one that owns property, and its view of society is forced upon all (including the workers) until a moment comes when they begin to question it.

Objective and Subjective Conditions   Each phase of the class struggle and each form of property relations differs in content from the preceding one. Bourgeois capitalism revolutionized the *objective economic conditions* of production. Division of labor, capital accumulation, technological progress—all these profit-inspired activities changed the world in the late eighteenth century and throughout the nineteenth. Marx conceded this, as we have seen. But by also creating a vast proletarian army, by divesting the lower classes of property, and by concentrating capital in a small number of firms, individuals, and banks, society finds it easier to replace the capitalist class. A mass of people begin to demand the end of capitalist rule and are ready to replace it. These are the *subjective conditions.* Thus capitalism, at one and the same time, creates the conditions for greater productive effort and lays the groundwork for its expropriation by the community at large. A point comes when objective conditions (technology, concentration of capital, the capability of the economy to provide abundance) coincide with the subjective conditions (i.e., the will and the consciousness of the workers to take over the industrial apparatus created by the capitalist and use it for the whole community). When subjective and objective conditions converge, it is the moment of revolution.

Note this carefully: The revolution is not, according to Marx, a matter of will, indignation, or even leadership. Conditions, both objective and subjective, must be ripe. The workers must gain full consciousness that they are a class and that they must demand the change in the existing property relations. Only then can revolution under the appropriate leadership be envisaged.

The Theory of the State

The State is viewed by Marx as part of the "superstructure." It is used to keep the majority of the people, who do not own the means of production, under the control of the small minority who do. While many (including Hegel) see the State as the embodiment of noble purposes — rationality, an agency for social justice and protection, the equitable distribution of goods, an impartial umpire keeping and administering the rules and laws equitably — Marx sees it as the instrument of the capitalist class. It is a repressive agency — a policeman!

But the State is not the only agency of domination. The whole superstructure, as we have noted, is fashioned by the ruling class. Religion inculcates observance of bourgeois values and respect for property; the family and the laws of inheritance perpetuate the rule of property; the educational system socializes everybody to respect the capitalist ethic and, most important, private property; art and literature extol the same virtues. No matter where they turn, the workers and their children will confront the same values and principles and many of them will be brainwashed into accepting them. The peculiar characteristic of the State, however, is that it is the only part of the superstructure that can use force. Hence it is necessary to use force against it.

The Revolution

Revolution, therefore, is necessary and unavoidable. "But what about democracy?" the student asks, "What about free and equal voting, freedom of association and of trade unions, of political parties and even of socialist parties?"

The answer is complex. First, when Marx wrote, trade unions were only beginning to develop; second, there were no socialist parties, although some were just making their appearance; third, political parties almost everywhere were just about to become national parties with national organizations and members; fourth, outside the United States, universal suffrage did not exist or could not be freely exercised. Most important of all, however, Marx did not really believe that a capitalist system and the capitalist State would ever allow socialist parties to gain ascendancy, nor did he believe that such parties would ever be allowed to directly challenge private property or to control production and the allocation of goods and services. If they did, the State would use force against them.

It is true that at times Marx wavered, and Engels did even more so. On occasions they both conceded that it was possible for well-established democracies, in which the parliamentary system and universal franchise had gained deep roots — *where in other words the superstructure was genuinely democratic* — to radically transform property relations and socialize the means of production. This might happen, but it was very unlikely: the use of force against capitalism and the State would be virtually inevitable everywhere. The workers therefore had to gain freedom from their oppressors, by force. They had to make a revolution when conditions were ripe, when and where there was a convergence of subjective and objective factors in the industrialized countries.

Marx gives us only a sketchy account of the communist society to come. In fact, he provides us with what amounts to a two-stage scheme. The first corresponds to the transitional stage toward socialism, and the second is the ultimate one, the utopian level of communism.

In the first, the revolution is followed by the "dictatorship of the proletariat." The workers take over the State and all the instruments of coercion that it disposed and use them against the capitalist class. "The development towards communism," he writes, "proceeds through the dictatorship of the proletariat; it cannot do otherwise, for the resistance of the capitalist exploiters cannot be broken by anyone else or in any other way."[5] In contrast to all other dictatorships, however, this is one by the majority against the minority. It is necessary, he claims, in order to avert a counterrevolution. Therefore, this is a dictatorship that corresponds to, and gradually becomes, a democracy of the people and the workers. The few—the capitalists—are excluded and suppressed by force.

What are the measures to be taken during this stage? Marx advocates abolition of the ownership of land, heavy progressive income tax, abolition of all rights of inheritance, centralization of credit and all means of transport, extensive socialization of factories and all means of production, equal obligation of all to work, public education, and so on. These measures will pave the way for the complete abolition of property and to the full and comprehensive socialization of the means of production.

As the State is now being used by the workers against the capitalists, its substance changes. It becomes the instrument of the many against the few. As the means of production become socialized, classes disappear, since there can be no classes without property. Without classes there is no need for coercion. *The dictatorship paves the way toward its own disappearance and to the establishment of a classless and stateless society.* The State simply "withers away."

The second phase corresponds to communism. The economy, both production and distribution, is now in the hands of the community. Nobody can exploit anybody; "bourgeois rights" (individual rights) give their place to "common rights." The final and ultimate phase is reached with the collectivization of all the means of production, with the harnessing of production to common purposes, with the transformation of the State from a coercive power to a purely administrative one. The objective conditions of production bequeathed to the new society from capitalism can now be used to make the slogan *"From each according to his ability to each according to his needs"* possible.

This is the apocalyptic or utopian element. And although Marx did not go to the lengths some earlier utopian socialists did, he shared their general optimism and was influenced by it. Crime would disappear, the span of life would increase, brotherhood and cooperation would inculcate

---

5. In *The Communist Manifesto,* cited in McLellan, D. *The Karl Marx Reader.*

a new morality, scientific progress would grow by leaps and bounds. Above all, with socialism spreading around the world, war, the greatest blight of humankind, and its twin, nationalism, would have no place. International brotherhood would follow. Engels waxes enthusiastic over the prospects and goes so far as to declare that, with the socialist revolution, humanity will complete its "prehistoric" stage and enter for the first time into what might be called its own history. Until the revolution, he claims, society submits to outside forces while the majority of humans within a society submit to a ruling class. After the revolution a united classless society will be able, for the first time, to decide which way to go and what to do with its resources and capabilities. For the first time we shall make our own history! It is a "leap from slavery into freedom; from darkness into light," he announced.

The skeptics were now confronted with the anatomy of capitalism, a theory of history, a theory of revolution, a theory of the State — all of them pointing in the same direction, to the communist society. With it, of course, the laws developed by Marx to explain the economy, the society, and the history would come to an end, for individuals and society would be free to make their own laws and shape their own future.

The Diffusion of Marxism: Success and Failure

Marxism represented the synthesis of many socialist writers and movements that were active before the body of Marx's thought became known and disseminated. The first volume of *Capital*, incorporating Marx's analysis of capitalism, was completed in 1867; it was translated from German into French (1873) and English (1886). Most of his other works, especially the many political pamphlets, including, of course, *The Communist Manifesto* of 1848, were translated, at least in French and English, almost as soon as they came out. They all were read by socialists, anarchists, utopians, and the many other radical groups of the time. The work of Marx helped shape ideas, create a firm ideological orientation, and ultimately brought together various sects and factions into well-organized large socialist movements and parties. It became an ideology.

In 1864, the International Working Men's Association (the First International) was founded by representatives of English, French, Italian, and German labor organizations. Marx wrote the basic guidelines for the International, including among others the need for a federation of all workers of various nations, the destruction of class domination, and the emancipation of the working class. With its headquarters in London, the First International never attained a large membership, and most of its efforts were devoted not so much to the organization of the workers but to fighting a strong anarchist faction. It held a few congresses and gradually disappeared.

The spread of Marxism took place after his death in 1883, with the development and consolidation of socialist parties not only throughout most of Europe but also in the United States. These were dedicated to the expropriation of the capitalist class, to class struggle, and to international-ism. The German Social Democratic party became the dominant Socialist party of Europe, receiving 4,250,000 votes in the 1912 elections — almost 35 percent of the total. In France, after many internal struggles, a Socialist party was founded in 1904 and in the election of 1914, on the eve of World War I, received over one million votes. By 1904 the British Labour party had been established — perhaps the only Socialist party of the world, however, that did not owe much directly to Marx. It made appreciable electoral gains. In Russia, a clandestine Social Democratic party was founded in 1898. The Socialist party of America was founded in 1901. It gained a million votes in the presidential election of 1920 — while its leader, Eugene Debs, was in the penitentiary for speaking against the war.

Many of these socialist parties, and others from Italy, Belgium, and Holland, were represented at the founding of the Second International in Paris in 1889, called to organize all workers against anarchism, to prepare them to combat the dangers of war that threatened Europe at the time, to commit them to class struggle and, of course to commit them to socialism and internationalism. "If war threatens to break out," the leadership of the Second International declared, ". . . the working class pledge themselves . . . to use their utmost exertions to prevent the outbreak of war by using the means which seem most effective to them. . . ." If war should break out, they pledged themselves "to work for its speedy termination and to exploit with all their strength the economic and political crisis induced by the war to arouse the people and thereby hasten the abolition of the class domination of capitalism."[6]

While socialist movements and parties were spreading all over the world, so was trade unionism. After the end of the nineteenth century, the freedom of workers to establish trade unions, to bargain collectively, and, in some instances, to strike, had became assured in most of the western democracies. Millions of workers in the advanced capitalistic countries, notably Germany, France, and England, became union members and engaged, legally or illegally, in strikes. Some theorists saw the strike as the special weapon of the working class — the ability to undermine the capitalist order. Others used it simply to extract local benefits from the employers and still others saw the trade-union movement as a prerequisite for the development of working class consciousness. One Marxist leader (Lenin), however, was fearful that trade unionism might divert the workers from revolution and limit them only to the search for immediate benefits within the capitalistic order.

Revisionism and Nationalism

The year of crisis for Marxism was 1914, as it was for socialism and for the Second International. There were at least two separate crises: revisionism and nationalism.

---

6. Quoted in Max Beer, *The General History of Socialism and Socialist Struggles,* Vol. 2. New York: Russell and Russell, 1957, pp. 157–158.

We have already discussed revisionism in regard to evolutionary socialism. It had abandoned revolutionary tactics to become increasingly gradualistic and reformist, and it accepted the principles of democracy and representative government. By 1914 virtually all socialist parties had become revisionist and paid only lip service to Marxist formulas and slogans.

Nationalism was a different and perhaps even more serious problem. Its tenacity, before, during, and also after World War I, indicated that the *class* consciousness of the workers was not as strong as their *national* consciousness. Although according to Marx the workers of all the countries shared the same predicament, and should have united against their common masters everywhere, the German, French, British, Austrian, and all other workers and socialists in all countries supported their government (with very few exceptions) and fought against each other in the war. Workers' international solidarity remained a dream, and the Second International was broken.

Revisionism and nationalism, the former questioning directly the validity of the Marxist theory and blueprint, the latter denying explicitly its internationalist aspirations, were only two forces that undermined and weakened Marxism. Criticism came from many other sources—from the left as well as the right. Anarchists already objected to the Marxist scientific scheme that subordinated revolution to specific conditions. They preferred to stress individual and revolutionary political will, but they also rejected the blueprint of the "dictatorship of the proletariat" and the imposition of socialism through State controls. Anarchists felt that the society envisioned by Marx provided little prospect for individual freedom and initiative, and that the communist regime would substitute one form of tyranny for another. Similarly, many socialists, as we have seen, shied away from the advocacy of force. They believed that change through persuasion and education would in the long run prove to be far more lasting and creative than one undertaken by force.

Many other philosophic assumptions and conclusions of Marx were criticized. Dialectic materialism came under attack by philosophers and also by the Church and the many strong religious organizations. Religious leaders argued that it reduced men and women to passive instruments whose fate and actions and ideas and beliefs were fashioned by the material conditions of life. The individual was deprived of his or her vaunted "freedom of will." A strong reaction among intellectual and educational leaders against dialectic materialism developed, often leading them to the other extreme of proclaiming the complete and unfettered freedom of individuals to choose and shape their own lives.

By 1914, therefore, Marxism as a philosophy and a revolutionary political ideology had become increasingly isolated. Socialist parties had accepted parliamentary democracy, negotiations, and compromises with their capitalist "masters" as well as the reality of the nation-states within which they lived. The hard core of the Marxist doctrine had been abandoned. It seemed like a monumental defeat.

But one man had recognized the reasons for the failure, had reflected on them, and was determined to revive Marxism. This man was Lenin; to his efforts, and the establishment of communism in Russia, we now turn.

Bibliography

Avineri, Shlomo. *The Social and Political Thought of Karl Marx.* New York: Cambridge U.P., 1968.

Berlin, Isaiah. *Karl Marx: His Life and Environment,* 3d ed. New York: Oxford U.P., 1963.

Bernstein, Eduard. *Evolutionary Socialism.* Translated by E. C. Harvey. New York: Schocken, 1961.

Bober, M. M. *Karl Marx's Interpretation of History.* New York: Norton, 1965.

Burns, Emile. *An Introduction to Marxism.* New York: International, 1966.

Bottomore, Tom (ed.). *Modern Interpretations of Marx.* Oxford: Basil Blackwell, 1981.

Cohen, G. A. *Karl Marx's Theory of History.* New York: Oxford U.P., 1978.

Cornforth, Maurice. *Communism and Philosophy: Contemporary Dogmas and Revisions of Marxism.* London: Lawrence and Wishart, 1980.

Djilas, Milovan. *The Unperfect Society: Beyond the New Class.* New York: Harcourt Brace Jovanovich, 1969.

Drackhovitch, Milorad M. (ed.). *Marxism in the Modern World.* Stanford, Calif.: Stanford U.P., 1965.

Fromm, Erich. *Marx's Concept of Man.* New York: Frederick Ungar, 1965.

Gregor, James. *A Survey of Marxism.* New York: Random House, 1965.

Heilbroner, Robert L. *Marxism: For and Against.* New York: Norton, 1980.

Kolakowski, Leszek. *Marxism and Beyond: On Historical Understanding and Individual Responsibility.* Translated by Jane Zielonko Peel. London: Pall Mall Press, 1969.

————. *Main Currents of Marxism.* Translated by P. S. Falla. (3 vols.) Oxford: Clarendon Press, 1978.

Kolakowski, Leszek, and Hampshire, Stuart (eds.). *The Socialist Idea: A Reappraisal.* London: Weidenfeld and Nicolson, 1974.

Lichtheim, George. *Marxism: An Historical and Critical Study.* 2d ed. New York: Praeger, 1965.

Luxemburg, Rosa. *Selected Political Writings.* Edited by Dick Howard. New York: Monthly Review Press, 1971.

Marx, Karl, and Engels, Friedrich. *Selected Works.* New York: International Publishers, 1968.

McLellan, David. *Karl Marx: His Life and Thought.* New York: Harper & Row, 1973.

————. *Karl Marx.* Baltimore: Penguin, 1976.

———— (ed.). *The Karl Marx Reader.* New York: Oxford U.P., 1977.

McMurtry, John. *The Structure of Marx's World-View.* Princeton, N.J.: Princeton U.P., 1978.

Meyer, Alfred G. *Marxism: The Unity of Theory and Practice.* Ann Arbor: University of Michigan Press, 1963.

Miliband, Ralph. *Marxism and Politics.* New York: Oxford U.P., 1977.

Plamenatz, John. *German Marxism and Russian Communism.* New York: Longmans-Green, 1954.

Seliger, Martin. *The Marxist Conception of Ideology: A Critical Essay.* Cambridge, England: Cambridge U.P., 1977.

Tucker, Robert C. (ed.). *Philosophy and Myth in Karl Marx.* 2nd ed. New York: Cambridge U.P., 1972.

————. *The Marx-Engels Reader.* 2d ed. New York: Norton, 1978.

Wolfe, Bertram, D. *Marxism: One Hundred Years in the Life of a Doctrine.* New York: Dial Press, 1965.

6 | Soviet Communism

*The organization of the Party takes the place of the
Party itself; the Central Committee takes the place of
the organization; and, finally, the dictator takes the
place of the Central Committee.*
LEON TROTSKY   Our Political Tasks

With Lenin, Marxist ideology and revolutionary tactics were given a new sharpness and urgency. Lenin was able to take the theoretical Marxist blueprint and adapt it not only to the revolutionary movement of Russia in the early part of the twentieth century but also to the independence movements of the colonial world. The first successful revolution in the name of Marxism, the Bolshevik Revolution, was made under his leadership in Russia on November 7, 1917.

Stalin succeeded Lenin in 1924 and became in a true sense the architect of Soviet communism. He remained in power for almost thirty years until his death in 1953. Collectivization, economic planning, rapid industrialization, the expansion of Soviet power, and also one-man authoritarian government are associated with his rule. Since Stalin's death, despite serious qualifications of the one-man rule Stalin had enforced, the same blueprint has been retained by the Soviet leaders. At the same time a number of communist movements have emerged that differ sharply from the Soviet model.

Leninism

Lenin faithfully accepted the body of Marxist thought and devoted a good part of his life to defending it against its many critics. He accepted the idea of dialectic materialism, endorsed and developed Marx's theory of the State, and sharpened and refined Marx's theory of revolution — especially revolutionary tactics. His two most important contributions to communist thought can be found in two pamphlets — *What Is to Be Done?* (1903), and

Imperialism, the Highest Stage of Capitalism (1917). In the first, Lenin developed a new theory for the organization of the proletariat through the Communist party; in the second, he attempted to show that the highest stage (and last stage) of capitalism was inextricably associated with colonial wars among capitalist nations. In a third long essay, *The State and Revolution* (1918), he elaborated on such key concepts as the revolutionary takeover of power, the period of the dictatorship of the proletariat, and the final stage of communism where the State was to disappear and material abundance become a reality. But his most important contribution, as the head of the Russian Bolshevik party, was to make a revolution and to preside over its consolidation.

Because of Lenin's theoretical contributions to the works of the founding fathers Marx and Engels, and also because of the political tactics he developed as a revolutionary, Lenin's name has been permanently attached to theirs. The new term of orthodox ideology became *Marxism-Leninism.*

Lenin's Revolutionary Doctrine

The greater part of Lenin's life was devoted to the development of a revolutionary doctrine. In *The State and Revolution* he summarized the Marxist theses: the State is the product of the irreconcilability of class antagonisms and the agency of the capitalist class; liberal democracy is another name for capitalism, ensuring domination of the workers; law and the State are instruments for the domination of the ruling class against the working classes; and, of course, revolution and the triumph of the working class is both desirable and inevitable.

The revolutionary stages Lenin envisages are the following:

1. The armed uprising of the proletariat, under proper leadership
2. The seizure of political control by the workers, in the form of a temporary "dictatorship of the proletariat," against the remnants of the capitalist classes

   Lenin's concept of dictatorship was as succinct as it was brutal. "The scientific concept of dictatorship (of the proletariat) means neither more nor less than unlimited power, resting directly on force, not limited by anything, not restricted by any law or any absolute rules. Nothing else but that."[1]
3. The socialization of the means of production and the abolition of private property
4. Finally, the slow "withering away of the State" as an instrument of coercion and class oppression, and the emergence of a classless, stateless society

1. Quoted in Bertram Wolfe, "Leninism" in Milorad Drachkovitch (ed.), *Marxism in the Modern World.* Stanford, Calif.: Stanford U.P., p. 69.

BROWN BROTHERS

Lenin (1870–1924)

Vladimir Ilyich Ulyanov ("Lenin" was originally a pseudonym, but became the better-known name) spent his childhood—a happy one according to all accounts—in the province of Kazan. After receiving his law degree he was arrested for revolutionary activity and exiled to Siberia. In 1900 he was allowed to go abroad where, as a professed Marxist, he pursued his revolutionary activity with remarkable energy. He formulated, and imposed on his followers, a program for a highly centralized party consisting of trained revolutionaries.

The collapse of the tsarist armies and the democratic revolution of February 1917 found Lenin in Switzerland. He managed to negotiate with the German government for a passage across the front line between the German and Russian armies; on the night of November 6–7, 1917, the Bolsheviks seized power and Lenin was made chairman of the new government. By 1918, Lenin had established what amounted to a dictatorship. He dissolved the Constituent Assembly after the Bolsheviks failed to get a majority in the elections, but his main attention was given to the war against the tsarist loyalists. Not until 1920 did the Russian Civil War come to an end with the victory of the communist forces.

The Communist Party

What does Lenin mean by a revolution of the working class *under proper leadership?* Marx's position was that objective economic factors and the class consciousness of the masses would move in parallel. The maturing of capitalism would mean the maturing of the social (i.e., revolutionary) consciousness of the workers.

Lenin posits from the very beginning, however, the need for leadership and organization, and stresses the inability of the masses by themselves to develop a proper social consciousness. The working class—and particularly the Russian working class—could never develop revolutionary consciousness by itself. An elite, organized into a Communist party, would have to educate the masses, infuse them with revolutionary spirit, and inculcate in them class consciousness. This would lead them toward the revolution and, ultimately, communism. *Dialectic materialism is brushed aside here to be replaced by a theory of voluntarism.* The Communist party is based on the will and dedication of Marxists. They are the revolutionaries. They can make the revolution irrespective of the prevailing social conditions.

A number of consequences, both at the theoretical and tactical levels, follow these assumptions.

Elitism   The party is to be composed of gifted individuals who understand Marxism and therefore understand the direction of history better than the rest of the people. The leaders of the party are particularly endowed with scientific knowledge and foresight that the common people lack. Leadership is likely to come not from the ranks of the working class but from "outside"—from middle-class intellectuals who are able to comprehend the totality of the society's interests and hence promote socialism. They are trained in Marxist dialectics and can discern the historical pattern leading to socialism. This party is the *vanguard* of the proletariat. It speaks and acts on behalf of the proletariat.

Organization of the Party   The rank and file of the party is united with its leaders by bonds of allegiance and common action, and also obedience and discipline. They must be prepared for any kind of action, legal or illegal, at any time. "The one serious organizational principle for workers in our movement," Lenin wrote, "must be the strictest secrecy, strictest choice of members, training of professional revolutionaries. . . ."[2]

The party, Lenin asserts, has to be organized on the basis of *democratic centralism,* according to which:

1. All decisions are to be made in an open and free debate by the representative organ of the party, the congress.
2. Once a decision is thus made, it is binding upon all. No factions are to be allowed within the party and no minority within the party is permitted either to secede or to air its grievances in public.

2. Ibid., p. 78.

3. All officers of the party—secretaries, the central committee, and other executive organs—are elected indirectly from lowest membership upwards.
4. All decisions and instructions of the party executive officials are binding upon all inferior organs and officers.

Thus, the party can be democratic if the principles of open debate and elections are followed, but it can also become authoritarian, and even autocratic, if emphasis is put on the right of the superior officers to command and the obligation of inferior officers to obey. The organization of the Soviet Communist party became, in fact, hierarchical. Orders for action flowed from top to bottom. Throughout his whole life Lenin was able, despite oppostion, to hold the supreme decision-making power in his hands and to control the nomination of local party leaders. The party did not tolerate dissent and, under Lenin's leadership, indulged in purges in the years after the revolution. He invented the notion "enemies of the people." It was during this same period that thousands of so-called wreckers, saboteurs, petit bourgeois, and many others were jailed, and sentenced to death.

From Lenin's model of the party, it is obvious that he had no respect for democracy. In his view, representation, universal and secret franchise, political parties, and periodic elections had no value in themselves. If suitable to the revolutionary struggle they ought to be defended, but if they proved to be obstacles to the proletarian revolutionary movement at one moment or another, they should be brushed aside without a moment's thought.

The second congress of the Russian Social Democratic Workers' party was held in Brussels in 1903. Writing of it, Sir Isaiah Berlin says: "There occurred an event which marked the culmination of a process which has altered the history of the world . . . Lenin and his friends [insisted] upon the need of absolute authority by the revolutionary nucleus of the party." When this concept was questioned one of the founders of Russian Marxism took Lenin's side with the statement that the "revolution is the supreme law." "If the revolution demanded it . . . everything—democracy, liberty, the rights of the individual—must be sacrificed to it."[3] Accordingly, Lenin had no scruples at all in dissolving democratically elected bodies whenever the Bolsheviks were in a minority in them.

Trade Unionism   One might have thought that Lenin would see in the growth of the trade union movement a proper medium for the development of class and revolutionary consciousness. This was not so. From the very beginning Lenin looked upon trade unions with apprehension. He feared that workers bargaining with capitalists through their trade unions would increasingly tend to pay attention to their conditions of work, to ways to improve conditions, and to their wages and benefits. If so, they would gradually adjust themselves to the capitalistic economy and learn to

---

3. Isaiah Berlin, "Political Ideas in the Twentieth Century," in *Foreign Affairs,* April 1950.

act within it. Instead of gaining revolutionary consciousness, they would, on the contrary, shed it in favor of opportunistic compromises and bargains.

There was also a second danger. If trade unions represented only a part of the working class — usually the most favored one and the better organized — the working class would split and lose its solidarity. A situation would develop in which some workers would have a great deal to gain by staying within the capitalistic system while others would want to destroy it. One part of the working class would be pitted against another. Trade union activity was therefore detrimental to revolutionary Marxism. According to Lenin, unionism is an infantile disease of the working classes and the faster they are cured of it the sooner they will reach adolescence and revolutionary maturity.

Colonies and World Revolution

In *Imperialism: the Highest Stage of Capitalism,* published in 1917, Lenin attempted to show that the highest and last stage of capitalism ("monopoly capitalism") corresponds to a period of control by the big banks and trusts that have investments in overseas colonies, and the division of the world into colonial areas of domination and exploitation, and wars. The most important thesis of the book, however, was that capitalist countries had divided the world and that, as a result, capitalism had become a world phenomenon despite the uneven economic development of the various countries and the backwardness of the colonies. From this he drew the conclusion that revolutions were advisable and tactically desirable irrespective of whether they take place in an advanced or backward country. Any revolution, anywhere, was legitimized because it was directed against capitalism as a worldwide phenomenon.

This account of *imperialism* appeared at a most opportune moment, shoring up the waverings of many Marxists. It explained why Marx appeared to be "wrong" in predicting the pauperization of the masses in industrially advanced nations. Now it was claimed that it was because of these nations' foreign colonies that this had not come to pass. Surplus values derived by the capitalists in the colonies was also shared in part by the workers of the imperialist powers. This in turn accounted for the delay in the development of working-class revolutionary consciousness and the successes of revisionism. It also explained nationalism and wars. Above all it vindicated revolutions in underdeveloped areas (including, of course, Russia). With this brilliant (no matter how inaccurate) pamphlet, Lenin revived Marxism and, indirectly, justified the revolutionary takeover of power in Russia in the name of Marx.

Telescoping the Revolution   If capitalism had indeed become a worldwide phenomenon, if the imperialist nations had divided the world among themselves, and if they had managed to blunt the revolutionary class consciousness of the workers by providing them with benefits and advantages that were being extracted from the colonial peoples, where would the revolution come from? For Lenin, as we have seen, it would have to come from trained revolutionaries, well-organized and sharing a common will. But where would the revolution take place?

One of the answers given by Lenin, with the support of Leon Trotsky, was that one should not wait for the stages of capitalistic development to unfold themselves. History could somehow be telescoped so that even if capitalism had not matured, and even if there were no strong working class, a combination of the peasantry and the workers could support a revolutionary seizure of power in the name of communism. The capitalistic stage could be combined with the socialist stage at an accelerated rhythm. It was therefore possible, and indeed desirable, to push for revolutionary seizures of power anywhere in the world rather than wait until each and every country had reached the level of maturity required by Marx and Engels.

This analysis provided a theoretical justification and also a powerful tactical weapon for colonial revolutions. Capitalism was not as strong on its colonial periphery as it was at its center. The capitalistic chain which bound the world had some weak links, particularly its colonies, where it was vulnerable when colonial peoples demanded what many liberal bourgeois leaders had advocated for themselves — national independence, political rights, equality, and so on. One part of the fight against the capitalists, therefore, was to try to snap their chain at its various weak links. Communists were asked, in the name of Marx, to promote revolutions in countries where the peasantry and not the workers represented the most numerous social group; they were to do this in the name of nationalism rather than internationalism. From a tactical point of view, every colonial independence movement that succeeded was a break of the capitalistic chain and hence a victory for Communist Russia.

It was a masterly tactical twist designed both to defend communism in Russia against potential enemies (and in so doing defend Russia as well) and also to expand and export the Communist revolution made in Russia. At this point we enter the stage of ideology where communism as a political ideology becomes very closely linked with the interests of Russia as a nation-state. This was a phenomenon that became particularly pronounced under Stalin.

Conclusion

Emphasis on political and revolutionary tactics, no matter what the objective conditions, are the hallmarks of Leninism: reliance on the human factors of will, leadership, and organization irrespective of their social contents; and the subordination of everything else to political organization and political will and leadership to make the revolution. Very often this is referred to as the theory of *substitutism*. With Marx, the working class develops the consciousness to make the revolution and establish communism, thus substituting itself for the whole of society. With Lenin the Communist party substitutes itself for the working class and speaks for the interest of the working class. Then, thanks to the principle of democratic centralism, it becomes the executive and higher organs of the party, the central committee, who speak for the interests of the working class, which speaks for the interests of the whole. But since the same central committee controlled the Third International it also spoke for the interests of all the Communist parties, which spoke for their respective working classes!

It takes only one more step for the single leader to substitute for all the others in order to arrive at the logical outcome of such an organization — the subordination of *everything* to the leadership of *one* man. Such was the essence of Stalinism.

Stalinism

The name of Stalin is becoming as remote to many students as that of Napoleon. But for many contemporary Communists, Stalin and Stalinism remain important and highly controversial. A member of the Russian Communist party and an associate of Lenin, Stalin succeeded him after his death in 1924. After five years, during which he managed to eliminate all opposition within the Communist party, he became its absolute ruler. While Lenin was backed by his enormous prestige and was respected for his intelligence and writings, Stalin relied on the organization he had built with the party as well as outright force. Stalin institutionalized in his own person the dictatorship of the proletariat: not bound by any law, indeed being above any law.

In 1929, Stalin undertook what became known as the Second Revolution, collectivizing agriculture, socializing all means of production, establishing a rigorous planned economy, and attempting to industrialize the country as fast as possible through massive capital investment. He controlled not only all the instruments of coercion at home, but through the Third International he managed to impose his will upon foreign communist parties. His personal rule emulated that of the tsars. Intellectuals, poets, novelists, and scientists were forced to pay constant homage to him. During his lifetime the term Marxism-Leninism became transformed to Marxism-Leninism-Stalinism — an indication that he was considered one of the "founders."

With Stalin an important transformation in communist ideology occurs. From a revolutionary ideology it becomes the official *status quo ideology*. Even after the 1917 Revolution with Lenin trying to consolidate it, Marxism was still a revolutionary movement. He hoped that what he had started in Russia would be only a spark to ignite a worldwide revolutionary conflagration.

Stalin succeeded Lenin at a moment when the revolutionary spirit in Russia, and everywhere else, was at an ebb. Long years of strife, civil war, and economic hardships had disillusioned a number of revolutionary leaders and undermined the morale of the rank and file of the party. The inability, or unwillingness, of the European working classes to follow the

BROWN BROTHERS

Joseph Stalin (1879–1953)

Born in Georgia, Stalin became the head of the Communist party of the Soviet Union after Lenin's death in 1924. Though originally a lesser figure among the Communist leaders who made the revolution, and lacking the literary, oratory, or intellectual talents of many of them, Stalin nevertheless assumed a controlling position within the organization of the party, becoming its Secretary General, and his rule prevailed. He launched what is generally called the Second Revolution, collectivizing agriculture and socializing all the means of production. His rule, which lasted until his death, saw the rapid increase of Soviet power, economically, internationally, and militarily. But it was in substance a personal dictatorship based on the most ruthless application of force and terror, and it is characterized by many as a great betrayal of the original principles upon which the revolution was predicated.

Bolshevik Revolution left the Soviet Union in a precarious economic and international position. Times no longer called for the revolutionary but for the administrator and the organizer. The period needed stability and reconstruction.

Stalin's rise to power reflected this basic desire. A party organizer above all, with all the qualities and limitations of an administrator, Stalin was able to succeed Lenin because of his administrative functions and position within the party. Patiently he wove within the central committees of the party and within the regional and district committees at large a web of personal and organizational contacts. He controlled the appointments of Communist party members to local and district administrative jobs; he was in charge of party admissions; he was asked to reorganize and purge the administrative apparatus of the State. He used these powers to the best of his ability in order to consolidate and promote his own personal position.

Almost a year before his death, Lenin dictated the following in his political testament:

> Comrade Stalin, having become secretary-general, has bound-less power concentrated in his hands, and I am not sure whether he will always be capable of using that power with sufficient caution.[4]

A man of rather limited philosophic and speculative capacities, Stalin did not share the broader outlook of other communists. He set for himself the task of reconstructing the economic and political institutions of Russia, without concern for worldwide socialism. Neither did he share the faith of the other party leaders in the possibility of a proletarian revolution in western Europe. In fact, he had a deep distrust, even enmity, for the western world about which, in contrast to the other Russian Communist leaders, he knew and understood little.

Gradually the terms Soviet Union and Russia came to be identified with communism, and the future of communism in the world became identifiable with the well-being of the Soviet Union. Loyalty to the one also meant loyalty to the other. With Stalin, what was a revolutionary ideology and a revolutionary movement became State and party orthodoxy. Speculation, argument, and debate gave place to imposition and dogma. Arguments, or even mere disagreements, were magnified to mean treason. Persuasion gave place to force, and the State and the party became the agencies to administer it. Marxism (so rich in speculative thought, and claiming to be a rational and scientific doctrine) was now presented in simple didactic terms to settle every dispute — especially when the presentation of the ideas was made by Stalin himself. It became a catechism repeated through all the socializing mechanisms available to the party — the party agitators, the press, the schools, the radio, the universities, the trade unions, and so on.

---

4. Richard Tucker (ed.), *The Lenin Anthology.* New York: Norton, 1975, p. 727.

The first element of Stalinism is a nationalism closely associated with the traditional patterns of Russian history. Stalin decided to forge ahead with socialism in Russia without much concern for the fate of communist revolutions in western Europe, though he continued to exert influence over all communist parties in Europe, China, and southeast Asia. He set before him the task of building "socialism in one country" (a phrase first used by Lenin) in Russia. His decision, though made in the name of socialism, evoked a genuine patriotic response among the members of his party and at least part of the Russian people. Russia was backward when compared to the West. The assertion that Russia alone could perform the miracle of building socialism was in itself an expression of faith in the strength of Russian society, a defiance of the West, and a proclamation of Russian independence and self-sufficiency.

The Organization of the Communist Party   The organization and functions of the Communist party under Stalin represent the ultimate development of what Lenin had started. The party remained an *elite* composed of loyal and energetic members. Its mission was to maintain and further the cause of Soviet socialism and to educate the masses into socialism. Its membership continued to be relatively small. Sometimes it was described as the "chief of staff of the proletariat" and sometimes as "the teacher" of the Russian masses and the "vanguard of the working class and the masses." It grew into an exclusive organization which controlled every aspect of governmental and social life of the Soviet society.

    The Leninist conception of the hierarchical relationship between leadership and rank and file hardened into an institution. The role of the leader began to be expounded upon in a semireligious, semi-Byzantine manner: he was omniscient and omnipresent, he was the father of the people, his word was law. There was in Stalinism a marked similarity to the despotic paternalism of the tsarist regime.

    The development of this concept of leadership is also related to the internal development of the party organization. Decision-making powers became concentrated exclusively in the hands of the executive organs of the party, and any semblance of democratic centralism was abandoned in favor of rigid centralization and control from the top. Nominations to party posts were made from above and not by the rank and file. Criticism was allowed only when leaders would permit it, and only on subjects selected in advance by them; periodic purges accounted for a constant turnover of the rank and file and middle-echelon officers and organizers.

No Internal Democracy   Another indication of the demotion of the status of the party was the lack of any genuine free deliberation and criticism among its assembled delegates. Congresses, whenever they were convened, spent their time in giving their approbation without any debate to the resolutions of the leadership. After 1927 not a single protest was raised;

not a single dissenting voice or vote expressed. The slate of candidates for the various executive organs was prepared in advance by Stalin and his immediate associates and was always approved unanimously.

The Police   The new organ, which in effect replaced the party, was the police, which operated directly under Stalin. It was the duty of the police to maintain communist legality. Lenin had used it to first operate against "deviationists" and "dissenters," but it was always understood that it was to be an adjunct of the party acting on its behalf. But by 1935 the secret police became the instrument of control and intimidation not only of society as a whole but also vis-à-vis the party. Party members were totally at its mercy as were high-placed party officials. The secret police gradually became the most feared coercive and punitive force. It had its own private army (including tanks), a huge network of spies and informers, and was in command of the forced labor camps where the inmates—variously estimated to range from 3 to 4 million to as many as 10 million over the whole Stalinist period—were interned. Terror thus became an instrument of government.

Stalinism and the Social Order   When the revolution took place in Russia in 1917, the attention of all intellectuals, socialist leaders, and the people of western Europe was directed to the first genuine revolutionary experiment to be made in the name of Marx. Expectations and hopes ran high for many and the leaders of the revolution shared them. Trotsky, for instance, on becoming Minister of Foreign Affairs, claimed that all he had to do was to publish the various secret (and imperialist) treaties signed by the victorious powers in World War I, issue some revolutionary proclamations, and then "close shop"—national boundaries would then melt away and internationalism would come about! The early policy of war communism—a blanket socialization of all property and the direct control by the socialist state of the economy—would pave the way to the transitional stage leading to communism. Throughout these first years, these social developments were carefully watched. Lack of democracy was consistent with the idea of the dictatorship of the proletariat, but many argued that it was fully compensated by the prospect of economic equality. The argument was repeatedly made that the West protected political (formal) rights while the Soviet socialist system was ushering in economic (substantive) rights.

Industrialization   Reality, however, differed sharply from expectations based on ideology. Communism failed to initiate any economic recovery, just as national boundaries had failed to melt away. Lenin, a masterful tactician, was the first to retreat. His New Economic Policy of 1921 reestablished freedom of commerce, agriculture, and manufacturing, but the State kept in its hands what he called the "commanding heights" of the economy—banks, steel, iron, coal, transportation, energy. The rest went back to private hands: private employers who could hire labor and presumably get surplus value and make profit, private tradesmen, and individual farmers who owned farms could buy land and employ farmhands.

This was the situation that Stalin inherited and he decided to resolve in 1929. All means of production and all private property were socialized and agriculture was collectivized. Marxism-Leninism became the convenient political instrument for controlling society and bending it to the task of rapid industrialization. This entailed a rigorous centralization and bureaucratic control of the national economy. Economic targets were formulated over five-year periods (the Five-Year Plans) with priorities and specific quantitative quotas. Capital investment — the building of factories and industrial equipment — and the training of the labor force took precedence over consumption. Education became an indispensable part of industrialization, because technicians, scientists, skilled workers, engineers, and service personnel such as doctors, administrators, accountants, and so on, were vital to economic growth. A crucial problem was to find the human resources to train, and Stalin's answer was a massive transfer of the population from the farm and the country into the new industrial urban centers.

Force and Incentives   The overall effort amounted to a radical overhaul of Russian society. In the name of socialism the task was to create what socialism should have inherited, an industrialized society. Three basic incentives could be used. The first was propaganda and persuasion: to extol the myth of socialism and incite people to communal efforts and sacrifices. But ideological exhortation has limits, and Stalin had to fall back on the two classic means of encouraging compliance: the carrot and the stick. The carrot was monetary incentive; the stick, force.

He who did not work would not eat. Income was to be proportionate to the quality and quantity of work done; inequality of income was declared to be unavoidable. Trade unions that favored equality of pay were put in their place — their leaders arrested and eliminated; the right to bargain was abolished, and the right to participate in the decisions of the plant manager were withdrawn.

The differences in pay created a salary structure that began to resemble that of the capitalistic societies, with the right of certain individuals to save and get interest, to pass on some of their gains to their heirs, to provide their children with better education, and to enjoy special advantages for vacation, leisure, and travel. There was even status — the recognition that they belonged to an elite class consisting of the top group of the *intelligentsia* (the Russian word denotes a very large class of people, comprising all groups other than workers and farmers). In recognition of their services and as an added incentive, they were allowed membership within the party — thus bestowing upon them political status as well. The percentage of workers and farmers within the party decreased correspondingly.

Force took a number of forms and served many purposes. It was used against those who did not work, or did not work regularly, and failed to live up to the quotas assigned to them. These people found their way to labor camps, and their disappearance was only a reminder to others of what they might have to face. Force was also used directly to create regiments of workers in labor camps who were responsible for tasks that nobody else would take (except for very high pay) such as mining of gold, lumber cutting, and road construction. In a more comprehensive sense, force was also a constant reminder, even to those who received a good pay for their work, that any relaxation or negligence would be followed by swift punishment.

Interpretations of Stalinism

Stalin and Stalinism can be viewed from three different points of view. Stalin can be considered, in line with Marx and Lenin, to be one of the chief exponents of communist philosophy and practice. One may also attribute to him the consolidation of the revolution in Russia. As Communist dictator in charge of the party, he expropriated the farms, socialized the means of production, and established economic planning. Finally, he may be viewed as a modernizer. He started Russia on the road to economic modernization. As Isaac Deutscher put it, he found Russia with the wooden plough and left it with atomic weapons.[5]

Stalin, in fact, may go down in history as another Peter the Great, as one of the great modernizers. Under his rule and in a short period of time the Russian economy and society underwent a great change with an emphasis on education, technology, mass production, urbanization, the movement from the farm to the city, the development of science, and above all a rapid economic growth. It was inevitable that rapid economic and industrial development would be linked to socialism and that in the process the political aspects of Stalinist rule would be glossed over. It was also unavoidable that the modernizing aspects of socialism would be emphasized and presented as the most attractive side of the Stalinist regime.

But the great loyalty to Stalin during his lifetime and to the Soviet system in general, by other communist parties and so many intellectuals in western Europe and elsewhere, is due to the profound impact of Marxism. As an ideology, it provided simple answers to the three most fundamental questions we ask about our society and our lives. Where are we going? How do we get there? What will it be like? By answering them, Marxism, like all great ideologies, gave a particular meaning and therefore direction of history: it is not haphazard; it is not indefinite; it is not aimless. We are moving in the direction of freedom, equality, and abundance to fulfill the ultimate goal of our nature as individuals and social beings. We can get there when conditions are ready but only by an act of our own will or by revolution.

5. Isaac Deutscher, *Russia, What Next?* New York: Oxford U.P., 1953.

History and its purpose may be realized through the most unexpected or repugnant agencies, but it moves inexorably to its predetermined goal of communism—and humanity's salvation! Stalin is thought of as a dictator, as a perpetrator of inhuman acts, as the murderer of friends and relatives. He is considered to have deprived millions of their freedom and their lives, and all of this is true, but to some he incarnated history. Jean-Paul Sartre spoke of the "monster dripping with blood," but still remained very sympathetic to the Soviet system and with it, of course, to Stalin. To attack *him* would have been to endanger the citadel of communism and with it the future of humankind. There *was* no alternative. Belief, a powerful ingredient of all ideologies, came to stifle critical inquiry. As we pointed out, an ideology is a lens through which some people share a view of reality. Reality cannot be used to disprove them since reality is what they see in terms of the ideology. It is only in the last two decades that intellectuals from the left—even communist ones, in Spain, France, and Italy and very recently in the Soviet Union—began to raise embarrassing questions about Soviet communism and Stalinism.

The Critics

Leon Trotsky: A New Revolution?   Leon Trotsky (1879–1940) was one of the architects of the Bolshevik Revolution and a theoretician and tactician just as brilliant as Lenin. Much of his work—after he was expelled from the Communist party and forced out of the country by Stalin in 1925—is remembered, however, for his criticism of the Stalinist system. It embodied all the shortcomings of "socialism in one country." Russia did not provide an adequate base for the building of socialism; economic growth and development would remain slow, and the bureaucracy would become the privileged class. Under Stalin it had, in fact, grown into an independent state—not responsive and responsible to the people. It had become a dictatorship that began to move against and to exploit the workers. The bureaucracy must be overthrown, and, to do so, in 1938 Trotsky urged the formation of an illegal revolutionary party in the Soviet Union and a worldwide revolution by the workers everywhere.

It was the last worldwide appeal for a communist revolution; Trotsky was assassinated in 1940. "National communisms" inspired by the Soviet leadership developed, but they began to pit themselves against the Soviet control and domination, as well as against each other. Without genuine internationalism, two alternatives to communism remained: "national communisms" or Soviet-controlled communisms.

Milovan Djilas: A New Class?   The most scathing critique of the Stalinist system, and also more generally a critique addressed against virtually all communist systems, has come from a Yugoslav communist, Milovan Djilas, in a book entitled *The New Class*. It was written only three years after Stalin's death and published in the United States in 1957. "Everything," writes Djilas, "happened differently in the Soviet Russia and other communist countries from what the leaders—even such prominent ones as Lenin, Trotsky, Stalin, and Bukharin—anticipated."[6] They expected, he points out wistfully, that the State would wither away, democracy would be strengthened, the standard of living would go up, and internationalism would supplant nationalisms. Exactly the reverse has happened; neither industrialization nor collectivization has accounted for economic improvement, let alone plenty. And the dream of a classless society remains a dream. In fact a new class has developed: it is the Communist party and "the Communist party State" with a huge bureaucracy. In the process of industrializing, and even after industrialization had been in part achieved, "the new class . . . can do nothing more than to strengthen its brute force and pillage the people. It ceases to create. Its spiritual heritage is overtaken by darkness."[7]

The new class legitimizes itself the way all classes have done in the past. It uses indoctrination and force, relies on handouts to secure loyal supporters, and develops a nationalist ideology to appeal to the same forces on which the bourgeoisie had relied in the past. The party oligarchy and its bureaucratic apparatus maintains not only a monopoly of political control but allocates to itself a disproportionate part of the national wealth and income. Despite their rhetoric, the communist regimes thus far, and Soviet communism in particular, have continued to perpetuate class rule.

Djilas' criticism is similar to that voiced by many liberal critics, even though he would not agree with them. Djilas states that all-encompassing direct economic planning, under which virtually every aspect of the society is controlled, not only leads to the formation of a huge and self-perpetuating bureaucratic apparatus, but also it is inherently inefficient. No bureaucracy can possibly take into account and satisfy the myriad of needs and aspirations of all individuals. Furthermore, putting so much emphasis on the government as the only decision-making mechanism can overburden it to the point of paralysis.

Antonio Gramsci: The Importance of Ideology   The person who gave us the best critical examination of Stalinism, even before the term was coined, was one of the early leaders of the Italian Communist party—Antonio Gramsci. Active in Italian politics from 1914 to 1926, he was arrested by the Italian Fascists in 1926 and kept in jail until 1937 where he died after a long illness. While in prison, he wrote voluminously about communism in general and about his own experience within the Italian Communist party of whose central committee he had been a member.[8] Gramsci addressed

6. Djilas, *The New Class*, p. 37.
7. Djilas, Ibid., p. 69.
8. A short account of Gramsci's life and writings is by James Joll, *Antonio Gramsci*, Penguin, The Great Masters Series, 1977. The student will find a biographical sketch and a succinct but excellent analysis of Gramsci's philosophy.

Born on the island of Sardinia in 1891, Antonio Gramsci moved to the University of Turin in northern Italy after completing his secondary education. Although constantly plagued with ill health, he became active in the Italian Socialist party and began to write for socialist periodicals and newspapers. He played an important role in the organization of the workers' strikes in 1919–1920. In 1921 he became a member of the Central Committee of the newly formed Italian Communist party. Active within the Communist Third International, he was also elected to the Italian Parliament. With utmost courage he spoke against the repressive legislation the Fascists had introduced. He was arrested in 1926 and spent the remaining years of his life in jail, where he died in 1937. It was in jail that he wrote what became known as the "Prison Notebook"—a major contribution to Marxism and indispensable to the understanding of the tactics of the Italian Communist party. *(Photo: Copyright G. D. Hackett. Reprinted by permission.)*

himself to the relationship between the superstructures (the State and other institutions such as the church, the family, the legal system, the universities and schools) and the economy (the infrastructure). We noted earlier that a mechanical way to view the relationships between infrastructure and superstructure is to assume that the economy and especially the class relations in a society determine the superstructure. According to this view all societal forces including the state and the ideas we hold—the prevailing ideology—are determined by the class that owns the means of production—the bourgeoisie. The State is nothing but a coercive force acting on behalf of the bourgeoisie to protect its economic interests. Therefore, it is only by destroying the State, after capturing it first, that economic relations and all societal forces including ideology can be changed. Lenin placed emphasis on capturing State power and using it to destroy capitalism, its institutions, and the ideology it had imparted, and to pave the way for the ultimate realization of socialist and democratic goals. Gramsci's answer was far more sophisticated.

While agreeing that the State represents the interests of the property-owning class and acts on its behalf, Gramsci argued that the State (part of the superstructure) has a great amount of autonomy and initiative. It was not simply and always the obedient gendarmerie of the bourgeoise. It can, under certain circumstances, take action that can change and mold the societal forces, including the economy and class relationships. This is particularly so with a democratic state that is, to a degree, responsive to the people at large.

A second observation made by Gramsci had a profound implication for the tactics of the Communist party. The state, in order to be obeyed, should be widely representative and should derive its authority from popular acceptance and consent. No state can live by force. This raises fundamental questions about the Leninist scheme favoring a revolution and a dictatorship of the proletariat. Once such a dictatorship had been established from where would it draw its support? Communists who take over the state by a revolution would find themselves holding only a small island—the state and its coercive institutions. In order to succeed, Gramsci argued, a communist revolution should be made only when the institutions and the ideology surrounding the state, that is, the civil society, had been modified and when people were prepared for it and receptive to it.

The Civil Society   It was therefore unavoidable that Gramsci would look more closely at the civil society—its institutions and its ideology. It was in the interstices of the civil society, he discovered, that the capitalist classes domination was exercised—not only by the State. Simply put, this meant that both the societal institutions—family, property relations, law, educational institutions, working conditions in the factory or the farm, urban and peasant life—and the prevailing ideologies about marriage, family life, child rearing, art and leisure, culture, politics, property, lifestyles, freedoms, discipline, and work, all reflected and buttressed the bourgeois way of life. In other words, the domination of the bourgeoisie was implemented through the shaping of the ideas people held about themselves and their society. This domination—what Gramsci called the "hegemony" of the bourgeoisie—was exercised through the control of the minds of the people. Ideology, not force, played the crucial role in explaining domination and hegemony.

The differences from Marxism, and especially Leninism, become apparent in the weight and importance Gramsci gave to the societal and ideological forces. In his eyes, they are "independent variables," independent forces that assume their own weight, force, logic, and roles, and cannot be viewed as instruments of the bourgeois class to be swept away by a communist revolution and reshaped by the dictatorship of the proletariat. The tenacity and strength of the societal forces in capitalism, where the capitalist class has asserted its hegemony, makes a genuine communist revolution virtually impossible unless it is carried out in a Leninist manner: by an elite well organized into a disciplined party that takes over the state to impose its rule. But if and when this happens, as it happened in Russia, then, according to Gramsci, the revolution would be unable to live up to its promise. Coercive practices would result, and imposition rather than consent and participation would become institutionalized. Undertaking a revolution under such circumstances would be a mistake, for it would not serve the democratic aspirations of communism. It would be advisable to gradually change the institutions of the civil society and the ideology, that is, the superstructure, from within, before a revolution took place. In this manner, the societal forces would become "prepared"; they would become hospitable to a revolution, and communism could develop side-by-side with popular participation and democracy.

Both participation and democracy were deemed by Gramsci to be absolutely necessary to communism. Therefore, the Communist party and progressive intellectuals should concentrate their efforts not on organizing for the conquest of power but on the gradual transformation of the bourgeois civil society and the ideas people hold about it. By penetrating and changing the institutions, allying themselves with liberal even if "bourgeois forces" and practices, while gradually modifying them, by getting deeply involved in local government, by attempting some reconciliations between party membership and religious and other bourgeois organizations, by democratizing the forces of production in the factory and the farm in a manner that would promote greater participation by the workers and the farmers, by gradually creating new centers of art and leisure and encouraging new forms of culture, the Communist party would "march through the institutions" (as Gramsci put it) of the capitalist society. It would accomplish this by opening up new forms of social and economic relations, inducing self-government and self-reliance and participation on the farm, while instructing the workers about responsible management and industrial organization. In a sense, therefore, the revolution would be made *before* and *without* a revolution! The bourgeoisie would maintain perhaps to the last the overt forms of coercion — the army and the police, the prisons and bureaucracy, but it would be deprived of the real source of strength and power — its hegemony — because of the change in the ideas and practices the civil society had undergone. The bourgeois state deprived of the consent and the ideological support of the civil society would find itself standing on a small island surrounded by stormy seas . . . destined to swarm over it in one form or another.

The Task of the Communist Party   This analysis by Gramsci gave the Communist party a new role — that of an educator to shape minds, to innovate and develop new institutions, or modify the existing ones, in short to create the new civil society within the shell of the old one. Human will armed with a vision and organized in a party would undertake day after day to modify the existing practices, ideas, and attitudes of the men and women living in the society. Political action (*praxis*) in this sense was not simply revolutionary action; it was the patient and everyday dialogue between men and women armed with a new vision against the recalcitrant societal forces that had been shaped by a *bourgeoisie* to buttress its hegemony and maintain its privileges and power. The path toward communism was paved with a myriad of actions undertaken at various levels in the society until they cumulatively had deprived the *bourgeoisie* of the supports it had manufactured over centuries. And the ultimate revolution to be undertaken, even if by force, would indeed be the uprising of the many against the very few. Hardly any dictatorship would be needed since the vast majority would be now in tune with socialism as an ideology and everyday practice.

Gramsci presaged some of the ideas we discuss about Eurocommunism. Above all, he influenced the attitude of the Italian Communist party. Palmiro Togliatti, its leader between 1945 and 1967, had been Gramsci's associate and friend; Enrico Berlinguer, the Secretary General of the Italian Communist Party until 1984, followed Gramsci. The Italian Communist party made alliances with many bourgeois forces. Catholics were allowed to join the party. It became increasingly an open mass party rather than an elite; its members were elected in local and city government to control the administration of some of Italy's major cities; it promoted cooperatives in the farm and workers' participation in the factories; it tempered, on a number of occasions, workers' and peasants' protests movements and prevented violence; it offered to participate in a government coalition with its foremost political opponent, the Christian Democrats; and it developed a truly and independent foreign policy, refusing to follow the cues provided by Moscow. The party waxed strong in elections, capturing about 30 percent of the vote.

Thus if communism is to come about, it will do so only if enough people liberate themselves from the prevailing ideology — from the "hegemony" of the bourgeois class. And it can come about only when the people become convinced (not forced) that the new ways and the new institutions proposed truly implement democratic values: the values of equality and liberty and the opportunities for individual fulfillment. Gramsci, while dying in his prison cell in the 1930s, proposed a communism with a human face, far different from Stalin's despotism.

Soviet Domination: The Comintern

How would the communist parties and the movements that sprang up almost everywhere after the Bolshevik Revolution be organized? The answer was the Third International — the Comintern — founded in 1919. The communist parties that formed in many countries agreed to coordinate revolutionary strategy and tactics. There were thirty-five national parties in the Comintern when it was founded. By 1939 — on the eve of World War II — the number had grown to about sixty.

The Twenty-One Conditions

What bound all these new communist parties and movements together in the Third International were the famous twenty-one conditions set forth by Lenin. The same (or almost the same) characteristics of discipline, organization, and loyalty that Lenin imposed upon his Bolshevik party were required of all other national communist parties. Some of the conditions for communist parties everywhere were as follows:

— They must accept absolute ideological commitment to communism.
— They were to assume direct control over their communist press and publications.

— They accepted the principle and practice of democratic centralism. (i.e., the compliance of the rank and file to the instructions of the higher authorities and the obligation not to allow any factions to exist within their party). Reformists, revisionists, trade unionists, were to be ruthlessly eliminated from their ranks.
— Underground and illegal organizations and activities were to be established and party members should be ready for illegal work.
— A pledge was taken to make special efforts to undermine and disorganize the national armies.
— Pacifists and pacifism were not to be tolerated.
— All communists undertook the obligation to give aid and support to revolutionary movements of the colonial peoples.
— They were ordered to break with all trade unions affiliated with the Second International.
— Communist members in national parliaments were mere delegates of the party.
— All communist parties in the world undertook to support the Soviet Union and "every Soviet republic."
— The communist party program for every country had to be accepted by the executive committee of the Third International.

In this manner Lenin transformed the communist movement into a worldwide organization to counter the worldwide grip that he claimed the capitalists had established. Any threats on the part of the capitalists against socialist Russia would meet with the resistance of this well-organized force everywhere outside of Russia.

With the offices of the Comintern in Moscow, the Soviet leadership was able to establish its control over all other parties. Aside from ideology, many organizational and financial ties linked the individual communist parties of various countries with the Soviet Union. Seven Congresses of the Third International were held and, in the beginning, there was freedom on the part of delegates from abroad to express their points of view and engage in dialogue. Soon the choice of these delegates became controlled by the Soviets, and the Congresses simply confirmed the "line" suggested by the Soviet leaders.

The Third International became the Vatican of the communist movement; in its various pronouncements it analyzed the worldwide forces at work and set forth the strategy and the tactics to be followed by the individual national communist parties and their leaders. The Soviet Union, through the International, maintained surveillance and control over all national communist parties. The most direct method of control was through the exchange of delegates. All communist parties were expected to have a delegate-in-residence at the headquarters of the Third International in Moscow; the Third International in turn dispatched its own delegates to the headquarters of the national communist parties. They sat at their deliberations and often shaped their decisions. Many of the national party leaders had served time as delegates. After World War II, almost all of the leaders of all communist parties throughout the world had been trained, if not "made," in the Soviet Union. Most behaved as Moscow expected; only a handful did not.

Major ideological pronouncements defining the party line to follow, with regard to both domestic and international politics, came from the Third International. The two most significant ones were the pronouncements made in 1928 (Sixth Congress) and in 1935 (Seventh and last Congress). In the Sixth Congress, the socialist parties were declared to be the principal enemies of communism and no cooperation with them was permitted. The socialists became known as "social-fascists."

In the Seventh Congress of 1935 the Communist party line changed by 180 degrees. It now favored cooperation with all democratic parties — not only the socialists, but also middle-class liberal parties and often conservative parties — that were opposed to Nazi Germany. This became known as the policy of the "popular front." It lasted until August 1939 when the Executive Committee of the Third International, under the control of the Soviet leaders, again reversed its position. The Soviets signed a "nonaggression" pact with the Nazis.

In 1943, the Third International was formally dissolved. The reasons given were that the various communist parties in the world were "mature" enough to take care of their own programs and tactics and move about in their own way. The dissolution, however, was meant to placate the western Allies (especially the United States) by showing that the Soviet Union was no longer bent on world revolution. But the Third International had played its role — it had coordinated tightly the communist movements throughout the world according to Soviet designs and had solidly infused the belief that the defense and protection of the Soviet Union was the ultimate duty of all workers.

Soviet Communism After Stalin

In 1956, after a short power struggle, Nikita Khrushchev replaced Stalin as General Secretary of the party and Chairman of the Council of Ministers of the Soviet Union and gave a "secret report" to the delegates of the Soviet Communist party at its twentieth Congress. He criticized Stalin sharply for the many crimes committed during his long stay in office.

Comrades! . . .

After Stalin's death the Central Committee of the party began to implement a policy of explaining concisely and consistently that it is impermissible and foreign to the spirit of Marxism-Leninism to elevate one person, to transform him into a superman possessing supernatural characteristics akin to those of a god. Such a man supposedly knows everything, sees everything, thinks for everyone, can do anything, is infallible in his behavior.

Such a belief about a man, and specifically about Stalin, was cultivated among us for many years . . . Stalin acted not through persuasion, explanation, and patient cooperation with people, but by imposing his concepts and demanding absolute submission to his opinion. Whoever opposed this concept or tried to prove his viewpoint and the correctness of his position was doomed to removal from the leading collective and to subsequent moral and physical annihilation. . . .

Arbitrary behavior by one person encouraged and permitted arbitrariness in others. Mass arrests and deportations of many thousands of people, execution without trial and without normal investigation created conditions of insecurity, fear, and even despair.[9]

The Nobel Prize novelist, Aleksander Solzhenitsyn, in his *Gulag Archipelago* describes the utter capriciousness behind the terror that Stalin used. One of the inmates is asked for how many years he was sentenced in the labor camp. "For ten," he answers. "What did you do?" "Nothing." His companion seems surprised. "Nothing!" he exclaims. "People usually get five years for doing nothing."

Since the time of the Khrushchev report, but particularly since 1961, Stalin's name has been virtually removed from every corner of Soviet life. Streets and villages and towns no longer bear his name. He is no longer part of the Marxist-Leninist-Stalinist trinity, and no longer regarded as a founder of the communist ideology. Occasional efforts to "rehabilitate" him have failed but similar efforts to rehabilitate some of the communist leaders who were put to death or "disappeared" during his reign seemed doomed. Many of the communist leaders executed by Stalin were prolaimed innocent, however, in 1988.

International Communism: Trends and Changes

The control that the Soviet leadership once exercised over the other communist parties in the world has declined. First it was Tito in Yugoslavia, then Mao in China, and then Eurocommunism, together with various "deviant" forms of communism that emerged in a number of countries, all of which we discuss in our next chapter. They all differed or claimed to be different from Soviet communism. References were now made to polycentrism, with multiple and independent centers of communist rule and to "national communism" where communist parties would follow a path dictated by specific national conditions and not by the Soviet leadership according to the Soviet model. The ability of the Soviets to impose their course of action declined.

9. Khrushchev's "Secret Report" to the Twentieth Congress of the Communist party of the Soviet Union, in Bertram Wolfe, *Khrushchev and Stalin's Ghost.* London: Atlantis Press, pp. 88–100.

Peaceful Coexistence   Communist leaders had posited the inevitability of a conflict between communist and capitalist blocs. After Stalin's death it was abandoned in favor of "peaceful coexistence," which assumed conflict between the two blocs but denied that it would inevitably lead to war. Such an admission in itself weakened Soviet control over other communist parties since war was no longer considered inevitable. Peaceful coexistence allayed the fears of many communists and gave them time to develop their own individual strategies and domestic politics. It is only within the eastern bloc — the Warsaw Pact countries — that Soviet control has been maintained, by virtue of the presence of Soviet military forces.

Domestic Developments   Stalin's rule has come under increasing criticism both with regard to the political practices he used and with reference to the overall kind of socialism that developed. The State had not withered away; on the contrary, many pointed out that it had blossomed forth in the form of excessive centralization and bureaucratization. Freedoms virtually disappeared, and the development of a consumer-oriented economy was still far off. Inequalities increased and coercive practices were still prominent even when more incentives were introduced.

Why was this so, many asked. Was Stalinism a phenomenon peculiar to Russia? Did it obey characteristics embedded in the Russian political culture and history? Was the continuing backwardness of the Soviet economy the inevitable result of its manifest backwardness at the time the revolution was made? As we pointed out, many communists and socialists considered that Stalinism was a temporary phase — inevitable, but destined to pass. Many hoped that democratization would be possible after Stalin's death. The disappearance of the cult of personality; the downgrading of the role of the police; the growth of intraparty democracy; the development of some degree of pluralism, and a more tolerant attitude to dissent — all of them would indicate that liberalization was at long last on the way.

The Cult of Personality   Stalin, as the leader — omniscient and omnipotent — was replaced by "collective leadership." The General Secretary of the party, however, continues to have ascendancy. Yet the servile adulation and deference is gone. Through the party, Stalin's successors continue to exercise control, but it is no longer the direct and personal iron grip that Stalin held through the police and through outright intimidation.

Succession   The problem of succession seems to have been resolved in a manner that allows for the peaceful removal of a leader and the designation of another. The organs of the party — the Central Committee and the Politburo — are consulted. The ousting of top leaders does not lead to their physical extinction. There will be jobs for them in Uzbek or in Taskent . . . or in other remote parts of the Soviet Union.

The Police   The police and their arbitrary practices have come under party control thanks to the development of some general rules and procedures. To be sure, Soviet legality may be a very flexible concept, but some search for legality has been going on and efforts to curb the police and to subordinate them to procedural and legal requirements have been made. People no longer disappear overnight; they are not sent to labor camps without proper investigation and "trial." Intimidation is not as pervasive as it used to be.

Dissent   There has been a great interest in dissent and dissenters abroad, with the obvious conclusion that it is still not open to Soviet citizens, Jewish or non-Jewish. Yet despite harrassment and persecution, dissenters remain active; they give interviews to foreign reporters, and they seem to be protected by the interest that world opinion has focused on them. Some are allowed to leave; others are not. The Nobel Prize winner Andrei Sakharov is again free, something impossible to imagine under the Stalin regime. The Soviet Union continues to show its reluctance to allow for freedom of criticism — even the kind of freedom that does not question the foundations of the socialist system, but rather attempts to reconcile it with political freedoms and civil rights.

All in all, little seems to have been modified in the official ideological orthodoxy of the party. The "dictatorship of the proletariat" continues to be proclaimed necessary and as long as there is a capitalist sector in the world it is to be maintained. The period of genuine communism as envisaged by Marx and Engels is still far off. Society is still going through a process of adjustment, allegedly to prepare the conditions for a truly classless society. The State in the hands of the Communist party maintains its coercive traits and is likely to continue to do so.

The "Opening": Glasnost and Perestroika

After becoming Secretary-General of the Communist party in March 1985, Mikhail Gorbachev consolidated his power in the Politbureau, the Central Committee, and within the party. By the middle of 1986, he was vigorously advocating a policy of "openness" — liberalization of the political system (*Glasnost*) and economic restructuring (*Perestroika*).

The aim of *Perestroika* is to dismantle the huge bureaucracy that plans, directs, and implements industrial and agricultural production and trade through a process of decentralization. The central bureaucracy will be replaced by smaller functional regional and local units, down to the businesses themselves and their managers. They will be free to plan production, secure labor and raw materials at the best possible cost, establish their own budget, and seek benefits from their products. "Profits" would be

The Passing of the Old Order?

On March 15, 1985, fifty-four year old Mikhail Gorbachev, first behind the coffin, replaced his departed leader Konstantine Chernenko—age 74—as First Secretary of the Communist party of the Soviet Union. The two previous First Secretaries, Andropov and Brezhnev, had held their posts until they were seventy-two and seventy-six respectively. In the coming of Gorbachev, many saw an end to the old order and the beginning of a vigorous and innovative leadership. (*Photo: Wide World Photos*)

realized through both an increase in productivity and efficiency, which will reduce costs, and through creative marketing practices, which will increase sales and income. Such moves would inject some flexibility into the system so that production can be increasingly geared to consumer demand, needs, and tastes. There could even be competition among firms: for example, differential profits and wages could be established and a special bonus for productivity could be granted. In other words, the Soviet economy would move in the direction of the "capitalistic" world in order to spur growth.

Glasnost is an effort to liberalize the political regime by allowing for greater public debate within and outside the political party, in the press, and on radio and television. Moreover, *Glasnost* seeks to develop procedures through which public officials—mostly party members—can be scrutinized and held accountable. This should not necessarily be interpreted as a movement toward democracy, though it may be a beginning. There is no pretense of abandoning the monopoly of the single party, nor is there a desire to publicize the deliberations of the higher decision-making units of the party. Some democratization at the grass roots level is envisaged, for example, the election of local officials, but not at the higher echelons of the party—notably the Central Committee—where deliberations remain secret, candidates are selected in advance, and only official accounts are given to the public at large. More important at this stage may be the effort to open up historical research and allow for some freedom of expression in poetry, literature, art, films, and the theater. Reducing the heavy hand of censorship in these areas may bring about some significant changes. "We are for a diversity of public opinion," Gorbachev proclaimed, "for a richness of spiritual life. We need not fear openly raising and solving difficult problems of social development, criticizing and arguing. It is in such circumstances that the truth is born and that correct decisions take shape." Gorbachev further asserted that critical inquiry should also be directed to Soviet history and the reconsideration of the role of revolutionary leaders—including, above all, Stalin and many of his victims. In short, Gorbachev was urging the Russians, for so long treated as subjects, to become citizens—free to participate, equal before the law, and protected from personalistic and dictatorial regimes, such as the one shaped by Stalin. He also opened a wide window to the world. "Peaceful co-existence," he seemed to indicate, was no longer enough. The present and the future require "interrelatedness" and "interdependence," cooperation and solidarity. This outlook is now necessary, he said, because of technological changes, the role of mass communications, world environmental and resources problems, the social and economic problems in the developing countries, and, above all, human survival from the dangers of nuclear weapons.[10] "Anti-Sovietism" was on the decline, he said, and he seemed to imply that the fear of the Soviets by the outside world had also subsided.

Without doubt the move toward economic freedoms (and efficiency) and political freedoms (and political responsibility) remains one of the most exciting prospects for the Soviet society. The inertia of the past, the heavy hand of a bureaucracy that has institutionalized itself over so many years, the preferential treatment and privileges that go with the top decision-making jobs—among the politicians, the managers, the bureaucrats, the Soviet intelligentsia in general, and also the military—may all be in jeopardy if public officials are to be freely scrutinized and criticized. As we have noted, however, ideology shapes attitudes and the political roles in any society. Soviet communism today and the legacy it embodies from the past legitimizes the status quo and protects the privileged groups—it is a status quo ideology. Unless the existing Soviet political elite begins to divide openly on ideological issues, which has not happened yet, there is little prospect for change. Not that the ideology cannot change or will not change to adjust to needs and circumstances, but rather that its changes, in scope and emphasis, continue to remain under the tight control of the leadership. The Communist party maintains a monopoly on political expression, and its ideology continues to rationalize the interests of those in power. A possible harbinger of change may lie in the present confrontation within the Communist party between the "reformers" under Gorbachev and the "conservatives" who cling to bureaucratic and centralized economic methods together with repressive political controls. No class, no

10. Quotes from excerpts of a speech printed in *The New York Times*, November 3, 1987.

orthodoxy, no caste has been immune to change. But for the student who watches Soviet developments, the prospect for change can be assessed only if and when the political monopoly of the Communist party is dented.

Communism in Crisis: The Specter of Capitalism

Like the crisis of democracy, and of the democratic and socialist regimes that we discussed, communism and the various communist regimes also seem to be going through a crisis — perhaps an even more serious one. It is a crisis of their economies, a crisis in ideology, and a crisis in their political institutions and structures. To paraphrase the famous battle cry of Marx, today the specter of democracy — even worse, the specter of capitalism — seems to haunt the communist world!

By the time Stalin died in 1953 the Soviet economy seemed to have successfully gone through the stages of what might be called primitive industrialization, as they had made massive investment in capital goods to produce steel, iron, cement, oil, coal, and the like. But the technological revolution of the sixties and seventies in western Europe, Japan, and the United States has left the Soviets behind. Central planning, nationalization of the economy, bureaucratic controls — the Soviet "model" — has not fared well. It has failed in agriculture and in technological modernization and has proven pitifully inadequate in satisfying consumer demand and the production of durable consumer goods. The Soviet Union is beginning to depend on the West not only for wheat and corn but also for technology. The bureaucratic centralization of the economy has created serious problems of distribution. A number of communist regimes, Hungary, for instance (to say nothing of the efforts that were made in the same direction in Czechoslovakia and Poland), have undertaken extensive decentralization and have introduced individual incentives including the profit motive. China seems to be moving in the same direction, and we shall briefly discuss the Yugoslav model.

Equally significant is the crisis in communist ideology. It is comparable in many ways to the crisis of Marxism in the decades before World War I. In great part it is due to the resurgence of nationalism — a resurgence to which the Soviet communist leaders contributed. "National-communisms" and various self-styled national communist regimes have broken from the communist international movement and its common ideological and political front. After World War II, both the efforts to bring together the communist regimes and parties under Soviet control and leadership and the efforts to impose the Soviet model of communism upon all other parties and communist regimes have failed.

But for many, it was the political arrangements and institutions in the Soviet Union and eastern Europe that began to provide the major reason for discontent and disaffection. For a long time western intellectuals accepted Stalin's rule and the terror associated with it as necessary to bring about economic well-being and equality. Political freedoms were to be put

AP/WIDE WORLD PHOTOS

Gorbachev's new policy of "openness" is reflected well in this picture of the new Soviet leader. Dialogue, debate, reexamination of the roots and the destiny of the Soviet society and the Soviet Union, and the liberalization of societal forces, including even the economy, are beginning to emerge. Will Gorbachev's efforts succeed?

on ice. But with the revelations of what Stalin's dictatorship was—capricious, despotic, and inhuman—even some of the most ardent pro-Soviet communist ideologues were profoundly shaken. Even the most skilled dialecticians began to doubt that Soviet communism was a one-way ticket to a better world. And most began to fear the journey! Many began to flaunt the Soviet model—even those from the left—and demands for genuine pluralism and democracy, decentralization of power, and accountability of the officeholders became more pronounced. The imposition of a military dictatorship with Soviet support in Poland in 1981 was "the last straw."

The deepening of the political, economic, and ideological crisis in the communist world, and among those who professed the communist ideology and claimed to be united by it, is both sharpened and obscured by one overriding reality—the growth of the Soviet military power. Sheer power in the international arena silences the critics of the Soviet system and stifles the voices of dissenters abroad and at home. As ideological mobilization begins to weaken, Soviet power is used in its place as an instrument of governance and domination. This is the crisis that the Soviet communist regime faces today as Mikhail Gorbachev attempts to liberalize the regime without managing to provide for a new ideology.

Bibliography

Bialer, Seweryn. *Stalin's Successors.* New York: Cambridge U.P., 1980.

Borkenau, F. *The Communist International.* London: Faber, 1938.

Brauntahl, Julius. *History of the International 1914–1943,* (2 vols.). New York: Praeger, 1967.

Conquest, Robert. *The Soviet Political System.* New York: Praeger, 1968.

Deutscher, Isaac. *Stalin.* New York: Oxford U.P., 1949.

Djilas, Milovan. *The New Class: An Analysis of the Communist System.* New York: Praeger, 1957.

Gorbachev, Mikhail. *Perestroika.* New York: Harper & Row, 1987.

Lenin, V. I. *What Is To Be Done?* New York: International Publishers, 1969.

————. "Imperialism: The Highest Stage of Capitalism" and "The State and Revolution." In *Lenin: Selected Works in One Volume.* New York: International Publishers, 1971.

McNeal, Robert H. *The Bolshevik Tradition.* Englewood Cliffs, N.J.: Prentice-Hall, 1975.

Medvedev, Roy. *On Socialist Democracy.* New York: Knopf, 1975.

Meyer, Alfred G. *Leninism.* New York: Praeger, 1957.

————. *The Soviet Political System: An Interpretation.* New York: Random House, 1965.

Schammell, Michael. *Russia's Other Writers: Selections From Samizdat Literature.* New York: Praeger, 1971.

Schapiro, Leonard. *The Communist Party of the Soviet Union.* rev. ed. New York: Vintage, 1978.

————. *The Government and Politics of the Soviet Union.* New York: Vintage Books, 1978.

Shub, David. *Lenin: A Biography.* New York: Penguin, 1976.

Simon, Gerhard. *Church, State, and Opposition in the USSR.* London: C. Hurst, 1974.

Solzhenitsyn, Aleksander. *The Gulag Archipelago* (3 vols.). New York: Harper & Row, 1974–1979.

Stalin, Joseph. *The Essential Stalin.* Edited by Bruce Franklin. New York: Anchor/Doubleday, 1972.

Tucker, Robert C. (ed.). *Stalinism: Essays in Historical Interpretation.* New York: Norton, 1977.

Ulam, Adam B. *The Bolsheviks.* New York: Macmillan, 1968.

————. *Stalin: The Man and His Era.* New York: Viking, 1973.

Wolfe, Bertram D. *Three Who Made A Revolution.* New York: Delta/Dell, 1964.

7 | Communist Variations

*The most successful, and the most fanatically
revolutionary and communist, group of followers . . .
found itself compelled to defy the claims of the
Kremlin to dominate unconditionally every
Communist Party of the world.*
ADAM ULAM   Titoism and the Cominform

The aftermath of World War II accounted for the consolidation of the
Soviet Union as a world power. In the name of socialism, and because of
the presence of Soviet forces, most of eastern Europe established communist regimes and came under the control of the Soviets: East Germany (the
German Democratic Republic), Hungary, Czechoslovakia, Rumania, Bulgaria, Poland, together with the small border states of Latvia, Estonia, and
Lithuania. Yugoslavia had already made its own socialist revolution while
the war was going on thanks to the organization of a strong partisan army
which fought the Germans under communist leadership.

In Asia it took only a few years after the end of the war for nationalist
forces and the Chinese warlords to give way to the communist forces led by
Mao. Though they had received some Soviet help, these forces were homemade and homegrown and, as in Yugoslavia, there was no direct Soviet
military involvement.

Would the communist bloc act as one? Would ideological ties overcome national rivalries? Would the Soviets manage to maintain their hegemony over the communist bloc — over its "satellites," as they came to be
known, in the name of ideological unity, and power? Would they be able
to extend their influence over other parts of the world, and especially
among the new nations?

A brief glance at two dissident movements, Titoism and Maoism,
indicates the emergence of ideological conflicts and national rivalries
within what we called the communist bloc. Eurocommunism, too, may be
viewed as an ideological movement among western European communist

parties claiming independence from the tight bureaucratic, organizational, ideological, and financial control that the Soviets had managed to impose in the years of Stalin and until the 1960s.

The result has been a break in Soviet control and in the monolithic kind of communism that many, especially American political leaders, had taken for granted.

Titoism

Titoism is the label given to the prevailing communist movement and the ideology of Yugoslavia. It began to develop after the German occupation of the country in 1941. Throughout the war, the Yugoslav Communist party under Tito assumed the leadership of the resistance and organized and fought a sustained guerrilla war against the Nazis. In 1945, the party assumed political control of Yugoslavia, but in 1948–1949, communist Yugoslavia and the Soviet Union disagreed on a number of issues. Ever since, Titoism has been synonymous with a national communist regime that has declared itself independent of the Soviet Union, and that differs on a number of domestic and international questions.

Adam Ulam writes that Titoism is "... a proper name for the historical moment of the break between Tito and Stalin, but not for an ideology...."[1] Yet he points out also that "Titoism ... has a broad meaning [that] might be translated as resistance on the part of a communist party to the domination of the Russian communists." We shall not be concerned here with the specifics of the historical moment — that is, of how Tito defied Soviet leadership and control — nor of the circumstances surrounding it. Rather, we will discuss the development of an ideology in terms of which the Yugoslav political, social, and economic experiment seeks an identity separate from that of Soviet communism.

The Nationalist Urge

As we have seen, it was Lenin's genius that knit together the various Marxist groups and parties into an international organization, the Third International. This was accomplished at a time when communism was still a movement whose chances of survival, even in Russia, were dim. How would the international proletariat react when communism had triumphed in a number of countries? Would they disregard their national borders in favor of cooperation? Or would they follow the way of the socialist parties on the eve of World War I and put their country above proletarian brotherhood and solidarity?

Stalin's answer was simply to subordinate the communist ideology and the communist movements to the national interests and needs of Russia. One might argue that this was only a tactical move and that if and

1. "Titoism," in Drachkovitch (ed.), *Marxism in the Modern World*, p. 137.

YUGOSLAV PRESS AND CULTURAL CENTER

Josip Broz Tito (1892–1980)

Josip Broz was born on May 25, 1892 in Croatia. Wounded in World War I and captured by the Russians in 1915, he eventually joined the Red Army and married a Russian woman (whom he later divorced). In 1920, Broz returned to Yugoslavia and joined the Communist party. He served a five-year prison sentence received in 1928 for subversive activities and was imprisoned in Lepoglava and Maribor. In 1934 he became member of the Provincial Committee of the LCY (League of Communists of Yugoslavia) for Croatia; in that capacity he was co-opted on to the Central Committee of the LCY and elected to the Politbureau. In 1935 and 1936 he was in Moscow wherefrom he returned to carry on political work. In 1937, he became Secretary-General of the Yugoslav Communist party. In June 1941, after the invasion of the Soviet Union by the Germans, Broz returned again to Yugoslavia under the name Tito to organize resistance against the occupation forces there. It was one of the most successful partisan operations of the war. In 1945, Tito became prime minister of Yugoslavia. His independent, nationalistic brand of communism eventually brought verbal attacks, along with threat of military invasion, from Stalin in 1948.

when communist regimes spread in other countries, then indeed cooperation among them would be spontaneous and would be carried out on a footing of equality. Again Stalin gave the answer: the communist regimes that emerged in eastern Europe in the wake of World War II were imposed and controlled by the Soviet leadership. Their leaders were handpicked; their economies were controlled; their relations with each other and with the Soviet Union were fully dominated by the latter. There was no semblance of international communism on a footing of equality, only the control of the Soviet Communists.

As they emerged from the war, Tito and his Yugoslav Communist party felt they merited special attention and looked forward to genuine cooperation with their Soviet comrades. There was in Yugoslavia, more than in any other country in Europe, a strong Stalinist faction in the Communist party. It had waged war against the Germans, tying down a number of their divisions and keeping them away from the Russian front. It was able to lead the resistance successfully enough to force the Germans out without the intervention of the Soviet Army. Tito's communist Yugoslavia was a homemade product with proper communist credentials, its own cadres, its strong popular support, its own roots and, therefore, freedom to claim its "own road" to the building of socialism.

The historical moment for breaking with the Soviets came after the end of the war when the Yugoslav leadership showed remarkable unity in resisting attempts by the Soviet Union to dictate their policies. The leaders took exception to Soviet spying and machinations; to the lack of open and fraternal discussions; and to Soviet "arrogance" and "interference." They asked the Soviet technicians and advisers to leave. The conflict which had been muted for some time came out into the open in the spring of 1948 and the Yugoslavs stood alone. It was like a mouse taunting the big bear . . . and the mouse survived.

The ability of the Yugoslav communists to resist was due to the strong national base that the Communist party had developed as a *national* party. Some time after the split, the Yugoslav communist leaders began to search for their own ideology and to take a foreign policy that differed from that of the Soviet Union. It was only then that Titoism became transformed into the *Titoist ideology*. This took at least two new directions: the establishment of, or at least the effort to establish, political and economic institutions that differentiate Yugoslavia from the Soviet Union, and the search for a foreign policy that differed from and was independent of the Soviets.

New Institutions

The Yugoslav Communist party numbered only some 15,000 members in the years before World War II. It was a Stalinist party like all other European communist parties: tightly organized and disciplined, committed to revolution, but always ready to follow the tactical shifts and changes that Moscow ordered. By the end of the war — within a matter of six years — it

Tito's partisans took the lead in fighting the occupying German forces in Yugoslavia. The struggle was hard but the successes often spectacular: here, partisans lead large numbers of enemy prisoners down from their mountain hideouts. (*Photo: Yugoslav Press and Cultural Center*)

numbered 120,000 members and had made a revolution at home by destroying the industrial and financial elites, expropriating the land of the landowners, reducing the middle classes, and gaining the support of the peasantry and the overwhelming backing of the workers. It also gained the support of the ethnic minorities. It was a remarkably youthful party, primarily recruiting from among those who had entered the partisan forces and who were waging war against the Germans. Thus the party developed a solid base that gave it the independence to defy the Soviets and the strength to maintain its separate course and ideological orientation.

Communism and Patriotism Nowhere in Europe was communism so deeply associated with national resistance against the Germans, and with patriotism, as in Yugoslavia. The communist leaders were the leaders of this resistance. They organized the partisans, provided for political and military direction, and gradually gained the support of many of the social strata of the population. The more brutal the German repression, the greater the support for the partisans, and the greater the influence and control of the communists over the countryside. Young men and women fled to the mountains to join the partisans. As the predominance of the communist leaders asserted itself, and as they gained greater popular support, the elimination of opposition became easier. Rival partisan formations, and groups that collaborated, were destroyed in what amounted to a civil war fought alongside the guerrilla war against the Germans.

In this manner a social revolution took place in the context of a vast patriotic uprising against the Germans and the collaborators. The Communist party emerged after the war with few enemies at home and with the backbone of the conservative forces broken. It had gained wide popular support.

After the Split: A New Communism?   This brief account of the role and the conditions under which the Yugoslav Communist party grew explains not only why the party managed to survive the split with the Soviet Union, but also it may explain the split itself. The party emerged with grass roots support, with faith in its own ability to lead, and with few enemies at home. The split with Soviet Russia forced it to consider alternative models of communist rule, and in fact, it triggered a search for a new model of communism which began to emerge some ten years later, by 1958.

The model is by no means complete. Yugoslav communists have been moving, and are still moving, into uncharted waters in the attempt to launch a new and different kind of socialism. The political regime and the ideology to sustain it have also been going through numerous modifications as they adjust to national and international pressures, demands and counterpressures. How the regime will evolve is uncertain since the very symbol of legitimacy, Marshall Tito, who played the role of unifier and ultimate arbiter for almost forty years, is now dead.

A Communist Society. Yugoslavia is a socialist society. Property belongs to the State, and to various State agencies, and to the people. Except for the farmers who own their farms (nobody is allowed to have more than sixty acres of land) and small artisans and shopkeepers, the rest of the economy is owned by the collectivity. Industry, manufacturing, mining — over 90 percent of the total nonagricultural economic activity — is in the hands of public bodies. Even in agriculture, publicly owned farms account for a significant percentage of the total production of some crops.

Economic Democracy? By 1958, Yugoslavia had definitely abandoned the Stalinist model of modernization involving State control and subordination of economic activities to a highly centralized bureaucracy. Instead, it put the premium on *decentralization* through the development of quasi-independent units of production with grass roots controls. This is in essence the principle of self-government in industry and the economy. The bureaucratic model has been turned upside down and economic activity has been returned, so to speak, to the producers. State socialism of the Stalinist model fixes production in advance, in the form of quotas, and it controls prices, wages, and consumption. The socialist model of Yugoslavia allows for competition among firms and decentralizes decision making on what and how much to produce. It allows, therefore, for self-regulatory mechanisms (i.e., for a market economy that generally determines prices, production, and consumption) as well as for a great degree of freedom for each and every individual firm. It encourages competition among enterprises and allows some to earn more while the others strive to do the same. Though property is "socialized," it is managed by thousands of separate firms and public enterprises. Efficient management brings higher profits from which everybody within the firm benefits.

Institutions of Self-management: Workers' Councils. Decentralization simply means that decisions are not made by one single central authority but are left in the hands of individual units and firms. Self-management, on the other hand, refers to the institutions and procedures under which decisions in a firm or in any other economic unit are made by all those who work in it.

The most important institution, which allows for such an internal democracy, is the workers' council in industry and in all other branches of the economy. The representatives elect the managers and have the right to dismiss them, and they review and deliberate on all aspects of the firm's decisions — what to produce, how much, how to distribute income, how much to allot for capital formation. They have a strong, and at times, the definitive voice on policies of hiring and firing, promotions, and standards for promotion.

No doubt tensions between managers and the workers' councils exist; firms everywhere may be run with a eye to profit (like capitalistic ones) at the expense of other social considerations. But Yugoslavia provides the best case of such a widespread participation of workers, and perhaps the unique case of workers' control. It is the only communist regime to have managed to embark upon industrial democracy.

What are the advantages of this system? They are social, economic, and political. Politically, the workers are increasingly allowed to participate. Even if it is for economic matters only, they are drawn into the system and, the more they benefit from it the more they are likely to support it and to support the political regime as well. From a social point of view, workers' councils and workers' control may overcome the sentiment of alienation and powerlessness that afflicts workers in industrial societies, including the Soviet one. They have a voice and a stake in what is being decided and what is being produced, and they benefit or suffer directly because of the decisions they make. Furthermore, in making decisions of an economic nature, they have to balance their own direct and immediate self-interest against the interest of the collectivity where they live and work, and those of society as a whole. The system, in contrast to bureaucratic ones, presumes that the workers may be able to learn how to balance these various interests and to shed gradually the selfish motivation that "economic man" displays.

But one of the advantages of the system is that it does not do away with private interest. On the contrary, it allows for the expression of self-interest and, within limits, legitimizes it. It gives the workers a sense of direct economic responsibility for their own well-being, since bad decisions may well mean less income. From a more general point of view the system allows competing self-managed firms to seek the highest possible efficiency in order to show a profit.

Toward a Political Democracy?

The present regime appears to be relatively open and free to a far greater extent than the Soviet Union and any of the eastern European regimes. The country is open to millions of tourists every year and, in turn, Yugoslavs are free to travel abroad. There is no *prior* censorship in the publication of books, and much of the press that is not directly controlled by the party is relatively free. But controls vary from one republic to another. Authors have been sentenced for their publications and some have found themselves in jail.

Within the various representative assemblies, debate is free and many policies are not agreed upon until an elaborate process of compromise has yielded agreement. The constitution provides for federal organs: a government and a parliament where national policies are hammered out; six individual republics and two autonomous provinces, each representing different ethnic and religious populations. The federal bodies represent the "nation" as a whole. Every effort has been made to avoid the domination of one nationality (i.e., Serbian) over others.

The overall purpose is to create a multinational political society in which all ethnic groups have equal representation and participation as well as freedom to use their own language and to enjoy their own ways, including the expression of their religious beliefs. The same is the case with another national institution, the army. Whereas in the past, the officer corps was overwhelmingly Serbian, we find today that only 46 percent of the generals and only 33 percent of the members of the high command are Serbian.

The League of Communists

Yugoslavia has a one-party system. The League of Communists of Yugoslavia (the new name for the Communist party) is a national organization with a membership of over a million and a quarter. It is both a horizontal organization cutting across republics and a vertical one reaching down into every republic, region, locality, firm, and social institution. Elective office is generally limited to the members of the league, because at election time candidates for office must be approved by it. Thus the league remains a monopolistic organization and competition for elective office is controlled by it.

There are three important considerations regarding the composition of the league that should be kept in mind. First, over 75 percent of its members have joined it since about 1960. They are still relatively young, and all came into the party *after* the Yugoslav-Soviet split. Their entry coincides roughly with the shift away from the centralized model of Stalinism in the direction of self-management. To them, the institutions of the workers' councils and direct participation and control *is* socialism. Second, every effort has been made, despite the inevitable growth of white-collar and managerial groups, to keep the league a working-class party. Workers, white-collar workers, technicians, managers, and students comprise a majority and are considerably overrepresented in comparison to their population strength. These are the more dynamic groups of the population that are interested in continuing modernization and anxious to maintain and enlarge their opportunities and advantages in the regime. Third, every effort has been made to make the league as faithfully representative as possible of the ethnic composition of the country as a whole.

What is the major function of the league today? "The league," writes Bogdan Denitch, ". . . even though it renounces the role of direct shaper of day-to-day policy and defines itself primarily as the leading ideological guardian of an essentially self-managing society and economy, is a key factor in the social changes taking place in Yugoslavia. . . ." "It is hard," he points out, "to imagine an active citizen . . . who is not a member of the league." The league "is the active vehicle for active political participation in the system as a whole." Finally, "The league functions as the representative of the new values of industrialization and modernization."[2] One might add that the league is also the major instrument for the organization and integrity of a multinational political society both against internal disruptive forces and external enemies. It is the custodian, in other words, of the nation, the State, and the official ideology.

The elite that constitutes the league is drawn from the population on the basis of their ability and achievement. It is an elite that believes in rapid modernization and progress, and takes it for granted that the communism they practice is the best way of bringing it about. The leadership is quite conscious that it needs widespread support and that force may be both costly and ineffective. Support is inculcated not only through education, socialization, and propaganda but through participatory mechanisms and rewards. Self-management and the workers' council promote participation, and the modernizing sectors and strata of the population, whether in industry, among engineers, white-collar workers, or managers, are rewarded with prospects of social mobility and higher material benefits. The league acts as a catalyst in providing and encouraging participatory politics and seeing to it that rewards will be channeled, in the name of modernization and socialism, to the more active and productive segments of the population—something that *both* motivates them and secures their support.

It is conceivable, however, that self-management and participatory politics may lead the citizenry to a point where the basic values of the regime may be questioned; in other words, when persuasive politics will give place to confrontation politics. The league stands as a guardian against such an eventuality. If dissent spills over the limits set by the

---

2. Bogdan Denitch. *The Legitimization of a Revolution: The Yugoslav Case.* New Haven, Conn.: Yale U.P., 1972.

ideology on which the regime is based, then it is inevitable that there will be a sharp confrontation between the league and the participatory and self-managing institutions it has created. But the league remains the only watchdog of the existing values, and together with the army, may have to protect them even by force. In the meantime, it acts as the nervous system of a highly complicated organism, promoting the acceptance of common values, facilitating compromise and decision making, reconciling ethnic or group antagonisms, supervising, from a distance, the effective application of self-government in industry and in all other social local institutions, while making sure that no rival force develops.

It is precisely this openness, within the limits that a socialist regime can allow, that has been both a source of pride for the Yugoslavs and a lever of criticism against the Soviet Union. The words of Tito show why Yugoslavs are led both to glorify their own regime and to criticize the Soviet system. To explain the Soviet-Yugoslav split Tito wrote: "Progress toward socialism has been arrested and the Soviet Union has become an enormous terror state. . . . The fundamental question on which Stalin failed is the problem of freedom of the individual in socialism, for there can be no socialism without freedom. These two concepts are identical."[3] But freedom and openness are tolerated only within a socialist context, where most property has been socialized and the Communist party enjoys a political monopoly.

An ideological profile is beginning to emerge; one of relatively open and participatory socialism, of decentralization and industrial democracy, of socialism with a market economy. However, it is a system whose democratic credentials depend, in the last analysis, upon what the League of Communists (i.e., the Communist party) will or will not allow.

Foreign Policy

It was far more difficult for Yugoslavia to develop a new image in the international world. Tito split from the Soviets and managed to survive in the name of national communism. He planted seeds then that have continued to grow, and are now thorns that plague the Soviet Union. The most important one is the concept of "national communism." It means that nations, despite their acceptance of communism, are fundamentally and irrevocably committed to their full independence and reject any intervention in any form. "Titoism" as national communism spread all over eastern Europe.

A second effort by Tito to find an image was his sponsorship of "nonalignment"—that is, the effort to organize nations, mostly in the Third World, which refused to become dependent politically, diplomatically, or militarily upon either the western world led by the United States or the communist world led by the Soviet Union. While these nations constitute a large bloc numerically, they are generally poor and torn with

3. Vladimir Dedijen. *Tito Speaks.* London: Weidenfeld and Nicolson, 1953.

internal disputes and conflicts. They have been unable to organize thus far and have failed to agree on any basic foreign policy objectives.

Faced by the Soviet power, Tito and the present Yugoslav leaders fell back discreetly on the only possible course of action left to a small state — support from the United States. There was no alternative. It will have to be so until Titoism develops elsewhere in eastern Europe and until fellow communist China, whose concerns and ideological posture parallel those of communist Yugoslavia, takes a more active part in European affairs. For the time being, the assertion of an independent stance by a communist state in the name of national communism, and its consolidation, remain Tito's most enduring legacy in international affairs.

Titoism Without Tito

On May 4, 1980, Tito died after a long illness, and as with the death of Stalin in 1953, the question was raised: After Tito what? The intensely personal element of the leadership he had provided, the deep respect and attachment of the Yugoslavs for their leader — irrespective of ethnic origin, religion, or language — made the question even more relevant for the people of Yugoslavia. Tito was "the founder." When the institutions did not provide the accommodation of conflicting points of view, especially among the nationalities comprising Yugoslavia, Tito could be counted upon to provide an authoritative solution or, if need be, to apply force. Without him the mosaic that had been written into the Yugoslav federal constitution giving autonomy and in substance a veto to various governmental units might not work, and the League of Communists of Yugoslavia itself might reflect the fragments of the many political forces at work rather than provide the glue to keep them together.

It is still too early, however, to answer the question. The remarkable thing is that more than a decade after Tito's death, Yugoslavia is united and its institutions have functioned. Conflicts among nationalities about the allocation of resources have been resolved, and there has been no change in the independent stance Tito imparted to Yugoslavia's foreign policy. Titoism remains very much alive. While the Party Congress held in June 1982, two years after Tito's death, was an indication of the durability of the regime, it was also an occasion to note the many strains and conflicts that have been aggravated by the world economic crisis. Disparities between the autonomous republics remain great. For instance, the per capita income in Croatia or Slovenia is about seven times as high as that of Kossovo, which is inhabited by Albanians. Efforts to distribute the economic activity evenly among the countries' autonomous republics, and thus equalize the national wealth, have not been successful so far. The economic problems aggravate existing ethnic and religious conflicts so much that the individual republics have developed separatist tendencies that divide and fragment the regime. The unifying force remains the Communist League and a long-term functioning of the regime will depend, as Tito's legacy begins to fade, upon its ability to generate and sustain the kind of ideology that will transcend individual particularisms and contain separatist movements.

Maoism

Like Titoism in Yugoslavia, Maoism is the label for the communist movement and its ideology that developed in China under the leadership of Mao Tse-tung. "Chairman Mao" was, for more than forty years, the undisputed leader of the Chinese Communist party and the head of the communist government in China after the civil war (1946–1949) and until his death in 1977.

Maoism represents the first, apparently successful, communist revolution in an underdeveloped non-European society and the first viable non-European communist regime. Like Yugoslavia, China broke off from the direct political and economic oversight of the Soviet Union to follow its own path to communism, but the reasons for the break can be traced to the very beginnings of the Chinese communist movement, as expounded by Mao Tse-tung.

Background

The Chinese Communist party, founded in 1921, at first accepted fully the twenty-one conditions imposed by the Third International. It accepted the "dictatorship of the proletariat" and subscribed to the concept of revolutionary class struggle. Yet at the express insistence of the Soviet leadership, the Chinese communist leaders abandoned their party's revolutionary position and gave their support to the leader of what appeared to be a middle-of-the-road coalition of political forces in China — the Kuomintang, led by Chiang Kai-shek. Almost immediately, Chiang turned against the communists, arrested and imprisoned thousands of leaders, cadres, and members, and shot many of them. The Communist party was destroyed in virtually all urban centers where it was supported by workers and intellectuals. Its proletarian base was wiped out. Perhaps it was from this moment on that the peasant base of the Chinese Communist party became indispensable in the eyes of Mao. He and many communist leaders withdrew into the vast countryside to develop intimate relations with the peasantry.

They gathered in strength in one of the relatively poorer provinces of China, Kiangsi, where they established a communist republic and ruled the province from 1931 to about 1934. It was at this time that the Red Army, later to become known as the People's Liberation Army, was founded. But through their "Kiangsi experience" the Chinese communists under Mao learned what they had to do if they were to receive support from the peasants. They realized that they had to relate their strategy and goals to the expectations of the peasantry. "The peasants came to see that the

WIDE WORLD PHOTOS

Mao Tse-Tung (1893–1977)

Mao Tse-tung (Mao Ze-dong) was born in Hunan. In 1918 he
became a librarian at Peking University where his socialist lean-
ings were strengthened as a result of contact with the works of
Marx and those of Li Ta-chao and Ch'en Tuhsiu, two professors
who with Mao were to help found the Chinese Communist party
(CCP) in 1921. Although attaining leadership positions in the CCP,
Mao's devotion to the peasantry as a revolutionary force, and his
theory of guerrilla warfare rather than urban insurrection, alienated him from much of the party leadership. After the persecution
and elimination of the communists in 1927, Mao proclaimed a
"soviet republic" in southwestern Kiangsi Province. In 1934 he led
his forces on the two-year "Long March" to regroup in northwest-
ern China. The Chinese communist forces finally triumphed over
their nationalist opponents in 1949 and established the People's
Republic of China, with Mao serving as President in addition to his
post as Party Chairman. Among Mao's major works are *On Contradictions, On Practice* and *Quotations From Chairman Mao,* an anthology that served as the textbook for the young Red Guard
cadres of the Cultural Revolution.

Communists worked for their interest. Their army was perfectly disciplined, neither plundered nor commandeered. What it needed it bought for cash and if it could not be supplied it went elsewhere."[4] Good relations with the peasantry, and the support they gave to the communists, was an important element of Mao's famous theory of guerrilla warfare.

The Pillars of Maoism

It was the support of and identification with the peasantry, as well as the increasing assumption by the communists of a nationalist posture, that accounted for their ultimate victory. But it was to a great extent also due to the development of a new revolutionary strategy — *guerrilla warfare.*

The Peasantry   The peasants invariably play a crucial role in all revolutions, and their grievances have been exploited by conservative, liberal, and communist leaders at different times. Lenin's slogan "land to the peasants" on the eve of the Bolshevik Revolution either directly rallied many of them behind the communists, or, and even more important, neutralized them. But Marxists believe that while the peasantry could at times be helpful it was only the working class and its leaders, the Communist party, that could develop the proper class and revolutionary consciousness,

Source of inspiration and training for China's Red Army was the communist stronghold at Yenan. Important army and party councils and assemblies were held in the mountains where the officers and soldiers came for political "revival." *(Photo: Wide World Photos)*

4. Fitzgerald, *Mao Tse-tung and China*, p. 39.

make the revolution, and establish socialism. Peasants' major preoccupation is the ownership of land: they are therefore considered to be fundamentally an obstacle to the building of socialism.

At the second congress of the Third International in 1920 the role of the peasantry had been explicitly recognized to act side by side with the working class. It was Mao who, for the first time, went beyond this to attribute to the peasantry a genuine revolutionary role and to build his revolutionary movement on a peasant basis. The revolution would be made in close association with the peasantry and in great part by the peasantry.

It may be argued that Mao's strategy was dictated by the circumstances. Since the urban centers were controlled by Chiang and the proletarian ranks of the Communist party were decimated, the communists had no alternative but to turn to the peasants. But there seemed to be more important reasons. Mao, the son of a fairly well-to-do farmer, had spent years in his native province of Hunan studying peasant conditions.[5] He described their miseries, deprivations, and the manner in which they were exploited by the landlords, but he also expressed his admiration for their stoicism, shrewdness, and courage. There was a genuine populist streak in Mao — an admiration for the innate goodness and spontaneity of the peasants. He also saw that the decades of deprivation and exploitation and the constant strife against the hated landlords made the Chinese peasantry a potentially powerful revolutionary force. All that needed to be done was to mobilize it under the proper leadership. Accomplishing this was Mao's major achievement. Without forgetting the importance of the proletariat, he built the Chinese Communist party on the basis of the peasantry and from the peasantry.

Nationalism   The slogans of the Bolshevik Revolution were both antinational and antiwar, but they were addressed against the top oligarchy. The Bolsheviks simply overthrew it and replaced it almost overnight. The revolution amounted to a swift replacement of the ruling elite by a revolutionary one. It was almost like a *putsch* though it had the most far-reaching social and economic consequences.

The situation in China was vastly different. First and foremost, the revolution took place over a long period of time in a two-front war against both the Japanese military forces, which had occupied the greater part of eastern China and against the Nationalist forces of the Kuomintang led by Chiang. The communists claimed to be the only truly national force, fighting not only the Japanese but, indirectly, the British and Americans who were supporting Chiang. Gradually, Chinese nationalism and China's independence became associated with the Communist party and Mao's People's Liberation Army.

---

5. "Report of an Investigation of the Peasant Movement in Hunan" (1927). In *Selected Readings from the Works of Mao Tse-tung.*

The Communist party broadened its appeal to include almost all those who were fighting the Japanese but who also favored full and un-qualified independence from all former imperialist forces—most notably the British and the Americans. Not only did they dig deep into the rich substratum of the peasantry, but their appeal was irrespective of class. The base of the revolution was broadened to include not only the workers and the peasants but also the middle classes, the intellectuals, and the lower middle classes. The "people" were defined in the broadest possible terms to include virtually all groups. The only "enemies" were the landlords and those who served the interests of the foreign powers, including, of course, those who collaborated with the Japanese.

Guerrilla War   In classic Leninist theory and practice a revolution is an act of force made by a trained, organized, and a highly disciplined revolu-tionary party (the Communist party) acting in the name of the working class. The revolution must be ruthless, just as it has to be swift. If successful, it will impose itself upon the society and the Communist party will assume all powers.

However, the broader definition of the "people" given by Mao, and the particular circumstances of the struggle for power in China, differen-tiate Maoism from this Leninist model. Mao relied on popular support and sustained collective effort. He put a premium on the motivation and the initiative of the masses more than on organization and discipline. Further-more, he knew that only one single uprising could not replace the ruling elite in China. The double struggle against both Japanese and Chiang could not be sustained without broad support. The Communist party could not monitor, let alone lead, every skirmish and every confrontation with its enemies. A certain degree of voluntarism and a great degree of decentralization were necessary and perhaps unavoidable. (We have noted that the same was the case with the Yugoslav Titoist movement when the partisans fought both against the Germans and the various collaborationist forces.)

Mao and his Communist party relied far more than did the Bolshe-viks on shaping "the minds and the souls" of the people, so that they would support his Liberation Army and provide the fighting forces with shelter, food, information, and new soldiers. In the long struggle which ultimately led to victory, a vast network of connections was built between the Communist party and the People's Liberation Army with the peasants and all other sections of the population. The Communist party spear-headed the movement, but the thrust of the spear depended on the strong links to social groups and the solidarity of supports that had developed.

Under these circumstances, then, the revolution in China was to be made over a long period of time. It was not to be simply the expression of force at a particular moment. To be sure, force is to all revolutionaries what the Bible is to missionaries: Mao's famous statement "Power comes from the barrel of the gun" shows that he had a great respect for force. But his theory of guerrilla warfare also shows that he understood the limitations of force and the gun when they do not take human factors into account: will, motivation, cooperation, initiative, moral support, and commitment. The barrel is empty without them. This is the basis of Mao's theory of guerrilla warfare; there must be the broadest possible participation, because unless the population is prepared and willing to give its support, fighting is impossible.

Chinese Communism in Flux

As some commentators have pointed out, what characterizes the communist regime in China thus far is a constant tug and pull between "institutionalization" and "transformation." The ideological goals of the regime still remain the transformation of social relations and the individual by establishing communism. Yet to do so, new institutions must be established in education, governance, the economy, and the army. However, institutionalization slows down change and inertia sets in; quite often vested interests develop which become obstacles to change. How can this be averted? Only by once more launching forth in the direction of transforming what is just barely institutionalized! The regime, founded on the commitment to change, becomes endangered by the very change to which it is committed.[6]

To allow a process of institutionalization that fosters and crystallizes hierarchical relations and a bureaucracy that becomes uncompromising toward popular needs, is to abandon hopes for transformation and change. Even more, it is going against the high hopes of Mao that popular participation and the tapping of the ingenuity and spontaneity of the people is the only safeguard of socialism. It is also to gradually give in to bureaucratic controls and directions similar to those existing in the Soviet system, and by so doing, to resort increasingly to force rather than relying on popular support.

There has been a high degree of fluidity, and at times downright instability if not chaos, in the development of the Chinese communist system. With the death of Mao and the virtual disappearance of all those who were in one way or another associated with the Long March and the civil war, a new generation may put the premium on institutionalization, stability, rapid industrialization, and modernization.

The following main ideological and institutional stages of the Chinese communist regime since its inception can be outlined:

1. A period of consolidation but also of education and mobilization in the principles of socialism (1949–1953).
2. The move in the direction of economic planning and socialism (1953–1956), followed by a period of liberalization known as the "Hundred Flowers" campaign.
3. A massive effort to industrialize — known as the "Great Leap Forward" (1957–1960).
4. A subsequent period of retreat from the goals of rapid industrialization that lasted until 1965, to be followed by

6. The thesis of institutionalization versus revolution is developed in Townsend's *Politics in China*. I am indebted to the author for many of my observations in this section.

5. The "Cultural Revolution" (1966–1969), again followed by a period of consolidation until 1972.
6. The period since Mao's death when, after a brief conflict between "moderate" leaders and "revolutionaries" (who hailed from the period of the Cultural Revolution and claimed to be Mao's intellectual heirs), the moderates have gained the upper hand. Their emphasis has been on stability, industrialization, and modernization, with the help of capitalist countries in western Europe, and even the United States itself.
7. In the 1980s we again witness a period of flux in which "capitalistic" incentives in the economy and especially in agriculture are being tried side by side with socialist modes of production—a period indeed in which China may alternate between the two.

The 13th Party Congress: Decline of Ideology?

The watershed in the evolution of China's communist regime was the 13th party Congress held in October 1987, long after Mao died. The party leadership was rejuvenated and communist ideology seriously qualified.

The way was shown by the party leader, Deng Xioping, 83 years old, who together with a number of his close associates of about the same age made way for younger leaders in the Politbureau. Together with Mao, Deng Xioping joined the party in 1920 when it was founded. They both saw the Bolshevik Revolution as a model for China to follow in order to attain its national independence; they accepted Stalin's formula of central bureaucratic planning as the best way toward modernization and industrialization; they both participated in the Great Leap Forward, which in the name of rapid industrialization caused havoc in the towns and the countryside. But Deng began to question the Stalinist model and when he took over the leadership of the party in 1979, he sought new formulas.

If it was the purpose of socialism to make China strong, industrialized, and independent, it was no longer ideology that counted but realizations. They were not encouraging. Deng proceeded to gradually dismantle the bureaucratic central controls. The rural communes gave place to private family farms, central planning to decentralization, and bureaucratic management to individual entrepreneurship—to independent units in production and trade where the managers would be able to allocate resources, including funds borrowed from state banks, at their discretion. The manager was to be free to fire and hire labor, buy the raw materials needed, develop and rationalize production with an eye to efficiency, and sell at the market. The profit shown would be the ultimate test of efficient management. The 13th Congress consecrated these changes formally and opened the way to new capitalist incentives. The economy has been growing at the rate of 8 percent a year, and during the last decade entrepreneurs have been thriving—in textiles, clothing, food processing, the services, glassware, and household utensils. In fact it is no longer the Soviet model that attracts the Chinese leaders. Rather, it is the model being used in South Korea, Japan, and Taiwan.

Another radical change that has taken place is the abandonment of Mao's policy of "self-reliance," similar in essence to Stalin's notion of "Socialism in One Country," whereby China would industrialize strictly from its own resources. China has now opened its doors to foreign investment and foreign trade, and trade with the outside world has increased sevenfold in the last few years. As a result, China now has the much needed foreign exchange to buy sophisticated technology and industrial equipment from abroad.

Does all this amount to the jettisoning of the communist ideology? Not quite. Political leadership and control remain in the hands of the Communist party. It maintains its political monopoly and can decide on the parameters of dissent it will allow and the degree of conformity it can exact. The economy is still under the control of the State: it owns the banks and all heavy industries. It channels investment on the basis of national priorities and despite concessions to the market, it can fix prices. But the political leadership has changed and its "ideology" is changing rapidly. The members of the Politbureau are much younger and far better educated than their predecessors—40 percent of them are engineers. For most of them Mao is simply a legend and Maoism a legacy to be preserved as a symbol of the national unity forged by his revolution. For the new leadership, the first priority now is modernization. How to catch up with the twentieth century before moving on into the twenty-first.

Modernization and growth, however, will be made in "Chinese colors" to suit Chinese needs. Pragmatic considerations will count above everything else—even the communist ideology. What "colors," one might ask? Again, Deng gave the best answer, which may well prove to be his own legacy in the future. It is not the color of the cat, he reputedly said, that counts. "It is whether or not she catches mice." Pragmatic considerations will be entertained, including individual economic freedoms, if they bring about modernization and growth in the economy. The cat may change many colors before this is done!

Conclusion

All regimes that spring from revolutionary ideology, and which take power through revolution, are shaped by the way in which they first managed to acquire power. The Bolshevik Revolution was the work of a handful of men and women who believed in organization and for whom the party was a paramilitary instrument for the conquest of power. The Russian communists, once in power, used the party as an army of a highly centralized political organization, governing the country from the top down through a highly centralized and bureaucratized apparatus.

The Chinese Revolution, on the other hand, and the communist takeover of power in China, was the work of a vast popular movement of guerrilla warfare that involved, in one form or another, virtually the whole of the countryside and many of the urban populations. Victory was won thanks to popular support and participation. To maintain their leadership, therefore, the communist leaders and the party have had to go back to the people, so to speak, to mobilize them, organize them, and work with them and for them. Coercion has been widely used but it could not in the long run succeed. It is education in socialism and mobilization for socialism that is best able to bring forth popular support.

This is perhaps the distinctive trait of Chinese communism.[7] Its ultimate goal is to provide and generate incentives and participation—to fashion men and women who ultimately become convinced of the advantages of a communist society. The building of socialism and the transformation of the individual must go hand in hand. But what if individuals begin to turn away from the socialist framework? And what if individual criticism and dissent begin to question the very citadel of power—the Communist party and its leadership?

The constant shifts and changes underlined by massive appeals to the party rank and file, and the people, together with the frequent attacks against bureaucratization and centralization, indicate that the system is seeking a middle ground between freedoms and constraints, between participation and repression, between orthodoxy and experimentation. It is still going through a period of change and transformation. The Chinese regime is still in flux.

Eurocommunism

The term Eurocommunism has been used to describe and identify new common trends, ideological and political, which have appeared since 1975 or earlier among some European communist parties within the western democracies, and particularly in France, Italy, and Spain. Eurocommunism represents a departure from the basic doctrinal and tactical guidelines of international communism as set forth in the twenty-one conditions, particularly the assertion of an independent stance vis-à-vis the Soviet Union.

Class Struggle

Eurocommunists began to reconsider the principle of class struggle, which, as we saw, is of crucial importance to the thinking of Marx and Lenin. The reasons are many. The distinction between the working class and "capitalists" is not as marked in advanced industrialized societies as it has been in the past. The vast majority of the gainfully employed are salaried—they form a large new middle class. The composition and income of the working class has changed radically to allow for relatively high incomes for skilled and white-collar workers, whose mentality and outlook also became increasingly middle class. The democratic process also

---

7. For a general discussion of Mao's political ideology and its implications, see Schram, *The Political Thought of Mao Tse-tung.*

bridges the gap between workers and capitalists and allows the communists, in combination with other parties, to seek, and hopefully to obtain,
political power. Eurocommunists, therefore, increasingly take a reformist
attitude, advocating change, compromise, "advanced democracy," a
"popular union" with other left-wing parties—not in order to establish
socialism but in order to form a government to prepare the conditions from
which socialism will develop.

Revolution

Electoral politics, the agreement of the communists and other left-wing
forces of European countries to seek power peacefully and through the
ballot, makes revolution obsolete. Eurocommunists no longer wish to take
power by force or to impose one class upon the rest of the society. They
prefer to cooperate with other groups to form a majority in parliament.
Antonio Gramsci, the Italian communist leader and theoretician, advocated the tactics of a broad penetration of various socioeconomic groups by
the communists to gain popular support and acceptance. Over recent
years the French communists abandoned their commitment to class and
revolutionary politics in favor of a broad "popular union." Communist
leaders there joined the Socialist government between 1981 and 1985. In
Italy, from 1974 to 1979 the famous "historical compromise" amounted to
a political cooperation of the communists with their archrivals, the Christian Democrats.

Parliamentary Democracy?

Many Eurocommunists therefore seemed to accept the logic of majoritarianism and the principles of democracy. The Italian communist leader
Enrico Berlinguer went further, stating that even if the Italian Communist
party got 51 percent of the vote they could not govern against the other 49
percent! He accepted the tactics of compromise and the necessity of getting
support from as wide a sector of the population as possible.

French Communists accepted the principle of governmental "alter-
nation," promising that they would accept the popular verdict: there
could be no question of dictatorship. The Spanish Communist leader (but
not the Portuguese one) committed himself to electoral and democratic
politics, and went so far as to accept the monarchy in Spain. They all agree
to respect the freedom of association and parties as well as individual and
political freedoms.

Democratic Centralism and Avant-Gardism

The principle of democratic centralism, as we noted earlier, makes for
hierarchical and leadership control within the Communist party and does
not allow the formation of factions. The party thus assumes a paramilitary

character, stressing obedience of lower-ranking organs to superior ones, and ultimately to the leader of the party. It is this democratic centralism that differentiates the Communist party from all other political parties, including the socialists. It is a practice that safeguards unity and militancy, which is necessary for a party committed to revolution and a dictatorship. The party is the "avant-garde" of the proletariat and the masses, leading them to socialism.

It would have seemed natural, therefore, for the European communist parties with their new profession of faith in democracy to have relaxed a rigorous application of democratic centralism and to allow for an open and free debate within their ranks. This has not come to pass. In fact the French Communist party silences all internal criticisms and does not allow its daily newspaper to publish articles of party members critical of the leadership and suggesting new policies. The same has generally been the case with the Spanish and the Portuguese communist parties, and even of the Italian party. The Eurocommunist parties do not seem ready to abandon their tight organization, discipline, and leadership control.

National Communism?

Ever since the death of Stalin the control of the Soviet Communist party over all European communist parties has progressively declined. National forces, as we have seen first with Tito, weakened Soviet control until it had to be reaffirmed through military intervention—in Hungary in 1956 and again in Czechoslovakia in 1968. But western European communist parties, the Italian one first and foremost, began to reassert their own intellectual and political independence in developing their program and their course of action. Their belief is that communism should manifest itself in its national colors, independently of Moscow.

A National Foreign Policy?

Will Eurocommunist parties in the name of the rediscovery of their "national colors" defend foreign policies independent of Soviet ones and even contrary to them? Or will they stay close to their previous line by identifying the interests of communism and the working class with the interests and policies of the Soviet Union? This may well be the ultimate test of the genuineness of the professed independence of the communist parties.

No clear answers can be given as yet. The establishment of a military dictatorship in Poland with the full support of the Soviet leadership in December 1981, however, may give us a clue—especially since the dictatorship had been directed against the newly formed Polish Trade Union, Solidarity. The French Communist party led the way for many European communist parties—including those of Portugal and Greece—in fully condoning the military coup and in giving its full support to the Soviet Union. It also supported the Soviet military invasion of Afghanistan in December 1980. On the other hand, the Italian Communist party sharply criticized

the Soviet Union for its moves both in Poland and Afghanistan and virtually accused the Soviet leadership of imperialist practices. The Spanish
Communist party followed the Italian lead. However, it has been going
through a severe internal crisis during which its leader and the foremost
exponent of Eurocommunism, Santiago Carrillo, was forced to resign. Similarly pro-Soviet factions maintain their control of the French Communist
party. Thus, Eurocommunism is still torn between its Soviet attachment
and its search for a truly European and independent stance.

Bibliography

Adamson, Walter L. *Hegemony and Revolution: A Study of Antonio Gramsci's Political
Theory.* Berkeley: University of California Press, 1980.

Barnett, A. Doak. *Communist China: The Early Years, 1949–1955.* New York: Praeger,
1964.

Bicanic, Rudolf. *Economic Policy in Socialist Yugoslavia.* New York: Cambridge U.P.,
1973.

Boggs, Carle, and Plotke, David. *The Politics of Eurocommunism: Socialism in Transition.* Boston: South End Press, 1980.

Brown, Bernard E. (ed.). *Eurocommunism and Eurosocialism:The Left Confronts Modernity.* New York: Cyrco Press, 1979.

Carrillo, Santiago. *Eurocommunism and the State.* New York: Lawrence Hill, 1978.

Chang, Parris, H. *Power and Policy in China.* University Park: Pennsylvania State
U.P., 1975.

Chen, Jack. *Inside the Cultural Revolution.* New York: Macmillan, 1975.

Claudin, Fernando. *Eurocommunism and Socialism.* Translated by John Wakeham.
London: New Left Books, 1978.

Dedijer, Vladimir. *Tito Speaks.* London: Weidenfeld and Nicolson, 1953.

Deleyne, Jan. *The Chinese Cultural Revolution.* Translated by Robert Leriche. London: Deutsch, 1973.

Denitch, Bogdan. *The Legitimization of a Revolution: The Yugoslav Case.* New Haven,
Conn.: Yale U.P., 1972.

Documents of Dissent: Chinese Political Thought since Mao. Translated by J. Chester
Cheng. Stanford, Calif.: Hoover Institute Press, 1980.

Drachkovitch, Milorad (ed.). *Marxism in the Modern World.* Stanford, Calif.: Stanford
U.P., 1965.

Fitzgerald, C. P. *Mao Tse-tung and China.* New York: Homer and Meir, 1976.

Godson, Roy, and Hasler, Stephen. *Eurocommunism: Implications for East and West.*
New York: St. Martin's Press, 1978.

Gramsci, Antonio. *The Modern Prince and Other Writings.* New York: International
Publishers, 1957.

———. *Letters from Prison.* Translated and edited by Lynne Lawner. New York:
Harper & Row, 1973.

———. *Selections from Political Writings (1919–1920).* Edited by Quinton Hoare.
Translated by John Mathews. London: Lawrence & Wishart, 1977.

Griffith, Samuel B. *Mao Tse-tung: On Guerrilla Warfare.* New York: Praeger, 1961.

Griffith, William E. (ed.). *Communism in Europe* (2 vols.). Cambridge, Mass.: M.I.T.
Press, 1967.

Joll, James. *Antonio Gramsci.* New York: Penguin, 1977.

Kaplan, Morton A. *The Many Faces of Communism.* New York: Free Press, 1978.

Karol, K. S. *The Second Chinese Revolution.* Translated by Mervyn Jones. London: Jonathan Cape, 1975.

Kriegel, Annie. *Eurocommunism: A New Kind of Communism?* Translated by Peter S. Stern. Stanford, Calif.: Hoover Institute Press, 1978.

Lange, Peter, and Vannicelli, Maurizio. *The Communist Parties of Italy, France and Spain: Postwar Change and Continuity: A Casebook.* Winchester, Mass.: Allen & Unwin, Inc., 1981.

Leonard, Wolfgang. *Eurocommunism: Challenge for East and West.* New York: Holt, Rinehart and Winston, 1979.

Mao Tse-tung. *Selected Readings from the Works of Mao Tse-tung.* Peking: Foreign Languages Press, 1971.

Pellicani, Luciano. *Gramsci: An Alternative Communism.* Stanford, Calif.: Hoover Institute Press, 1981.

Price, R. F. *Education in Communist China.* rev. ed. London: Routledge & Kegan Paul, 1976.

Rakovski, Marc. *Towards an East European Marxism.* New York: St. Martin's Press, 1978.

Schram Stuart (ed.). *The Political Thought of Mao Tse-tung.* New York: Praeger, 1963.

Sher, Gerson S. *Praxis: Marxist Criticism and Dissent in Socialist Yugoslavia.* Bloomington: Indiana U. P., 1977.

Tannahill, Neil. *Communist Parties of Western Europe: A Comparative Study.* Westport, Conn.: Greenwood Press, 1978.

Townsend, James R. *Politics in China.* 2d ed. Boston: Little, Brown, 1981.

Ulam, Adam. *Titoism and the Cominform.* Cambridge, Mass.: Harvard U.P., 1952.

Urban, G. R. (ed.). *Eurocommunism: Its Roots and Future in Italy and Elsewhere.* New York: Universe, 1978.

Zukin, Sharon. *Beyond Marx and Tito: Theory and Practice in Yugoslav Socialism.* Cambridge, England: Cambridge U.P., 1975.

Part Three

Nazism and Fascism: The Totalitarian Right

Preventing the sick from making the healthy sick . . . this ought to be our supreme object in this world . . . But for this it is above all essential that the healthy should remain separate from the sick, that they should not even associate with the sick. . . .

NIETZSCHE   The Genealogy of Morals

Right wing totalitarian movements like those of the Nazis and Fascists developed everywhere in Europe soon after World War I. They spread to central Europe, Portugal, Spain, and the Balkans in the 1930s. They affected countries with strong democratic traditions like France, and even England. Liberal democracy was threatened everywhere.

The Fascist and Nazi regimes did away with some of the most basic freedoms that the civilized world had built up over many centuries. They proclaimed force at home and war in the international community as the highest of values. Their discrimination against certain races, nations, and creeds was taken to the point of not only advocating, but actually implementing, their methodical destruction.

As often pointed out, right-wing totalitarianism is couched in terms of negative themes: against liberalism, against individualism, against reason, against equality, against parliamentary institutions, against democracy, against international law, against the bourgeois society and its culture, and against big cities. The twentieth-century right-wing movements signified a culmination and a synthesis of a multiplicity of "antis," most of which were developed throughout the nineteenth century, side by side with the development of liberal democratic thought and democratic regimes. They are also based on a body of thought that is deeply antirational, stressing the importance of emotions and intuition as opposed to scientific inquiry and reason, and seeking to find in communitarian values and solidarity the key to political obligations and stability.

In this part we shall give an overview of the intellectual roots of nazism and fascism and discuss their ideology. We shall also outline some of the extremist right-wing movements in the United States and note briefly the resurgence of the extreme right in Europe.

8 | Nazism and Fascism: The Background

(Fascism) . . . is the general reaction of modern times
against the flabby materialistic positivism of the
nineteenth century.
      BENITO MUSSOLINI   The Doctrine of Fascism

Nazism and fascism, like the other totalitarian regimes and extremist right-wing movements that developed in Europe and elsewhere after World War I, had deep roots. They did not spring from the wickedness of a leader such as Hitler; they were not the product of deviant personalities; they were not initiated by adventurers and veterans of World War I seeking redemption from defeat or boredom. In fact, they were well-organized and well-structured political movements representing, at one and the same time, a very powerful reaction against both liberal democracy and communism and the communist parties that had developed in the wake of the Bolshevik Revolution. They were movements that reaffirmed, in the strongest possible terms, national solidarity and unity, order and discipline. They drew heavily from the body of antidemocratic and antiliberal thought, and from the ideology and practice of Leninism.

In other words, right-wing totalitarian movements and regimes cannot be dismissed as exceptions to the democratic norm any more than communist totalitarian systems. They drew their inspiration, whatever the specific historical circumstances that brought them to power, from deep roots that had been planted in fertile soil. These roots have not yet been fully removed. We must not consider nazism and fascism something that happened in the past and should be forgotten but as a political ideology that is still with us. The ideology and the movements they generated remain alive.

The Intellectual Roots

Many authors, philosophers, sociologists, anthropologists, and political scientists contributed to the formulation of an antiliberal and antidemocratic body of doctrine. Some would have taken pride in the movements and regimes that borrowed from their thinking; others would have rejected them outright as a gross distortion of what they had thought, written, and taught. The major ideas used by the right-wing parties were elitism, racialism, Social Darwinism, irrationalism, the exaltation of violence, the notion that the group has a reality superseding that of the individual, and nationalism. Lenin's conception of a revolutionary party based on will also played an important role, as did the reaction against industrialization by many social groups who felt threatened by it.

Elitism

Liberal assumptions of equality and participation had not been accepted by many conservatives. The latter spoke in terms of natural leaders, that is, persons with special endowments and with a special stake in the country that entitled them to have special leadership roles. Throughout the nineteenth century a number of authors advanced new arguments to justify the rule of the few, whether by government or by an elite, and they believed that the majority was simply incapable of self-government.

Elites derive superiority from intelligence, knowledge, manipulative skills, or from sheer physical courage. One sociologist distinguishes between gifted individuals and the mass of mediocrities who follow them.[1] He asserts that competition takes place only among elites—the people follow like sheep. Democracy, he claims, is nonsense, a better name for it would be "mobocracy." Robert Michels, in a much-quoted book on political parties, had observed and documented the same phenomenon of elitism within socialist parties that claimed to be open, egalitarian, and democratic.[2] They were run by an elite. In all such organizations there is an "iron law" of oligarchy.

The German philosopher Nietzsche reached even more extreme conclusions. He identified leadership with the "heroic man" who has the will to power and the desire to dominate. The "superman," he predicted, would emerge and rise to power to impose his law and his will upon the "spineless multitude" with its Christian "slave morality." The future belonged to heroes unconstrained by law and conventional morality who would set their own morality and make their own law for all to follow. Lenin, too, without subscribing to the "superman" theory, emphasized that only a few, an elite, could organize the Communist party and speak on behalf of the workers and lead them to the promised land of communism.

1. Vilfredo Pareto, *The Mind and Society.* New York: Dowe, 1963.
2. Robert Michels, *Political Parties.* New York: Free Press, 1962.

Irrationalism

Early in the nineteenth century another German philosopher wrote a book characteristically enough entitled *The World as Will and Idea*.[3] It began with the ominous phrase, "The world is my idea. . . . " What this means is that rational and scientific discourse is inadequate to provide us with the understanding of the world surrounding us and that "knowledge" is a matter of intuitive communication that alone can provide full "understanding." Knowledge thus becomes entirely subjective. Much later, the French philosopher Bergson also stressed the intuitive aspects of learning—the mystical communication of the subject with the outside object.[4] It is thanks to intuition that we "know" an object by "entering into it." Science, reason, measurements, observation give us only a relative, partial, and fragmented knowledge; intuition supplies an "absolute" one. . . . "The spirit has never had more violence done to it than when mere numbers made themselves its master," wrote Adolf Hitler.

Myths and Violence

But what is the relevance of intuition or instinct to politics? Simply that logic, persuasion, and argument cannot move people and cannot sustain a political system. In politics the counterpart of intuition is the "myth," that is, an idea, a symbol, a slogan that moves people into action because it appeals to their emotions. They become attached to it and they feel for it. The "crowd" or the "masses" act and can be much more easily moved when their emotions are aroused. They act in terms of stereotypes, prejudices, and instincts, not in terms of reason and proof. The myth unites them and gives purpose and meaning to their lives far better than logical exposition and reasoning. After all, it was the great philosopher Plato who had defined a myth as a "golden lie" to be propagated by the philosopher king in order to keep the people united and under control. All people were to be taught that they were brothers and sisters because they had the same parents, and were to accept inequalities as natural. Myths can take a variety of forms—racial supremacy, racial purity, national superiority and strength, the dictatorship of the proletariat, the resurrection of ancient empires, the reassertion of tribal bonds, the emergence of the superman, and so on.

Georges Sorel, the French revolutionary syndicalist (1857–1922), used the myth explicitly as a vehicle for moral, economic, and social revival.[5] The myth that he considered as potent as the Christian belief in the Second Coming was that of the general strike, by which he meant the development of a state of mind among the workers favoring the violent

---

3. Arthur Schopenhauer, *The World as Will and Idea*. Translated by E. P. Payne, New York: Dover, 1968.
4. Henri Bergson, *The Two Sources of Morality and Religion*. Notre Dame, Ind.: University of Notre Dame Press, p. 177.
5. Georges Sorel, *Reflections on Violence*. New York: Macmillan, 1961.

destruction of the existing social order. Violence would organize the workers, form the battle lines, and marshal them to war against the society. Their "sentiments," properly aroused by an elite, would lead to revolution. The myth of the general strike, therefore, called for a state of permanent violence. Violence, Sorel argued, is ennobling in itself, but it also helps people develop the moral courage to distinguish them from bourgeois cowardice and rationality. He wrote:

> Proletarian violence, carried on as pure and simple manifestation of the sentiments of class war, appears . . . a very fine and heroic thing; it is at the service of the immemorial interests of civilization. . . . It may . . . save the world from barbarism.[6]

Lenin never accepted Sorel's overall philosophy, but he nonetheless endorsed the need for violence.

Social Darwinism

Charles Darwin's theory of evolution and the notion of the survival of the fittest was quickly, and unwarrantedly, transferred to the social and the international order. In its new setting it became known as Social Darwinism. According to Darwin, "survival" means that some species survive while others perish in the course of adjusting, or failing to adjust, to the environment and to each other. Transposed to human society the term was taken to mean that those who manage to survive or to succeed are superior to those who are unsuccessful or perish. Conflict between individuals and groups, and especially races and nations was declared to be a natural and necessary process for the selection of the best and the elimination of the weak and incompetent. The elites in power arrive at their position through struggle; but they are likely to be displaced through struggle if they begin to lose the qualities that brought them to the top. The struggle for survival is likely to affect them just as it affected the dinosaurs.

Social Darwinism has been used by liberals to justify economic competition and economic individualism. Right-wing totalitarianism has used it to justify competition and conflict, especially among elite races and nations, and to legitimize the supremacy of some individuals on the grounds of biological superiority. Some nations are considered superior to others and need more territory than others; some races are considered superior to others. Those that are superior are the "master race," while those that are inferior are the "slave races."

Throughout the nineteenth century, sympathy for racial theories was widespread, and Social Darwinism reinforced previously developed racist theories. French and British authors had discoursed on racial differences and were responsible for the establishment of cultural, biological, and moral criteria of superiority and inferiority. They concluded that the

---

6. Cited in Lane W. Lancaster, *Masters of Political Thought*, Vol. 3. Boston: Houghton Mifflin, p. 296.

Concentration camps; death camps; prisons and cemeteries. This photo taken at Auschwitz is a poignant reminder of what the "One Thousand Year Reich" would have meant. (*Photo: Stock Boston/Berndt*)

white race, and some of its various branches, was superior. The Nazi regime came to a most horrifying decision to exterminate the Jews—a fate that was also reserved for other "inferior races."

The Group Mind

As we pointed out, liberalism freed individuals from all attachments to groups and status that defined and structured their activities. The individual became the driving force within the social and political system. The formation of associations, and even the existence of the State, was traced ultimately to contractual and voluntary relations and individual consent. There was nothing "real" outside of the individual, to whose will, consent, and rationality all economic, political, and social institutions were traced. Throughout the nineteenth century, however, this position was strongly contested by those who argued that "individuals," as such, were a mere fiction, and that their ideas and values, and ultimately their reasoning, derived from group values. Marx argued, too, that individual attitudes and ideas were determined by the class to which an individual belonged.

Anthropologists and sociologists claimed to have discovered the "group mind" in tribal groups. People living in tribal societies could not clearly distinguish between "I" and "we"; individual morality, value judgments, and attitudes coincided fully with tribal or collective values and attitudes. In this way the group was larger than its parts, the individuals, and preceded them. Even more, group and collective ideas had a coercive character: the individuals were constrained by them, and their lives were to be understood only in terms of conformity and compliance to such groups. It was group solidarity, not individual morality, that counted most.

Thus, studying and understanding groups was a better way of understanding society than studying the individual who was nothing else but the sum total of the group images and pressures weighing upon him. Only the group was real. It took but one step to move to larger collectivities, notably the nation. The nation was real and not the individuals who made it; the morality of the nation was the morality of the individual; individual judgments had to yield to national judgments and imperatives. Therefore, the nation and nationalism became a superior moral force.

Escape from Freedom

Erich Fromm published a melancholic book in 1941, entitled *Escape from Freedom*. He claimed that there was one basic psychological need that liberalism had ignored. It was the individual's desire to belong, to be attached to groups or to hierarchies that make decisions, and to be part of the whole with fixed obligations to it and fixed rights deriving from it. Feudalism had provided such a setting, and its destruction had uprooted the individuals from their traditional groupings. Individuals found themselves desperately in need of similar ties to anchor their existence — ties that liberalism and industrialization had broken. Totalitarianism was in essence a return to group values and to authority; it was a response to the intense need for "belongingness," which, he claimed, was much stronger than reason and self-interest. Liberalism and the historical phase of liberalism were therefore nothing but an interlude between the structured life of the feudal society of the past and the subjection to the totalitarian regimes of the future. The latter amounted to a revolt of the individuals against the burdens of freedom and free choice that liberalism had imposed upon them.

Against the Bourgeois Mentality

Bourgeois values were a major target of criticism throughout the nineteenth century. The peaceful but unheroic existence of the citizen; the constant search for material gains and satisfactions; the compromising spirit that democratic liberalism fosters; the smugness of the wealthy and their ability to manipulate representative institutions to their advantage, while paying lip service to equality and freedom; the subordination of all values to material considerations — all this was repugnant to many intellectuals and philosophers, as well as workers. In a reaction, many writers extolled courage, violence, emotions, and instincts. They sought to find new binding ties in common adventures that liberalism downgraded and to help the "true" individual realize himself or herself; to find a way of life that was closer to nature but further away from reason; closer to instinct

The "group mind" in action: the Führer arrives at a mass rally, Nuremburg, 1935. (*Photo: Wide World Photos*)

and intuition but further away from material interests; closer to feeling but away from science. It was in essence an exaltation of bygone romantic values of valor, adventure, and physical strength.

The Historical Setting

As we have pointed out, ideas may hibernate for a long time until the right conditions bring them back to life and transform them into political ideologies and movements. This was the case with the antiliberal and antidemocratic ideas outlined above. Until World War I, democratic liberalism and democratic liberal regimes remained strong. Even socialist parties had joined, for all practical purposes, democratic practices and regimes. Rightwing extremist movements received only little support.

It took two major upheavals to transform totalitarian ideologies into powerful movements and for liberal democracy to find itself on the defensive almost everywhere.

World War I accounted for unprecedented destruction, loss of life, and socioeconomic and political upheavals throughout Europe. It spawned bitterness and distrust in the political institutions of almost all countries involved—both the defeated and the victorious, with the possible exception of England and the United States. In Russia it created the conditions that accounted for the triumph of the Bolshevik Revolution in November 1917. In Germany the semiauthoritarian system collapsed to give place to a democratic constitution, but conditions remained chaotic and democracy was never given a genuine chance to gain respectability. Defeat haunted many Germans, and the democratic constitution established in 1918 was for them the symbol of defeat. In France a strong communist faction emerged and divisions between the left and the right became sharper. Italy (a latecomer in the war on the side of the victorious powers) felt betrayed by its allies when it came to the final settlement at the Treaty of Versailles. In central and eastern Europe extreme left-wing radicalism, often supported by Russian communism, alternated for a while with right-wing authoritarian reactions.

The war brought forth new popular demands and had serious political implications. The people of all nations were mobilized into the war effort. They fought for four years in the trenches where a new spirit of egalitarianism and camaraderie were fashioned and where distinctions of birth, wealth, and education were blurred. Wartime sacrifices were translated into demands for a better life and more comforts, and these were pressed hard on national governments. Failure to provide them brought quick political reaction, and more often direct and violent action. Resentment increased and took the form of left- or right-wing extremism. In some countries, as in Russia, the "system" broke down; in others, notably in Germany, inflation deprived a great number of people (particularly the middle classes) of their savings and their pensions, and dislocated economic activity. The liberal democratic states seemed unable to cope.

The Great Depression

It is against this background that the Great Depression of 1929 should be assessed. The depression was particularly severe in Germany, where almost half the labor force found itself without jobs. But throughout the whole of central Europe, as well as in France and England, unemployment spread. The faith in liberal economic and political institutions was severely shaken. For the left, depression was a clear indication that Marx had been right in foreseeing the collapse of capitalism. For the right wing, the depression was an equally clear manifestation that liberal economic and political institutions could no longer function. A new formula was needed, avoiding both Marxist revolutionary politics and putting an end to economic liberalism.

The remedy suggested was that of a strong State which would overcome internal divisions and cleavages: a new economic system that would set aside private interests and even private profit in favor of unity and cooperation with common social and national goals. It was the formula used in Italy by the Fascists and in Germany by the Nazis, and by all other right-wing nationalist movements throughout Europe.

Because of the depression it appealed to a growing number of people and voters. Unemployed workers, farmers, the lower middle classes, and particularly the middle classes, war veterans, university students, found the combination of nationalist and unifying slogans, together with the promise of economic reform, irresistible. Status quo groups, fearing loss of status, joined forces with the disaffected, the romantics, the nationalists, and the unemployed. During the period of the depression, right-wing extremism swelled into powerful political movements everywhere.

Special Reasons

There were other reasons for right-wing totalitarianism's victorious emergence in Italy and Germany. In both countries, as well as in many others that followed their example, democracy had never gained legitimacy. Elites, intellectuals, associations, and interest groups never developed a strong working attachment to democratic regimes. They had not become integrated into the system. Neither the educational system nor the family socialized the young into the principles and practices of democracy. As a result, both the Italian Republic and the German democratic constitution were faced with hostility and indifference instead of affection and support. Nationalism in both countries remained a powerful force. Germany's defeat and the nonrealization of national claims for Italy intensified the search for nationalist solutions.

The economic difficulties facing these countries right after World War I and the inability of their political institutions to cope with them, to provide employment and to arrest inflation, further undermined whatever attachment the people had to democracy.

Similarly, the existence of strong communist parties in both countries played a dominant role. A sharp reaction against them was couched in strong nationalist terms. There was also a strong resentment against the Versailles Treaty, which settled the war, imposed heavy reparation payments upon Germany, and gave the victorious powers—England, France, and the United States—a dominant position in world affairs.

If we review the various factors that accounted for the coming and spread of right-wing totalitarianism in a number of European countries, we find the following:

1. Defeat or feeling of deprivation in and after World War I in 1918
2. Intensification of nationalism because of the relatively late national unification (Italy and Germany)
3. Inflation, unemployment, and in general, economic depression

4. Loss of status among low-middle and middle classes or fear of further deterioration of their position
5. Fear of strong communist and revolutionary movements and parties
6. Reaction against the international order and the settlement after World War I
7. Lack of legitimacy of democratic institutions

Thus the stage had been set for the eruption of powerful and anti-democratic and antiliberal totalitarian mass movements. The individual and the individualistic ethic, which had hardly come into their own, were shoved aside in the name of the group, the party, and the nation. What Aristotle had termed "reason without passion" — the law — to regulate human intercourse and to safeguard peaceful and stable relationships was to become a laughing stock subject to the whim and caprice of political leaders and tyrants.

Bibliography

Abel, Theodore. *The Nazi Movement: Why Hitler Came to Power.* New York: Atherton, 1965.

Adorno, T. W., et al. *The Authoritarian Personality.* New York: Norton, 1969.

Arendt, Hanna. *The Origins of Totalitarianism.* New York: Harcourt Brace and World, 1968.

De Felice, Renzo. *Fascism: An Informal Introduction to Its Theory and Practice.* New Brunswick, N. J.: Transaction Books, 1976.

Delzell, Charles F. (ed.). *Mediterranean Fascism 1919–1949.* New York: Walker and Co., 1971.

Friedrich, Carl J. (ed.). *Totalitarianism.* Cambridge, Mass.: Harvard U.P., 1954.

————, and Brzezinski, Zbigniew. *Totalitarian Dictatorship and Autocracy.* 2d ed. New York: Praeger, 1965.

Fromm, Erich. *Escape from Freedom.* 1941. Reprint. New York: Avon Books, 1965.

Gregor, A. James. *The Ideology of Fascism.* New York: Free Press, 1969.

Hitler, Adolf. *Mein Kampf.* Boston: Houghton Mifflin, 1962.

Laqueur, Walter (ed.). *Fascism: A Reader's Guide.* Berkeley: University of California Press, 1976.

Mosse, George L. *The Crisis of German Ideology: Intellectual Origins of the Third Reich.* 1964. Reprint. New York: Fertig, 1978.

Mussolini, Benito. "The Doctrine of Fascism." In *Communism, Fascism, and Democracy,* edited by Carl Cohen. 2d ed. New York: Random House, 1972.

Nietzsche, Friedrich. *Beyond Good and Evil.* New York: Vintage, 1956.

————. *Thus Spoke Zarathustra.* Baltimore, Md.: Penguin, 1961.

————. *The Will to Power.* New York: Vintage, 1968.

Oakeshott, Michael. *The Social and Political Doctrines of Contemporary Europe.* New York: Cambridge U.P., 1942.

Shirer, William L. *The Nightmare Years, 1930–1940.* Boston: Little, Brown, 1984.

Talmon, J. L. *The Origins of Totalitarian Democracy.* New York: Norton, 1970.

Turner, Henry Ashby. *German Big Business and the Rise of Hitler.* New York: Oxford University Press, 1985.

Weber, Eugen. *Varieties of Fascism.* New York: Van Nostrand, 1964.

Woolf, S. J. (ed.). *European Fascism.* New York: Vintage, 1969.

9 | Nazism and Fascism: Ideologies and Regimes

For the Weltanshauung *(the ideology) is intolerant
... and peremptorily demands its own, exclusive,
and complete recognition as well as the complete
adaptation of public life to its ideas.*
                    ADOLF HITLER   Mein Kampf

The intellectual background of antiliberal and antidemocratic thought and the particular historical circumstances in Europe after World War I affected all nations—particularly Germany and Italy. It is in these two countries that the special reasons we mentioned triggered powerful totalitarian movements. It is to these two movements and regimes, the Nazis and the Fascists, that we turn now.

The Nazi movement and regime are discussed first, despite the fact that the Italian Fascists came to power a decade earlier, because Nazism was far more "successful" in accomplishing what it professed. Italian fascism was less comprehensive and far less effective in mobilizing society. But the Nazis managed to bring virtually all Germans and all elements of German society under their control. Germans were made to "march in step" to the tune of the Nazi party. This was the meaning of the famous term *gleichschaltung*—the "synchronization" of all aspects of social life with the political ideology and objectives of the Nazi party. Not so in Fascist Italy. Many did not march at all, while others dragged their feet, and still others marched to different tunes than the one played by the Fascist party. It was said that the Italian Fascists made the Italian trains run on time; Hitler and the Nazis made the nation run in unison into disaster.

German Totalitarianism

A historian of Germany entitles his chapter on German National Socialism "Germany Goes Berserk."[1] It is only a mild comment on what occurred in

1. K. S. Pinson, *Modern Germany*, 2d ed. New York: Macmillan, 1966.

one of the most advanced and civilized nations of the world. Nazism should be a constant reminder to all of us—no matter how special the conditions in Germany appear to have been—how fragile the bonds of reason and law are and how vulnerable we *all* may be to political fanaticism under certain circumstances.

German totalitarianism became a political reality when the leader of the National Socialist Workers' German party, Adolf Hitler, came to power in January 1933. Hitler immediately set about organizing the new system, the Third Reich,[2] implementing many of the promises he had made. Most notably these included the abolition of the institutions of democracy and the preparation for an expansionist war to establish German worldwide domination.

The Road to Power

The beginnings of the Hitler movement can be traced directly to the aftermath of World War I, and also to the rich background of German antidemocratic literature and right-wing political extremism.

Defeat in World War I caused a great disillusionment and eventually a desire for revenge. The discontent was focused on the Versailles Treaty, which had stripped Germany of its colonies and imposed a heavy burden of reparations, but there were also other factors. First, the galloping inflation of the early 1920s was unprecedented in the economic history of any nation. The inflation wiped out savings, pensions, and trust funds and made salaries and wages dwindle with the passage of every day, week, and month. It created a state of acute panic among the middle classes.

A second important factor was the reaction to communist revolutionary movements. Revolutions actually took place right after World War I, and communist regimes were installed temporarily in parts of Germany. Private groups and armies, led by officers and war veterans, took it upon themselves to stop the leftists. Often aided by the police and whatever remained of the German Army, they began to wage war against the communists and their sympathizers. Many of these veterans and their organizations rallied to the Nazis and formed the hard core of the Nazi party.

The Nazi party was founded in 1921 as the extension of the German Workers' party (DAP) over which Hitler managed to gain control. Its original program included the usual nationalist and racist themes but also promised social and economic reforms that were downright socialist: land reform, nationalizations, and the "breaking of the shackles of capitalism." It also attacked the political and economic elites, and identified the "domestic" and "outside" enemies of Germany as the victorious powers—notably England and France, the Jews and "international Jewry." It was a small party at first—a sect, with not more than a few thousand members as was quite typical of many other extremist nationalist groups. Few paid

---

2. Third Reich was an expression intentionally used to indicate continuity with the German Empire (1871–1918) and the Holy Roman Empire.

Adolf Hitler (1889–1945)

The Führer, ironically enough, was a non-German. Hitler was born in Austria in 1889. A poor student given to prolonged moods of melancholia and daydreaming, he found himself in the army where he served with the rank of a corporal with apparent diligence and courage. Defeat enraged him and he sought scapegoats in the "cowardice" of the civilians and the "conspiracy" of the Jews. Without any formal education—he wanted to be an architect and tried painting—he had read much of the great nationalist literature.

  After World War I he found himself in Munich, capital of Bavaria, where he founded the NDASP (the Nazi party) in 1921. After the abortive effort to seize power in 1923, he received a light sentence and spent the months of his imprisonment writing what became the political bible of Nazism, *Mein Kampf* (My Struggle). It was the Depression and the frustrations and political conflict associated with it that provided the climate for his ascent to power. On January 30, 1933, President Hindenburg asked him to become Chancellor of Germany and he assumed full powers until his "Thousand Year Reich" ended with his suicide in the ruins of Berlin on April 30, 1945.

attention to its founding. When the economic situation improved, it seemed destined to oblivion—particularly so after 1923 when Hitler attempted to take over power by force in Munich. The coup failed dismally and Hitler found himself in jail and the party was outlawed.

In 1924, running in the legislative election under various camouflage labels, the Nazis managed to get thirty-two deputies elected in the legislature and received 6.5 percent of the national vote. Thereafter, its electoral fortunes declined. After 1928, however, and especially after the depression of 1929, the Nazis began to make rapid gains and soon emerged as the strongest single party (see Table 9-1).

There were a number of reasons for the rapid growth of the Nazi party. It managed not only to survive but also to become the sole spokesman of all right-wing extremist groups. Hitler paid particular attention to its organization and managed to create what amounted to a paramilitary party. Leadership was consolidated in the hands of the leader—the Führer. Uniforms, a special salute, pomp and ritual, and above all, discipline and activism appealed to many, especially the young. In 1931, some 35 percent of the party members were below the age of thirty. Party membership began to grow—especially after 1928–1929 when there were about 100,000 members, to 1.5 million by 1933, and up to about 4 million at the beginning of World War II.

Special shock formations were established. The SA (Brownshirts) and, after 1934, the SS (Black Guards) grew in numbers to almost equal the German army. At the slightest provocation they engaged in street fights or attacks against leftists and opposition leaders whose headquarters they sacked and burned. Anti-Semitic demonstrations and acts of violence were common. All this was testing the will of the Nazis, preparing them for further action and intimidation.

Yet Hitler and his associates pledged to respect "legality" and in effect promised not to use violence in order to come to power. Many political leaders believed them, especially among the conservative and centrist groups, thus allowing the Nazi party to operate. They were convinced that it would never receive a majority and that even if allowed to form a government it would abide by the constitution and act according to the rules and procedures of the parliamentary assemblies. After the 1932 election when the Nazis, 196 strong, entered the legislature, Hitler left no doubt at all as to what he meant by "legality." "We come as enemies," he wrote. "Like the wolf coming into a flock of sheep, that is how we come!"[3]

A number of front organizations were created to strengthen the party's appeal and to recruit more members and sympathizers. In 1931 the Hitler Youth numbered only about 100,000. In 1933–1934 it was close to about 4 million members and at the outbreak of the war almost 9 million. In addition there was a Hitler Student League, an Officers' League, a Women's League, a workers' Nazi organization (the Labor Front), and many others representing

---

3. Cited by Bracher, *The German Dictatorship,* p. 142. This is an excellent account of Hitler's Germany, and I am indebted to the author for many of my observations.

TABLE 9–1   Elections and the Nazi Vote

LEGISLATIVE ELECTIONS		
1924 (May 4)	1,918,300 (32 deputies)	6.0%
1924 (Dec. 7)	907,300 (14 deputies)	3.0%
1928 (May 20)	810,000 (12 deputies)	2.6%
1930 (Sept. 14)	6,409,600 (107 deputies)	18.3%
1932 (July 31)	13,745,800 (230 deputies)	37.4%
1932 (Nov. 1)	11,737,000 (196 deputies)	33.1%
1933 (March 5) (Nazis in power)	17,277,200 (288 deputies)	43.9%
1933 (Nov. 12) (Nazis in control)	39,638,800 (661 deputies)	92.2%
PRESIDENTIAL ELECTION		
1932 (March)		
1st ballot	11,339,288 (Hitler)	30.1%
2d ballot	13,418,051 (Hitler)	36.8%

Reprinted with permission of Macmillan Publishing Company, from *Modern Germany,* 2nd ed., by Koppel S. Pinson. © 1966 by Macmillan Publishing Company.

every academic, social, and professional group in the country. The party gradually became a state within a state with its private army, tribunals, police, and military formations all spreading the Nazi doctrine far and wide and creating within Germany a strong Nazi subculture. It had its own cult, slogans, and morality; they were antirepublican, racist, and nationalist.

With the economic depression the Nazis made the breakthrough that led them to power in 1933. They became a mass party as the election results show, but they also attracted the attention and support of the conservative forces and the army. The business community and the financial elites opened up their purse, and the party's treasury was again full. The Nazis and their leader broadened their appeal to catch, if possible, every group, every section, and every occupation and profession.

Nazi Pledges

To the farmers the Nazis promised "green democracy" and "soil-rooted" pure communitarian values as well as protection and subsidies. They pledged to uphold the rural values and traditions that were menaced by urbanization.

To the workers they promised jobs. Between 1929 and 1932 unemployment had shot up from 1 million to 6 million. Many employed and unemployed workers began to join the party and to vote for it. The depression had weakened the trade unions, and left-wing workers were hopelessly divided between socialism and communism.

To the army the Nazis promised rebuilding and an end to the Versailles Treaty.

To the middle classes, they promised special measures to arrest the decline of their income and give them security; above all, they promised to do away with the dangers from the left by eliminating communism. These promises appealed especially to the lower middle classes — merchants, artisans, shopkeepers, civil service personnel, clerical personnel, and so on.

The Nazi party promised a special place to the young. The future was theirs. "Make room for us, you old ones," was one of their battle cries.

Propaganda was developed into a fine political art along clear-cut lines suggested by Hitler: repetition of the same simple slogans and themes; appeal to the emotions; propositions that clearly distinguished the negative from the positive — "this *is* the truth, *they* lie," "*we* can, *they* cannot"; simple answers to complex problems — "*we* shall solve unemployment by giving jobs to all"; emphasis on nationalism and national togetherness — "*we*" (Germans) against "*they*" (Jews, plutocrats, capitalists, communists, and so on). These propaganda themes were to be strengthened by direct action taken against opponents. Truth lay not in demonstration but in belief *and* in action. A Nazi was someone who believed and strengthened his belief by acting. Force became the best vindication of belief.

The Nazi pledges were powerful. Party membership in 1930 and 1934 clearly shows that the Nazis had a wide appeal among virtually all groups (see Table 9–2). In the 1932 presidential election the Nazi candidate, none other than Hitler himself, received 36.8 percent of the vote. More than one-third of German voters wanted him as their president!

Who were the Nazi voters? The great majority of farmers voted for the Nazis as did the majority of the people living in small towns and, in general, in rural areas. Protestants tended to vote for them more than

TABLE 9–2   Composition of the Nazi Party

	1930	1934	PERCENTAGE OF POPULATION
Working class	28%	32%	46%
White collar	25.6	20.6	12.4
Independent business	20	20	9
Civil service and teachers	8.3	13	5
Farmers	14.7	10.7	9

From Karl Dietrich Bracher, *The German Dictatorship: The Origins, Structure and Effects of National Socialism.* © 1970 by Praeger Publishers, Inc. Reprinted by permission of CBS College Publishing/Holt, Rinehart & Winston (subsidiaries of Harcourt Brace Jovanovich), and George Weidenfeld & Nicolson Ltd., London.

Catholics. A great percentage of the middle and the lower middle classes voted Nazi. But so did four out of every ten workers, many among the unemployed. Seymour Martin Lipset wrote that the "ideal type Nazi voter in 1932 was a middle class, self-employed Protestant who lived either on a farm or in a small town and who had previously voted for a centrist or a regionalist political party strongly opposed to the power and influence of big business and big labor."[4] Yet the Nazis received a sizable working-class vote, even though trade union members, socialists, and communists remained, for a while, beyond their reach. In 1932 the Nazi party had become a truly mass party — cutting across classes, religions, and occupations.

The Nazi Ideology

Nazism as an ideology and a political movement began as a gesture of negation, but there was also the formulation of a number of "positive" themes and propositions on the basis of which the new society would be constructed. Some of them were addressed to the immediate situation, others to long-range social, economic, and political problems created by liberalism and the threat of communism.

Negative themes   The negative themes of Nazism were many:

1. *Against class struggle:* The notion of class, developed by Marx and endorsed by all communist parties, was inconsistent with national unity. As such, it was only an extension of the idea of conflict and competition developed by liberals and Marxists. The Nazis claimed that the notion of class was incompatible with the communitarian values of the German people and the German nation. Germany was "one"!

2. *Against parliamentary government:* According to the Nazis, parliamentary government leads to the fragmentation of the body politic into parties and groups jockeying for position, compromising their particular interests, and forming unstable governmental coalitions. The "real" national interest was neglected. A common purpose could not develop from such a fragmentation of the national will. "There is no principle which . . . is as false as that of parliamentarianism," wrote Hitler in *Mein Kampf.*

3. *Anti-trade union:* Unions express the sectarian and class interests of the working class. However, the workers were also Germans and citizens. They had to be integrated into the community like all others instead of pitting themselves against other Germans.

4. *Against political parties:* Like representative government, political parties expressed special ideological or interest particularisms, splitting the nation. The national purpose called not for parties but for one movement embodying it. Such a movement, even if it were called a party, should be given monopoly of representation. Hence all other political parties should be outlawed, and a one-party system instituted.

4. Seymour Martin Lipset, *Political Man.* New York: Doubleday, 1963, p. 148.

5. *Against the Treaty of Versailles:* The Versailles Treaty, imposing an inferior status upon Germany that deprived it of its army and required it to pay reparations, had to be eliminated. But more than that, the existing international system that perpetuated the supremacy of some nations — notably England and France — should be drastically altered to give freedom and space to Germany.

There were a number of other comprehensive negative themes that inevitably blend with some of the "positive" formulations of the Nazis.

6. *Anti-Semitism and racialism:* Anti-Semitism had been a common phenomenon in many countries of Europe stemming from religious prejudices, cultural differences, and economic rivalries. The Jews were blamed as responsible for both liberal capitalism *and* for communism. There were extravagant myths attempting to show that the Jews were plotting the domination of the world. This was the case with a document (fabricated by nineteenth-century anti-Semites) called *The Protocols of the Elders of Zion,* in which the Jews were said to set forth their plans to conquer the world. This was widely used by the Nazis. They added a new twist, however — that Jews were biologically inferior. They were therefore not only dangerous because of their ideas, their beliefs, and their plans to conquer the world (how inferior people could do it was never explained), but because their very presence within Germany endangered the purity of the German "race." There were only half a million Jews in Germany at the time Hitler assumed power and over 65 million Germans — that is less than 0.7 percent. More than 200,000 Jews managed to escape the country by 1938. Those who remained were viewed as a germ just as virulent as botulism. It had to be isolated first and then exterminated.

As soon as the Nazis came to power, they began to reduce the German Jews to the status of nonpersons. They could not keep their businesses; they could not receive any social benefits. They were relegated to special neighborhoods; they were constantly harassed and intimidated by the members of the Nazi party, the SA, and its various front organizations; they were arbitrarily arrested, could not engage in any gainful occupation, had their belongings confiscated, and were forced to pay special levies to the state authorities that invariably went to the Nazi party members. Intermarriage was prohibited, and existing intermarriages annulled. The Nazis developed the long-range policy of exterminating all Jews that led actually to the destruction of European Jewry wherever the Nazi armies gained a foothold.

Given its basis, German anti-Semitism left no room for compromise. But the same biological discrimination also threatened other groups and nations that the Nazis found dangerous or "impure" — Slavs, blacks, and so on.

7. *Anticommunism:* If anti-Semitism derived from racist allegations, anticommunism stemmed primarily from political and international considerations. It was aimed not only against communists at home, but against the "fatherland of communism," the Soviet Union. It called not only for the elimination of the German Communist party, but also for the elimination of international communism as spearheaded by the Soviet Union. The

ideological crusade against communism would thus serve the secular strategic, economic, and geopolitical goals of Germany. It was part and parcel of the *Drag Nach Osten* — the German drive eastward.

There were other reasons for anticommunism inherent in the totalitarian ideology of nazism. The German Communist party was well-organized and disciplined. It also had an ultimate vision of total control, as did Soviet communism. There was an incompatibility, therefore, between two intensely ideological and inherently totalitarian movements. As soon as they came to power, the Nazis outlawed the Communist party, arrested its leaders, and jailed and murdered many of them. The party was dismantled. The same fate awaited the Social Democrats, also a Marxist party in name, that had also opposed the Nazis. But it was not until 1941 that the main clash between communism and the Nazis took place, when the German armies invaded Russia.

"Positive" Themes   Every negation advanced by the Nazis (what they planned to do away with) naturally called for an affirmation (what they planned to do instead). It is therefore only in this sense that I am using the term "positive."

Anti-Semitism suggests racialism and the purity of the race; antiindividualism, a communitarian ethic transcending the individual; antiliberalism, a new political organization; and the anti-Versailles posture, the erection of some new kind of international order. It is the combination of the reasoning behind many of the negations that resulted in the new and dynamic synthesis of social and national life. No matter how morally repugnant, it must be analyzed and discussed if we are to grasp the full and ominous implications of the Nazi movement and regime.

1. *Nationalism and racialism:* To understand the character of Nazi German nationalism we must distinguish it from other nationalist movements. There were liberal nationalist movements in the wake of the French Revolution of 1789 identifying with the principle of nationality and demanding that people sharing the same national background — a common history, culture, language, religion — live within a given territory, the nation-state. This is basically the principle of self-determination, allowing peoples to form their own State. There have also been conservative nationalist movements which have extolled national virtues and asserted their superiority over others; they stress national integration and unity at the expense of particularisms, regionalisms, and even individual freedoms. But such nationalist movements are content to see the values they assert cultivated and strengthened within the nation-state. They are not expansionist.

Nazi nationalism was both racialist and expansionist. While insisting on the superiority of Germanic values, it also proclaimed the superiority of the German race and the desirability of imposing its superiority upon others. Aryans were superior not only to Jews but also to Slavs, Turks, Greeks, French, and so on. And among the Aryans, the Germans were the superior race because they had managed and, thanks to the Nazis, forever intended to keep their race "pure." They would not allow for a "mongrel-ization" similar to what they claimed had occurred in the United States. They were the *master race* destined to dominate all others. This racialist doctrine, coupled with extreme nationalism, led to the inevitability of war.

2. *Expansionism:* The valor of the race could not be proven by assertion only. It had to be demonstrated on the proving ground of war and conquest. The master race was to be a race of warriors subduing lesser races. Germany was to conquer and Berlin would become the capital of the world. But in addition to racism there were ideological, economic, and strategic reasons to justify an expansionist and warlike policy. A totalitarian system is "total" at home because it tries to subordinate everything to its ideology and control. It cannot allow competing units to exist. But the same is true in international terms. The logic of totalitarianism calls for the elimination of competing centers of power everywhere.

Economic reasons were also advanced. One was the notion of "proletarian" nations; another that of "living space." According to the former, World War I had allowed some nations to control the world's wealth—for example, England, the United States, France—while other nations like Germany, Italy, and even Japan were poor, "proletarian," without colonies, raw materials, and resources. Similarly, some nations had ample space at their disposal: the French, British, and Dutch had their colonial empires. The Soviet Union and United States had immense land at their disposal. Other nations did not, however, and Germany, without colonies, was squeezed into the center of Europe, while its population was growing and its needs increasing. Land would therefore have to be reapportioned to meet the German needs. To this argument yet another one was added— the distinction between "young" and "old" nations, suggesting growth against decay. In historical terms, Germany was "young" compared to England or France and needed "living space" and land into which to grow.

Thus the conquest of territory and the destruction of neighboring nation-states became an essential element of the Nazi ideology, and a long-range policy goal. It could not be attained overnight. The elimination of Soviet Russia (an old bulwark against German expansion to the east and also an ideological foe) and France (the spearhead of the "plutocracies," especially England and the United States) would have to come first. The Japanese and the Italians were offered only tactical alliances in the expansionist German ambitions. Their position in the international order that the Nazis would build would have to be settled later.

3. *Communitarianism:* The elimination of all freedoms and their replacement by a single "freedom"—that of obeying the party that represented the German community and the leader of that party—was the essence of German totalitarianism. It was central to the building of a new political system that would replace liberalism and capitalism. All parties, all organizations, all associations, all religious groups, and churches would become subordinated to the communitarian will. After the Nazis came to power, freedom of press, of association, and of speech ceased to exist. All parties were abolished. The individual—alone, free, independent, thinking

his or her own thoughts—would give place to the "new individual" imbued with communitarian and nationalist beliefs as dictated by the leader and the party. The individual and the community would become one. Dissenters were, of course, not to be tolerated; they were executed or sent to concentration camps. But individuals who tried to remain aloof and distant from the national community were declared to be "asocial." They had failed to respond to the demands of the party and the community; they were not fully mobilized; they were not one with the nation.

Communitarianism called for constant participation; it aimed to inculcate a spirit of individual attachment to the whole and a readiness not only to obey but also to sacrifice everything for the general interest as defined by the Nazis. Communitarianism also suggested the need to subordinate private interest in the economic sphere to general social goals and, thereby, the subordination of the market economy to the party and the leader. The early Nazi ideology was distinctly anticapitalist, and it advocated the supremacy of national goals over all economic interests.

4. *Leadership ("Führerprinzip") and the party:* In what ways do communitarian values manifest themselves? One way is the direct participation of all in decision making—claimed to be the practice of the early Germanic tribes. A second way is for the community to select its representatives. This notion of representation was given a particular twist by the Nazis. They accepted it but they rejected free elections. The Nazi party "represented" the German people because it was in tune with the people and expressed directly the desires of the nation. Within the party its leader instinctively and intuitively acted for the whole. It is the leader, therefore, who best expresses the communitarian values.

Within six months after it came to power the "monopoly" of the Nazi party was legalized. The National Socialist Workers' party constituted the *only* political party in Germany. Whoever undertook to maintain the organizational structure of another political party or to form another political party was to be punished with penal servitude up to three years.

Communitarian aspirations gave a populist trait to Nazism. It claimed to embody values and principles that stemmed directly from the people—the *volk.* It was the "people's spirit"—the *volksgeist*—that was tapped by the party and was represented by it. Hence the party, in the name of this unique representative quality, claimed to be the only vehicle of representation and the very essence of direct democracy. But because of this, it also claimed to be an entity above the State and to control the State while acting on behalf of the community. In the last analysis, the State was nothing but an agency, an instrumentality of the party, and all its offices and officials were subordinate to the party.

The leadership principle is the cornerstone of Nazism and the institution that best combines authority and control with "representation." It is a principle that cannot be easily defined since it can be only "understood" by those who experience it. The leader decides everything and everybody must obey. He can delegate his authority to others but can never give it up. He is the law and hence above the law. He can legislate and then change that legislation overnight. His will is arbitrary, absolute, and superior. He can set procedures and change them at will. He is free to appoint his successor, just as a Roman emperor could make his horse a consul and send him to the slaughterhouse!

Yet the question remains: From where does the leader derive his representative quality? The answer is very difficult. First, it is his capacity to speak on behalf of the national and popular spirit. It is also his special ability to persuade his followers: he has a special charisma that convinces the many to obey. It is also his intuition: his ability to sense what is right and wrong; what must be done and what must not be done; his feeling for what is good for all.

But what about the leader's authority? Why do people obey? The link is the mystical and intuitive link between leader and followers. He speaks for the people and the people agree with him because he speaks for them! And where his authority does not quite prevail, the leader has at his disposal formidable instruments of coercion, intimidation, and downright terror to elicit obedience.

While it is relatively easy to describe the omnipotence and omnicompetence of the Führer, it is far more difficult to explain it. How would a civilized nation, even one in which democratic values and institutions had not gained roots, accept it? And how can one explain the German people's fealty to the Führer until Germany had been reduced to ruins? In the last analysis, there can be no explanation except the very trite one. Hitler, his totalitarian regime, and his leadership principle combined with nationalism, racism, and expansionism, must have had, under the particular circumstances, a strong appeal to some prominent traits of German political culture.

The Subordination of the Society

The vast majority of Germans acquiesced in the Nazi takeover, often with enthusiasm. They showed remarkable loyalty throughout Hitler's stay in power. Many did so out of self-interest; how many submitted out of fear is difficult to tell. Let us see how the various "social groups" reacted to the coming to power of the Nazis and their regime.

The Army   Diminished in status, reduced in numbers, bearing the brunt of defeat, and hostile to communism and left-wing movements, army officers saw, in the coming of the Nazis, the prospects of their rehabilitation. Never at ease with republican institutions, the army's position was that it either should be a dominant force in the society or a separate and distinct entity for training soldiers, maintaining order, and making war. It would not play a subordinate role. After World War I, many of its officers joined right-wing vigilante organizations against communists and leftists. Throughout Hitler's rise to power, prominent officers cooperated with him or gave him a helping hand. He promised the rehabilitation of the nation and saw war as an answer for past failures. As General Blomberg testified at the Nuremburg trials: "Before 1938–1939 the German generals were not opposed to Hitler. There was no ground for opposition since he brought them the success they desired."[5] It was only when the fortunes of the war began to turn against Germany that a number of generals became impatient with Hitler and some even conspired to assassinate him.

Civil Service   German civil servants, federal and state, responded with satisfaction to Hitler's program and supported his regime. The Nazis seemed to represent the basic values of order, centralized authority, and national integrity to which they were accustomed. Once it became clear that party members would not replace them, the support of the bureaucracy was overwhelming. It was strengthened by generous promotions and increases in salaries.

Yet bureaucracies are accustomed to an orderly way of doing things. They accept hierarchical relationships and a careful structuring of inferior-superior lines of command. They are committed to a rational, detached, and impartial way of reaching decisions and implementing them; they are concerned with efficiency. The Prussian, and later on German, bureaucracy was always considered to be both well-organized and efficient. As a result, the frequent intrusions into it of the Nazi leaders, and the ultimate power they had to intervene and make decisions themselves, alienated some civil servants, forced the resignation of others, and often created confusion. However, at no time during the Hitler regime was there an open defiance on the part of the civil service.

The Church   Religious groups tried to maintain a certain distance from the Nazis, but an effort was made to eliminate some and to bring the two major churches, Catholic and Lutheran, under control. Jews were quickly isolated and their synagogues burned; Jehovah's Witnesses were persecuted. A Concordat was signed with the Vatican giving the Catholic Church some autonomy — the right to hold services, raise funds, and distribute pastoral letters to the faithful. But the Concordat also legitimized the Nazi State in the eyes of many Catholics. They were particularly receptive to the Nazi anticommunist pledges and during the war they considered it their patriotic duty to support the fatherland, especially when at was against the Soviet Union.

The Lutheran Church maintained a distance from the State, distinguishing political from spiritual matters. Political obedience was one thing, and the worship of God another, but the Lutherans gave their support to the Nazis as citizens, whatever their innermost thoughts might have been. Even to those for whom Hitler was a tyrant, obedience to the State was an obligation and prayer the only answer.

Individual Catholic prelates and Lutheran pastors occasionally raised their voices against the Nazi regime and its atrocities, but they were the exceptions to the general passivity of the churches.

5. Cited in Pinson, op. cit., p. 508.

Business Groups   As for business groups, they gave their full support and cooperation once the "socialist" pledges that were in the original platform of the party were abandoned. Neither private property nor business profits were tampered with, and the antilabor and antitrade union measures satisfied them fully. Business elites cooperated closely with the Nazi leaders, trading favors and benefits with them.

The Middle Class, Farmers, and Workers   Germany had never experienced a genuine middle-class liberal movement as had England, France, and the United States. Rapid industrialization was grafted upon semifeudal and authoritarian social structures. Paternalistic and hierarchical relationships were the rule. The middle classes *fitted* themselves into these structures instead of creating their own kind of political and social relationships — egalitarian and participatory. They felt more at home with authoritarian solutions and hierarchical relationships, and hence they were inclined to accept nazism and the authoritarian and nationalist philosophy it represented. Furthermore, the Nazi anticommunist ideology and its intention of doing away with trade unions reflected the middle-class fear of the working class and their political parties. The overwhelming majority of middle-class voters voted for the Nazis and supported them throughout their stay in power. The lower middle classes — the petit bourgeoisie — insecure, patriotic, and antisocialist — gave them their full support as they sought a niche in the Nazi order.

Similarly, the farmers gave the Nazis overwhelming support. The rustic virtues the Nazis extolled were also theirs: protection in the form of higher tariffs provided them with added revenue; anticommunism appealed to their traditional nationalism and conservatism. Small towns and rural communities voted overwhelmingly Nazi.

It was only the workers, then, who seemed to demur. But even among them it was only the politically and ideologically organized and committed, those who belonged to trade unions or were in the communist and socialist parties, who provided the opposition. The unemployed, as we pointed out, tended to join the party in return for promises of employment. With the coming of World War II in 1939, full employment was attained and the labor force was by and large materially better off than it had been at any time since before World War I. There was no organized opposition.

The Economy

The Nazis failed to implement their original economic program. They did not nationalize the monopolies; on the contrary, every effort was made to encourage concentration and cartelization; they did not confiscate war profits or unearned income; they did not undertake land reform, and they did not take over uncultivated lands and transform them into peasant cooperatives. Populist and socialist promises were forgotten when they came to power. The Nazi party's socialist leaders, many of whom had taken these promises seriously, were massacred in 1934.

Nazi economic policy consisted of a series of improvisations to meet the political objectives of rearmament and war. There is no doubt that the economy was subordinated not only to political and ideological exigencies, but also to the necessity of planning or waging war. From the very start, controls were put on foreign exchange. Special efforts were made to promote investment and direct it to key areas of economic activity; to secure raw materials and, when it became necessary, to produce them at home (as, for instance, with synthetic gas and rubber). In general, the emphasis was put on reducing imports and promoting self-sufficiency. Priorities were established, wages controlled, and labor scarcities met through the importation of foreign, often slave labor—especially in the war period. However, cartelization proceeded through the amalgamation of firms or the takeover of smaller ones, and profits remained secure, even during the war. Property, both individual and corporate, was respected.

Political imperatives prevailed. But the economy was not absorbed by the State; it was not nationalized. It became subordinate to the State and the party—a subordination that most other countries had experienced in time of war. There was nothing original about the Nazi economy—it produced no new blueprint for production, trade, growth, or consumption. It made no effort to establish a new framework for labor-capital relations other than to disband all trade unions.

Conclusion

With an ideology that appealed, at least in part, to some of the basic cultural traits of the German people, with a militant party to mobilize the people behind it, with a magnetic political leader trying to resurrect the national demons of the Germanic racial and national superiority while exploiting all the weakness of a deadlocked parliamentary government, the totalitarian state came to Germany with far greater support than anywhere else.

The Nazis were a mass party—far more so than the Russian Bolsheviks in 1917, the Italian Fascists in 1922, or the Spanish Falange from 1936 to 1938. In free and open elections, they received a greater percentage of votes than any other totalitarian party in Europe, or for that matter, than any other party in Germany. They were welcomed by most social groups and classes, including an appreciable part of the workers, and by the important elite groups, including the churches and the military. Nazism was a homemade product. It was "made in Germany" by the Germans.

Italian Fascism

The Fascist party emerged in Italy at just about the same time as the Nazis did in Germany. But the Fascist State came into being much earlier. The Fascists took power on October 28, 1922—a decade before Hitler. By 1923, when Mussolini was setting the foundations of the new Italian order, Hitler was still a political upstart and in jail for the abortive Munich *putsch*.

The similarities in the way the Fascists and the Nazis took power are striking:

1. Fascism capitalized on the nationalistic fervor which followed World War I because Italy did not receive the territorial compensation for the war effort that the Italians thought they deserved.

2. Italy's parliamentary institutions could not cope with the problems facing the country. There were many political parties, sharply divided on ideological and policy matters. Governments consisted of short-lived coalitions, and cabinet instability was the rule.

3. Democratic institutions were not valued by major sections of the population, and Italy's experience with democracy and representative government had been limited. A small elite consisting of the northern industrialists, landowners, and the Catholic hierarchy ruled the country. The middle classes, the lower middle classes, and the peasantry were either weak or unable to exercise political influence and bring about necessary reforms.

4. The workers joined powerful leftist movements, some led by the Socialist party, some by anarchists and syndicalists, and some by the communists, who after 1921 began to assume an important position in many trade unions. A strong minority endorsed extremist programs and direct action. They were organized for a revolutionary takeover and used the strike as a vehicle for weakening the State. They occupied factories and led the farmers to the occupation of land. Socialists showed remarkable strength at the polls, gaining 1,834,792 votes and 156 deputies in the legislature in the election of 1919. Again, in the election of 1921, their respective strength was 1,631,435 votes and 138 deputies. This "red menace" threatened not only the conservative forces, the Church, the industrial elites, and the monarchy, but also the middle classes, the lower middle classes, and the peasants in regions where the Church was particularly influential.

5. In this context, as in Germany, vigilante nationalist groups began to mushroom. They were led by former army officers and veterans. They took the law into their own hands in fighting the leftists, with the complicity of national and local governmental authorities. Gang wars developed in the cities and the countryside. The newly formed Fascist party began to play the leading role in combating the "the reds."

6. Inflation, and the relative success of trade unions in maintaining their real wages through collective action while the middle and lower middle classes suffered, accounted for a sharp right-wing reaction on the part of the latter. They were losing income and status, and they were increasingly forced down to the economic and social levels of the workers.

7. In contrast to Hitler, Mussolini, the founder of the Fascist party, was not a newcomer to politics. But the similarities with Hitler are remarkable. They both came from the lower middle classes; both had read what they

found congenial to their activist and romantic dispositions and admired the many writers who criticized liberalism and extolled will power and communitarian nationalist values. Mussolini, too, had fought in World War I and had been wounded. He, too, was a great orator. Like Hitler, Mussolini at first propounded ideas that had strong socialist overtones: confiscation of war profits, socialization of industries, workers' participation in the running of firms, the utilization of unused land by those who could work it, and appeal to the poor and the workers with promises of social and economic equity.

8. As with Hitler, Mussolini did not have to shoot his way into power. He was received by the King and appointed by him.

The Fascist Party

The term Fascist comes from the Latin word *fasces,* which was an emblem carried by ancient Roman magistrates as a symbol of their authority. It consisted of many rods tightly banded together, with an axe protruding on top. It conveyed remarkably well the underlying philosophy of the Fascists: the combining of individuals together in order to generate both power and authority.

The Italian Fascist party was founded in 1919. At first the Fascists did not fare well. In the election of 1919, in which the socialists gained 156 seats in the Chamber of Deputies, the Fascists failed to gain a single seat. Mussolini himself, a candidate in Milan, received less than 5,000 votes out of 346,000 cast. The program of his party contained the socialist slogans to which we have referred: an eight-hour working day, minimum wage policy, participation of workers in the management of industries, welfare measures with comprehensive sickness and old age protection, a capital tax leading to the expropriation of the wealthy, and the confiscation of the property of religious organizations and of war profits.

Within two years of the founding of the party its membership had grown to 300,000. In the 1921 election, the Fascist party secured thirty-five seats in the legislature and 19.6 percent of the vote (1,289,556). But what strengthened them even more was the private war they began to wage against all leftists. Left-wing clubs, newspapers, trade unions, and party headquarters were sacked. Agricultural cooperative societies were destroyed. The Fascists, like the Nazis, appeared as the strong men of "law and order" where government failed to provide protection. Their program also began to swing to the right. Mussolini now attacked the "Russian myth" of communism, spoke of rural democracy as opposed to collectivization, rejected class war in favor of national unity, and promised to protect the workers but only in accordance "with the interests of production." Subsequently, in a party congress, the concepts of both economic liberalism and a strong State were endorsed. The party declared itself neutral on the question of the monarchy, which it had previously opposed. There was no mention of confiscation of lands held by religious organizations. Thus both the monarchy and the Church were placated.

THE BETTMAN ARCHIVE, INC.

Benito Mussolini (1883–1945)

The son of a socialist blacksmith and a Catholic schoolteacher, Mussolini broke with the Italian Socialist party over his support for World War I, and became editor of the nationalist *Il Popolo d'Italia.* In 1919, he founded the Fascist party, and on October 22, 1922, King Victor Emmanuel IV asked him to become prime minister. Mussolini began to put into effect his philosophy of a totalitarian one-party state by abolishing republican institutions. He also attempted to realize plans for a "new Roman empire" by embarking on a series of military adventures, including the conquest of Ethiopia (1935–1936), support of Franco in Spain (1936–1938), and the occupation of Albania (1939). In June 1940 Italy entered into World War II on the side of the Germans, but its forces were unable to make any genuine contribution to the German war effort. Expelled from office on July 25, 1943, after the invasion of Sicily by allied forces, he was arrested and subsequently executed by partisans on April 28, 1945.

Mussolini provided some good formulations of the Fascist ideology, notably in his *The Doctrine of Fascism; Fascism: Doctrine and Institutions;* and in his *Autobiography.*

A general strike organized by the socialists and the communists late in 1922 gave Mussolini the opportunity for his "March on Rome" and takeover of power. Actually he did not march; he simply took the train from Milan! His Fascist squads, however, had occupied various localities and tens of thousands had moved into Rome and its outskirts. The King received Mussolini and asked him to take office. Thus, the Fascist State was born.

Ideology

Fascism, like nazism, was to be the answer to liberal democracy, doing away with competition, individualism, the quest for profit and material gain, divisions, fragmentations, and particularisms. Instead, a new regime would be established to create unity and cooperation, discipline and joint effort for the realization of collective purpose under the State. "Believe; Obey; Work; Fight" was one of the mottos of fascism. "Everything within the State; everything for the State; nothing outside the State" was another.

The argument favoring the inclusiveness and the primacy of the State is, as we know, an old one. For the Fascists it meant the subordination of all social activities and organizations, all individual interests, all cultural manifestations (including religion), and all rights—material, political, and moral—to the State. Without the collectivity of the group, there can be no individual life and freedom and of course no common purpose. The State expresses them all. Morality can no longer be based on individual rational calculations: it exists when we share fully the collective purpose of the State and we obey the State. "Fascism is for liberty," wrote Mussolini, but ". . . for the only liberty that can be taken seriously, the liberty of the State. In this sense fascism is totalitarian and the Fascist State the synthesis and unity of all values . . . [It] interprets, develops and gives power to every aspect of the life of the people."[6] The State, therefore, is a truly moral creative force.

Mussolini went beyond even this by saying that the Fascist State is truly democratic, for democracy in its purest form is "what ought to be." Fascism provides this kind of morality of substituting for the will of the many that of the few and by subordinating the few to the will of one. The will of the leader becomes their will and, in turn, the will of all.

Side by side with the concept of State, and often used interchangeably with it, is the nation. In fact, it is the combination of the two—a combination that is "indissolubly" cemented—that the Fascists stressed. The nation and nationalism provide the ultimate spiritual focus to bind people together within the State that embodies it. Nationalism "is the central inspiration of the human personality living in the civil community; [it] descends into . . . and makes its home in the heart of the man of action

6. Cited by Herman Finer, *Mussolini's Italy.* New York: Henry Holt, 1935, p. 201.

as of the thinker, of the artist, as of the scientists." Nationalism "becomes the very soul of the soul" in all of us.[7]

Nationalism and statism, the quest for the absolute ethical ideal, theoretically divests fascism of material considerations. To live dangerously, to navigate on the high and perilous seas, to be able and prepared to fight at any time at any risk gives to life a heroic quality which the drudgery of the "economic man," constantly concerned about his insurance, his wage, and his benefits, is incapable of showing. The rational man must give place to the heroic man and material considerations to dreams of great exploits. The real man must replace the mechanical man produced by liberalism. This rationale, in part, accounts for the influx of younger people and university students into the Fascist movement.

The Leader (Il Duce)   This effort to fashion a new society and a "Fascist man" called for leadership and for the right kind of institutions to organize it and lead it. The Fascist party and the leader (Il Duce) play the key roles. The leader speaks for the party and the State. He combines in his person the highest offices of the State and the party. The party represents the movement that speaks for the leader and the State and acts on their behalf. Party officials occupy virtually all the important posts in the State. In fact, almost all civil service positions were reserved by law for party members and officials, which assured the party of patronage. The party also organized and structured all social activities and mobilized the rank and file to provide for support and watch out for deviant manifestations. Finally, the leader, with top party officials, controlled the economy, which, like everything else, was supposed to be subordinate to the State and its ideology.

The Development of the Party   The Fascist party held the monopoly of representation, the virtual monopoly of officeholding, and the monopoly of mobilization and recruitment, but it did not develop a private army as the Nazis did through the SS and SA formations. Throughout the Fascist period the army and the officer corps maintained their autonomy. The Fascist militia remained relatively unimportant.

The party also controlled a number of "front organizations" among civil servants, retired officers, Fascist trade unions, teachers, students, and so on. A total of at least 4 million people were involved in these organizations. Thus about 6 to 7 million Italians were members of the Fascist party or party front organizations. In sheer numbers the Fascists permeated the whole of Italian society.

The party controlled opinion, the education of the youth, and all the media; it outlawed all opposition and through its various agencies intimidated those who were of a different mind. All agencies of the State were in the hands of party members. One is tempted to say that fascism had become the

---

7. Alfredo Rocco in Adrian Lyttelton (ed.), *Italian Fascism.* New York: Harper & Row, 1973, p. 262.

The Ten Commandments of the Fascist Fighter[8]

1. God and Fatherland: all other affections and duties come after these.
2. Whoever is not ready to give himself body and soul for his country and to serve the Duce without discussion, is not worthy of wearing the Black Shirt.
3. Use your intelligence to understand the orders that you receive and all your enthusiasm for obedience.
4. Discipline is not only a virtue of the soldiers in the ranks, it must also be the practice of everyday.
5. A bad child and a negligent student are not Fascists.
6. Organize your time in such a way that work will be a joy and your games, work.
7. Learn to suffer without complaining. . . .
8. In actual circumstances, remember that the good lies in audacity.
9. Good actions, like actions in war, must not be done by halves: carry them to their extreme consequence.
10. And thank God every day for having made you Fascist and Italian.

only dominant force in the Italian society. There were only few pockets of resistance — notably in the Church.

The Corporatist State

We have left the discussion of the economic organization of Italy under fascism until last. It took the form of corporatism — used to denote cooperation between capital and labor as opposed to class conflict. Corporatism comes from the word *corpus*, body, and its institutions are designed to bring workers and owners together into "one body," in which there is a cooperation and consultation before decisions are made. It is an old theory, stressing the organic relationships between two groups or classes which according to Marx are inherently antagonistic. It suggests harmony and common interest.

"We have created the Corporate State," Mussolini proudly announced in 1927. The regime established twenty-two corporations. Among them, the most important were those for cereals, fruit, vegetables and flour, beets and sugar, lumber and wood, chemical trades, textiles and engineering, credit and insurance, building trades, sea and air, inland communications. Every such corporation, corresponding to a broad area of economic activity, included representatives of all interests involved in all the branches of economic activity included in it— employers, employees,

---

8. Adapted from Tannenbaum, *The Fascist Experience.* This is one of the better books on Italian fascism and I am indebted to the author for some of my observations and figures in this section. Also Finer, op. cit., pp. 426–454 contains a survey of Fascist youth organizations.

Mussolini is shown, in civilian dress, leading his Fascists on their "March
on Rome," 1922. (*Photo: Brown Brothers*)

managers, owners, and so on. All corporations in turn elected the General
Corporate Assembly consisting of eight hundred members. This was the
Corporate Chamber. In each corporation, employers and employees were
equally represented, but in each one there were also members of the Fascist
party representing "the public." The trade unions from which representatives of the employees were selected were, of course, Fascist
trade unions. A corporation was declared to be an organ of the State, an
official body.

What were the functions of the corporations? They were mostly to
reconcile conflicts among the various branches of activity that were included in it, to better coordinate their respective activities, and to regulate
employment and the technical training of its members. They were also
expected to provide for discipline in production and, with the approval of
the State, to fix prices for goods, services, and wages and supervise the
working conditions in various firms and services.

The Fascist State had the first and last word. "The corporations were
the links in the chain which bound the citizens tightly to the State."[9] They
were presided over by a Fascist minister, and most decisions could be made

9. Lyttelton, op. cit., p. 31.

only with the approval of the State. The old trade unions had been destroyed and the Fascist unions guaranteed the domination of the Fascists. Thus the corporative mechanism turned out to be an instrument to control the workers and provide a link between the Fascist State and the business and industrial elites. This was a far cry from what corporatism was meant to be. It forced the workers underground and did nothing to alleviate class conflict.

Nazism and Fascism: Interpretations

In discussing nazism and fascism we alluded to some of the underlying causes of right-wing totalitarian movements. It is time now to restate briefly some of the interpretations that have been advanced, and to raise some questions about the present status of right-wing totalitarian ideologies. Were nazism and fascism passing phenomena or, on the contrary, can they be considered as ideologies that are likely to endure? Are nazism and fascism dead?

The Abnormality and Uniqueness Theories

A widely held notion a few decades ago was that totalitarianism and its specific manifestations in Germany, Italy, and elsewhere were deviations from the democratic liberal norm. It was a disease, like measles. It could not affect the normal and inevitable progress of societies in the direction of open and democratic politics any more than contagious diseases normally affect children's growth.

An equally widely held belief holds that Italian and German fascism were unique phenomena which correspond to the particular histories of these countries (late unification and defeat or dissatisfaction in World War I) or their particular political cultures (primarily the lack of democratic political tradition and institutions and the corresponding development of powerful left-wing revolutionary movements). In both cases the inference drawn was that the right-wing extremist totalitarian phenomenon was self-contained. It would not spread elsewhere.

The Marxist Theory

A classic interpretation widely used by many authors was the Marxist one, formally endorsed by the Communist Third International. According to it, fascism and nazism correspond to the "last stage of monopolistic capitalism." It is spearheaded by the most racist and expansionist elements of the capitalist class in an effort to maintain its rule at home and subjugate other peoples and their economies. Expansionism and war are two of the remaining means available to the capitalists faced with economic depression and the growing contradictions of their system that Marx had anticipated. The evidence was considered clear: both nazism and fascism geared the economy to war, distracting the people from their economic problems by appealing to their nationalism and by preparing them for war. They maintained private property and profits and destroyed the trade unions and working class parties.

The Modernization Theory

Another theory views totalitarianism as a movement that corresponds to a stage of economic modernization. As the industrial and nonagricultural sectors gradually gain, there is a shift of power from the traditional landed and commercial elites to industrial and banking groups. Rapid industrialization accounts for an influx of farmers into the cities and for urbanization and for a rapid growth in the numbers of industrial workers. These shifts bring about a new type of political mobilization and new political parties that attempt to recruit the new workers, the urban masses, and also the disgruntled peasants. Invariably, such a mobilization frightens the middle classes and the industrial elite groups who begin to favor repressive and integrative solutions. One author considers the optimal condition for the development of fascism to be when the nonagricultural occupational groups have increased, at the expense of agriculture, to the point where they represent about 40 to 50 percent of the gainfully employed. This is of course not an assertion that all such societies will develop fascism, simply that it is one of the many conditions propitious for its emergence.[10]

It is precisely the many other conditions that account for fascism that are missing both from the Marxist theory and the modernization theory. For instance, if the highest and last stage of capitalism accounts for fascism, why did it develop in Germany but not in equally or even more advanced economies? Similarly, if we take the theory of modernization to explain Italian fascism, what accounted for its absence in other countries going through roughly a parallel stage?

Psychological Interpretations

Totalitarianism has been viewed by many authors as a psychological mass phenomenon. People react to a "threat" or to "alienation," both of which occur during the development of industrialization and the concomitant creation of a "mass society." The first accounts for large-scale, impersonal organizations with a high degree of division of labor and specialization. A mass society corresponds to the breakup of most intermediate social structures—village, family, neighborhoods—and many traditional institutions which structure and shape individual values, attitudes, and life. The ultimate result is the "atomization" of society. As the old groups disintegrated,

10. A. F. K. Organski, "Fascism and Modernization," in S. J. Woolf (ed.), *The Nature of Fascism*. New York: Random House, 1968.

the individuals find themselves alone and lonely. A reaction sets in, as we saw in discussing Fromm's *Escape from Freedom,* in favor of communal and integrative ideologies.

The perception of threat strengthens totalitarian appeals when the threatened individuals belong to groups that are comfortable, relatively well-off, and satisfied with their lot. Such is the case with the middle classes that enjoy a higher income and a better status than farmers or workers or lower middle class people. They are, according to some authors, the key to the door to power for right-wing totalitarian leaders. They can keep the door closed or they can open it when special economic conditions begin to account for a loss of income and when special social conditions make them feel that they are in danger of losing their position in society. There is hardly any doubt, as we have seen, that the middle classes, both in Germany and Italy, gave their full support to the Nazis and the Fascists in order to protect themselves against threats to their income and status. They sought protection against trade unions and workers, and found it.

As with the previous theories, this psychological interpretation fails to provide a satisfactory and general explanation. If Germany was a mass society in 1933, so were the United States and England. Why did right wing extremism gain the upper hand in one country but not in the others? Similarly, if the middle classes were "threatened" in Germany, so were they threatened in other industrialized systems, including the United States, during the Great Depression. Why did they seek defense in a totalitarian system in Germany but not elsewhere? Why were antidemocratic solutions sought in some countries and not in others? A theory that does not provide us with the explanation of as many occurrences as possible is not satisfactory.

Managerial Revolution?

Totalitarianism and totalitarian regimes have been viewed by some as representing a "managerial revolution" to replace the inept political leadership of democratic regimes. The economic structure of capitalism, they argue, has changed. Property is not in the hands of only a few; it is widely dispersed among stockholders. Property owners cannot and do not make decisions: their managers do. Decision making is therefore increasingly concentrated in the hands of a managerial elite that enters into close contact with other elites, not only in the economy but also in the army and the civil service; it even enters into close cooperation with labor leaders. In other words, it is a coalition of persons with technical skills in production, management, administration, and group organization.

It is this new managerial elite, then, that makes the major decisions in the economy (often through planning): production levels, the establishment of economic priorities, the utilization of resources, the supply of money, income distribution, wage policy, and so on. Gradually the democratic institutions become an obstacle to this *de facto* government of experts and managers who control the heights of the economy and society.[11] Totalitarianism in the form of fascism or nazism have been viewed accordingly as the triumph of the technocrat and the expert—of a power elite which finally does away with democracy for the sake of efficiency and organization.

The difficulty with this interpretation is that it assigns a role to rationality, knowledge, and technical expertise that neither the Fascists nor the Nazis valued. On the contrary, in both systems there was a constant struggle between the political ideological propositions, utopian or downright irrational, and the imperatives of rational management. There were constant conflicts between the economic managers and the party or the State, between the army officers and the party, and between the economic planners and the party leaders. In fact, fascism and nazism amounted to the predominance of politics over technical roles and considerations such as competence, organization, management, and efficiency.

Personality Theory

Considerable ingenuity has gone into efforts to show that totalitarianism appeals to and receives widespread support from individuals with a particular type of personality—the "authoritarian" or "potentially authoritarian." A number of attitudinal traits combined constitutes a "syndrome" or a "pattern" of the authoritarian personality: anti-Semitism, nationalism, fear of outsiders or aliens, conservative political outlook, strict family upbringing. Persons showing this syndrome are likely to be found among the lower middle classes, the workers, and the uneducated. Similarly, persons suffering from various types of anxiety, even paranoia, who are unable to make decisions and choices and often are afraid of the outside world, divest themselves easily of their freedoms in favor of authoritarian leadership which provides some degree of fixity and stability in their lives.

But there is no adequate evidence to attribute fascism or nazism and membership in and support for totalitarian movements to particular personality types. To begin with, both Nazi and Fascist movements received strong support from the middle classes, to say nothing of university students—persons, that is, with relatively comfortable backgrounds and higher education. Support was lowest from the working classes, where many of the traits associated with an authoritarian personality would be found. Second, even if we concede that there is an authoritarian upbringing in German and Italian families, a random distribution of political attitudes, ranging from authoritarian to democratic, would show only marginal differences for various countries of Europe and elsewhere. To assume that there was a preponderance of authoritarian personality types and syndromes among the Germans and the Italians, as compared to other nationalities, requires statistical proof that is not available and is unlikely to

11. James Burnham, *The Managerial Revolution*, Bloomington: Indiana U.P., 1973.

be found. "Personality" may in some instances be a contributing factor, but it is a very marginal one.

Conclusion

All the interpretations given of totalitarian movements provide us with only parts of an explanation. In some cases it may well be that levels of modernization provided a setting; in other cases, the lonely uprooted individual may have sought shelter in unity and communitarian effort; in others, authoritarian solutions were sought by business and financial groups to defend the economic system that provided them with profits; in still others, the middle classes and the lower middle classes, confronted with loss of income and status, revolted against democracy and liberal institutions.

No single interpretation will do; and even if all of them are put together they do not point to the set of conditions that will *inevitably* lead to totalitarianism. They do help us, however, in identifying the conditions under which political systems may be susceptible to totalitarian assault. The study of right-wing totalitarian movements, therefore, becomes not the study of unique manifestations but the comparative study of a potentially universal phenomenon.

Are Nazism and Fascism Dead?

As we have noted, ideologies often go through a process of ebb and flow. Right-wing extremism and totalitarianism have deep roots, and it is not at all unlikely that, given certain conditions, they may surface again. This does not mean that they will take a form identical to that taken in either Italy or Germany, only that they will follow the same general themes of nationalism, antiliberalism, and antiindividualism in order to impose a national, communitarian, and integrative ideology.

Many of the conditions for the rise of totalitarian movements and regimes continue to be present. The mass society has become even more impersonal and atomized because of rapid modernization and technological development. Individuals are very much alone, and their discontents and frustrations may lead them to espouse unifying and communitarian themes. The liberal ethic that continues to emphasize individual effort and to promise material well-being has raised high expectations for abundance. But it has also undermined some of the basic control mechanisms of society — the Church, the class, elite groups, the structure of deference, and mutuality of respect. Even the modern political party seems unable to hold people together around common programs, and to pattern and regulate their expectations accordingly. The democratic society has been reduced to a myriad of competing and conflicting groups (some refer to them as molecular groups), each one of which tries to maximize its benefits and advantages. It is not unlikely, therefore, that new ideological and totalitarian parties may try to capture the frustrations and discontents of the many who are not satisfied with their position and material well-being.

International tensions may cause a revival of nationalism, defensive or expansionist, that will be used to subordinate individual and group demands, and also result in a loss of freedoms to absolutist nationalist myths and ends. The ruling elites seem to have regrouped into a more coherent "power elite," consisting of the major decision makers in society — economic, political, labor, and military — and the temptation to safeguard their positions through repressive measures cannot be excluded. As for the middle classes, the rate of inflation and the prospects of an economic depression in many societies may cause the same threat and panic that it caused in pre-Nazi Germany.

All that may be needed for virulent extremist movements to emerge is a severe international crisis or another serious economic crisis. Such a crisis could cause a resurgence of revolutionary leftist parties, of one denomination or another, that would put the elites and the middle classes on the defensive. It could bring forth a movement or a regime that would attempt to control group particularisms, to replace representative institutions, to set aside political competition, and to manipulate public opinion around nationalist and communitarian themes. Force would replace consent, even if only to a degree, and propaganda would replace persuasion. In other words, the prospect of extreme totalitarian movements remains very much alive. So does the rich ideological background from which they can draw.

The Extreme Right in the United States

"Extremism," writes Seymour Martin Lipset with particular reference to American political history, "describes the violation, through action or advocacy, of the democratic political process." Despite sporadic flareups from what has come to be called the American "extreme" or "radical" right, the democratic process in the United States has held remarkably well. Extremist movements hardly ever succeeded in synthesizing their various negations into a program or an ideology or in transforming them into some kind of positive political formula in order to seek, let alone gain, broad national support and political power.

The strains and stresses of American society have spawned extremist movements. Most but not all of these have come from the right. They have been movements of disaffection appearing in "periods of incipient change"; they are addressed to groups that "feel deprived" or feel "that they have been deprived of something they consider important" and also to particular groups whose "rising aspirations lead them to realize that they have always been deprived of something they now want."[12] Under

---

12. Lipset and Raab, *The Politics of Unreason,* p. 428.

such circumstances, and unless there is a deep commitment to democracy, the growth of authoritarian movements becomes a distinct possibility. Underlying economic factors have always played a crucial role in the rise of extremist movements, but in the American experience ethnic, racial, and religious factors have been more important. Only since World War II have economic as well as international and genuinely ideological political factors begun to gain prominence.

The Know-Nothings

One of the earliest extremist movements was the Know-Nothing party that developed in New England, with particular strength in Massachusetts, in the 1820s. It was primarily composed of workers and artisans who feared that the influx of immigrants would depress their wages and drive them out of work. They advocated the exclusion of immigrants and wanted to prevent their participation in politics. Direct action was often taken against foreigners: members were supposed to "know nothing" about such action. Even if wages appeared to be the central issue, psychological factors played an important role. In an expanding economy, there could be work both for immigrant workers and also for the indigenous Anglo-Saxons. But the very fact that "foreigners" would attain the income of the native workers appeared to the latter an affront to their position and status within the community.

The Ku Klux Klan

The Ku Klux Klan (KKK) emerged in the South right after the Civil War, to intimidate blacks and thwart the federal measures taken to give them citizenship and extend constitutional rights after they had been freed. It was a regional movement based on community and vigilante organizations and gangs, designed to keep blacks out of politics and the economy, to deprive them of access to property, and to keep them at the level of farmhands and unskilled workers. It also kept a tight control on all whites suspected of showing tolerance and sympathy to blacks. In the years following World War I the Klan had a particularly strong revival, emerging not only as the advocate of white supremacy but also as the champion of "Protestant" and native superiority over all immigrant and non-Protestant religious groups. It became the proponent of the purity of Americans — against Italians, Jews, Mexicans, Japanese, and so on. At one point in the 1920s, it numbered more than 4 million members and extended beyond the South into the Southwest and California. It exerted a strong influence over the Southern state legislatures.

The Klan did not directly challenge the Constitution. It gave it, however, a special interpretation favoring state rights and state autonomy. It was unwilling to see individual protection and civil rights extended to the groups and the minorities it had singled out. It favored restrictive and repressive legislation, and when they were not forthcoming, resorted to direct violence with burnings, intimidation, evictions, and not infrequently, lynchings.

Like the Know-Nothings, the Ku Klux Klan's membership consisted of low-income and low-status groups: artisans, shopkeepers, unskilled workers, and farmers who had moved from the farm to small towns. Their leadership came from petty officials — police officers, small-town businessmen, realtors, and an assortment of veterans. Local ministers of various Protestant denominations played an important role and added biblical zest and justification to the movement, especially in the campaign against Catholics and Jews. In general, the movement preached religious orthodoxy and conformity, the simple values of rural life and the small town against the big city, and was against American entanglements abroad. It was fearful of industrialization and modernization because they were changing American society and shifting the weight of population and economic and political power into the cities and away from the countryside. The movement against the immigrants was a desperate effort to vindicate the position of white, small-town, low- and middle-class Protestant America, and to maintain their economic, social, and political status in a changing world.

Father Coughlin

The first genuine ideological and national extremist right-wing movement was developed by Father Coughlin, a Catholic priest, between 1928 and 1940 — the years of the Great Depression. Unemployment peaked at a level of about 9 to 10 million until 1939, despite the New Deal measures. Not only did blue-collar and white-collar workers suffer, but also the farmers, the middle classes, and many of the manufacturing and trading groups. Fascism had triumphed in Italy, and the Hitler movement had begun its upward climb in Germany. Democracy, as we have seen, was on the defensive, and socioeconomic conditions in the United States were ripe for a strong movement against it. Father Coughlin tried to exploit all this.

His movement had many of the characteristics of a totalitarian right-wing movement similar to those in Italy and Germany. First, it purported to be a mass movement. According to surveys conducted at the time, almost one-third of the American people "approved" of what Father Coughlin said. What he said was not addressed to native Americans. It did not pit them against immigrants: it almost did the reverse. It struck at the major American institutions and the elites, pitting the "small man" against the "establishment."

A second important feature of the movement was its anti-Semitism. It endorsed the racist doctrines of the Nazis and described Jews in the same racist terms. But there were other special reasons — one of them manifestly religious, exploiting the Catholic bias against the Jewish faith. It viewed the Jews as an "internationalist element," distinct from the American melting pot. The infamous and malicious *Protocols of the Elders of Zion*, which, as we have seen, Hitler had publicized, were frequently broadcast and printed in the various pamphlets of the movement.

Its third feature was anticommunism. Communism was a threat both because of its antireligious appeal and also because of its emphasis on class. This was in opposition to the national and communitarian philosophy Father Coughlin wished to impart.

Although a staunch nationalist and an isolationist, Father Coughlin began to lean increasingly in the direction of the Nazi and the Italian models, favoring support of both countries. Just before the demise of his movement in 1940 (by this time its popularity had waned, and at the beginning of the war it was outlawed) he identified fully with the cause of the Nazis to the point of declaring himself to be a "Fascist."

His program had all the familiar "antis": it was anti-elite, anti-Semitic, anti-internationalist (except, as noted above, his support for Hitler and Mussolini), anti-democratic, anti-liberal, anti-capitalist, and against the Constitution. It was one of the first movements to directly advocate the overhaul of the Constitution of the United States. It also suggested a new social order against *both* big capital and big labor. The name of the movement, characteristically enough, was The Union Party for Social Justice, and it merged with other extremist groups to form the National Union. It preached unifying and communitarian themes.

The social configuration of its support was not dissimilar from the one found in the early stages of nazism and fascism. It came from lower middle class groups and from rural areas and small towns; there was considerable support among the middle classes, and higher support among Catholics and the unemployed in the urban and industrial centers.

Joseph McCarthy

It was a convergence of many factors that both sharpened and deepened the content and the thrust of the American extreme right in the 1950s. The major ones were similar to those that accounted for the emergence of fascism in Italy after World War I: profound discontent with the settlement that followed World War II. Many in the United States felt that the Russians had strengthened their position, and began to search for scapegoats. Senator Joseph McCarthy found one in "international communism" and its agents in the United States. Singlehandedly, he began to mount a campaign against not only communists but also their sympathizers—left-wingers and liberals—the so-called "fellow travelers." The term included intellectuals, university professors, members of the "Northeastern establishment," bankers, and supporters of the United Nations. Not only Democrats but also Republican leaders—even President Eisenhower—were accused. McCarthy, in many highly publicized appearances and through investigations conducted by his Senate Committee, discovered "hundreds" of card-carrying communists in the State Department. He claimed that agreements at Yalta and Potsdam during and after World War II were

Senator McCarthy, whipping up anti-communist hysteria in New York, 1954. (*Photo: UPI*)

engineered by the fellow travelers to give undue benefits and advantages to the Soviet Union and to deprive the United States of its victory.

While McCarthy never managed to organize a national movement, national response was widespread and positive. This was the period of "The Great Fear,"[13] when wholesale purges of "crypto-Communists" occurred in the federal government, in universities, the army, and the trade unions. It was also a movement which began to show clearly the impact that the media of communication, especially TV, can have in creating a "national" state of mind. McCarthy and his activities were widely publicized.

Conspiracy theories are common in extremist movements. With Hitler it was the conspiracy of the Jews and the failure of the civilians to support their soldiers in war that played an important role. The conspiracy of the communists against the United States was a notion that satisfied many conservatives and appealed to others who felt that the international position of the United States was slipping. In a peculiar way the McCarthy crusade also appealed to the forces of nativism that we found in the Know-Nothings and the Klan. There were the "ins," the good Americans, and the "outs," the communists, fellow travelers, crypto-communists, immigrants, left-wing liberals, and so on.

13. David Caute, *The Great Fear: The Anti-Communist Purge Under Truman and Eisenhower.* New York: Simon & Schuster, 1978.

The John Birch Society

229

*Nazism and
Fascism:
Ideologies and
Regimes*

Founded in 1958 by a candy manufacturer, Robert H. W. Welch, Jr. (who died in 1985), the John Birch Society has maintained that it exists to educate the public on the threat of communism. Its official ideology can be found in the John Birch Society Blue Book, and it should be noted that in contrast to other extremist organizations it does not espouse political violence.

The movement, named after a captain in World War II killed by the Chinese and seen as the first "hero" of the Cold War, opposes social and welfare legislation. Its followers consider social security as socialism and they call for the elimination of a graduated income tax. They claimed that Presidents Roosevelt, Truman, and Eisenhower were communists and conspired with Russia to deplete U.S. power. The John Birch Society disapproves of all efforts leading to an arms treaty with the Soviet Union and would like the United States to withdraw its recognition of the U.S.S.R. In addition, they oppose the United Nations. Welch said that he wanted the country to move toward "a militant form of Americanism."

During its heyday in the 1960s, the Society had 100,000 members, an annual budget of $8 million and 400 bookstores nationwide carrying its message. Recently, under the leadership of Thomas Hill, membership seems to have stabilized to around 50,000. It publishes a monthly newsletter, the *Bulletin*, and *American Opinion*, a magazine issued eleven times a year. Its headquarters are in Belmont, Massachusetts.

Fringe Movements

Minuscule groups of extremists keep mushrooming throughout the land. They constantly question political compromise and political tolerance, sometimes through the pulpit and the ballot, often with overt acts of defiance and violence. By and large, they preach white supremacy and many trace their origins to the KKK; many are overtly anti-Semitic and some are against Catholics and the new immigrants from Asiatic and Latin American countries. They all share a common anticommunist and anti-Soviet posture, drawing from the literature of the John Birch Society and the legacy of McCarthyism. In line with the evangelicals, they actively preach a return to traditional and moral values but they do not shy away from violence. They appeal to poor farmers and the marginal groups in small towns in Middle America—the region most threatened by economic changes. It appears that each group acts independently of the others and that the seeds of intolerance and militancy they sow have not found fertile soil. What are some of these movements? And what is their overall impact, if any?

(a) "Minutemen" was the label for an extremist vigilante organization founded in 1960 by Robert DePugh, a Missouri businessman, with the purpose of training Americans in guerrilla warfare. They would be used to fight the communists after they had taken over the United States (an event the Minutemen saw as highly probable) either through internal subversion or invasion. Membership estimates ranged from DePugh's claim of a high of 25,000 to a low of 500. Several groups of Minutemen were seized with illegal arms caches that included rifles, submachine guns, explosives, mortars, and antitank weapons. DePugh himself was arrested in July 1969 and sentenced to a ten-year prison term. Little has been heard of the Minutemen since then.

(b) The Populist party, founded in 1984 as an arm of the Liberty Lobby, is intensely nationalistic and racist. Their motto is "America First." Claiming to be a revival of the nineteenth-century Populists, the party managed to receive 66,000 votes in the 1984 presidential race (they were on the ballot in more than twelve states). Its chairman, Robert Weens, Jr., formerly involved with the National States Rights party, had links with the KKK and has cooperated with a paramilitary group, the Christian Patriots Defense League (CPDL).

The agenda of the Populist party is quite clear. "(It) will not permit any racial minority, through control of the media, culture distortion or revolutionary political activity, to divide or fractionalize the majority of the society in which the minority lives." Its weekly newsletter, *The Spotlight*, claimed a subscription list of "over" 50,000 in October 1984.

(c) Lyndon LaRouche has formed a group within the Democratic party with some notable success in party primaries. He claims that there is an international conspiracy against the United States that includes Pope John Paul and Queen Elizabeth of England and has accused many prominent American statesmen of conspiring with Soviet leaders to impair U.S. power.

In 1980 LaRouche received 177,784 votes in Democratic presidential primaries, representing .09 percent of the total votes cast. In 1982 a LaRouche candidate opposing Maryland Congresswoman Barbara Mikulski, Debra Freeman, won 19 percent of the Democratic primary votes.[14]

(d) Some of the smaller groups include (1) The Liberty Lobby, founded in 1955 in Washington, D.C., which claims a membership of some 200,000 who subscribe to the *Liberty Ledger* and the monthly *Liberty Letters*; (2) the Nationalist Socialist White People's Party, under the leadership of Lincoln Rockwell, with a handful of members; (3) the National Socialist Party of America, based in Chicago; (4) the National Association for the Advancement of White People, with about 6,000 members; (5) the National Socialist Movement, founded in 1975 with chapters in twenty-two states; (6) the White Aryan Resistance, based in California with about 5,000 members; and (7) the Invisible Empire of the Knights of the Ku Klux Klan, committed to the "protection and maintenance of distinctive institutions, rights, privileges, principles and ideals of pure Americanism and to the defense and preservation of the Constitution as originally written and intended."

A feeling of frustration, resentment, and impotence has always provided the best climate for the growth of extremist movements, which

---

14. "The 'LaRouche Democrats,' " by Steven Strasser and Ann McDaniel, printed in *Newsweek*, April 16, 1984, p. 31.

invariably come up with simple answers to complex problems and nationalist solutions to deepset social and economic difficulties. The extremist movements we mentioned are but an expression of such a mood. Currently, they are dispersed, without central direction, and weak. But in a turbulent political landscape, the voices of violence and "unreason" could grow loud, if they find a leader. Under certain circumstances—economic depression or military setbacks—these voices could unite to test the foundation of constitutional government and democracy.

The Return of the Extreme Right in Europe

Almost half a century after the defeat of the Nazis and Fascists in Europe, right-wing extremism, whose intellectual roots we discussed in Chapter 8, is surfacing again. The ideology revolves around the same old staples: racism, xenophobia, and nationalism. Its springboard is also what it was in the early thirties: the insecurities and anxieties that arise from an economic crisis, unemployment, and international tensions. Its political manifestations, tame for the time being, may well become increasingly intransigent.

The spearhead of the extreme right today is in France—it is the National Front, a party organized and led by Jean-Marie Le Pen. It is dedicated to the preservation of the purity of the French nation and its culture, and is directed against the immigrant workers (and their families) in France. There are more than 4.5 million immigrants in France today and at least half of them are Muslims from North Africa or from the African colonies of France. Le Pen's movement seeks to deny them citizenship, education, and employment and to repatriate them. Muslims speak a different tongue; they have a different religion (mosques have sometimes been built close to the French medieval cathedrals), different laws and customs (some practice polygamy), and they produce children at a much higher rate than French citizens or Europeans. They refuse to assimilate; they want to maintain their cultural, religious, and linguistic identity as well as their attachment to the countries they came from. However, since they also want to and do work in France, they are accused of depriving French citizens of jobs at a time when unemployment remains high.

In the elections for the European Parliament in 1984 and again in the legislative election of 1986 the French National Front received almost 10 percent of the vote; and finally to the surprise of all Jean-Marie Le Pen received 14.4 percent of the vote in the presidential election held on April 24, 1988. In many opinion polls more than one-third of the French "agree" or "agree more or less" with the positions taken by Jean-Marie Le Pen.

Economic depression afflicts most of Europe, with unemployment averaging about 13 percent in the countries belonging to the European Common Market. There are large numbers of immigrant workers in the Federal Republic of Germany, England, Holland, Belgium, and Denmark, as well as in Switzerland and Sweden, which are outside the Common Market. They are increasingly being looked upon with suspicion and even hostility and their repatriation is under serious consideration. Right-wing parties like the French National Front had been formed or are being formed in England, Belgium, and Holland, while similar movements are developing in Denmark and the Federal Republic of Germany. In the legislative election held in Denmark on May 9, 1988 the right-wing "Progress Party" received 9 percent of the vote. They have all taken up the same slogans of nationalism, xenophobia, and racism, although they have not yet challenged democracy and the democratic institutions of the countries where they have surfaced. A severe economic or foreign policy crisis could propel them into action against the "aliens" and the "undesirables" in the name of national unity and national independence, and in the process they could jettison the protections that constitutional government and democracy provide.

Bibliography

Abel, Theodore. *The Nazi Movement: Why Hitler Came to Power.* New York: Atheneum, 1965.

———. *The Nazi Movement.* New York: Atherton Press, 1965.

Allen, William Sheridan. *The Nazi Seizure of Power: The Experience of a Single German Town.* New York: New Viewpiont, 1973.

Aycoberry, Pierre. *The Nazi Question.* New York: Pantheon Books, 1981.

Bracher, K. Dietrich. *The German Dictatorship.* New York: Praeger, 1970.

Bullock, Alan. *Hitler: A Study in Tyranny.* New York: Harper & Row, 1971.

Carsten, F. F. *The Rise of Fascism.* Berkeley: University of California Press, 1967.

DeFelice, Renzo. *Interpretations of Fascism.* Cambridge, Mass.: Harvard U.P. 1977.

———. *Fascism: An Informal Introduction to Its Theory and Practice.* New Brunswick, N. J.: Transaction Books, 1976.

Finer, Herman. *Mussolini's Italy.* New York: Grosset & Dunlap, 1965. First published in London: Victor Gollancz, 1935.

Gallo, Max. *Mussolini's Italy.* New York: Macmillan, 1973.

Germani, Gino. *Authoritarianism, Fascism, and National Populism.* New

Gregor, A. James. *Fascism: The Contemporary Interpretation.* Morristown, N.J.: General Learning Press, 1975.

———. *Young Mussolini and the Intellectual Origins of Fascism.* Berkeley: University of California Press, 1979.

———. *Italian Fascism and Developmental Dictatorship.* Princeton, N.J.: Princeton U.P., 1980.

Heiden, Konrad. *Der Fuehrer.* Boston: Beacon Press, 1969.

Hitler, Adolf. *Mein Kampf.* Boston: Houghton Mifflin, 1962.

Joes, Anthony James. *Fascism in the Contemporary World: Ideology, Evolution, Resurgence.* Boulder, Colo.: Westview Press, 1978.

King, Desmond S. *The New Right: Politics, Markets and Citizenship.* Chicago: The Dorsey Press, 1987.

Langer, Walter C. *The Mind of Adolf Hitler.* New York: New American Library, 1978.

Laqueur, Walter. *Fascism: A Reader's Guide.* Berkeley and Los Angeles, Calif.: University of California Press, 1976.

———, and George Mosse. *International Fascism.* New York: Harper, 1966.

Merkl, Peter H. *The Making of a Stormtrooper.* Princeton, N.J.: Princeton U.P., 1979.
————. *Political Violence Under the Swastika.* Princeton, N.J.: Princeton U.P., 1975.
Mussolini, Benito. *My Autobiography.* New York: Charles Scribner's Sons, 1928.
Neumann, Franz. *Behemoth: The Structure and Practice of National Socialism.* 2d ed.
    New York: Oxford U.P., 1944.
Reich, Wilhelm. *The Mass Psychology of Fascism.* New York: Farrar, Straus & Giroux,
    1970.
Schoenberger, Robert A., ed. *The American Right Wing.* New York: Holt, Rinehart
    and Winston, 1969.
Shirer, William L. *The Rise and Fall of the Third Reich.* New York: Fawcett-World, 1978.
Smith, Dennis Mack. *Mussolini's Roman Empire.* New York: Viking, 1976.
Tannenbaum, Edward R. *The Fascist Experience.* New York: Basic Books, 1972.

The American Right

Barnhart, Joe Edward. *The Southern Baptist Holy War.* Texas Monthly Press, 1988.
Bell, Daniel (ed.). *The Radical Right.* New York: Doubleday, 1964.
Bozell, L. Brent. *Dialogues in Americanism.* Chicago: H. Regnery Co., 1964.
Buckley, William F. *Right Reason: A Collection.*
Crawford, Alan. *Thunder on the Right: The "New Right" and the Politics of Resentment.*
    New York: Pantheon Books, 1980.
Epstein, Benjamin, and Forster, Arnold. *The Radical Right.* New York: Vintage, 1967.
Fachre, Gabriel J. *Religious Right and Christian Faith.* Erdmans, 1982.
Kymlicka, B. B., and Mathews, Jean V. *The Reagan Revolution?* Chicago: The Dorsey
    Press, 1988.
Liebman, Robert C. *New Christian Right: Mobilization and Legitimation.* Aldine Pub-
    lishing Co., 1983.
Lipset, Seymour Martin, and Raab, Earl. *The Politics of Unreason: Right Wing Extrem-
    ism in America, 1790–1970.* Chicago: University of Chicago Press, 1978.
Macedo, Stephen. *The New Right v. the Constitution.* Cato Institute, 1986.
Roelfs, H. Mark. *Ideology and Myth in American Politics: A Critique of a National Political
    Mind.* Boston: Little, Brown, 1976.
Shapsmeir, Edward and Frederick. *Political Parties and Civic Action Groups.* West-
    port, Conn.: Greenwood Press, 1981.
Viguerie, Richard A. *Establishment vs. the People: Is a New Populist Revolt on the Way?*
    Chicago: Regnery Gateway, Inc., 1984.

Part Four

Old Voices and New: Nationalism, The Third World, Feminism, Liberation Theology, Revolution

What is truth? asked jesting Pilate, and would not stay for an answer.

FRANCIS BACON   "Of Truth"

This part will deal with several significant movements and ideologies now being voiced throughout the world. They include (1) nationalism and ethnonationalisms; (2) Third World ideologies, in which nationalism played, and continues to play, an important role; (3) feminism, in which one can find an expansion of liberalism but with some radical and even revolutionary overtones; (4) liberation theology — calling in the name of God for revolutionary action and borrowing from Marxism; and (5) some relatively new and extremist ideologies of revolution that put the emphasis on human will and action — on *praxis*.

All these ideologies and movements, so disparate at first glance, have a number of things in common: all of them borrow a great deal from past ideologies — nationalism, anarchism, early Christian thought, utopian socialism, Marxism and Leninism, and even liberal and democratic thought. The wine seems to be the same old heady wine, but one will find it mixed with many recent vintages. All of these ideologies demand the realization of long-unfulfilled imperatives: they all show the same impatience with the injustices that history has heaped upon the backs of so many; they all seek redemption "now and here." "This is our world" and "we must set it right," they all seem to affirm. They all share a profound, almost religious, sense of righteousness, of what is morally right and must be done and what is morally unacceptable and has to be destroyed. Above all, they put great emphasis on human will—on our freedom to change and improve radically the circumstances that surround us.

Even if many hail from the past, these new voices are extremely powerful and convey a sense of urgency as they confront old values and institutions: the state, the church, the family, individual rights, property rights, and established political institutions, including the State.

10 | *Nationalism*

Without a country . . . you are the bastards of humanity. Soldiers without banner . . . you will find neither faith nor protection.

MAZINNI   to the Italians c. 1850

People who once every four years watch the Olympics or who occasionally turn their TV to United Nations debates cannot help but marvel at the number of nation-states with their delegates, their flags, their athletes, their diplomats, and their national anthems stressing the same themes — pride and strength, unity and loyalty to the fatherland or the motherland, military glory, a call to action and sacrifice, an assertion of superiority and a demand for utter devotion. "Our fight for our land will never cease; it was ours and it will be ours forever and ever" (Uganda); "Fatherland, fatherland . . . thy sons swear to breathe their last on thine alter" (Mexico); "Onward sons of *la patrie* . . . The day of glory is before you" (France); "Germany, Germany above all others" (West Germany); "Sweet land of liberty . . ." and so on. Today are more than one hundred and seventy nation-states with their own armies, navies, language, and tariffs. Within nation-states there are also many "nationalities" — Basques, Bretons, Catalans, Corsicans, Armenians, Macedonians, Ukrainians, Georgians, Ibos, American Indians, and so forth — each asserting their own identity.

Ours is a world of nation-states. Nationalism has proven to be one of the most tenacious ideological bonds binding human beings together into separate political communities. Its values may vary, the particular content of the citizen's attachments may change, but fundamentally the nationalist feeling is described in terms of a common feeling of togetherness that identifies the "we" against the "they." Nations are invariably defined in terms of a *"community"* and in terms of the *loyalty* of the individual to the community. It is a common mind, common habits — moral, social, civil, and political — common ancestors, common character, common race, common symbols, common language, common culture, a corporate will, and a common soul. Loyalty is invariably described in terms of dedication, sacrifice,

238

*Old Voices and
New:
Nationalism, The
Third World,
Feminism,
Liberation
Theology, and
Revolution*

subordination, love, and affection. Nations are either a motherland or a fatherland, evoking the obedience and affection that children owe to their parents.

Even if we take it for granted, nationalism is something relatively recent. It is primarily a political ideology that developed in Europe in the latter part of the eighteenth century and throughout the nineteenth century. After the end of World War II, in 1945, it spread to the so-called Third World (the then colonies in Africa, Asia, and the Middle East), and also Latin America. Like all political ideologies, nationalism is an instrument for the acquisition of political power by certain groups and the organization of political power on the basis of new principles — notably popular participation. Hugh Seton-Watson defines nationalism as "a policy of creating national consciousness within a politically unconscious population"[1] and he notes that its purpose was precisely the mobilization of a population behind new leaders and new leadership groups.

Nationalism was, and remains, a unifying ideology aimed at manufacturing consent on the basis of a strong appeal and symbols of identification. It generates emotional supports, creates an emotional state of exaltation and sacrifice, and provides for loyalty to new political elites. Nationalism solidifies a community, creates allegiance, establishes uniformities, and attempts to absorb the citizen into the purpose and the life of the nation-state.

Nationality, Nation-States, States, and Nationalism

Some clarifications are needed in order to better understand the dynamics of nationalism.

Nationality denotes an ethnic and cultural identity, based on common values. *A state*, on the other hand, is a political organization holding and exercising supreme power through its various agencies over a given people within a given territory. A state may include a number of "nationalities." The most illustrious example of such a state was the Austro-Hungarian Empire that until 1918 was a political administrative organization governing Slavs, Slovenes, Croatians, Italians, Montenegrins, Hungarians, Poles, Austrians, Czechs, and quite a few others. A state, in other words, may be "multinational." The best examples today are the Soviet Union and Yugoslavia.

A *nation-state*, in contrast to a nationality (which is not a state) and to a state (which is not necessarily based upon a common nationality), is supposed to be *both a state and a nationality*. Political power stems from and applies to a given ethnic national group within a given territory, so there may be nationalities without their own state, and there also may be states

1. Hugh Seton-Watson, *Nations and States*, p. 449.

that do not derive their legitimacy and identity from a nationality. Catalonia is an example of the first and the Soviet Union an example of the latter.

Nationalism is the ideology that asserts the right of a given nationality to form a state and becomes a movement to obtain it. Nationalism rationalizes such a demand; it becomes a powerful political movement mobilizing all nationalities to form their states. It was the case with the Greeks throughout the centuries of their occupation by Turkey; the case of Poland as it has attempted throughout most of its history to reaffirm its nationhood by creating an independent Polish state; it has been also the case with most of the erstwhile colonies after World War II. Nationalism is the ideology that has led to the mushrooming of nation-states and continues to be a force that propels every single nationality—no matter how small—to become a nation-state.

"Political Nations" and "Historic Nations"

The difference between "nation-states" and "states" corresponds to the differences that some German scholars have suggested between "culture nations" and "political nations," respectively. The *Kulturnation* is based on the criteria of nationality: history, common language, common religion, shared memories of the past as they have unfolded themselves in the arts and the literature, and a communality of customs and traditions. Most European nations in this sense are "historic" or "culture" nations—they have a commonly shared past and culture. On the other hand, political nations—the *Staatnation*—are supposed to lack strong cultural and historical attributes. Usually there is hardly any communality of religion; there are different languages spoken; and there are many ethnic minorities. Their common bond is political—the existence of a regime that is accepted by all. They are simply "states." Even such diverse countries as the United States and the Soviet Union are defined in such terms—they are "political nations." If you accept the Constitution and live by it you are an American. And those who live under the communist regime are citizens of the U.S.S.R., irrespective of whether they are Russians, Uzbeks, Armenians, Georgians, or Ukrainians.

It is impossible to find *Staatnations* and *Kulturnations* in their pure form. Even the French, who are proud of their "culture" and their past, concede that within France there are elements that are "foreign" in terms of a strict definition of a common "cultural nation." There are Catholics, Jews, Protestants, Muslims, and at least 4 to 5 million immigrants who may become "naturalized" French citizens. On the other hand, nobody can deny that political nations like the United States or the Soviet Union have common cultural traits—in the common sharing of the past, common traditions and values, and common lifestyles. Even if the American melting pot has not fully refashioned the immigrants, it has nonetheless produced citizens that, irrespective of their ethnic, cultural, or religious background, share certain values and traditions. And in the Soviet Union there is a Soviet fatherland beginning to transcend all nationalities.

240

*Old Voices and
New:
Nationalism, The
Third World,
Feminism,
Liberation
Theology, and
Revolution*

Nationality and Nationalism:
Objective and Subjective Criteria

The familiar controversy as to the primacy of the group or the individual reappears in the various theories of nationalism. The nation-state may be viewed, to put it very simply, as the creature of the individuals who comprise it; it exists and derives its existence from the support and the consent the individuals give to it. As a French publicist put, *it is the result of a contract or of a "daily referendum."*[2] The terms "nation" and "nationality" began to appear only in the seventeenth century, to denote the emergence of a consciousness of a common identity of people in a given territory. People in a given location began to gain awareness of something they had in common as distinguished from others. There is a common sharing and a common predisposition for sharing it. A people's feelings and will create the nation.

The nation may also be viewed as having a separate reality outside and beyond the consent of the individuals who make it up. It is an objective and historical reality that overwhelms the individuals. Historical and other reasons give it a transcendental quality and a moral superiority that impose themselves upon the individuals. According to this view, individual freedom and morality cannot be attained except within the nation and in terms of the national values and beliefs. The nation, in other words, is "real"; the individual is not.

Objective Factors. The most common traits with which nationality is associated remain: (1) language; (2) religion; (3) a consciousness of common traditions and history and a will to maintain them; and (4) a common territory. When no common territory exists, as was the case with the Jews and occasionally with the Greeks, the fourth trait is the memory of the territory that was occupied sometime in the past and a desire to recover it. Different authors and nationalist movements have stressed at different times one or another of the various "objective" factors:

Religion was particularly important in the period of the formation of national consciousness. Religious wars were fought to both emancipate the State from the papacy and to create internal unity, which was endangered both by the papal control or by the existence of religious minorities. People were expected to have the religion of their king within a nation.

Language was an important criterion used by a number of authors, especially German. It was a common and distinct vehicle that bound people together, creating a special bond among its users. But, as the case of Switzerland shows conclusively, it is not a necessary condition.

Race was used primarily, as we have seen, in the twentieth century by the Nazis to show the unique traits of the German nation. It is supposed to refer to specific biological traits which are not always clearly perceived or agreed upon.

2. Ernest Renan, "What Is a Nation?" In Hans Kohn, *Nationalism, Its Meaning and History*, pp. 135–140.

Ethnicity is a broader term that may or may not include race but usually refers to a number of the common cultural attributes. Both race and ethnicity are terms indiscriminately used in Europe as well as in Asia and Africa. Some groups perceive themselves or are perceived by others as a "race" or as an "ethnic group" and often as both.

The *common past* has been constantly invoked and when it could not be easily found, every effort was made to manufacture it by rewriting history.

Geography — a common territorial basis — is invariably invoked. Nations like an individual had to have "a home," a space under the sun.

Subjective Factors:
Nationalism and Self-Determination

All the objective traits we outlined — religion, language, common history, and so on — may exist and may be commonly shared by a given "nationality." Nationalism, however, becomes an ideology and a movement only when it translates this self-consciousness into a demand to form a nation. The subjective element is an element of will and purpose. Nationalism asserts the validity of the objective factors of nationality for *certain* political purposes; it affirms their uniqueness and often their exclusiveness. It is not only the will to live together but to have a government. It is the assertion that such a purpose has an inherent claim to be heard and to realize itself; it is a purpose that is presumed to be morally just. In this sense nationalism is, as Elie Kedourie writes in one of the most penetrating studies on the subject, "a doctrine *invented* in Europe at the beginning of the nineteenth century . . . [It] holds that humanity is naturally divided into nations, that nations are known by their characteristics . . . and that the only legitimate type of government is national self-government."[3]

Nothing better exemplifies the differences between those who stress objective factors from those who rely on subjective ones in defining a nation — the first relying on history, language, religion, and tradition and the second on subjective factors — than the conflict between Germany and France over the provinces of Alsace and Lorraine occupied and annexed by the Germans in 1871. Renan, the French publicist, in his famous essay *What Is a Nation?* (1882), was willing to accept the verdict of the people given through a referendum. The Germans, on the other hand, asserted their claims in terms of historical right. "These provinces are ours by the right of the sword," wrote a German nationalist, "and we shall rule them by the virtue of a higher right. . . . *We desire, even against their will, to restore them to themselves.*"[4]

Self-determination is the demand made by a nationality to become a state. It became a doctrine when it was expressly stipulated in the famous

3. Elie Kedourie, *Nationalism*, p. 77.
4. In Hans Kohn, op. cit., p. 61.

242

*Old Voices and
New:
Nationalism, The
Third World,
Feminism,
Liberation
Theology, and
Revolution*

Fourteen Points that President Woodrow Wilson issued as the guidelines for building a new political order in Europe after World War I.

"Self-determination," Wilson declared, "is an imperative principle of action, which statesmen will . . . ignore at their peril." World War I, he claimed, "had its roots in the disregard of the rights of small nations and of nationalities which lacked the union and the force to make good their claim to determine their own allegiance and their own form of political life." He suggested among other things, in the form of guidelines for the Peace Conference that was to follow the hostilities that ended in 1918, "a readjustment of the frontiers of Italy . . . along clearly recognizable lines"; "the freest opportunity of autonomous development" for the peoples of Austria-Hungary; the redrawing of some of the frontiers in the Balkans "along historically established lines of *allegiance* and *nationality*"; "an absolutely unmolested opportunity of autonomous development" for the national minorities within Turkey; "an independent Polish state . . . inhabited by indisputably Polish populations."[5]

It is in the name of nationalism and self-determination that old multinational political organizations and empires gradually broke down until by the end of World War I most European states became nation-states. The Austro-Hungarian Empire, the Ottoman Empire, the Russian Empire broke up under the force of nationalist movements.

Rousseau and Nationalism

Everybody seems to agree that the great French philosopher, Jean Jacques Rousseau (1717–1778) is the "father" of modern nationalism. For some he was a romantic—stressing emotions instead of reason and believing that psychological attachments were far more potent than agreements derived from rational calculations and expectations. The nation was an emotional and a spiritual entity. For others his theory of popular sovereignty helped identify the state with the people; still others consider that Rousseau was the first to see in nations the best form of expression of community life. Others see in him the precursor of totalitarianism—the development of irrational and conformist national themes couched in terms of national superiority that led to the subordination of the individual.

It was Rousseau's theory of the "general will," but more particularly the distortion of this theory by others, that leads us directly to the exaltation of communitarian and national feeling. For Rousseau the general will was in fact the will of all the people—but only on condition that they were right! The people were sovereign and would and could act rationally only if they abandoned their direct and immediate personal interests and acted as social beings by putting the interests of the whole above their own. It

5. Presented on February 11, 1918. Cited in Alan P. Grimes and Robert H. Horowitz, *Modern Political Ideologies*, New York: Oxford University Press, 1959, pp. 501–503.

assumed that people in a community could reach a consensus. But under what conditions, and how?

Nationalism was to become the answer. By injecting the same values and feelings, by stressing unifying themes, by exalting what unites, by inculcating through education, ritual, and at times even force common national bonds or strengthening those that exist, nationalism would shape the people as a whole to develop a common frame of reference from which an agreement, a general will, would result. Nationalism becomes thus a unifying ideology — a powerful emotional force. "Everything for my fatherland; nothing for myself." The citizen becomes a patriot.

The political leader, the prophet, the legislator, is called upon to distill the rules and the institutions that will establish and consolidate a common frame of reference — a feeling of togetherness, a national mind. Moses, according to Rousseau, "gave" to the Jews their nationality of which they were only dimly aware. He built "a nation out of a swarm of wretched fugitives who possessed no arts, no arms, no talents, no virtues, no courage and who — with not a single square foot of territory that they might call their own — were in truth a troop of outcasts upon the face of the earth. . . . He imposed rites upon them and ceremonies to be performed within the bosom of their families. . . . It was Moses who dared transform this gang of servile migrants into a political body — *a free people*."[6]

Mazinni (1805–1872), an Italian nationalist, expressed Rousseau's nationalism even more forcefully by telling the Italians, who were still divided into many states: "Without a country you have neither name, token, voice, nor rights, no admission as brothers into the fellowship of the Peoples. *You are the bastards of humanity*. Soldiers without banner, Israelites among the nations, you will find neither faith, nor protection; none will be sureties for you."[7]

The French Revolution

It was the French Revolution of 1789 that asserted the sovereignty of the people *and* the nation. But it was also the French Revolution that through its various stages highlighted the distortions of Rousseau's ideas. The revolution began as an assertion of individual freedoms and popular sovereignty. It finished with an absolutist ruler — Napoleon — and an expansionist nationalism that changed the map of Europe.

With the overthrow of the monarchy in 1792, the French Revolution quickly established patriotism as the highest ideal and as the most intimate bond among the people. Rituals, national festivals, symbolisms, national songs were all used to create a solidarity among the French. A system of national education was instituted to propagate patriotic values. Every attempt was made to wipe out regional and linguistic particularisms in favor of cultural unity, territorial integration, and centralization. The republic

6. In "Considerations on the Government of Poland," in Grimes and Horwitz, op. cit., p. 469.
7. In "The Duties of Man," ibid., p. 496. Italics added.

244

*Old Voices and
New:
Nationalism, The
Third World,
Feminism,
Liberation
Theology, and
Revolution*

was to be "one and indivisible." Compliance with the revolution and its policies was promoted everywhere, requiring coercive measures that gradually were transformed into an outright tyranny. A revolutionary leader spoke of "the *tyranny of liberty* against despotism."

The last phase of the revolution produced an expansionist nationalism and a desire to conquer and subdue other peoples in the name of liberty *and* France. French men and women were made to "march in step" with the nationalist ideology, not only in Napoleon's battlefields but also at home. "The citizen is born, lives and dies for the fatherland" was the inscription that all French could read in every municipality where they lived. "Oh sublime people! Accept the sacrifices of my whole being. Happy is the man who is born in your midst; happier is he who can die for your happiness," exclaimed Robespierre. The citizen-patriot gradually became transformed into the citizen-soldier, willing to die for his country.

Thus we find in the manifestation of French nationalism the traits that were to be repeated elsewhere in Europe: a revolutionary fervor associated with the destruction of the aristocracy and the economic and social order it represented; an effort to devise slogans to unify the country and to break down all internal barriers; the creation of new national symbols to mobilize the people and inculcate in them common values, and thus elicit their support; and, finally, the assertion of national virtue and right over individual citizens, and over other peoples as well.

Throughout Europe, nationalism played the same important role in forging tightly integrated communities. It was strongly related to the rise of the middle classes and the destruction of the feudal structures. Politically speaking, it was a vehicle for the acquisition of power by the middle classes by mobilizing the masses as they had never been mobilized before. Controlling "their minds and souls" was a source of far greater power than any ruler or class appealing to status, tradition, authority, or divine right had ever claimed or possessed before.

Traditional Nationalism

The French nationalism that came with and after the French Revolution was an intensely ideological phenomenon that broke from tradition and the past. It attempted to restructure society and formulate a new way of life, a new nation. This was not the case with traditional nationalisms as they grew in response to the French nationalism, especially in Germany. French nationalism was man-made and future-oriented. Traditional nationalism, on the other hand, sought its source in the past. The nation was portrayed as a natural phenomenon, not an act of political will.

German nationalists, influenced by Rousseau, naturally selected from his writings what suited them best. Herder (1744–1803) sought the German national spirit in the "people" — the *Volk* — as it had developed from the time of the German tribes. Herder also "legitimized" nations and nation-states by claiming, as so many others have claimed since, that they

The Romantic painter Delacroix (1798–1863) painted "Mother-France" and her children flocking behind the flag and mounting the barricades in the name of Freedom. *(Photo: The Bettmann Archive, Inc.)*

were "willed" by God and that the diversity of nations represented His will. Men and women could best fulfill themselves within nations.

Traditional nationalism was reinforced not only by biological and racial arguments but also by cultural ones. The purity of the German language indicated, among other things, its cultural superiority. A German writer, Fichte (1762–1814), called upon Germany to assert its "cultural" supremacy. Some asked that all those speaking the German language be united into one fatherland. Others, long before the Nazis, asserted the racial purity of the Germans. Unification and independence was in the air, and German philosophers extolled the State as the embodiment of the purest ideals of the Germans. It was the Prussian state that ultimately was to become the vehicle of German national unification in 1871.

What characterized German nationalism, therefore, was its conservative emphasis. It looked to the past; it appealed to the establishment groups; it was imposed, not made as it was with the nationalism of the French Revolution. The same was true with many eastern European nationalisms, notably the Russian one, stressing religion as one of its primary forces and only indirectly race and language.

British and American Nationalism

The early awakening of nationalism in England in the eighteenth century and in America in the decades before and after the Declaration of Independence were closely associated with individual freedoms and toleration. Pride in the Constitution and individual liberties, including religious freedom, characterized this early Anglo-Saxon form of nationalism. It derived from an individualistic ethic: it reflected the proclamation of the virtues and the initiative of the individual, not of the collectivity. Even a conservative like Edmund Burke, who admired the British national institutions, never subordinated religion, tradition, and rights to the nation. He remained a committed patriot only as long as his country served them well. One must love one's country, he pointed out, only if it is "lovely."

As for the United States, the main assertion of nationalism lay in the creation of a republic best exemplified in the Constitution. The country remained wide open to immigration and as succeeding waves of immigrants came from England, Scandinavia, Germany, Ireland, Italy, Poland, and elsewhere it lost whatever distinctive ethnic, cultural, or religious characteristics it might have claimed. As for its history—Lexington, Concord, Bunker Hill, the Boston Tea Party, etc.—it was repeated in the schools and in literature. It strengthened and maintained the political symbolism of individual freedoms and constitutional government. American "nationalism" remained political in character: it meant an attachment to the Constitution and to the individual rights spelled out. It was *civic* loyalty that counted.

Both in England and in the United States, of course, the assertions that the fatherland is above the individual were made, but not as often and not as convincingly as in Europe. No nationalist ethic developed that subordinated the individual to the collectivity; no religious, historical, or cultural bonds were imposed upon the individuals in the name of the nation; no uniformities of thought and action were shaped in the name of an overriding national reality and goals.

Of course, such views about American and British nationalism must be taken with a grain of salt. It is true that the two countries have remained relatively far more open and tolerant than others and that nationalism never managed to mobilize the people in one overriding conformist ethic as other nationalisms did in Europe. But there were frequent assertions of national supremacy in both countries. In England, Rudyard Kipling and many others spoke of the "white man's burden"—the self-appointed duty for the British to civilize and educate the masses of the colonial peoples, "the lesser breeds," that were under their control. Both cultural and racist considerations entered into the formulation of English nationalism. In the United States, by the end of the nineteenth century, there was a strong nationalist ideology and vocabulary. There was, it was claimed, a "manifest destiny" for Anglo-Saxon nations like the United States to play an important role in world affairs and to assume its own share of domination and tutelage of "lesser" peoples. Considerations that were religious, political, economic, and not infrequently racist entered into it. And the effort to exact civic conformity and loyalty around national symbols was and remains ever present. Deviations from the national and political ethos of American liberalism have been often branded as "un-American" and at times became almost synonymous with treason.

The Nation-State and Ethnonationalisms

It appears that nation-states are beginning to get a taste of the heady medicine of nationalism that brought them into being. It is *ethnonationalism* — the search and the expression *within* the nation-state of particular ethnic, cultural, regional, religious, or linguistic *autonomous* or *separatist* movements. They range from demands for outright independence and the assumption of statehood to requests for "self-government." Such manifestations sometimes have clear-cut territorial bases — linguistic, ethnic, religious, racial, or cultural groupings that are easily identifiable within a given region of the nation-state. For instance, the French-speaking minority in Canada, which is also predominantly Catholic, live in Quebec — a province of Canada; the Georgians or Uzbeks or Armenians in the Soviet Union, the Corsicans or the Bretons in France, the Scots and the Welsh in the United Kingdom, Sicilians in Italy, some Indian tribes in the United States, the Ibos in Nigeria, they all can be located in certain regions of the states in which they live.

But not infrequently a territorial identification of an ethnic minority is difficult — the particular people who share specific ethnic attributes are spread throughout the nation-state. This is the case, for instance, with the blacks in the United States, and also with virtually all other groups — Italian-Americans, Greek-Americans, Irish-Americans, German-Americans, American Jews, and so on. The same is true for Protestants in France, for Catholics in England, and for Jews in the Soviet Union.

Ethnonationalist Ideologies

Ethnonationalist movements have become so widespread in our day that generalizing about them is just as difficult as undertaking a detailed study of each and all of them, in Belgium, the United Kingdom, France, the United States, the Soviet Union, Nigeria, China, Iran, and so on. There is virtually no modern nation-state where the phenomenon is not present. In each and every case it has generated ideological manifestations that assume the following patterns: (1) they are downright *nationalist*, borrowing from the nineteenth-century ideology of nationalism; (2) they are *reformist*,

248

*Old Voices and
New:
Nationalism, The
Third World,
Feminism,
Liberation
Theology, and
Revolution*

calling for basic reforms in the direction of increased federalism and de-centralization; (3) in an attempt to reformulate a theory of democracy, they stress *direct participation, loyalty, and control* by the citizens within local or small units.

Of particular interest for our discussion is the nationalist forms that ethnonationalism displays. They exist when a basic ingredient of nationality differentiates a given people living within a state from the rest of the population. This ingredient of nationality may be a different religion or language, or a common past, or racial and cultural characteristics. There are cases where, as we noted, such a situation is clear. The people of Quebec, Canada, speak French, worship as Catholics, and have common memories that identify them with France and French history and culture. Scots and Welsh claim to have distinctive cultural or religious or linguistic traits from the English. Flemings and Walloons in Belgium speak different languages and occupy different parts of Belgium. In Cyprus, where Greeks and Turks are separated, everything divides the two populations: religion, language, culture, and common history, all of which intensify the differences between the two peoples.

Quite often, economic considerations reinforce ethnonationalism. In some cases an ethnic minority lives in a region that is relatively poor: for instance, the Quebecois in Canada, the Welsh in Great Britain, and the Macedonians and Albanians in Yugoslavia. There are theories of "internal colonialism," according to which some ethnic populations and regions are exploited for the benefit of others within one and the same nation and, more particularly, for the benefit of the ruling elite. A commonly shared feeling of being exploited strengthens ethnonationalist sentiments in favor of separation.

Black Separatism in the United States

A little more than 10 percent of the people in the United States are black. Brought to America until 1808 as slaves or born and raised in slave plantations until 1863, they were people without rights under the law, without property, without skills and education. In some states, slaves were not allowed to learn to read or write. They were at the mercy of their white owners. The Civil War led to their emancipation and even to their political enfranchisement. But soon thereafter discriminating practices developed. The blacks were for all practical purposes disenfranchised in the majority of states and remained without protection of the law, the right to vote, or the opportunity to learn the skills that would provide for a better life and income. They were excluded from the American liberal mainstream. Yet in contrast to most all other ethnic minorities in so many other parts of the world, the prevalent ideology among blacks in the United States has been to join, rather than to reject, the mainstream of American liberal values, to become part of it and to be integrated within it. Louis Hartz's *The Liberal Tradition in America* provides perhaps the best answer for the lack of black separatism. The overwhelming liberal ethos in America — stressing equality of opportunity and individual effort — could not be arbitrarily interpreted to exclude men and women because of their color. At the same time, it exercised an overwhelming attraction for blacks—it promised them the equality that they wanted and of which they were deprived.

There were many other reasons, however, for the lack of a black separatist movement. One reason was the lack of education among blacks for a long period of time, which made it difficult for them to gain a consciousness of their position and to translate it into a distinct and organized political movement. Second, they lacked a clearly identified territorial base—a territory in which they lived, as is the case with the Basques in France, or the French in Quebec, or the Croatians in Yugoslavia, or even the Scots and the Welsh in the United Kingdom, and the Corsicans in France. To be sure, a preponderant percentage of blacks lived in the South, but after World War I, and even more so since World War II, the blacks who moved in search of employment to the urban centers of the North and the West began to outnumber those who remained in the South. The black population dispersed throughout the United States. Their predicament, economic or social, remains a national phenomenon; it is not associated with a given region, area, or state to which national resources have not been properly allocated, as is the case with Corsica, for instance. The arguments of "internal colonialism" and "regional deprivation" could not be advanced in order to reinforce territorial separatist claims. Third, in contrast to most separatist movements, no common and different language existed for the blacks. They all spoke and wrote—when they were allowed to learn it—English. Finally, as the economy developed and the most overt forms of discrimination ended, blacks appeared less and less a homogeneous social force. They became increasingly differentiated on the basis of income, status, skills, and lifestyles. Some had fully entered the "mainstream" and became its supporters; to others, the mainstream continued to beckon. Even if most blacks remained out of the mainstream, the hope had been kindled that they too would "overcome," and become a part of it.

Without a clearly identified territorial base, without a commonly shared consciousness of their traditions and past, without a common and separate language, without a common social and economic identity or even a commonly shared sense of exploitation—which goes with "class"—the blacks, excluded and invisible to all others for so long, became increasingly visible to each other and to all as Americans. Only the church and black religious leaders provide a distinct center of community life and leadership.

Separatist Movements   The most spectacular phenomenon of the American society remains the lack of black separatism and the lack of ideologies to promote it. There are only a few ideologies that can be mentioned. Black "nationalism" is associated with Marcus Garvey (1887–1940) and his movement, the Universal Negro Improvement Association, founded in 1914 in Jamaica and transferred to Harlem in 1920. Its platform advocated Negro nationhood, Negro race consciousness, inculcation of "ideals of manhood and womanhood" in every Negro, self-determination, and racial self-help and self-respect.

250

*Old Voices and
New:
Nationalism, The
Third World,
Feminism,
Liberation
Theology, and
Revolution*

As stated in the platform, Africa was to be "territory" for the blacks in the same way that Israel was to be a home for the Jews, according to the Zionists. This meant that the liberation of Africa, virtually all of which was under colonial rule at the time, had to be undertaken. In the meantime, race consciousness would enhance the unity and cultural identity of all blacks — and Garvey was a segregationist. Racial self-help required the development of black capitalism and a black economy, and again Garvey was particularly instrumental in the building of black businesses and co-operatives. The founding of the African Orthodox Church just about completed all the elements of "nationality" to be imparted, namely economic autonomy, cultural autonomy, religious autonomy, and racial separateness. Self-determination would follow with a plea for the political independence of all blacks in Africa and of those who went to Africa and for the political independence of Africa from the colonial yoke.

It is interesting to note that at no time did Garvey assert or claim any territory of the United States as a "home" for the blacks. It was only in the years after World War I that a small group, under communist inspiration, asked for a "Negro republic" in the "Black Belt" of the South, a proposal that was not seriously considered by any of the black leaders. Instead Garvey's dreams died with him, and until almost 1965 the theme focused instead on ending all discriminatory practices and attaining integration in education, jobs, law and political representation, and social life. This theme was strengthened by the massive move of blacks from the South to the booming industrial centers in the North, the Midwest, and the West, and also by some critical decisions of the Supreme Court in favor of integration. It was also strengthened by the assertion of the blacks themselves in favor of integration under the leadership of Martin Luther King, Jr., and others and in cooperation with liberal groups among the whites and a number of white political leaders — notably John F. Kennedy and Lyndon B. Johnson. Boycotts, marches, and demonstrations gradually brought down segregation.

Malcom X   Yet it was at this juncture that a strong black nationalist movement emerged in the late 1960s first under Malcom X (1925–1965), the leader of the black Muslims and the Organization of Afro-American Unity and later by the Black Panthers, and among other groups, including white radical organizations like the Students for Democratic Society. Malcolm X gradually began to view the situation of the American blacks in the broader contexts of American capitalism. It was American exploitive capitalism, he argued, that accounted for their inferior status, and it was the destruction of capitalism that would liberate the blacks. It was not, therefore, a matter of appealing to black nationalism. Nationalism in itself could become, Malcolm X argued, a reactionary force and, even after emancipation, could keep black people under subjection. Black nationalism should become simply a component in the struggle against class oppression and exploitation everywhere in the world. Only a *revolutionary* nationalist movement could attain this. Only a movement such as socialism, which promised profound and radical change in the structure of the economy and the society, could liberate the blacks and the downtrodden.

The Black Panthers   The Black Panthers moved a step closer to this revolutionary position. Inspired in part by the revolution in Algeria against the French, the victory of Castro in Cuba, and the independence of almost all colonies in Africa during the 1960s, they saw the situation of the blacks as a phenomenon of "internal colonialism" and hence the redemption of the blacks only in terms of a revolutionary struggle against colonial masters in the United States and everywhere. The Black Panthers asked for "independence" at home; they set up their own cabinet with various ministers and organized paramilitary formations for self-defense. But they viewed the success of their movement in the context of a worldwide revolutionary struggle in which nation-states would give place to ethnic and cultural groupings cooperating with each other in a socialist world. This is what was meant by *intercommunalism*. No other specifics were given and no demands were made for any form of black autonomy or "territorial" autonomy within the United States. If the class structure in America was altered and if capitalism were superseded by a socialist commonwealth, only then would the position of blacks become safe and their lot equal with those of whites. Black nationalism is viewed as almost identical with the colonial emancipation movements. Its vision, however, remained far more difficult to realize for lack of a territorial base or "home." For Garvey it was Africa; for the Panthers, the world — a socialist world.

Garvey, Malcolm X, and the Black Panthers, and other small black organizations that advocated positions ranging from separateness and autonomy to revolutionary struggle and socialism, never captured the following of even a minority of the blacks in the United States. In the last thirty years only a handful attempted to reject completely their "Americanism" — stressing their roots and their past with Africa or Islam. Some reached out to their black-Hispanic origins stressing their ties with Cuba and the Caribbean, some converted to Islam, some even tried to familiarize themselves with African dialects. Only tiny minorities began to seek identities outside of the American world to which their ancestors had been forcefully transplanted and which was the only world they had known.

In 1984 and again in 1988 the political symbol and leader of the blacks became Jesse Jackson, who ran for the presidential nomination of the Democratic party within the "system." Throughout his candidacy, Jackson asked for the support of all people (even if particular emphasis was put on the so-called Rainbow Coalition of blacks, women, Hispanics, and other minority groups) and sought equal representation in the electoral process and within the Democratic party for all minorities and blacks. He also reached out to solicit the support of whites. Jackson identified the blacks in political terms — as a political force that could be organized within the context of democracy and had to be counted upon, just as other ethnic groups and movements were, including labor, in the past. In this sense, he remained solidly in the tradition of Martin Luther King — the tradition favoring the full integration of the blacks as citizens within the United States on the basis of equality of opportunities for all and equal treatment to all. Today the only true separatist movement is represented by a religious leader, Reverend Farrakahn, but he has a very small number of followers.

Conclusion: A World of Nations

A noted English author writing forty-two years ago (when World War II had come to an end and with it, many had thought, the dawn of a new era of internationalism) pinpointed all the defects of nationalism. "What had to be challenged and rejected," he wrote, "is the claim of nationalism to make the nation the sole rightful repository of political power and the ultimate constituent unit of world organization."[8] The same argument can be made today. We live in a world of nations.

Nationalism has deeply colored our thinking and our perceptions. The nation-state and nationalist ideologies have not been superseded by any regional arrangements, military or economic, and all efforts to translate liberalism or communism into a genuine ideological transnational movement have failed. In fact, nationalism has shaped communism just as it had shaped liberalism. National communist states have rebelled against the Soviet Union in the name of their independence, their cultures, and their way of life, seeking to find their own path to communist development just as liberal regimes developed their own national institutions and practices. Communist regimes have developed the same rivalries that liberal regimes developed, rivalries that are couched in nationalist terms. No regional efforts and no "pan"-movements in Africa or Asia, in the Atlantic area or in Europe, have managed as yet to supersede the appeal of the nation-state and the affective attachment to it.

Large or small, nationalism continues to shape the minds and the attachments of all of us. It provided a moment of exaltation to the Argentines when in 1982 they sent their navy and army into the Falkland Islands (the Malvinas as they call them), miscalculating the immediate and profound nationalist response on the part of the British. A bitter war went on for three months over these remote and inhospitable islands in which both British and Argentines became emotionally involved. Nothing could show better how seductive the old-time religion of nationalism remains. Like Rupert Brooke, a young British poet buried on a small Greek island after dying in combat in World War I, many of the British soldiers buried in the Falklands will continue to whisper to the generations to come:

> Think only this of me:
> That there is a corner of a foreign field
> That is forever England . . .
> A dust whom England bore, shaped, made aware.

If nationalism is, as it has been alleged, "the last refuge of scoundrels," most of us continue to remain scoundrels in our hearts and minds!

8. E. H. Carr, *Nationalism and After*, p. 63.

Bibliography

Carr, Edward Hallet. *Nationalism and After*. London: Macmillan, 1945.

Deutsch, Karl W. *Nationalism and Its Alternatives*. New York: Knopf, 1969.

———. *Nationalism and Social Communication*. 3d ed. Cambridge, Mass.: The MIT Press, 1981.

——— et al. *Political Community in the North Atlantic Area*. Princeton, N.J.: Princeton U. P., 1957.

Gerassi, John. *The Coming the New International*. New York: World Publishing, 1971.

Hayes, Carlton T. H. *Essays on Nationalism*. London: Macmillan, 1937.

Hinsley, F. H. *Nationalism and the International System*. London: Hodder and Stoughton, 1973.

Hobson, John A. *Imperalism*. Ann Arbor: University of Michigan Press, 1965.

Kedourie, Elie. *Nationalism*. Rev. ed. London: Hutchinson, 1961.

Keohane, R. O., and Nye, Joseph. *Transnational Politics*. Cambridge, Mass.: Harvard U. P., 1972.

Kohn, Hans. *Nationalism: Its Meaning and History*. Rev. ed. New York: Van Nostrand, 1965.

———. *The Idea of Nationalism*. New York: Collier, 1967.

McNeil, W. H. *The Rise of the West*. Chicago: University of Chicago Press, 1963.

Meinecke, Friedrich. *Cosmopolitanism and the National State*. Princeton, N.J.: Princeton U. P., 1970.

Ronen, D. *The Quest for Self-Determination*. New Haven, Conn.: Yale U.P., 1979.

Seton-Watson, Hugh. *Nations and States*. Boulder, Colo.: Westview, 1977.

Smith, Anthony. *Theories of Nationalism*. London: Duckworth, 1971.

———. *Nationalism in the Twentieth Century*. New York: New York U. P., 1979.

Tilly, Charles (ed.). *The Formation of the National States in Western Europe*. Princeton, N.J.: Princeton U. P., 1975.

Waltz, Kenneth. *Man, the State and War: A Theoretical Analysis*. New York: Columbia U. P., 1954.

11 | *Third World Ideologies*

In the 1950s the French philosopher and political activist Jean-Paul Sartre advised all young ideologues and political activists to pack their bags and move somewhere in the Third World where the flame of revolutionary ideology burned bright, arming all of us a with a new vision for our world. The Chinese had made their revolution, and by 1950 Mao and the communists were in control. In Vietnam, Ho Chi Minh was challenging the French rule, soon (in 1954) to bring it down. In the same year, the Algerian rebellion rose against the French administration in what was technically a part of the French Republic. India, the most precious jewel in the British Crown, became independent in 1947 after a long and bitter struggle of civil disobedience. In Malaya, Indonesia, the Middle East, Egypt, the Philippines, the whole of southeast Asia, and even in the African hinterland and in the Latin American republics, a struggle against the established order and foreign domination was expected to produce new ideologies and new political movements that would lead us to a new order of peace, fraternity, and socialism. The future was being born in the new crucible of political struggle and the ideas fashioned in the Third World.

The Third World Countries

More than 100 of the 170 states in the United Nations belong to the Third World. It would be virtually impossible to generalize about their political ideologies. In all these countries there has been a constant quest for new political formulas and ideas, different experimentations with the organization of the economy and the society, but nowhere can we say that a political synthesis and new political ideologies have taken final shape.

*"Wandering between two worlds, one dead
The other powerless to be born"

254

Most of the political ideologies fashioned are, to a great degree, derivative—they are borrowed; only a few provide an ingenious combination of derivative themes and indigenous cultural and traditional forces and ideas. Few if any of the ideologies have managed to provide for sustained organization and mass mobilization. Even if they appeared at times intensive and highly mobilizing—and this was particularly the case with nationalism, a staple ideological commodity invented by the Europeans—they quickly lost their appeal and lost converts. In many of the Third World countries, parties and ideologies have given way to military rule.

All we can do is identify and discuss some of the most common ideological propositions that have developed in Third World countries—especially the most prevalent one, namely, nationalism. In fact, there are many "isms" but ultimately they can be understood only when preceded by "nation." Scratch the various terms that we find—federalism, socialism, scientific socialism, Marxism-Leninism, culturalism, humanistic socialism, self-reliance, communalism, populism, democratic dictatorship, guided democracy, solidarism, developmentalism, islamism, pan-Arabism, pan-Africanism, continentalism, antiimperialism, transitionalism—and you will invariably find nationalism written in capital letters.

Nation-states mushroomed in Europe throughout the nineteenth century and after World War I. But the rest of the world remained relatively immune to nationalism. Colonial empires—British, French, Dutch, Belgian, Portuguese—covered the whole of Asia (except for China and Japan), the Middle East, and Africa. In Africa, on the eve of World War II there were no independent states other than South Africa and Liberia. Today there are some thirty-five independent states in Africa, some seventeen in Asia, and nine in the Middle East, including Cyprus—more than sixty new states in Africa, Asia, and the Middle East alone!

Any chronology of contemporary world history will show the rapid pace of national independence movements after World War II. By the end of the 1950s, independence belonged to North Vietnam, Indonesia, India, the Philippines, Iraq, North Korea, South Korea, Israel, Jordan, Laos, Cambodia, Somalia, Libya, Madagascar, Tunisia, Morocco, and Ghana. In the early 1960s the movements toward independence became an avalanche. The Algerian rebellion led to independence in 1962; uprisings in Cyprus led to an independence, which did not, however, resolve the conflicts between the Greeks and the Turks until the island was divided into two separate and independent ethnic states in the 1980s. All the French African colonies became independent in the early sixties, with Guinea leading the way in 1958. In eastern Africa, independence was won by Kenya, Tanzania, Uganda, and Rhodesia. In the seventies, the movement was virtually completed with the unification and full independence of Vietnam, the revolt against the aging emperor of Ethiopia, and the independence of Djibouti, Mozambique, Guinea Bissau, and Angola. In the meantime, virtually all the small islands in the Caribbean archipelago, with the exception of Martinique and Guadeloupe (French departments) and Puerto Rico and the U.S. Virgin Islands (U.S. territories) gained the coveted status of independence and

256

*Old Voices and
New:
Nationalism, The
Third World,
Feminism,
Liberation
Theology, and
Revolution*

membership in the United Nations. Few today are the self-proclaimed national entities that live under foreign dominion.

Even within established states, such as China or Ethiopia, and more particularly Latin America where statehood with fixed and generally agreed borders had been achieved long ago, nationalist movements against foreign interests or powers assert themselves. This is evident in Mexico, Peru, Chile, and the Central American "republics" where social revolutions are couched in the name of national emancipation and independence. The target is often the United States and its economic interests; the struggle is against imperialism and the various forms of deprivation endured by the people of these countries. Nationalist ideologies become social and revolutionary ideologies, addressing themselves not only to the independent position of the country in the international community but also to the domestic social, political, and economic structures in an effort to refashion the polity and the economy.

A number of factors that had been at work converged after World War II to bring forth the nationalist independence movements. One of the most important was the weakening of the European colonial powers and the emergence of two non-European powers, the United States, and the Soviet Union, both favoring, for different reasons, colonial emancipation and independence. Underlying all these independence movements was a political phenomenon: the growth of native elites aspiring to political power. As with European nationalism, colonial nationalism became an ideology for mobilizing and organizing the quiescent masses. It proved to be a potent force, just as it had in Europe after the French Revolution.

From Assimilation to Rejection

The intrusion of the colonizers during the nineteenth century into Africa and Indochina, and much earlier in India and other Asiatic countries, undermined the organization, lifestyles, authority structures, and the economy of native societies. Traditional societies were opened up; the village life was disrupted; new forms of economic organization and production were introduced; and there was a massive exposure to new types of goods for consumption purposes. The traditional values of authority and deference and the group life that many tribal societies had practiced from time immemorial were seriously weakened. The child of European liberalism and capitalism, the individual, was also fostered in the colonial world.

For some the exposure to western influence was welcome. It was a chance to learn new ways. Indigenous elites sent their children abroad — to London, Paris, and elsewhere — to learn the new ways better. Some became assimilated, as was the case with French colonial natives, and some married French women. Assimilation of European ways and learning of European culture might have been one way to overcome colonial status. It was limited, as might be expected, to only a handful.

Whatever this assimilated minority sought to accomplish, however, in alliance with the colonial powers and their leaders, was thwarted for two reasons. First, the European elites — army, financiers, businesspeople, investors, administrators — were not willing to relinquish their roles, positions, and profits. The indigenous elites could play only a subordinate role. Second, there was the inevitable phenomenon of discrimination and inequality.The Europeans lived in their own world, with their own clubs, servants, schools, and hospitals, eating their own food and drinking their own water and liquor. They lived in a separate world that was equated with status. Natives could not penetrate it, even if they had studied at Oxford or the Sorbonne.

Together with the impenetrability of status went the difference in color, making the separation even more blatant. Gradually, therefore, it became clear that assimilation was not possible. "We could assimilate mathematics or the French language," wrote Leopold Senghor, a Senegalese leader and intellectual who had received his doctorate at the Sorbonne, "but we could never strip off our black skins or root out our black souls."[1]

The alternative to the unattainable goal of assimilation was rejection. The feeling of being discriminated bred an abiding resentment against the colonial master and created the moral indignation that brings out the prophet and the saint. The destruction of the traditional patterns of existence produced a large population which had lost its attachments to authority and traditional lifestyles — one that began to discern, even in a confused way, the discrimination to which it was subjected, but even more, the deprivation to which it was condemned. Without structured and patterned relationships, moving from the countryside into the urban slums, isolated from each other, the indigenous populations became, in Frantz Fanon's words, the *Wretched of the Earth*. Their color symbolized their lowly status, and sealed their fate. But they were easy to mobilize and organize, and they became the base of subsequent nationalist liberation movements.

It was at this juncture that two of the most powerful European ideologies joined forces. Nationalism and Leninism combined to fashion the national independence movements in the colonial world. The ideological aspirations of these movements went even beyond what communism and nationalism could promise. There was, Kedourie claims,[2] a powerful millenialist spirit in the colonial world, something like the religious vision of the Second Coming. It promised a new heaven and a new earth. For the poor and downtrodden a new vision of paradise also became a call for action.

It was a call for action that knew no limits. Nationalist guerrillas in Kenya, the Mau Mau, took the following chilling oath:

1. In Sigmund, *The Ideologies of Developing Nations*, p. 248.
2. Kedourie's *Nationalism in Asia and Africa* is an excellent anthology with a penetrating introduction by the author to whom I am indebted for both.

258

*Old Voices and
New:
Nationalism, The
Third World,
Feminism,
Liberation
Theology, and
Revolution*

I speak the truth and vow before our God
That if I am called to go to fight the enemy
Or to kill the enemy — I shall go
Even if the enemy is my father and my mother, my brother or
sister[3]

Nationalism

Colonial ideologies of national independence borrowed directly from European nationalism: the same assertion of a natural right to be a nation; the same search in the past for tradition and culture in terms of which the claims could be justified, the same emphasis on the basic factors of religion or language or ethnicity, as the occasion suited, and, finally, the same liberal vocabulary about equality, individual rights, and self-determination.

Where is the "Past"?

The Germans found their past in the Germanic tribes. The modern Greeks similarly had no difficulty: in their solemn declaration of independence on January 27, 1821, they asserted their glorious past to be the cornerstone of their future as a nation. "We, descendants of the wise and noble people of Hellas . . . believing it to be unlawful for us . . . to live henceforth in a state of slavery suitable to unreasoning animals than to rational beings. . . ."[4]

In Africa, however, the search took many nations to a mythical past. Ethiopians found it in the Bible: "Ethiopia shall soon stretch out her hands unto God." Why not unto Eritrea and Somaliland as well? The Israelis, as Jews, claim valid historical credentials to most of the land they now have, including Jerusalem. African nations looked for past African empires such as existed in Mali and Ghana, and Arab nationalisms invariably found past glories in the days when Islam controlled most of North Africa and had moved deep into Spain. Pakistan also sought its own past in its Moslem heritage, claiming to be the historically "oldest" of the ten nations that had existed in the Indian subcontinent.

Language and Culture

The search for the past meant the search for a language. Again, the example of the modern Greeks trying to resurrect the ancient Greek language illuminated the way for the new nations. "Every word in our language, with the exception of scientific terms, must be in Turkish, if possible, and if not possible at least Turkified. . . ."[5] declared the Turkish leaders in the

---

3. Cited in Kedourie, op. cit., pp. 466–468.
4. Cited in Kohn, *The Idea of Nationalism,* New York: Knopf, pp. 116–117.
5. Cited in Kedourie, op. cit., pp. 207–215.

1920s. But language proved to be a serious problem for India and many of the African nations where tribal dialects could in no way coincide with national boundaries. English and French continue to be widely used.

The search for a common language also led to a desperate search for a common past culture — even if it could be identified in the remote past — in traditions, ideas, ancestral tombs, epics, and arts and crafts that could be resurrected to provide the much-sought identity. For some of the African peoples, it was particularly difficult to find a given "national" identity, distinct from a common "African" heritage. It was relatively easier for the Arabs, given their Islamic religion and the Koran, to say nothing of the period of the great flowering of Arab culture, scholarship, art and commerce, and their expansion in the Mediterranean world and beyond more than a thousand years ago. Most of the Arab nationalisms referred to a common "Arab nation," a common religion, and a common cultural heritage.

Race

Race began to play a prominent role and became a powerful motive in the rejection of the European colonialists. No other than Marcus Garvey, president general of the Universal Negro Improvement Association in the United States, had proclaimed the purity of the Negro race and the purity of the white race: he was against intermarriage. In his search for "ethnicity" for the blacks in Africa — what he called "negritude" — Leopold Senghor spoke of an "antiracial racialism." Negritude was the "whole complex of . . . values — cultural, economic, social and political that characterize . . . the Negro African world."[6] God was declared by many black nationalists to be black. He was the "glorious Father of the blacks." One of the leaders of the Congo (now Zaire) declared himself to be "the banner of the dominion of the black race." Race leads to the exaltation of its characteristics and suggests that every effort should be made to maintain its purity. Native leaders fell into disgrace because they had married European women.

Sometimes the search for identity in the past, in religion, in language, took on absurd manifestations. For instance, European-trained African doctors began to use magic and witchcraft for cures; and there were desperate efforts made to find and imitate primitive African art. But emphasis on race was not exclusively anti-European and antiwhite. In East Africa and southeast Asia race was used against diverse minorities, especially Chinese and Indians.

Irrespective of the many extreme manifestations, the independence movements had a genuine claim which could not be denied: self-determination and self-government. Its logic, since it had been advanced and practiced by the Europeans, was irresistible. Even pan-African movements failed to gain momentum in the face of claims for the national independence of specific populations in given areas. Thus colonial nationalism followed the footsteps of European nationalism.

6. Cited in Sigmund, op. cit., pp. 248–250.

Leninism

*Old Voices and
New:
Nationalism, The
Third World,
Feminism,
Liberation
Theology, and
Revolution*

Marxism appealed to many of the colonial elites seeking independence. It rejected liberal capitalism, which was taken to be synonymous with the capitalist exploitation of the colonial world, and it provided a vision of a new world of equality and prosperity. But it was Leninism that had a far more profound impact, both because of its analysis and explicit condemnation of imperialism, and because it provided a theory and an organizational tool for revolution.

From a tactical point of view, as we saw earlier, Lenin considered colonies to be the "weakest link" in the capitalistic chain and pledged Soviet support to colonial national revolutionary movements. The second congress of the Third International in 1920 provided a number of "theses" on "national" and "colonial" questions.

> With regard to those states and nationalities where a backward, mainly feudal, patriarchal, or patriarchal-agrarian regime prevails, the following must be borne in mind: (1) All Communist Parties must give active support to the revolutionary movements of liberation. . . . (4) It is of special importance to support the peasant movements in backward countries against the landowners and all feudal survivals; above all, we must strive as far as possible to give the peasant movement a revolutionary character, to organize the peasants and all the exploited classes into the Soviets, and thus bring about the closest possible union between the Communist proletariat of Western Europe and the revolutionary peasant movement of the East and of the colonial and subject countries; . . . (5) It is the duty of the Communist International to support the revolutionary movement in the colonies and in the backward countries. . . .[7]

The Third International under the leadership of the Soviet Communist party stressed, therefore, three basic elements in the struggle for colonial emancipation and independence: first, nationalism; second, an outright appeal to the peasantry (since both the middle classes and the proletariat were virtually nonexistent); and third, the role of a well-organized party to provide for leadership and direction, and to bring the people to the appropriate level of mobilization and militancy. It was to consist of trained revolutionaries.

National Independence Movements

The double impact of Leninism and nationalism, and particularly the adoption of political organization inspired by Lenin, accounted for the

---

7. Cited in Kedourie, op. cit., "Theses of the Second Congress of the Communist International on the National and Colonial Questions," pp. 540–551.

authoritarian and paramilitary characteristics of the national independence movements in many colonies. They purported to be "mass movements," including everybody who favored independence from the colonial power, but the leadership was carefully selected, trained, and disciplined. Thus, while the base was as broadly popular as possible, the leadership was exclusive. All liberation movements developed their own special armies to wage war against the colonial power—a war that could range from acts of sabotage and terrorism to full-fledged military encounters. The party was the political arm acting on behalf of and organizing the people; the guerrillas were the military arm operating under the direction of the party but with the support of the people. Gradually national liberation movements became like states with their own army, tax collectors, tribunals, and political leaders and warriors.

As in Europe more than a century before, nationalism proved to be a powerful ideological force in the colonial world. For the first time apathetic and indifferent populations became mobilized; they were gradually given a political consciousness and a cause. The national movements became vehicles for the acquisition of power by native elites while the native populations found in the independence wars an identity and a sublimation from anonymity and past miseries. Above all, they were given hope about their future. Thus nationalism, skillfully manipulated by a small group of leaders, gradually asserted itself to lead virtually all colonies to independence and statehood.

Communism and the Third World

There are a number of Third World countries where "communism" (sometimes referred to as "scientific socialism") has become the official ideology—among them are Cuba, Vietnam, Ethiopia, perhaps Mozambique, and Angola; there are others where "popular guerrilla movements" in the name of communism and nationalism strive to attain power and to impose it: for example, Nicaragua, El Salvador, Zimbabwe, the Philippines, some of the small Carribbean islands, and Guatemala.

There were a number of reasons to expect a rapid spread of the communist model, especially the Leninist, among new nations. It provided a way to rapidly mobilize the population. It suggested a way to industrialize and modernize, as Stalin had done, through collectivization, nationalization, and economic planning. So in the 1950s and 1960s many colonial leaders claimed to be Marxists and Leninists. The revolution was a matter of political organization, they claimed—a matter of leadership capable of exploiting and marshaling the moral indignation of the colonial peoples against their masters. Both Castro and Ché Guevara felt that this should be the basis for revolution in Latin America, where the proximity of the United States and its "colonial" practices, in cooperation with despotic and corrupt regimes, accounted for a spirit of moral indignation and deep resentment. Some of the more sophisticated of the colonial leaders began

*Old Voices and
New:
Nationalism, The
Third World,
Feminism,
Liberation
Theology, and
Revolution*

to look beyond Lenin into some of the early works of Marx where revolution had its sources in a moral protest against deprivation as well as exploitation.

Emphasis on will and organization, the appeal to moral imperatives, the support of the peasantry—all these led to the concoction of a "doctrine" in terms of which some colonial revolutionary leaders called themselves Marxist and Leninist and waged war to gain their independence. In so doing they were, of course, cooperating fully with other social and political groups and leaders for whom national independence, not communism, was the primary consideration. The question of the applicability of the communist model came, therefore, with special urgency *after* independence had been proclaimed and after the colonial powers in India, Burma, Malaysia, Indonesia, the whole of Africa, and most of the Middle East had withdrawn. In some of these countries communism has been a negligible force; in others, lip service has been paid to the communist doctrine; only in a few has a fairly strong and politically conscious communist leadership and an organized Communist party developed. In most, the communist doctrine has been used to hide military authoritarian regimes—as, for instance, in Ethiopia.

A communist regime that was an approximation of the Soviet model established itself only in very few countries. Vietnam is one; Castro's Cuba is another—but it is only an approximation. So, too, Chinese communism has, as we have seen, basic differences from the Soviet model. In Indonesia, the Communist party came close to assuming a controlling position in the government and establishing a one-party rule, but it was crushed. In Africa, only Ethiopia, Mozambique, and Angola have an official Communist party, although other African regimes and leaders call themselves Marxist.

In most other countries the doctrine proclaimed favors the establishment of some form of "humanistic" or "democratic" socialism in which the State claims to control the major economic activities without, however, eliminating the market economy. But in virtually all of them there is a one-party system representing "democratic" unity and "communitarian" values.

Thus one might conclude that the Soviet model, important in shaping the doctrine and the organization that led to guerrilla warfare and to independence, has not been adopted by most of the new nations, nor has it been radically modified to suit specific circumstances. The reasons are many. First and foremost was the problem of national integration and consolidation after liberation. The Stalinist model, based on indoctrination and a well-organized party and force, could not be used. There were simply no well-organized communist parties; it was difficult to indoctrinate illiterate and apathetic groups. The very use of force might split the population of the new nations into their tribal or ethnic, linguistic, or religious components, rather than uniting them. "Nation-building" can be accomplished by force only when there is a powerful group or party that can use it and impose it.

Second, communism as a set of political tactics and organization developed by Lenin was welcome to many, but not as a way of life. Most of the African elites viewed their struggle for liberation in moral and religious terms, and sometimes even in the liberal terms in which nationalism had been couched in Europe in the nineteenth century. Marxism-Leninism was "materialist" and "atheistic." For a good number of Asian, African, and Moslem leaders, it was "another religion" that would threaten the existing ones. It was therefore unacceptable.

Finally, there were practical considerations stemming from the international political situation and the willingness on the part of the Soviet Union and the United States to offer economic aid. Former colonies maintained ties with the colonial powers: France, for instance, very quickly renegotiated economic, cultural, and military accords after the independence of its African colonies. The same applied to some of the British colonies in Africa in their relations with Britain. American business groups, as well as the American government, had every reason to invest or to give aid so that the new countries would not turn to the Soviet Union. Whatever the affinities were, therefore, between the new leaders of the new nations and the Soviet Union (and there was a debt to the Soviets for the moral and often material support given to them during their independence struggle), it would have been unwise to abandon the ties with the capitalist and democratic West. In fact, as the years went on after independence the Soviet leaders did not show themselves to be particularly generous nor did they provide aid, whether economic or military, without attaching strings. Aid was often clearly subordinated to Soviet strategic considerations that would force many of the leaders of the new nations to directly confront the West and the United States.

Democracy and Socialism in the Third World

While a number of the moral assumptions of liberal democracy—individual freedom, human dignity, religious freedoms—have been endorsed in the abstract by many of the leaders of the new nations in Asia and Africa, political and economic freedoms (what we have called the political and the economic core of liberalism) and also the democratic institutions themselves, were given new interpretations. This has happened to such an extent that democracy has come to mean something very different from what it has meant in western Europe or the United States. Basic principles like pluralism and basic institutions like representative government and the political parties, which allow for dissent and competition, have been rejected. Instead, they have been superseded by the search for a "popular" or "communitarian" will, one that is often expressed by a single party or very often by a single leader. The terms "democracy" and "republic" are used even when in practice the system is a dictatorship—with powers concentrated in the hands of one leader or a military junta that claims to represent the community as a whole."Democratic dictatorship," "guided democracy," "controlled democracy" are the expressions one finds frequently.[8]

In fact, in most of the Third World countries the factors that accounted for liberal democracies in the West and the United States were not present. Virtually unknown to the new states were the separation between church and state, economic individualism and entrepreneurship, laws to provide for the resolution of conflicts, the notion of separation between the individual and the state—essential to pluralism and to the limitations it imposes on the state—and, finally, the levels of prosperity that western societies attained, which allowed individuals to follow intellectual and artistic pursuits. In sharp contrast with western experience, what has developed in the new countries is a communitarian and statist ethic, according to which the state, acting on behalf of the community, could trace and dictate individual pursuits and control the civil society. As a result, democracy was equated in the eyes of many with communitarian values that transcended the individual and with statist controls that precluded the expression of individual self-interest. Democracy, even when advocated, was the democracy of all against all outsiders rather than the freedoms of individuals to coexist and even to differ within the whole. Democracy was interpreted in "totalist" terms, which had also been voiced by some of the makers of the French Revolution. Minority rights and the survival of minorities were ideas that were not seriously entertained.

Other reasons for the failure of liberal and democratic ideologies to gain roots stemmed from the history and the experiences of many of the national liberation movements. In almost all cases the emancipation of the colonies was the outcome of the collective and communitarian effort. It called for mobilization and organization of the population; their hearts and minds had to be conquered. This called for a highly disciplined political party and the development of total control with an ideological and political conformity. This was seen as the only way to sustain the fighting men and women. In Mao's expression, the population was to the guerrillas what water is to fish. It sustained, sheltered, and nourished them; it provided them with a built-in hiding place. In Algeria, in Vietnam, and in some African colonies, efforts to build totalitarian control were made during the national liberation wars. It sought conformity, discipline, and obedience to leadership.

It was this tight political organization and control that accounted, above all, for the ultimate victory of independence movements and the withdrawal of the colonial powers. But it carried its legacy after independence. The party remained a disciplined paramilitary force allowing no freedoms and competition. Its energy was now directed to other ends—national integration, economic development, the elimination of internal dissent and counterrevolutionary forces, and the subjugation of traditional elites, whether religious, linguistic, tribal, or economic, that might obstruct its efforts. Total effort led to "total" regimes, after liberation.

---

8. Sigmund, op. cit.

In institutional terms this meant that competition and political plu-ralism could not be accepted and representative assemblies could not be allowed to serve as the voice of particular and competing interests. Instead, they should speak for a whole and united community from which they derived their mandate. If they would not, then the leader would become the spokesman for the new nation.

The one-party system has been defended as truly democratic. "Does democracy necessarily imply several parties?" asked Jomo Kenyatta (of Kenya). "We say no," he answers. Political parties, according to him, are a reflection of classes and economic interests, but when no diversity exists or is permitted to exist in terms of interests and classes, then many parties are not needed. One is enough. Many political parties would divide the peo-ple and give rise to rivalries that would disrupt national unity.

In the same vein the leader of Guinea, President Sekou Touré, spoke of a "democratic dictatorship." "If the dictatorship exercised by the gov-ernment apparatus emanates directly from the whole people, this dicta-torship is popular in nature and the State is a democratic state. . . ."[9] The late leader of Egypt, Gamal Abdel Nasser, rejected a multiparty system. The latter would serve the interests of the colonial powers by dividing the Egyptian people. His answer was the formation of the Arab Socialist Union — a mass popular organization representing *all* the people.

Only few of the new nations have accepted economic liberalism. Many of them claim to be "socialist." Socialism is distinguished, however, from Marxism and communism, and though there is widespread admira-tion for the Soviet system, none of the new states has fully endorsed its model of economic organization. Generally the control of the State is accepted for the key economic activities and for investment. There is a public sector controlled and manned by the State. But there is also a private sector with a fairly wide margin of initiative in commerce, farming, and manufacturing.

Almost all of the Third World countries claim to be socialist, with notable exceptions, such as India, Indonesia, Malaysia, Morocco, and Saudi Arabia. In the Third World, however, socialism is very broadly defined to mean that the individual should be free from exploitation in all forms and enjoy an equal opportunity to have a fair share of the national wealth.

Socialism, almost everywhere in Africa (but in parts of Asia too), has been defined in "humanistic" terms. The African intellectual, Leopold Senghor, suggests that African socialism should develop in the form of a synthesis that brings together the works of Marx, the utopian socialists, trade unionism, and democratic socialism. It represents a reaction against both "capitalistic and communist imperialism." In many of the new nations, espe-cially in Africa, religious beliefs continue to play a more important role than material and economic considerations. Even more important, religions and religious values make the acceptance of Marxism difficult.

9. Ibid., pp. 162–163.

266

*Old Voices and
New:
Nationalism, The
Third World,
Feminism,
Liberation
Theology, and
Revolution*

Thus most of the new nations pay lip service to democracy but reject dissent, political competition, and pluralism and endorse the one-party system or personal authoritarian leadership. They strive to consolidate the unity they have acquired and want to defend it against the outside interventions that internal divisions may invite.

Modernization

The basic ideological propositions of socialism are all profoundly colored by the western experience that the Third World countries attempt to emulate. That experience is, in one word, modernization. Socialism, whether humanistic or scientific, democratic or Marxist and Leninist, or directed by an authoritarian elite, represents an ideology of modernization. The leaders of the Third World countries realize that their nations are far behind in economic well-being and even more so in technology and the application of industry and technology to social problems such as health, education, communication, and so on. They appear determined to close the gap that separates them from the rest of the world. Underneath the ideological labels there is a grim reality of poverty and dependence and the effort to transcend both. The question is, how to do it.

There have not been, as yet, any enduring indigenous ideologies that have fashioned a "non-Western" approach to modernization. Modernization tactics may differ and may pit political elites within one and the same country against each other, but the modernization strategy is by and large the same and borrows from the western experience. Briefly, the process is: to find the capital to build a basic economic infrastructure in communication and in the training of technical personnel; invest as much money as possible in industrial development, focusing on intensive exploitation of natural resources; increase the gross national product and the per capita income; and establish control over the distribution of the income to individuals and groups. State controls become necessary to avoid wasteful competition and also, hopefully, to avoid foreign domination and to provide a more egalitarian distribution of wealth. The tactics of modernization are, with some notable exceptions, nationalist, statist, antiforeign, and "independentist," irrespective of whether the professed official ideology is socialist, Marxist-Leninist, populist, or democratic. And the new and under-developed nations share the same urge to skip as many steps and stages of economic growth as possible in order to reach the promised heaven of modernity as soon as possible.

Under these conditions, the instrument of modernization is the modernizing elite organized in a party—a single party in the great majority of cases—and the obstacles to modernization appear to be the traditional groups (religious and tribal) and some of the interests associated with foreign and even international economic forces that often provide both capital and markets. Almost everywhere in the Third World, the parties associated with independence used nationalism as a major mobilizing force. New party cadres were organized and assumed power by controlling and directing economic resources. In Egypt, Syria, Iraq, Algeria, in Ghana and Mali, and in Libya, the revolution for modernization in the name of socialism also meant a political revolution in which control was wrested from the traditional elites by a new political class: in Egypt, the Arab Socialist Union; in Syria and Iraq, the Arab Renaissance (Ba'th) parties; in Mali, the Union Soudanaise; in Ghana, the Convention People party; in Guinea, the Guinean Democratic party; in Tanzania, the Tanzanian African National Union (TANU) — all were parties committed to modernization and socialism.

Third World socialism developed some particular characteristics especially with regard to its overriding emphasis on social justice and equality and on the common theme of attaining solidarity for heretofore apathetic, disparate, and parochial groups. But in many of the Third World countries, the socialist parties either disappeared to give way to military governments or came to terms with the military. Ideology as a mobilizing force became divorced from its political roots and from the party and the people it represented. Modernization became the affair of the military and the administration. In the process, the nature of the socialist experiment was distorted. The military assumed control in Egypt; the army took over Ghana in 1966; the army came to power in Mali in 1968; in Iraq and Syria the reality of power lies now with the army, which is also the only force that provides a backbone to Qadaffi of Libya. With the death of Sekou Touré in French Guinea, the army executed a swift coup and assumed power in 1984. The gradual weakening of the socialist ideology throughout most of Africa and the Middle East can be plotted in terms of the decline of socialist parties and increased military takeovers in the 1970s and early 1980s.

Some Original Efforts: Socialism and Tradition

There have been some notable efforts to establish original forms of economic modernization and organization and rationalize them in ideological terms that accommodate traditional and religious values. Gandhi's emphasis on village industries in the name of self-reliance and self-sufficiency may well be considered one of the most original efforts to promote for India a special, nonwestern, type of modernization, adjusted to Indian community and village life. Gandhi turned against rapid industrialization involving mass capital investment and the inevitable creation of an urban proletariat. But village industries and village community forms of production did not develop. Large-scale industry and the extensive use of mechanization in agriculture have supplanted Gandhi's notion of smallness and self-sufficiency. Today, there is nothing special about modernization and the organization of economic life in India. It is a mixture of state ownership and private enterprise, of state and foreign investments in an effort to industrialize very much along the lines of the western prototype.

268

*Old Voices and
New:
Nationalism, The
Third World,
Feminism,
Liberation
Theology, and
Revolution*

Libyan Leader Col. Qadaffi
His philosophy is a mixture of nationalism, populism, and pan-Arabism. *(Photo: Wide World Photos)*

More interesting perhaps are the ideological propositions of the Ba'th Party in Syria and Iraq, and also of Qadaffi of Libya, to combine modernization with socialism, populism, and Islamism, and those of Nyerere in Tanzania to develop, somewhat along the lines of Gandhi, village agricultural communities with an emphasis on self-sufficiency and community building.

In the Middle East   The Ba'th party in Syria and Iraq and more recently Qadaffi's military-populist regime in Libya are attempts to combine socialist and revolutionary objectives by appealing to religious and traditional forces. The constitution of the Ba'th party, drafted in 1956–1957, represents perhaps the best formulation of "Arab" or "Islamic" socialism. The "Arab nation" is declared to be one, having a right to exist "within a single state." It is described as a "cultural unit." Its stated mission is "the reformation of human existence and the enhancement of human progress." The Ba'th party is declared as a "universal Arab Party." Yet it is "nationalist." It is also a socialist party claiming that socialism derives from "genuine Arab nationalism." It is also a revolutionary party working to reawaken Arab nationalism and build socialism. It is finally populist in the sense that power "belongs to the people" and the party "depends upon the people."[10]

There are several strains, therefore, in Middle East "socialism." First, there is a strong nationalist appeal to each and every Arab state; second, there is a call for unity—to transcend in the name of Arab culture the individual states and move in the direction of pan-Arabism; third, there is an effort to blend indigenous traditional values such as religion with economic reforms and move in the direction of socialism. Finally, there is the appeal of a single populist party that speaks for all the people. This populist urge coincides with nationalism and the appeal to the people coincides with the reality of their religious attachments. The faithful will make socialism

10. Desfosses and Levesque, *Socialism in the Third World,* pp. 77–95.

create their national unity in the name of the Islam, but the revolution, too, will provide for social justice and equality in the name of socialism.

Under Qadaffi all these elements were brought together and constitute his "universalism." "Our socialism is the Socialism of the Islam," he proclaimed.[11] Libyan socialism was declared to be the socialism of the true faith. To bring it about the Arab Socialist Union and the Revolutionary Command Council were established; the former being a party organized by the Qadaffi that was responsible for mobilizing the public and supporting leadership, the latter being for government.

Despite the populists' assertions, the Revolutionary Command Council and the Arab Socialist Union abandoned all pretense of free discussion and democracy. As with some other Third World countries, emphasis was placed on modernization. The Council maintained that broadening the democratic base and indulging in the luxury of free debate would impede the progress of the movement. "Much as we want to hear the view of the majority, we shall continue to implement our own decisions which we consider to be the interests of the Arab society of Libya without heeding the views of the majority."[12] In an effort to eliminate all organized centers of opposition, Libya undertook its own cultural revolution between 1973 and 1975. Arms were distributed to the people (under careful army supervision and screening), and efforts were made to unite with Egypt and prepare for a "war of revenge" against Israel. The administrative apparatus was completely overhauled; old cadres were dismissed and new and loyal ones were recruited. The "politically sick" were duly eliminated, and moreover, all symbols and forms of media associated with western culture in the universities, libraries, and schools were extirpated. The Koran was proclaimed the law of the land.

To implement this radical overhaul of Libya's political, administrative, legal, and economic institutions, so-called people's committees were set up to control towns, villages, government agencies, farms, hospitals, schools, universities, and public utilities. The committees had the power to replace "bourgeois" elements with true representatives of the people. The movement took unprecedented proportions, and soon Qadaffi could proclaim that there was no state and no government and no leader in Libya. The people governed and he spoke with and for the people. Even embassies became "autonomous" representatives and delegates of the people working to enact the people's will. Foreigners were chased out of the country, books were burned, "traitors" to the people executed, and opponents of the revolution gunned down. To Libya, universalism meant the universal extinction of opponents, the destruction of Israel and imperialism, and the utilization of all methods, including terrorism, to accomplish it. "Brotherhood" was reserved for only those who agreed to follow the path to salvation that the Qadaffi proclaimed. It is a universalism by the few and for the few!

11. Ibid., pp. 99–119.
12. Ibid., p. 114.

270

*Old Voices and
New:
Nationalism, The
Third World,
Feminism,
Liberation
Theology, and
Revolution*

In Tanzania   Tanzania's efforts under Nyerere to combine socialism with indigenous and traditional values and practices in order to build socialism were based on different assumptions and values.[13] It was "inward-looking" and largely pragmatic, calculated to bring the citizens—especially the peasantry—into cooperative activity at the village level and thus strengthen the local community. The basis of socialism, agrarian socialism, was to be the extended family at the village level. It was *ujama*, or family-hood, that described Tanzanian socialism.The major national economic activities, banking, communication, industries, imports, and exports—the "commanding heights" of the national economy—were to be nationalized. But the core of socialism that would affect the majority of the citizenry was the village and the extended family in the village. With massive support from the center but with the proper grass roots enthusiasm and participation, they would become communal units of production.

Two conditions had to be satisfied, however. First, work incentives and a sense of self-reliance and self-sufficiency had to be introduced. Second, an organization to promote the inculcation of incentives had to be established to mobilize the villagers. The first condition was provided by work ethic. It was used to motivate the villagers to work, thanks to the realization that self-reliance and independence could be attained only through hard work and individual and collective efforts. To provide for it, however, material incentives had to be added to the moral and political exhortations. The economy in the villages had to show improvement. But collective self-reliance required not only collective effort but also collective leadership, which was provided through the single party—the TANU. The relationship between the party and the masses, however, had to be carefully monitored to prevent mobilization from giving way to imposition. Nyerere admitted that one could not force people to "live socialist lives"; indeed, an effort to build model socialist villages proved unsuccessful. Opposition groups spread; the villagers seemed disenchanted with hard work and self-reliance without the appropriate material rewards. Just as with Gandhi's village industries, the village socialism that had evoked so many hopes has failed to gain momentum.

Conclusion

Our discussion of Third World ideologies suggests that ideologies and institutional practices are not easy to import. Democracy has been reinterpreted by the new nations and differs greatly from its original meaning; also, in many instances, has communism. Democratic institutions virtually do not exist in the Third World, and the one-party system adopted by many of the new states has failed to mobilize the people and impose its control.

The Third World continues to be very much in flux. The quest for national independence has been realized but the hopes associated with it have not materialized. Ideological shifts and political instability have been

13. A good discussion can be found in Desfosses and Levesque, op. cit., pp. 216–244.

the rule, as has the search for a new international order that will provide for a more equitable distribution of our planet's wealth. It is perhaps in their continuing search to build societies that provide for well-being and equality, in their constant refusal to accept "western values," and their rejection of the European and North American forms of industrialization that the new nations continue to pose the same question. Will they discover new ways to harness economic modernization and growth to qualitative considerations? Or will they follow the model of early capitalism, even if under state direction and control? Will they reconcile their aspirations for communitarian and societal values with individual freedoms? Will "humanistic socialism" prevail or do they face a long period of military or "democratic" dictatorships? The ideologies we have surveyed only underline the flux, and in many instances, perhaps, the confusion that afflicts the Third World.

Bibliography

Albright, David E. (ed.). *Communism in Africa*. Bloomington: Indiana U.P., 1980.

Betts, Raymond F. *Assimilation and Association in French Colonial Theory, 1890–1914.* New York: TMS Press, 1970.

Desfosses, H., and Levesque, J. (eds.). *Socialism in the Third World*. New York: Praeger, 1975.

Chilcote, Ronald H. *Theories of Comparative Politics*. Boulder, Colo.: Westview Press, 1981, chap. 7.

Emerson, Rupert. *From Empire to Nation: The Rise of Self-Assertion of Asian and African Peoples*. Cambridge, Mass.: Harvard U.P., 1960.

Fanon, Frantz. *The Wretched of the Earth*. New York: Grove Press, 1965.

Friedland, William H., and Rosberg, Carl G. (eds.). *African Socialism*. Stanford, Calif.: Stanford U.P., 1964.

Goldthorpe, J. E. *The Sociology of the Third World: Disparity and Involvement*. Cambridge, England: Cambridge U.P., 1975.

Hodgkin, Thomas. *Nationalism in Colonial Africa*. New York: New York U.P., 1967.

Kedourie, Elie. *Nationalism in Asia and Africa*. London: World Publishers, 1970.

Kilson, Martin (ed.). *New States in the Modern World*. Cambridge, Mass.: Harvard U.P., 1975.

Langley, J. Ayo. *Ideologies of Liberation in Black Africa 1856–1970: Documents on Modern African Political Thought from Colonial Times to the Present*. London: Rex Collings, 1979.

Nasser, Gamal Abdel. *The Philosophy of the Revolution*. Buffalo, N.Y.: Smith, Keynes & Marshall, 1959.

Nyerere, Julius K. *Freedom and Socialism: Uhuru na Ujamaa, A Selection from Writings and Speeches 1965–1970*. Dar es Salaam: Oxford U.P., 1968.

Senghor, Léopold Sédar. *On African Socialism*. New York: Praeger, 1964.

Sigmund, Paul E. (ed.). *The Ideologies of Developing Nations*. 2d rev. ed. New York: Praeger, 1967.

Von Der Mehden, Fred R. *Politics of the Developing Nations*. 2d ed. Englewood Cliffs, N.J.: Prentice-Hall, 1973.

Worsley, Peter. *The Third World.* Chicago: University of Chicago Press, 1965.

12 | *Feminism: A Movement or an Ideology?**

*"Look at my arm! I have ploughed and planted and
gathered into barns and no man could head me—and
ain't I a woman? I could work as much and eat as
much as a man—when I could get it—and bear the
lash as well. . . . And ain't I a woman? I have born
thirteen children and seen most of them sold into
slavery . . . and when I cried with my mother's grief
none but Jesus hear me—and ain't I a woman?"*

SOJOURNER TRUTH, 1851

Like communism, socialism, and liberalism during the nineteenth century,
the liberation and revolutionary ideologies and movements since World
War II have promised to free the individual from oppression and subjection. Their major theme has been to restore what individuals had lost: the
autonomy of their wills, the freedom of their consciences, and equality for
all. Feminism shares the same overall goals—to establish equality for
women with men and to liberate them from submission to men.

We may define feminism as a set of ideas espoused by a number of
people—women and men—to form a movement whose goal is to attain
the full equality of women in terms of politics, economics, and civil rights
vis-à-vis men. In certain respects this movement (and the ideology that
spawns it) may not differ substantively from other liberating ideologies:
for blacks, minority groups, workers, or farmers. It may be more of a movement than an ideology.

According to a more comprehensive view of feminism, however, the
liberation of women will bring about a radical change in our society and its
values. It assumes that throughout history the roles women have played
and the images held about women have been shaped by men. In the
process women became alienated, viewing themselves in a mirror made
for them by men. They accepted a false set of images—a false ideology—

*As indicated in my Preface Elizabeth Windrove, a graduate student in Politics at Brandeis,
did a great deal of research in the form of notes and drafts for this chapter. She is not
responsible, however, for the judgments made here!

and they identified with it. They lost their individuality, a loss that adversely affects all of us, since it deprives women of their true selves, their spontaneity, and their potentiality. This broader view of feminism postulates therefore that "feminine values" and their realization will build a better world for all. The feminine ingredient, fully liberated, will become the leaven that will radically transform our values and our world.

In this chapter we will discuss both views of feminism and the underlying ideology. The first follows closely the ideology of liberalism, or even socialism and communism. We shall label it "liberal," or "egalitarian." The second has spawned movements in the direction of a radical overhaul of the society, movements that claim to be truly revolutionary. We shall label this view "radical," or "reconstructive." Before we begin, however, let us give an overview of the condition of women over the centuries. Actually, it is more of a predicament than a condition.

The Subjection of Women*

Aside from some rare circumstances where under special socioeconomic conditions "matriarchical" societies (societies in which women rule) appeared, the common lot of women has been subjection to men. Their roles and positions, their physical living conditions, including the disposition of their bodies, were determined by men—fathers, grandfathers, husbands, or sons. Subjection did not necessarily manifest itself in the actual use of force, though force was ever-present; it resulted from the dominant ideology. Women, even if exalted as mothers or wives or as talented courtesans, and even if often relied upon by men because of their talents, were considered inferior to men and were held in inferior positions. In most societies women had no rights until the middle of the 19th century. They could not participate in the economy or the political life of the society; they had no property and were not allowed to manage property bequeathed to them; they could not choose their own husbands; they had no access to education and the professions, and if they did, education was specially arranged or specially tailored for them.

Despite notable shifts and changes in ideology, the subjection of women remained constant, and still exists in many parts of the world today, especially among the less developed countries of the Third World. In many of these countries women are simply not valued; they work hard for little pay and receive little protection from the public authorities. Medical care is noticeably of lower quality (if any at all) than what is available to males; less food is available to them whether through the market, the family, or the distribution agencies that attempt to cope with famine in many Third World countries. They have less access to the educational facilities that are available. Although international agencies, the United

---

*This is the title of John Stuart Mill's essay (1869). It was recently reprinted with an introduction by Susan Moller Okin, *The Subjection of Women*, Cambridge: Hackett Publishing Co., Inc.

274

*Old Voices and
New:
Nationalism, The
Third World,
Feminism,
Liberation
Theology, and
Revolution*

Nations, and also religious organizations have noted women's tragic conditions and the compelling need to improve them, poverty and subjection continue to afflict women more than men in the underdeveloped world. It is important that we constantly keep their predicament in mind as we outline the significant changes that have taken place in the position of women elsewhere.

The reasons given for women's subjection have been many: Some societies deemed women as "weak" and "irrational." Roman law referred to the "imbecility" of the sex and put women under the tutelage of men. The Christian fathers, despite their professed compassion for all, considered women "sinful" and inferior; man was "complete," woman was a "part of" man; she came from Adam's rib.

The reality of subjection written into the law was reinforced by the writings of philosophers, intellectuals, and theologians. Few came out to plead for women's equality, freedom, and inherent rationality. Plato, it is true, allowed them within the "guardian" class and provided for the same education given to men, but their ultimate function was to provide male children of high quality for the ruling elite. For Aristotle, subjection was "natural": like slaves, women were by nature "defective." Christian theologians, even though they admired chastity and the "obedient wife," saw women as the embodiment of Satan — vile creatures of the flesh. The liberal philosophers did not consider them capable of facing the responsibilities of a citizen and coping with the cruel but necessary world of the capitalist market. Their paramount obligations to produce and rear children and maintain the conjugal family were emphasized to the point where women were excluded from political participation and the management of property.

It is true that John Stuart Mill pleaded their cause by asking that education be provided to them, but then education was for John Stuart Mill the cure for all inequities for all people. Even Karl Marx paid little attention to the special situation of women, assuming that the collectivization of the means of production — communism — would provide liberation for them, as it would for all the exploited and underprivileged groups. Engels, following Marx, attributed their enslavement to the property relationships established under capitalism, especially that of the conjugal family in which the husband owned everything and reigned supreme, but Engels did not explain why subjection was also prevalent in noncapitalist societies. In general Marxism paid no attention to the specifics of women's subjugation and provided no programmatic cures under communism.[1]

Egalitarianism and Liberalism

Liberalism provided the first impetus toward the emancipation of women. But as Simone de Beauvoir wrote, "It might have been expected that the

---

1. See Susan Okin, *Women in Western Political Thought* and Alison Jagger, *Feminine Politics and Human Nature.*

(French) Revolution would change the lot of women. It did nothing of the sort."[2] Throughout the nineteenth century women remained in an inferior position to men. The French Civil Code and the jurisprudence that followed consecrated the supremacy of the husband in the household. No civil or property rights were provided to married women as well as no political rights. Divorce remained outlawed in many countries in Europe and difficult for women elsewhere. As for the women who entered the labor force in factories of the rapidly industrializing societies or who did piecework at home, primarily in the booming textile manufacturing, no legislation protected them, despite the "frailty" of their sex. In fact, until almost the end of the century, women had worked longer hours and for less pay than men. On the farm (more than half the population of most European countries, the United States, and England were farmers) women labored hard in the fields while at the same time taking care of the household, giving birth, and raising children.

Protests were mounted throughout the nineteenth century by intellectuals, political leaders, and women's organizations. They all advocated the improvement of women's position and opportunities in the marketplace, the factory, at home, and in politics. There were demands to grant women the right to vote, the right to own and dispose of a business, equal civil rights, the right to an equal education, and access to the professions.

Demands for the right to vote raised passionate debates and conflicts. It was not until the turn of the nineteenth century that women were granted the right to vote, first in Australia, New Zealand, and the Scandinavian countries, and in some of the western states in America. Woman suffrage became law for all states in the United States with the passage of the Nineteenth Amendment in 1920; in England it became law in 1928. It was only after the end of World War II that universal suffrage became the norm. Legislation was enacted as late as 1945 in France and even later in Greece, Spain, and Portugal. Switzerland has the distinction of being the last liberal democracy to grant it—in 1971.[3]

The Suffragette Movement in England

The women's movement to gain the right to vote (the "suffragette"[4] movement as it became known) began in 1857 with the establishment of the Sheffield Female Political Association demanding voting rights for women, as well as full civil and property rights. It was followed with the establishment of the Kensington Society under the leadership of Miss

---

2. Simone de Beauvoir, *The Second Sex*, p. 100.
3. Two Swiss cantons, however, do not allow women to vote in local elections!
4. "Suffragette," the term used at the time, had and continues to have a condescending ring; hence the quotes.

276

*Old Voices and
New:
Nationalism, The
Third World,
Feminism,
Liberation
Theology, and
Revolution*

Helen Taylor, stepdaughter of John Stuart Mill. In 1870 the *Women's Suffrage Journal* appeared. Local committees sprang up all over the country and in 1867 Parliament was petitioned for the first time to enact legislation granting women the right to vote. Petitions were regularly submitted to Parliament and they were regularly ignored or rejected. Between 1876 and 1880 demonstrations and meetings were organized throughout the country, and in 1883 the Liberal Party Conference voted a resolution in favor of women's suffrage. Yet the Reform Act of 1884 extended voting rights only to males.

THE BETTMANN ARCHIVE/BBC HULTON

The majesty and the panoply of "the law" were brought to bear upon the "suffragette" leaders in England asking for nothing more but the right to vote. (c. 1910)

It was during the first decade of the twentieth century, under the leadership of Christian Pankhurst, that the movement grew both in scope and militancy. In 1903 the Women's Social and Political Union, a large umbrella organization, was formed. It gradually grew into a force that included millions of women and men, and it received the support of labor and liberal political leaders, trade unionists, and intellectuals. At first the movement used educational tactics: sermons, lectures, meetings, and pamphlets and other publications, as well as peaceful demonstrations, marches, and lobbying. But eventually it took violent forms. Women broke up public meetings and stopped traffic; they were arrested and jailed; in jail they went on hunger strikes and were force-fed. Increasingly the "weaker" sex showed its fortitude and became confrontational, throwing

stones at the police, burning public and private buildings, physically as-
saulting political leaders. More women were arrested; more of them went
on hunger strikes. The movement was briefly interrupted with the coming
of World War I in 1914 when women (despite many pacifists in their ranks)
began to work in munitions factories and in paramilitary services. Only a
limited franchise was granted in 1920, but the battle had been won. Full
voting rights were granted in 1928.

The Suffragette Movement in the United States

Ever since the drafting of the U.S. Constitution, women's rights and especially the right to vote, remained a salient issue until it was finally granted,
first by some states and then for the country as a whole in 1920. Intermin-
gled with demands for the right to vote were powerful moral and religious
issues; the antislavery movement, in which some women began to play an
important role; and later the temperance movement against the sale and
distribution of liquor, spearheaded by the Women's Christian Temperance
Association, which was founded in 1874. Demands for opportunities in
securing employment, the right to divorce, equal rights with men in education, access to professions and commerce, and the right to own and
dispose of property also played an important role.

The women's movement began in earnest with the Seneca Falls Convention in 1848. It was a convention "to discuss . . . social, civil and religious rights." Although the first day of the meeting was supposed to be
exclusively for women, the gathering of several hundred people also included many men, and after two days a Declaration of Principles was
drafted which, in the spirit of the Declaration of Independence, called for
the complete enfranchisement of women. In addition, other civil rights
were addressed. Most important of all was a change in the law to give
women rights over their property and income, which at that time remained under the control of their husbands; women were also granted the
freedom to engage in business and commerce. The Convention ended
with a ringing affirmation of the need for women's emancipation: "The
history of mankind is a history of repeated injuries and usurpations on the
part of man toward woman, having in direct object the establishment of
tyranny over her."[5]

Conventions were again called in 1849 and 1851. The movement
gained momentum. Susan Anthony, brought up in an abolitionist family,
assumed the leadership shortly after the Seneca Falls Convention, together with E. C. Stanton. Black women and men—most of them freed
slaves—also joined. One of them, Sojourner Truth, spoke at the convention of 1851 on race and liberation. Countering the arguments that women
should not be given the right to vote because they were "weak" and

---

5. For the full account see Flexner, *Century of Struggle.* I am indebted to the author for much of
the account I give here.

278

*Old Voices and
New:
Nationalism, The
Third World,
Feminism,
Liberation
Theology, and
Revolution*

"helpless," she spoke with the same passion we find in some of Martin
Luther King's speeches:

> Look at my arm! I have ploughed and planted and gathered
> into barns and no man could head me—and ain't I a woman? I
> could work as much and eat as much as a man—when I could
> get it—and bear the lash as well—And ain't I a woman? I have
> born thirteen children and seen most of them sold into
> slavery . . . and when I cried with my mother's grief none but
> Jesus hear me—and ain't I a woman?[6]

The Fourteenth (1868) and Fifteenth (1870) Amendments, which
abolished slavery and gave blacks extended civil and citizenship rights,
including the right to vote, also gave the "suffragette" movement renewed
determination and militancy. It was triggered by the fact that the citizenship rights were given only to *males.*

In their struggle to gain the right to vote, American women used
tactics similar to those used in England: pamphlets and other writings,
meetings, lectures, and lobbying. And as in England, women were arrested
and kept the jails crowded; they went on hunger strikes and were force-
fed. They abandoned peaceful tactics and took to civil disobedience.
Women activists picketed the White House, refused to participate in war
work (there were a significant number of pacifists among them), and some
activists promised to "punish" President Wilson. By 1917 the leading women's organization, the National Women's Suffrage Association, had a
membership of 2 million. Women's organizations singled out congressmen
and senators, both Democrats and Republicans, promising support and
help to friends and threatening to bring the enemies down in defeat.
Friends and enemies were defined in terms of where they stood on the
issue of the women's franchise.

The Struggle for Equality: Forward and Backward

Equality has many facets. For women, being able to influence the public
authorities through their vote was only one, but an important, first step in
their struggle for equality. Beyond lay many other disabilities that had to
be confronted and eliminated before genuine equality could be attained.
Economic rights loomed large: training for employment, the right to be
employed, full access to all jobs, upward mobility within the job, nondis-
crimination in hiring and firing by employers, and equal pay and benefits.
The social position and roles of women also had to be reconsidered. Their
virtually exclusive role as mother and housekeeper, while their husbands
worked, had to be modified. This would involve a restructuring of family
values to allow for greater, indeed equal, sharing by the husband. Another
important issue involved what we could call personal freedoms: the right

6. Cited in Flexner, op. cit., p. 91.

to have or not have children within or outside marriage, the unfettered right of divorce, protection against abuse to which women continue to be subjected, and ultimately the right to terminate pregnancy. It was not only a long list—and many of women's aspirations remain as yet unfulfilled— but one whose goals were difficult to realize without a drastic change in the values and ideas that even modern societies hold about women.

With the enactment of the Nineteenth Amendment on August 18, 1920[7] (after it was ratified by the thirty-third state, Tennessee), women entered the mainstream of political life as voters. In concrete terms, they could now make the weight of their numbers and organization felt on both national and state elections and legislation. But for at least two decades thereafter, their impact was limited and only incremental at best.

However, there were some steps taken to improve the position of women. Maternity and pediatric clinics were established by the states with matching grants from the federal government; some legislation for improved working conditions and shorter working hours for children and women was also enacted but in most cases (unless health hazards were particularly obnoxious), they were not implemented. The courts found legislative regulations to be contrary to the Fourteenth Amendment, which guaranteed employers and employees their freedom to contract.

The New Deal

It was in terms of its overall reforms rather than specifics that the New Deal had a positive impact on the status of women. Inasmuch as women constituted almost one-fourth of the labor force, they benefited from legislative measures such as the National Industrial Recovery Act of 1933 and the National Recovery Administration, measures designed to expand employment opportunities and safeguard jobs. Employed women also benefited from wage raises, shorter working hours, and a broader range of employment possibilities.[8] Since maximum hour and minimum wage provisions applied to *all* workers, women in low-paying jobs under "sweatshop" conditions saw their status upgraded. But all these provisions applied only to industry and trade, and women engaged in domestic service, clerical work, and on the farm were not helped. The establishment of the National Labor Relations Board, however, gave women workers, especially in the textile industries, the right to bargain collectively for better wages and working conditions.

Thus one may say that the benefits women received during the New Deal legislation were derivative: they came from legislation and programs addressed to overall social and economic predicaments, especially unemployment. There was no specific effort to advance the position of women materially or otherwise. It was only World War II that gave women new and unprecedented opportunities in the labor market, at least while it lasted.

---

7. When the amendment was passed in 1920, twenty-two states did not allow women the right to vote.
8. Susan Ware, *Holding Their Own.*

280

*Old Voices and
New:
Nationalism, The
Third World,
Feminism,
Liberation
Theology, and
Revolution*

Even if the New Deal did not address itself to particular women-related problems, however, a number of women in the Roosevelt administration kept women's issues alive — most notably the president's wife, Eleanor Roosevelt, and the Secretary of Labor, Frances Perkins, as well as many women who worked in the federal relief programs. There was a growing sensitivity to these issues within the political elites and especially within the Democratic party.

Recent Realizations

With the formation of the Women's Joint Congressional Committee in 1930, women began to lobby in earnest. For the first time birth control issues were debated by the House Judiciary Committee, and gradually birth control measures were legalized. In 1945 federal agencies provided funds for the establishment of some day care centers. In 1960, under strong pressure from many women's organizations, President John F. Kennedy appointed a Committee on the Status of Women, chaired by Eleanor Roosevelt. The report issued in 1963 was fairly tame and disappointing to many women activists. It avoided a number of pending demands and urged only greater educational and training facilities for women.

A major landmark was the Equal Pay Act (1963), which prescribed equal pay for men and women for the same job and prohibited discriminatory practices against women. This was broadened by the Civil Rights Act of 1964, expressly prohibiting all discrimination on the base of race *and* sex,[9] and an Equal Opportunity Employment Commission was established to oversee its implementation and enforcement. With the formation of the National Organization of Women (*NOW*) in 1966 and the Women's Bipartisan Caucus in 1971, feminist demands for equality grew. These groups disseminated information, mobilized the voters, and lobbied Congress. In 1972, the Education Act prohibited sex discrimination. Finally the courts, reticent if not outright hostile at first, became increasingly well-disposed to women's issues and demands and began to strike down discriminatory legislation and practices. In the famous *Roe v. Wade* case (1973), a state's anti-abortion law was deemed unconstitutional, and in the same year the Equal Rights Amendment (ERA) was overwhelmingly endorsed by Congress.

Equality at Last?

The franchise that was won and the subsequent expansion of civil rights, affirmative action for women, no-fault divorce laws, solid educational opportunities, the availability of birth control measures, and the freedom to exercise choice in having or not having children all seem to have brought to a realization many of the earlier feminists' demands for equality. Table 12–1 shows the gains made by women over the last fifteen years.

9. Ironically enough the word "sex" had been inserted by conservative Southern senators in the hope that this would defeat the proposal!

TABLE 12–1 The Gains of Working Women	1970	1986
Managerial and professional specialty (administrators, financial managers, buyers, etc.)	33.9%	43.4%
Professional specialty (lawyers, teachers, writers, etc.)	44.3	49.4
Sales occupations	41.3	48.2
Administrative support, including clerical	73.2	80.4
Service occupations	60.4	62.6
Precision, production, craft, and repair (mechanics, etc.)	7.3	8.6
Operators, fabricators, and laborers	25.9	25.4
Transportation and material moving occupations	4.1	8.9
Handlers, equipment cleaners, helpers, and laborers	17.4	16.3
Farming, forestry, and fishing	9.1	15.9

"The Gains of Working Women," from *The New York Times*, July 17, 1987. © 1987 by the New York Times Company. Used by permission.

Many of women's goals now appear within reach in the United States, the Scandinavian countries where the most noticeable advances have taken place, and also in England, New Zealand, Australia, Canada, and some European democracies. Women have become "assimilated" into a liberal society and a liberal ideology; they have joined the mainstream of society as consumers, producers, and professionals and increasingly share the same opportunities with men. They have settled into formerly male-dominated occupations and to all intents and purposes appear to be "equal."

But many battles remain to be fought: special benefits for mother-hood and childbearing, the expansion of day care centers, strong measures against child and wife abuse and, above all, the uncontested choice to have or not to have children. Similarly, there is a crying need to expand welfare support for women who are heads of households (⅗ of all families below the poverty line are headed by women—often referred to as the "feminization of poverty"), to expand educational opportunities, and to provide access to high-paying jobs. However, in spite of what still has to be done there is little doubt that the liberal democratic state has at long last accepted women as full-time citizens.

Has there been any change in the liberal ideology because of feminine gains? Are women playing the "masculine roles" they have fought for in a manner different from men? Is their participation changing any of the values of our society? It may be too early to tell.

Women's growing participation as full-time citizens has not yet brought about any significant changes on the political scene. Although

282

*Old Voices and
New:
Nationalism, The
Third World,
Feminism,
Liberation
Theology, and
Revolution*

there have been some minor flirtations with independent women's political parties, women still follow the same path as men in choosing parties and platforms. Only in Iceland is there a small "women's party," pledged to qualitative social changes that stem directly from women's concerns and that are different from those of other parties. Women's full citizenship has done little to mitigate the overall social and economic hardships of their male-dominated society. They distribute themselves on the political spectrum just as men do: by socioeconomic category and income; they vote their pocketbooks and interests just as men do; they follow the trade union and lobbying tactics set up by men.[10] Given this situation, one could ask: If the goal of the feminist movement was to fully assimilate women to the social norms set up by men, what is left of feminism?

Beyond Liberalism: Radical Feminism

Some women activists and some of their organizations have turned to socialism for the preconditions of women's liberation. By doing away with private property, which they have viewed as an institution controlled by the husband, they hoped to eliminate the basic source of male domination. Thus women's liberation would simply *derive* from the collectivization of the means of production and the changing industry-labor relationships. This is an assumption, however, that is beginning to be contested by many.

There is no convincing reason to assert that women's inferior status was caused by capitalism and the private ownership of the means of production—it predated them; and there is nothing inherent in the socialist

---

NOW

The organization that best expresses women's demands within the context of American democratic liberalism and continues to push for the full realization of equal rights is the National Organization of Women (NOW). Founded in 1966, it currently has a membership of about 200,000. In lobbying for women's causes it has been an active political force, supporting or opposing candidates for Congress, the Senate, and the White House. It challenges legislative measures that adversely affect women and promotes legislation favorable to them. It is without doubt the major feminist organization, advocating full participation and equality of women, as well as special provisions for women who are both mothers and workers. NOW insists on child care arrangements for working women, liberal policies for maternity and parental leave, affirmative action in hiring, free choice for and subsidizing of abortion, and of course equal pay. Like so many other groups NOW is asking for full integration of women into the society but not a change in the liberal society as we know it.

---

10. In 1988 there were only two women senators and only a handful of congresswomen and state governors. Even in state legislatures women are grossly underrepresented—they comprise about 15 percent of the total membership in the fifty states.

ideology to bring about women's equality except the hope that it will radically change societal beliefs and values. In many socialist societies, notably the Soviet Union, the status of women as such has not improved any more than in the liberal democracies. In fact, many argue convincingly that the status of women — their freedoms and equality with men — has improved far more rapidly in recent years in liberal democracies like France, West Germany, England, the United States, and the Scandinavian countries.

There is yet another reason why socialism is no longer broadly advocated. It lies in the historical fact that in most democracies the majority of women activists' organizations have had a great deal of success in securing equal property rights and equal opportunity for high-paying managerial and professional jobs. Women's movements, nurtured in the liberal ideology, found it difficult to turn against it, especially when many of their demands have been met.

Radical feminists go beyond socialism. They address squarely and confront directly the values that a male society has propagated about women. Radical feminists make a distinction between sex, on the one hand, and gender, on the other. The first is strictly biological and relates to pregnancy and motherhood. Women can do something that men cannot do — bring forth children. The second, gender, comprises all the sex-related institutional arrangements, notably the role of women in the family and their obligations for childrearing.

Are there any special characteristics that are directly attributable to sex *other* than the biological reality of pregnancy and motherhood? Simone de Beauvoir refers to a woman's state of immanence. Women are immersed in motherhood and childrearing; conversely, men are portrayed as "transcendent," in part because they are free from the burden of motherhood. Men strive to conquer and transform their environment through an active interplay with it. This is another way of repeating the stereotypes: women are "passive" and men are "active." Women submit to what is given; men strive to change it. How fixed, if true, are these traits? Where did they arise from, if not from the difference in sex? Can they be modified?

Another distinction between men and women stems, according to some, not only from sex but also from the assigned gender role in the family and childrearing. Women have particularistic attachments and concerns, mainly the children and the family. Men, on the other hand, direct their attention to broader interests — public life, for instance. In contrast to women's particularistic concerns, they display more universalistic ones. These distinctions correspond once more to the stereotypes of women's traditional attachment to the family and the household, while men soar over and beyond them. Again, how fixed, if true, are these traits? Are they sex-determined or gender-related? How can they be changed?

While sex accounts for some specific and unalterable traits, such as motherhood, it is doubtful that it accounts for the sex-related arrangements in our society, especially the responsibility for raising children. As mothers, women have assumed the primary role in childrearing in accordance with the existing norms of the society. However, it seems equally true that men

284

*Old Voices and
New:
Nationalism, The
Third World,
Feminism,
Liberation
Theology, and
Revolution*

can raise children and that significant changes can occur within the present conjugal family. Some new arrangements are already in evidence. In some households, for example, fathers have taken on a partnership role in childrearing, and day care centers for preschoolers have further freed mothers to pursue careers outside the home.

Many therefore argue that women's equality can be attained when the bringing up of children from the earliest age is shared by others—the father, child care centers, communal programs, or even public agencies. Such changes may or may not alter the conjugal family as we know it. But they may go a long way in doing away with what Betty Friedan called the "feminine mystique"—the exaltation by a male-dominated society of women's role in the household and in childrearing duties during a good part of their lives. In reality, this mystique is a drudgery that prevents women from developing their own talents outside of the home. When the mystique is lifted and the drudgery gone, women will be freer to share the same roles within the society that men play and become truly equal. Men's roles will change correspondingly when the present division of labor in the family gives place to a genuine cooperative sharing.

Some radical feminists go even further by questioning the institution of marriage. Some, like Shulamith Firestone, who assume that there is a constant dialectic struggle between men and women just as there is between workers and owners, call for the elimination of marriage. They advocate motherhood without marriage and the formation of communal associations for childrearing. Such ideas were suggested in the past by the utopian philosophers, and even Plato, who saw the family as the germ of private and often irreconcilable interests, egoisms, and conflicts.

Thus the crux of radical feminism lies in the elimination of all sex-related institutions and arrangements that have been attributed to women and separate them from men, especially childrearing. In addition to the complete abolition of the conjugal family the extreme feminists want sweeping reforms to protect the unmarried mother. Most advocate radical changes in the workplace to ensure special maternity leaves and allowances. And they all favor the unqualified right to choose contraception and abortion. In contrast to liberal feminism, therefore, radical feminists stress personal rights and major structural institutional changes.

The Rise and Fall of the Equal Rights Amendment (ERA)[11]

Immediately after women gained the right to vote in 1920, a movement for a constitutional amendment to provide "equality of rights" between the two sexes was initiated. It was not until 1970 that the amendment— "Equality of rights under the law shall not be denied or abridged by the

11. For a full account of the history of the ERA see Mansbridge, *Why We Lost the ERA.*

United States or any state on account of sex" — passed the House of Representatives by a vote of 350 to 15, well beyond the requisite two-thirds. In 1972 it passed the Senate by 84 to 8. By 1977 thirty-five state legislatures had ratified the amendment and only three more states were needed for the amendment to become part of the Constitution. It did not come to pass. The deadline for ratification by the requisite three-fourths of the states, after being extended, expired in 1982.

The purpose of the amendment was to formally guarantee women equal rights with men across the board by prohibiting any differential treatment. But many of the extreme activists envisioned radical changes. They saw the ERA not only as the formal recognition of equality but also as the symbol of the elimination of all gender distinctions. It was at this juncture that support for the ERA weakened. To many it had become a symbol of radical feminism, away from the mainstream of the liberal feminist movement. It also became increasingly linked to the proabortion forces and those who demanded radical changes in the institution of marriage and family.

The perception that the ERA had become the mantle of radical feminists was strengthened by the fact that in the 1970s many of the women's claims began, as we have seen, to be realized. Through legislation or court decisions women were granted equal protection before the law, equal educational opportunities, affirmative action for securing jobs and against being removed from them, and, finally the right to have an abortion when in the *Roe v. Wade* case (1973) the Supreme Court struck down a Connecticut law forbidding abortion. The Court ruled that the Connecticut law was an intrusion on privacy. At a time when women's rights were being supported and strengthened, many advocates thought that the ERA embodied only a symbolic affirmation of liberation with no tangible benefits. Other began to fear, rightly or wrongly, that its enactment might actually *deprive* women of many of the gains they had realized. For widows, divorcées, older women, and in many instances for young women too, the ERA could impose burdens: for example, serving in the army, being deprived of a husband's pension, being denied custody of a child, or losing the preferential treatment obtained through affirmative action in the workplace.

Conservative groups and religious activists were the first to seize on these issues and distort them in an effort to preserve the traditional status of women. The political parties began to divide, with the Republicans taking an increasingly anti-ERA stance[12] and the Democrats paying only lip service to it. While it is true that the amendment to the federal constitution lost because it failed in two Southern states (but also in Illinois), it is equally true that ERA amendments to state constitutions failed in "progressive" states. In 1975 ERA amendments to the New York and New Jersey constitutions failed with 57 percent voting against it in New York

---

12. There were also women and some women's organizations that opposed the ERA. They became known derisively as "Auntie Toms."

286

*Old Voices and
New:
Nationalism, The
Third World,
Feminism,
Liberation
Theology, and
Revolution*

SCHLESINGER LIBRARY, RADCLIFFE COLLEGE

Susan B. Anthony (1820–1906)

Susan B. Anthony was born in South Adams, Massachusetts, on February 15, 1820, the second oldest of eight children. Her mother was a devout Baptist and her father a Quaker. As with the rest of her sisters and brothers, she received fairly extensive early education and was trained for the only profession then deemed suitable for a woman—teaching—to which she devoted fifteen years of her life.

Along with her early interest in abolitionism (many of the most prominent abolitionists, including William Lloyd Garrison, visited her family), she was committed to the temperance movement. In 1847 she joined the Daughters of Temperance, and in 1852 she organized the New York State Women's Temperance Association.

From about 1850 on, she and Stanton devoted themselves in earnest to the cause of women's suffrage. Between 1868–1870, she produced in collaboration with Susan Anthony a feminist magazine entitled *The Revolution.*

In 1872 she was arrested along with several other women for voting in the presidential election and was brought to trial. When asked by the judge after she had pleaded not guilty, "You voted as a woman, did you not?" She replied, "No, sir, I voted as a citizen of the United States." In response to the $100 fine that was imposed, Susan stated "resistance to tyranny is obedience to God, and I shall never pay a penny of this unjust claim." She never did.

She doggedly wore the "Bloomer" outfit and by the time she died she symbolized women's rights and determination.

and 51 percent voting against it in New Jersey. Subsequently it failed in
Iowa (1980) and in Maine (1984).

287

*Feminism: A
Movement or an
Ideology?*

Liberal and Radical Feminism:
Areas of Convergence

There are some significant areas of convergence between liberal and radical feminists. Two programs have been suggested—one is fairly old and
needs only comprehensive implementation; the other is relatively new.
The first calls for a broad extension of the day care centers that are subsi-
dized by the federal, state, and local authorities. (Incidentally, such centers
have been established in the Scandinavian countries and in some European countries.) Child care would be available to all children regardless of
whether they come from a conjugal family or a single parent. For liberal
feminism, this is an extension of women's rights and women's independence, indeed emancipation from the "feminine mystique." For radical
feminism, this provides an opportunity for single women to have and
bring up children if they want to do so while fully employed.

A second, more controversial, proposal entails what may be called a
"mother salary": women working at home and raising their children
would be provided with a subsidy linked to other benefits—health and
social security. This proposal is advocated both by liberal and even some
radical feminists who deem it to be proper recognition and compensation
for a woman's worth and work as a mother and housekeeper. But it is also
advocated by many conservatives who see it as the only way to maintain
women in their "proper" role and at the same time save the conjugal
family. They see it as a means of keeping women away from the marketplace and the professions—away from masculine roles.

Conclusion

Feminism—liberal or radical—may be viewed in the last analysis as the
consecration of the moral and universal values of equality held at bay for so
long by the supremacy of males and the ideologies developed to legitimize
it. Even though the feminist movement does not advocate a revolution, it
is nonetheless what revolutions are all about: to undermine the power of
some (men) and enhance the power of others (women). It proposes cooperation instead of subjection and equality instead of discrimination. In this
sense, feminism is one of the many protest movements for the liberation of
the powerless against the powerholders.

But is feminism anything else or anything other than a movement
advocating change in social (and power) relations and in socially defined
roles? All revolutionary ideologies attempt not only to change the position
and roles of those in power in a given society but also to transform the
values of the society as well. Granting that feminism as a movement aspires
to restore women to the full equality and power sharing to which they are

Charlotte Perkins Gilman (1860–1935)

Charlotte Perkins Gilman was born in Hartford, Connecticut, and raised by her mother under truly dire circumstances.

She had a limited education but did manage to attend the newly opened Rhode Island School of Design for a short while. After reaching adult age, Charlotte supported herself for several years as an artist, art teacher, and governess. Although never a member of the Socialist party, she did attend the London convention of the International Socialist and Labour Congress in 1896. There she met Sidney and Beatrice Webb and George Bernard Shaw, and it was at this time that she developed a great interest in their Fabian socialism.

In 1898 she published *Women and Economics*, a feminist manifesto on the need for economic independence for women, arguing that due to the material conditions of their oppression, women were indeed dependent creatures. Her book was an immediate success, arousing both ardent support and passionate denouncements. It was translated into seven languages, including Russian and Japanese. In 1899 *The Nation* described her book as "the most significant utterance on the subject since Mill's 'Subjection of Women.'"

Charlotte Gilman actively supported the suffrage movement throughout her life but considered suffrage only a small step. Her claim was always that a much more profound restructuring of feminine and masculine roles would be necessary if the world was really to change. In this sense, she was quite a visionary feminist, making claims that are voiced again today among radical feminists.

entitled as human beings, how will this change the society's norms within which men and women interact? What will the new norms be? In what way will children be reared to espouse new norms and values? Will there be a radical change in property relations? In matters of war and peace? In working conditions? In education? In the production and distribution of goods and services? Will there be new outlets for individual self-realization? To return to our original question: Will the "feminine ingredient," fully liberated, become the leaven of a new society, or will it simply assimilate itself, once liberated, to the values that have been developed by a male-dominated society?

The answer is not at all clear because the theory underlining feminism is not yet clear. Feminists argue that there are no innate differences between women and men other than the biology of pregnancy and motherhood. All other differences, they claim, are socially determined. If that is true, how will their full and equal participation in the society transform the society? Unless special qualities — other than biological — are attributed to women, how and why can we expect the society to be changed? In what sense will women's liberation lead to a social transformation? In other words, will women become fully part of our society as we know it, or will they, in becoming fully part of it, change it?

It still remains for feminist theory to identify what new values and new characteristics will transform our society. Otherwise, feminism as an ideology is but another movement toward freedom and equality for all — very much in line with the egalitarian and universalistic promise of the liberal ethos. However, inasmuch as it offers another building block in the development of the universal values of equality, freedom, and friendship, this in itself may amount to a significant qualitative change.

Bibliography

Bradshaw, Jan (ed.). *The Women's Liberation Movement: Europe and North America.* Pergamon Press, 1982.

Brownmiller, Susan. *Against Our Will: Men, Women, and Rape.* New York: Simon & Schuster, 1975.

Bunch, Charlotte, and Nancy Myron (eds.). *Class and Feminism.* Baltimore: Diana Press, 1974.

Daly, Mary. *Gyn/ecology: The Metaethics of Radical Feminism.* Boston: Beacon Press, 1978.

de Beauvoir, Simone. *The Second Sex.* New York: Bantam Books, 1961. (First published in 1952.)

Eisenstein, Zillah. *The Radical Future of Liberation Feminism.* New York: Longman, 1980.

Elshtain, Jean Bethke. *Public Man, Private Woman: Women in Social and Political Thought.* Princeton, N.J.: Princeton U.P., 1981.

Firestone, Shulamith. *The Dialectic of Sex: The Case for Feminist Revolution.* New York: Morrow, 1970.

Flexner, Eleanor. *Century of Struggle: The Women's Rights Movement in the USA.* rev. ed. Cambridge, Mass.: Harvard Paperbacks, 1975.

Forster, Margaret. *Significant Sisters: The Grassroots of Activist Feminism, 1839–1939.* New York: Knopf, 1984. (This is a book on early movements in Britain.)

Friedan, Betty. *The Feminine Mystique.* New York: W. W. Norton, 1963.

Gay, Virginia. *Feminism and the New Right.* New York: Praeger, 1983.

Gilman, Charlotte Perkins. *Women and Economics, 1898.* New York: Harper and Row, 1966.

Gurko, Miriam. *The Ladies of Seneca Falls.* New York: Schocken Books, 1974.

Hole, Judith, and Ellen Levine. *Rebirth of Feminism.* New York: Quadrangle Books, 1971.

Jaggar, Alison. *Feminist Politics and Human Nature.* Totowa, N.J.: Rowman and Allanheld, 1983.

Jenner, Leslie. *Voices for Women's Liberation.* New York: New American Library, 1970.

Klein, Ethel. *Gender Politics.* Cambridge, Mass.: Harvard U.P., 1987.

Mansbridge, Jane. *Why We Lost the ERA.* Chicago: University of Chicago Press, 1986.

Millett, Kate. *Sexual Politics.* Garden City, N.Y.: Doubleday, 1970.

Mitchell, Juliet. *Women's Estate.* New York: Vintage Books, 1971.

Okin, Susan. *Women in Western Political Thought.* Princeton, N.J.: Princeton U.P., 1979.

O'Neill, William. *Everyone Was Brave.* Chicago: Quadrangle Books, 1969.

Ware, Susan. *Beyond Suffrage: Women in the New Deal.* Cambridge, Mass.: Harvard U.P., 1981.

———. *Holding Their Own: American Women in the 1930s.* Boston: Twayne, 1982.

13 | *Liberation Theology: The Voice of the Church and the Poor**

Now it is high time to awake out of sleep; for now is our salvation nearer than we believed. The night is far spent, the day is at hand; let us therefore cast off the works of darkness, and let us put on the armour of light.

ST. PAUL   Letter to the Romans Ch. XIII, II

Most all great religions ordain our temporal lives in terms of transcendental values, setting forth a code of behavior that guarantees the spiritual rewards of eternal life. When we think of religion we think of contemplation, inwardness, and a preparation for the life hereafter. "My kingdom is not of this world." The kingdom of God is separate and very different from earthly kingdoms. The church does not assume or exercise temporal powers. The "secular sword"—politics—is in the hands of kings, monarchs, peoples, and governments. It obeys its own rules and has its own logic. The "spiritual sword," though far mightier, is less visible. It is addressed to matters of sin and salvation and binds the faithful in an intricate web of faith, ritual, and sacraments.

Within the civil society, it is the mission of the church to "evangelize"—to spread the "good tidings" of the gospel and the word of God, to convert pagans and agnostics and make them aware of the church and

*I want to acknowledge with thanks and appreciation the help two students at Brandeis gave me in the writing of this essay—Joshua Spero, a graduating senior, and Perry Sekus, first-year graduate student—both in politics. Sekus prepared a paper on some of the doctrinal issues of liberation theology and Spero dealt with some of the issues relating to the "base ecclesial communities."

292

*Old Voices and
New:
Nationalism, The
Third World,
Feminism,
Liberation
Theology, and
Revolution*

the prospects of salvation. The mission of the church has been to save us *from* the world in which we find ourselves temporally.

In this discussion we are exclusively concerned with Christian churches in general and the Roman Catholic church in particular. Granted, there are doctrinal and organizational differences among various Christian churches and there are variations and frictions among the different orders within one and the same church. But certain common overall doctrinal positions characterize all Christian churches:

1. The role of the church is "sacerdotal" — to administer the sacraments — and "evangelical" — to convert non-Christians and "bear witness" to the gospel. The "pastoral" activities of the church and the clergy relate to these matters. The church and the clergy should not, however, assume directly political roles and become political or social activists.
2. The word of God is addressed directly to individuals in order to save their souls.
3. "History" is but a temporary stage lasting only until the return of the Lord and the new life of the hereafter. Not only is history beyond the scope and power of the church but also it is outside of the church's concern.
4. Social action — to change and reform and infuse institutions and social structures with Christian love and the teaching of the gospel — should not preempt the spiritual commitment of the church, which is to help us avoid sin and to prepare us for our salvation by following the word of God. If matters of state belong to Caesar, the world of the spirit belongs to God and is administered by the church.

Liberation theology, as it has developed in the last thirty years, goes against the limited conception of the church's role in society. It is a call for action, headed by some bishops, many clergymen and lay members, addressed to all but especially to the poor and the downtrodden of the Third World in order to redress, in the name of Christ, the social wrongs inflicted upon them, such as abject poverty, illiteracy, exploitation, and powerlessness. Liberation theology has spawned new forms of religious organizations that question the hierarchical organization of the church — especially the Catholic church. It has gained roots and seems to be spreading among populations where poverty has been endemic, where illiteracy is widespread, and where the law provides no security or protection. It claims to be a new religious movement addressed and applicable to the underdeveloped societies of the world, and it has been particularly in evidence in Latin America: Colombia, Brazil, Peru, Nicaragua, Chile, El Salvador, and Guatemala. Though many of its leaders received training in European religious institutes, the Catholic University of Louvain in Belgium, for instance, or the Catholic University in Paris, it is a truly indigenous intellectual and ideological movement addressed by native theologians and

His major work, *Liberation of Theology*,* was based on his lectures at Harvard University in the spring of 1974. Its focus is largely on the development of a new theological methodology. Of particular value are the three chapters on ideology and faith, in which Segundo elaborates on the distinction between the two and the need to combine both.

Segundo was born in Montevideo, Uruguay, in 1925. Like Gutierrez, Segundo studied both in Latin America and in Europe at the University of Louvain in Belgium, where he received a licentiate in theology in 1956. He also received a degree of Doctor of Letters from the University of Paris in 1963. He has written a number of articles and books on the sociology of religion and liberation theology. *(Photo: Courtesy of the Maryknoll Fathers)*

*Juan Luis Segundo, *Liberation of Theology*. Translated by John Drury. Maryknoll, New York: Orbis Books, 1976. Originally published by Ediciones Carlos Lohle, Buenos Aires, 1975.

intellectuals to the social ills plaguing Latin America. Its major inspiration, however, came from the Second Vatican Council (1962–1965) and from a number of papal encyclicals that reversed the traditional posture of the church and called upon the church and Catholics to undertake social and political action.

Background

By the end of World War II it was clear that evangelization alone, the "Christianization" of individuals, was losing ground. Industrialization, urbanization, secularization of values, intense social strife arising from social predicaments and inequalities, and even more, the rise of powerful secular ideologies — especially communist movements — provided a strong appeal to workers and the poor and challenged the church's aloofness. In effect, communist movements became rival ideologies, promising heaven on earth. In France and Italy, the Communist party could be counted in the millions. Its ascendancy among the workers, and in many cases among the farmers, could not be discounted. There was also the Third World — a world in misery, engulfed in social and revolutionary strife.

The Worker-Priests Movement

Nothing showed better the difficult position of the Catholic church in France, and also in other European countries, than the so-called worker-priests movement. By 1945 it was discovered that the vast majority of the

294

*Old Voices and
New:
Nationalism, The
Third World,
Feminism,
Liberation
Theology, and
Revolution*

French urban proletariats was in effect de-Christianized. Workers, orga-nized in trade unions spearheaded by the Communist party, had shed their religious consciousness while acquiring a social one. The sacraments were becoming increasingly foreign to them. The question was how to re-Christianize them. Catholic mission groups were established for this purpose and priests were allowed to become workers; they shed the cloth, undertook to work under the same conditions as the other workers, par-ticipated in their trade unions, and assumed the same professional respon-sibilities held by others. They lived in workers' neighborhoods and shared the workers' lifestyle. Their mission was to bring to the workers an aware-ness of the spirit of the church — to evangelize them and, if possible, recon-vert them. Their goal was to infuse religious feelings and religious aware-ness in an attempt to bring about a return to religious practices to a part of the population that had developed a strong secular social and political organization (often communist) and with it a revolutionary consciousness.

The experiment failed in a manner that was embarrassing to the church and the Catholic missions that had been established. Few, if any, workers were "evangelized"; some of the priests, on the other hand, were converted to the workers' ethos and adopted *their* social and political consciousness. They led the trade unions, participated in strikes, organized demonstrations against their employers, the government, and against France's ally, the United States, and the Atlantic Alliance, and spoke the same language communist leaders spoke. They became engaged not in the name of the Bible and the Lord but in the name of a special political doctrine and a secular ideology, and their engagement led them to direct political action. They absorbed the "proletarian consciousness" and acted in terms of it.

Some of the priests came to the conclusion that evangelization was but a bourgeois practice, that the church wanted to maintain the status quo values and keep the working class in a state of bondage. In a poignant document published in 1952 (when the movement was coming to an end), some of the worker-priests declared that "in order to 'bear witness' among the workers to divine revelation the priests must develop a new expression of faith that is based on proletarian consciousness." Religious sacraments no longer sufficed. The priests declared that it was "their task to adapt religion to social needs as defined by the working class." Hence they would rather be-come workers in the full sense of the term rather than remain priests.[1] Under the circumstances, both the Vatican and the French bishops were forced to put an end to the mission of the worker-priests. It virtually came to an end by 1954 after having lasted only a few years.[2] Some of the worker-priests "sub-mitted" to the bishops and the pope; others joined communist political orga-nizations; some developed their own political groupings that collaborated with the Communist party; many returned willingly to the church.

1. Quoted in Adrien Dansette. *Destin du Catholicisme Francais, 1926–1956.* Paris: Flammarion, 1956. (Author's translation.)
2. For a good documentary account of the worker-priests movement, see *The Worker-Priests: A Collective Documentation,* translated from the French by John Petrie. London: Routledge and Kegan Paul, 1956.

The Roman Catholic church in a number of famous encyclicals had often taken a position with regard to political and social problems in the name of "justice."[3] But it was in 1962–1965 in the Ecumenical Council in Rome (referred to as the Second Vatican Council or Vatican II) that the church developed comprehensive guidelines. While individual salvation continued to be the cardinal doctrine, a close relationship between it and social and political life was acknowledged. Vatican II and the encyclical that came out of it, *Gaudium et Spes*,[4] is the source of liberation theology.

The orientation of the Catholic church that emerged from Vatican II was not doctrinal but pastoral—how the church should act. Revealed truth is the only truth, and it is the function of the church to teach the eternal truth. However, a much greater emphasis was placed on worldly relevance—on how to make the gospel immediately and directly relevant to existing situational and social realities. The church acknowledges change and attempts to interpret it. In so doing, it realizes that the individual is not only a person but also a social being. The church stressed, as never before, social interdependence and solidarity. Salvation must be geared to the individual not only as an individual but also as a member of the community and of his or her role in the community. Therefore salvation relates to the "living out" of one's beliefs in the community and for the community. "To the extent that earthly progress contributes to the better ordering of human society it is of concern to the kingdom of God."[5] The church therefore becomes a force within temporal history—it becomes an agent of history and change. Even more, emphasis on the community and its betterment requires an acceptance of a social ethic (as opposed to a purely individual one) in terms of which the "common good" can be evaluated and the proper institutions that help actualize the values of dignity, equality, and freedom can be established.

Nothing could be more calculated to open the gates to social and political action and social, economic, and political reformism. The dimensions are spelled out in *Gaudium et Spes*. According to it, the church and also the Catholic laity is to become an "authentic witness" of the gospel (i.e., agent of justice). Its obligations are now to make sure that equality is guaranteed, that a Christian communitarian ethic of love and justice for all is developed and implemented, that gross inequalities in the living conditions of peoples in different parts of the world and nations are avoided, that peace prevail and nuclear wars are prevented, that political participation is assured to all, that associations and groups in one and the same nation are given autonomy and freedom to act. "Earthly progress to the extent that . . . it can contribute to the better ordering of human society,

---

3. A very useful introduction to Catholic social theory is David J. O'Brien and Thomas Shannon, *Renewing the Earth: Catholic Documents on Peace, Justice and Liberation.* New York: Doubleday (Image Books), 1977.

4. O'Brien and Shannon, *Renewing the Earth,* pp. 178–283.

5. Ibid., p. 175.

*Old Voices and
New:
Nationalism, The
Third World,
Feminism,
Liberation
Theology, and
Revolution*

Dussel's *A History of the Church in Latin America**
is a comprehensive account of the historical evolution of liberation theology as a theological
doctrine and as a movement. Dussel traces the
evolution of the Roman Catholic church from
the late fifteenth century to the present in three
distinct phases: the Christendom of the West In-
dies (1492–1808), the Agony of Colonial Christendom (1808–1940), and the church and Latin
American Liberation (1962–1979).

Dussel was born in Mendoza, Argentina, in
1934. He received degrees from the University of
Mendoza (philosophy), the University of
Madrid (philosophy), the Sorbonne (Paris) (history), and the Catholic University of Paris (theology). He also studied in Germany and Israel.
One of the themes recurrent throughout his
many books and articles is the need to adapt the
teachings of the church to the present situation
in Latin America. *(Photo: Courtesy of the Maryknoll Fathers)*

*Enrique Dussel. *A History of the Church in Latin America: Colonialism to Liberation (1492–1979).*
Translated and revised by Alan Neely. Michigan: William B. Eerdmans Publishing Company,
1981.

is . . . of vital concern to the kingdom of God."[6] In other words, even if
Christ's kingdom is not of this world, the encyclical proclaims that "the
Kingdom of God is in the midst of us."[7]

After *Gaudium et Spes,* the Catholic hierarchy, first under Pope John II
and since 1978 John Paul II, seems to have entered into social and political
action on an unprecedented scale. The papacy restated the social and
political tasks for the church and for Catholics in general with a growing
urgency, if not impatience, in 1967 with a new encyclical, *Populorum
Progressio*[8] (The Development of Peoples), and in 1971 with an Apostolic
Letter, *A Call to Action.*[9]

In *Populorum Progressio* we note the emergence of a new worldwide
social theology addressing itself to the world problems of our day—the
growth of poor nations, the ever-increasing inequalities between poor and
wealthy nations, and the growing concern of the church for the predicament of the poor everywhere. Aside from the individuals and questions of
individual sin and salvation there are *oppressive social structures*—with regard to both the distribution of property and the "abuse of power"—that
deny to the individual his or her vocation and fulfillment. The encyclical
states categorically that property is not an absolute right and that, for the
sake of common good, expropriation and socialization may be undertaken.

6. Ibid., p. 212.
7. St. Luke, 17:21.
8. O'Brien and Shannon, *Renewing the Earth,* pp. 313–346.
9. Ibid., pp. 312–383.

297

*Liberation
Theology:
The Voice of
the Church
and the Poor*

Property must never be exercised to the detriment of the common good. Laymen are urged " . . . to take up as their own proper task the renewal of the temporal order. . . . If the role of the hierarchy is to teach and to interpret authentically the norms of morality to be followed . . . it belongs to the laymen, without waiting passively for orders and directives, to take the initiative freely and to infuse a Christian spirit into the mentality, customs, laws and structures of the community in which they live."[10] This is an urgent call of action addressed to all Catholics—indeed to all Christians—to become each and all missionaries for a just society, a just political and social order, and for peace.

The same theme is repeated with the same urgency in many papal communications. "Politics," proclaimed the pope, is "a demanding matter"; it requires us to live out our Christian commitments to the service of others.[11] Catholics need to "become involved in action." Christians must "give witness," i.e., act for justice, solidarity, and equality. They must see to it that:

1. People should not be hindered from attaining the development they deserve.
2. Through mutual cooperation, all people should be able to become the principal architects of their own economic and social development.
3. Every person, as active and responsible members of human society, should be able to cooperate for the attainment of the common good on an equal footing with other people in other nations.

Echoes in the Third World

The student will recall from our discussion of Marxism that one factor that influenced Marx and Engels was the dismal conditions under which the workers and their families lived in the industrial centers of Europe and especially England in the middle of the nineteenth century. A sense of moral indignation permeates the works of the "young Marx." In the same sense, churchmen, Catholic or not, began to experience a growing sense of dismay and indignation at the poverty, misery, and helplessness of the mass of people in many of the underdeveloped areas of the world. In Latin American countries, daily income, social assistance, educational facilities, and health services are dismally low or nonexistent. Redress is impossible in these societies ruled by dictators and military regimes—another characteristic of underdevelopment—that often shield the ruling class. From a political standpoint, the poor are powerless. They are unable to organize

10. O'Brien and Shannon, op. cit., pp. 319–322.
11. O'Brien and Shannon, *Renewing the Earth*, p. 341.

298

*Old Voices and
New:
Nationalism, The
Third World,
Feminism,
Liberation
Theology, and
Revolution*

and articulate their demands, unable to participate in any decision, constantly at the mercy of a minority that abuses its power instead of promoting a degree of sharing that would raise the level of consciousness and participation of the masses. How to raise the people from their poverty and ignorance and give them a place consistent with their humanity?

One answer has been economic modernization, and many regimes, including military ones, have espoused it. But modernization in Latin America has involved an imitation of western methods: a growth of investment (by borrowing from abroad), and a reliance upon free enterprise and the market. It has been advocated by intellectuals and economists and by some theologians too. It was to be a modernization decreed from above, consistent with the social, political, and economic structures that prevailed; it was to be gradual and incremental.

This type of modernization as an answer to problems of poverty was disavowed by others. The reasons given were briefly the following: the Latin American economic structures were so closely tied to the world economy, or rather the United States economy, that they were in a state of "dependency." They could not develop the autonomy and freedoms and the means to modernize in order to serve their own needs and purposes. They were but an adjunct of American capitalism. Their situation was interpreted in the context of world capitalism to amount to a state of exploitation and semicolonialism in which production was geared to the interests of powerful foreign economic interests. These interests had every reason to continue to use Latin American countries as a source of raw materials and as a market of their own goods. When investments from abroad were made, their purpose was to produce goods at low costs, thus providing for a large margin of profit for foreign companies and interests. In effect, foreign capital, it was argued, robbed the underdeveloped societies of their own wealth and deprived them of the opportunities of growth consistent with national needs. It kept them in a state of dependency that amounted to exploitation. The reasons for poverty were to be found therefore in the international (i.e., American) exploitive capitalism. There was no way to break the cycle of dependency except by undertaking major structural reforms of the economy and the society in the direction of socialism.

The Doctrine

To the theory of dependency and the answer given as to how to overcome it, a new social and political orientation was needed. The church doctrine began to change accordingly. The pope himself in the *Populorum Progressio* had pointedly referred to the uneven distribution of goods among nations and in a number of his pronouncements had sharply criticized both the

In his major work, *Jesus Christ Liberator,** Boff discusses Christology based on the contextual variables of Latin America, i.e., oppression and poverty. His conception of Christology is characterized by (1) the primacy of the anthropological element over the ecclesiological element, (2) the primacy of the utopian element over the de facto element, (3) the primacy of the critical element over the dogmatic element, (4) the primacy of the social element over the individual element, and (5) the primacy of orthopraxis (correct action) over orthodoxy (true belief).

Boff was born in the town of Concordia, Brazil, in 1938. He pursued his studies in Brazil (Petropolis, Curitiba) and Europe (Ludwig-Maximilian Universitat in Munich, Wurzburg, Louvain, and Oxford). He is a Franciscan. Boff has been a professor for over a decade at the Petropolis Institute for Theology and Philosophy, where he teaches courses in systematic theology. He has written a number of books and numerous articles of theology and liberation. He is perhaps best known for his recent summons to Rome in September 1984 to explain his views on liberation theology before the pope and the Congregation for the Doctrine of the Faith, headed by Joseph Cardinal Ratzinger. One of his more recent books, *The Church: Charisma and Power,* was formally criticized in March 1985 by the Congregation. *(Photo: National Catholic News Service)*

*Leonardo Boff, *Jesus Christ Liberator.* Maryknoll, N. Y.: Orbis Books, 1978. Originally published as *Jesus Christo liberador: Ensaio de cristologia critica para o nosso tempo.* Petropolis: Vozes, 1972.

Liberation Theology: The Voice of the Church and the Poor

abuse of power and the abuse of wealth and property; he had expressed his particular concerns for the poor. On three occasions—at Medellin in 1969, in the *Letter Addressed to the People of the Third World* (1976), and in the Council of Latin American Bishops at Puebla in 1979—the changes as they related to the Third World became apparent.

Medellin

The Second General Council of the Latin American Episcopate was held in Medellin, Colombia, between August and September of 1968. One hundred and fifty-six cardinals and archbishops, along with one hundred priests, assembled to discuss the role of the church in Latin America. The theme of the conference was "Latin America in the Light of Vatican II." The general purpose of the conference was to update the Latin American church and bring it in line with Vatican II, but in many ways the conference went way beyond. Discussions centered around such issues as the low education level in their countries, the inadequate legal system, poverty,

300

*Old Voices and
New:
Nationalism, The
Third World,
Feminism,
Liberation
Theology, and
Revolution*

injustice, alienation, and exploitation. These problems were identified as structural (i.e., societal) problems that needed to be overcome. Change, it was agreed, would have to be social change.

It is at Medellin that capitalism is identified with the exploitation and oppression of the ruling elites throughout Latin America and abroad. The "imperialism" of the United States and other colonial powers is identified as having been the cause of much of the social and economic inequity and injustice that plague the Latin American people. The church hierarchy that remained wedded to the interest of these governing elite had to be replaced by church officials who identified with the poor, the exploited, and the oppressed. Similarly, the religious and doctrinal dependence of the Latin American churches on the Roman Catholic church would have to give place to the new Catholic message developing in Latin America for the Latin American people.

Two of the most significant documents signed at Medellin were the "Medellin Document on Peace" and the "Medellin Document on Poverty." They reflected the new-found commitment and aspiration of the Latin American church, and they identified the underlying causes of the social, economic, and political problems.

The Document on Peace   The "Medellin Document on Peace" pinpointed three major tensions existing within Latin America:

1. Class tensions and internal colonialism
    a. Diverse forms of marginal existence
    b. Excessive inequalities between social classes
    c. Rising expectations coupled with growing frustration
    d. Power exercised unjustly by ruling sectors
    e. Growing awareness of the oppressed sectors
2. International tensions and external colonialism
    a. Economic aspects
        (1) Growing disparity in international commerce
        (2) Plight of economic and human assets
        (3) Tax evasion and flight of corporate profits
        (4) Increasing debts
        (5) International monopolies and imperialism
    b. Political aspects
        (1) Indirect and direct imperialism and intervention
3. Tensions between nations of Latin America
    a. Excessive nationalism
    b. Arms races

The "Document on Peace," in addition to providing a comprehensive definition of peace, considered the issue of violence. If violence was to be the tool by which the ruling elite governed, then the oppressed had no recourse other than to adopt similar means in order to survive and strive for peace. Illegal actions in an unjust society, it stated, may be legitimate. To

301

*Liberation
Theology:
The Voice of
the Church
and the Poor*

support this claim, the document made reference to the Hebrew Exodus, which in the eyes of the Egyptian pharaoh was illegal but for Moses was a legitimate act. Since Medellin, the bishops at times have spoken of "legitimate revolution" and the overthrow of organized violence that manifests itself through military dictatorships. Finally, it is important to note that violence is defined also as "institutional violence," arising from the inequitable and unjust social, political, and economic institutions in existence throughout Latin America. Structural societal changes are the proper and necessary means to overcome this form of violence.

The Document on Poverty   The "Medellin Document on Poverty," focusing on a theme that ran throughout the Medellin conference, identified the central mission of the church as one committed to the service of the poor. Specifically, it called for priests to renounce the honorific titles and fees, to live with the poor and perform manual labor, and to share goods among all in religious communities. Identification with the poor, it stated, was essential to the mission of the church, whose purpose becomes to transform socioeconomic and political structures in a manner that will alleviate poverty. Economic reform and political development, and ultimately liberation, is the aim to which the church aspires.[12]

Letter to the "Third World"   The sentiments of the Latin American bishops were embodied in "A Letter to the Peoples of the Third World." Originally conceived at Vatican II, this letter was drafted and signed by eighteen bishops of the Third World in 1976. The letter summed up the general orientation of church leaders throughout the Third World, signaling their dissatisfaction with the traditional orientation of the European church and its failure to understand the historical and cultural specificity of the church in the Third World. Specifically, the letter proclaimed the peoples of the Third World as the "proletariat" in today's world. It asserted the need for drastic action and revolution to overcome the oppression imposed by authoritarian regimes throughout the Third World. It spoke of the need for the church to disassociate itself from systems of rule that were unjust and ill-suited to the needs of the present. Explicit mention was made of the need for "authentic socialism." It referred to "financial" and "cultural" imperialism and spoke of the right of each man to own property. "Property," it stated, however, "should be shared among all."

Puebla, Mexico: How to Save the Poor

From January 27 to February 13, 1979, 218 bishops convened in Puebla, Mexico, for the Conference of Latin American Bishops.[13] What emerged

---

12. For a discussion and the documents, see *Renewing the Earth,* pp. 547–573.
13. *New York Times,* Jan. 28, 1979, p. 1.

from Puebla was the influential "Preferential Option for the Poor," primarily composed by Father Gutierrez. The Peruvian reverend was resolute about the Catholic church's commitment to the poor. Even John Paul II endorsed it in moving terms:

> ... neither a handout nor a few crumbs of justice [are sufficient for the poor] ... we must act promptly and thoroughly; we must implement a bold and a thoroughly innovative transformation.[0]

Going one step further, Gutierrez asserted:

> The re-reading [of the Bible] involves a remaking, and the remaking must be done by the victims or there will be no significant remaking. ... We shall not have our great leap forward, into a whole new theological perspective, until the marginalized and exploited have begun to become the artisans of their own liberation — until their voice makes itself heard directly, without mediations, without interpreters.[0]

Thus the Catholic church (although the same is true for almost all of the Christian denominations) moved increasingly to take its place within the temporal order and improve it. This is especially so if we take into account the many recent pronouncements of Pope John Paul II in favor of the poor and the downtrodden, equality among nations, peace, the injustices of capitalism, and the need for action by the poor and the oppressed against their oppressors. What belongs to Caesar is not exclusive: the church is asking for its share in reforming the civil, social, and political order. What is even more significant is that inasmuch as matters of equality and justice are moral matters, their implementation becomes the responsibility of all moral men and women and above all of all Christians and Catholics. To educate men and women, to make them conscious (*conscientize* is the term used by liberation theologians) of their vocation and their worth as human beings, to do away with the very source of the evils of power and wealth and their abuse, to change social and political structures that preempt the poor and the many from exercising their human rights — they all become the job of the church and its flock. Every church, bishopry, and parish in this sense may become a center not only to propagate the faith and evangelize but also to promote the social order and to politicize.

Since Vatican II and the pronouncements that followed, many bishops have taken the lead in promoting a political and social consciousness everywhere and especially among the millions and millions of poor and oppressed in the Third World. For the first time perhaps in its history the church, without ever forgetting that its primary task is to save our souls,

---

14. *New York Times,* May 1984, p. 3.
15. Gustavo Gutierrez, *A Theology of Liberation.* Maryknoll, N.Y.: Orbis Books, 1973, p. xii.

Gutierrez's *A Theology of Liberation**** is considered by many scholars to be the definitive statement on the theology of liberation. Gutierrez's emphasis is on the theoretical rather than on the ideological movement associated with liberation theology itself. Gutierrez traces the origins of theological reflection since the early days of Christianity to a new and evolving orientation which stresses social *praxis,* a commitment to critical reflection, and a renewed commitment on the part of the church to the disenfranchised, the poor, and the destitute.

Gustavo Gutierrez was born in Lima, Peru, in 1928. He began his higher education at the National University in Lima, studying medicine. During the time that he attended the National University, Gutierrez was active in a number of political groups. After five years Gutierrez discontinued his medical studies and enrolled in a course in philosophical and theological studies and sought to enter the priesthood. These studies began in Chile but soon Gutierrez traveled to Europe, where between 1951 and 1955 he studied at the University of Louvain. He is a professor of theology at the Catholic University in Lima, Peru, and a national advisor for the National Union of Catholic students. (*Photo: National Catholic News Service*)

**Gustavo Gutierrez, *A Theology of Liberation: History, Politics and Salvation.* (Originally published as *Teología de la liberación,* Perspectives by CEP, Lima, 1971.) Maryknoll, N.Y.: Orbis Books, 1973, p. 308.

has taken into urgent consideration how to save our world. Whatever the reasons, the stage has been set for a new ideology that combines theology with reformist and even revolutionary politics. It is this combination that best describes liberation theology as an ideology and a movement to which we now turn.

The Philosophy of Liberation Theology

A new body of thought developed before and ever since Vatican II that raises fundamental questions on the historical role both of Christ and the church and even more searching questions about the role and position of the church in society. Let us try to outline the philosophic assumptions of the theory of liberation theology and then discuss it as a political movement.

The Theory

Traditionally the church viewed history as a temporary stage in our lives as compared to eternal life. The objective historical circumstances were not a

304

*Old Voices and
New:
Nationalism, The
Third World,
Feminism,
Liberation
Theology, and
Revolution*

matter of concern to the church when viewed with reference to the splendor of life hereafter. Orthodoxy, the maintenance of the true faith regardless of historical circumstances, was the church's central concern. In contrast, liberation theologians consider the church to be a vital agency of history, molding historical conditions and reflecting on these historical conditions. The gospel itself, and especially the role of Christ, is viewed as a historical basis for reform and change. The church ought to continue in this tradition, a tradition of action, to bring about change. Christ took the lead in attacking not only sin but social inequalities; he became the champion of the poor and spoke of a new social order. He was truly a liberator and reformer in addition to being God's son. Liberation theology therefore places its major emphasis on action—on the proper action—on the correct praxis or orthopraxis (*ortho* meaning correct and *praxis* meaning action) as opposed to orthodoxy (*ortho* meaning correct and *doxia* meaning belief). Indeed, the true faith can be found only in the proper action in line with Christ's life and teachings. It is argued that religious leaders and priests, especially Catholic, can find the true faith in the logic of social action. Until now, to paraphrase Marx, they had tried to understand God and explain His teachings; it is now time to *understand and change the world in line with His teachings.* Praxis—*action*—therefore becomes the essence of the faith.

Orthodoxy and Orthopraxis   Central to the theology of liberation is the notion of praxis. It is praxis which in fact gives liberation theology its unique quality. Orthodoxy represents the traditional doctrine of the European church, that is, the doctrine considered to be true, regardless of time and space. Orthodoxy characterized a church divorced from the concerns of secular society. Liberation theologians view this as largely ahistorical and couched in obsolete tradition. In the eyes of many Latin American church officials, it is a position that is largely irrelevant to the needs of present society—a society characterized by rapid social transformation. Orthopraxis, on the other hand, seeks a more accurate understanding of faith and Christian life through an appreciation of concrete realities and constructive commitment to service. The emphasis in orthopraxis is on service and action, and calls for the adaptation of Christian beliefs to the present conditions. In its focus on orthodoxy, the church had failed to live up to God's commitment to service, and had left service in the hands of nonmembers and nonbelievers. Orthopraxis seeks to make up for this deficiency.

Critical Reflection   Not only does the concept of orthopraxis signal the significance of service and action, but it also requires that theology become a form of critical reflection, not just in a doctrinal sense but with regard to economic, political, and social issues. If praxis is to be advocated, guidance must be provided as to when and how to act. Critical reflection, derived from secular theories and the reading of the "signs of the times," serve to guide praxis. Present realities are confronted, and through the proper reflection the seeds of future praxis are implanted. Praxis situates the

305

*Liberation
Theology:
The Voice of
the Church
and the Poor*

church within historical realities and demands of it specific commitments and service. This means that the theologian should become engaged where domination and oppression run rampant, and where the poor clamor for their own salvation here on earth. But what is the truth behind the needed action—behind the correct ("ortho") action?

Following the Second Vatican Council, the church, with a new definition of purpose and commitment to service, called for an effort to identify the signs of the times in order to discern truth and reach conclusions about the correct action to be taken. The need to discern the signs of the times through critical reflection leads the liberation theologians to adopt a new theoretical concept: the "hermeneutic" circle. (Hermeneutics is derived from the Greek word *hermeneia* which means "interpretation.")

The hermeneutic circle is a method that involves a continuous change in the interpretation of the Bible, thereby permitting analysis of God's word in terms of the continuous changes that take place in the world today. It allows the theologian to transcend the static interpretation of the Bible that was maintained over centuries by the European church. Basic questions are continually asked to reorient the theologian's understanding of social, political, and economic realities. It is a method for reevaluating the scriptures and sacramental practices, the church, and the concept of God itself in terms of the existing social realities and needs; i.e., by studying society.

In analyzing society, liberation theologians use new tools to evaluate the present social, political, and economic realities. The analytical tools that help in critical reflection are derived from the social sciences: sociology, economics, politics, anthropology, and the behavioral sciences.

The Marxist Temptation

The urgent task before Christians is to change society in order to improve the lot of the poor—indeed in order to eradicate poverty. But poverty arises because of faulty societal and economic structures—both national and international. Poverty can be alleviated by radical economic reforms in the direction of socialism. As Gutierrez put it, the preferential option for the poor is a socialist option.

The socialist option stems from an *analysis* of the society that—and here is the major source of controversy—borrows from Marxism. As we have seen, Marxism assumes the confrontation of two classes: those who own the means of production and those who do not—the workers for Marx, or the "poor" for the liberation theologians. In the same manner in which Marx assumed the workers would gain consciousness of their predicament and would rise to replace the property holders and socialize the means of production, the liberation theologians want to impart a reformist and even revolutionary consciousness to the poor to undertake the same task. The poor must improve their position by their own action and their own organization as the level of their awareness and consciousness improves. Self-reliance, community action, and spontaneous movements for

306

*Old Voices and
New:
Nationalism, The
Third World,
Feminism,
Liberation
Theology, and
Revolution*

reform and rectification of social evils are the means available to the poor, for the poor, and by the poor. In the process, local, community, regional, or national movements of the poor in their respective societies must keep their distance from international capitalism, which is blamed for the dependency of so many Third World countries and the concomitant subjugation of the poor to a local capitalist or bourgeois class. Liberation movements have to confront both their local oppressors and the international capitalist forces. When it comes to Latin America this means "Yankee Imperialism."

In the eyes of liberation theologians, the church assumes the task of leading a revolutionary movement by one class, the poor, against the local and international forces of capitalism that account for their plight. It becomes, in the name of an inevitable class struggle, an agency of revolution and reform to bring about socialism and social justice. According to Gutierrez, class struggle is an "objective reality" and "the liberation" of the poor is "not an act of generosity or charity or Christian brotherhood" — though it may include them. It is in his words "a demand for the construction of a new social order."[16] Class struggle pitting the poor against the capitalist class appears to be inevitable and perhaps desirable if the poor are to regain their position as human beings by their own efforts. In this sense, commitment on the part of the clergy for the poor and their liberation appears to be, even in the name of class struggle, the epitome of religious commitment.

In choosing to associate its theology with secular theories, which explicitly or implicitly adopted Marxist analysis and terminology, Latin American liberation theology became associated, at least in the eyes of western observers and some Vatican officials, with Marxism. In fact, the terms used (i.e., class struggle, alienation, dialectic, imperialism, proletariat, and so on) were directly borrowed from the Marxist vocabulary.

Collective Sin

Liberation theologians, particularly Leonardo Boff, suggest the notion of institutionalized violence and sin. It derives from and is embedded in the social structure; it relates directly to groups and classes; it says that the owners of the means of production or wealth (the landowners, for instance) who oppose and exploit the poor are — by virtue of belonging to the same group or class — all sinners, that collectively they represent a regime bent upon violence, which is sinful.

According to this notion, the redemption of the poor and the exploited lies in their collective struggle against the class that commits the sin. Violence must be met by counterviolence — by revolution. That is the only way to achieve liberation. This premise comes close to the Marxist theory of class struggle and the ultimate liberation of the proletariat by revolution. The Marxist categories are used even if couched in terms of theology. The

16. Gustavo Gutierrez, *The Power of the Poor in History*. Maryknoll, N.Y.: Orbis Books, 1983.

307

*Liberation
Theology:
The Voice of
the Church
and the Poor*

individual is viewed by his position in a given group rather than by his or her own volition, his or her own acts, and his or her own morality and reason. "When Christians take cognizance of the link between the personal and the structural levels," writes Boff, "they can no longer rest content with conversions of the heart and personal holiness at the individual level. They realize that if they are to be graced personally, they must also fight to change the societal structure and open it up to God's grace."[17] Injustice is embedded in a given structure that must be changed or destroyed, if necessary. God's grace should extend beyond the individual to the structures: to groups, to classes, to political regimes. The church therefore has an obligation to act here in our world to change the socioeconomic structures that account for injustice.

The Voice of the Poor and Political Action (Praxis)

In Latin America and in general in the Third World, the poor constitute the vast majority of the citizenry: peasants, a good percentage of Indians, the landless migrant farmhands, migrant workers, marginals, the urban poor. They remain separate from the centers of power and decision making, uneducated and unorganized. The church provided them with inadequate help and services, and its emphasis on evangelization was not consistent with everyday needs and expectations. The last rites were still administered, but on a social scale it was far more urgent to see to it that infants did not die at birth and that life expectancy increased. Love your neighbor — yes; but what if your neighbor is the policeman who put your son in jail? There was also another problem, closely associated with the role of the church to help the poor. There were not enough priests even for religious services, let alone societal education and reorganization. For the whole of Latin America there are fewer Catholic priests than in France, although the Catholic population of Latin America is about eight to nine times larger. Where to find the priests? And what kind of priests?

It soon became necessary to dispense with the formal education of priests and to establish seminars and workshops in which priests could be quickly trained (and some ordained). A Theological Education by Extension (TEE) program was developed, comprising study centers, lay training centers for missions, clinical pastoral education centers, community-based educational centers, pastoral education cells, groups for study and mutual care, centers of reflection on liberation movements, and a number of ad hoc centers to discuss immediate community problems. Here is how an author describes the development of new training centers and their educational role:

> . . . TEE began at a small, denominational institution in Central
> America in 1963. . . . By 1977 there were 133 known programmes
> with 19,384 students in Latin America and the Caribbean. . . .

---

17. Boff, *Church: Charisma and Power,* p. 85.

308

*Old Voices and
New:
Nationalism, The
Third World,
Feminism,
Liberation
Theology, and
Revolution*

In 1968 an association of extension programmes . . . was formed in Brazil, and in 1973 a similar association . . . developed for the Spanish-speaking countries, in addition to the associations established previously by the residential schools. In May 1980 representatives met to form a common association for theological education in the northern region of Latin America (ALIET). The major residential institutions in Latin America now have their own extension programmes, and they are playing an important role in the preparation of leaders and materials for the extension movement. The Latin American Biblical Seminary, for example, has initiated a continent-wide extension network of university-level studies comparable to its residential programmes. . . .

. . . The Theological Community of Chile runs an enormous extension programme with up to 4,000 students, mostly Pentecostal. . . . In Buenos Aires, the dean of the Protestant theological institutions in Latin America is now developing extension courses, and the Association of Seminaries and Theological Institutes, which serves Argentina, Bolivia, Chile, Paraguay, and Uruguay, is running a series of intensive workshops for writers of extension textbooks. The International Baptist Theological Seminary of Buenos Aires initiated an extension programme for Argentina in 1968; it now has 13 centres with 600 students.

In Brazil . . . when The Association for Extension Programmes celebrated its tenth anniversary in 1978, there were extension programmes with about 5,000 students. . . .

The author notes similar trends in Africa, Asia, and elsewhere among many churches.[18]

What will be the role of the newly trained "priests" or "missionaries" who take the gospel far and wide into the remotest areas of ignorance and poverty? Let the same author answer our question:

. . . One of the essential goals of theological education by extension must be to let the church be the church, or more specifically, to let the people of God become the primary agents of ministry. This is actually happening today in many parts of the world, but nowhere more dramatically than in Brazil. . . . No longer is pastoral action the exclusive prerogative of professional, highly qualified priests, carried out in isolation from social realities. It is now regarded as the work of the entire Christian community, inspired by pastoral agents, who can be bishops, pastors, catechists, workers, peasants, men or women. . . .

18. F. Ross Kinsler. *Ministry by the People — Theological Education by Extension.* Maryknoll, N.Y.: Orbis Books, 1983, pp. 7–8.

309

*Liberation
Theology:
The Voice of
the Church
and the Poor*

... Another central goal of theological education by extension must be to enable the church to understand and carry out holistic ministry. The biblical concept of salvation clearly includes physical, emotional, and social as well as spiritual health or wholeness. Christian congregations are called to be caring, healing communities. New approaches to primary health care, which are of great importance to people in all parts of the world, require a base of support such as these congregations can provide and local health promoters who understand and are accepted by their people. . . .

... A third major goal of theological education by extension during this decade must be to equip the church for the ministry of liberation, justice and development in each local and national context.[19]

Evangelization (the teaching and the bearing witness of the gospel), is superseded by the notion of social service. What would a priest — a lay or ordained "priest," a "missioner," a "delegate" be expected to teach the peasantry or the poor? The word of God, to be sure. But in various discussion groups and meetings and seminars social questions — about the lack of water, the lack of schools and health clinics, the heavy taxes, the exactions of those in a position of political or military power, the lack of food and housing — questions of everyday life and the need to satisfy urgent wants will have to be raised. Religious and moral questions will have to be related to the everyday needs and predicaments. How can we all be brothers, according to the Bible and Christ's teaching, when we live under such unequal conditions? Where is mercy and kindness when only few have access to a clinic but the many do not? Where is the "humanity" of the many, without access to a school or even to a church? A theological seminary that discussed these questions inevitably becomes transformed into a social sciences or social services seminar!

A point invariably comes when the answers cannot be detached from the social and even political action that is needed. What kind of action will the clergy or the surrogate priests suggest? And in suggesting action, will they too become involved in action? On behalf of whom?

The dialogue between the church and the vast masses of the poor produced its one consequence. The call for social reform and political participation of the Second Vatican Council could only strengthen the missionary zeal of many clergymen — and also the urgency shared by lay Catholics (as well as other Christians) to reach out to the masses and help improve their lives. What developed was literally an explosion of new community ecclesiastic organizations not only to educate and evangelize but also to organize and make the poor conscious not only of their predicament but also of their potential power. To put it simply, new parallel

19. Kinsler, op. cit., pp. 26–28.

310

*Old Voices and
New:
Nationalism, The
Third World,
Feminism,
Liberation
Theology, and
Revolution*

"churches" were established under the name of "base Christian communities"—*communidades ecclesiales de base*. This is how an author (and activist) describes them.

> ... We are in Santiago [Chile], in a *población*—a poor section of
> the city made up of wooden huts that look for all the world like
> the sheds you generally find in a backyard. There is a little chapel.
> One priest, a non-Chilean, has the care of three parishes whose
> total population is about fifty thousand. He is helped by two Ca-
> nadian lay missionaries. This means that the bulk of the pastoral
> work must be carried out by the lay persons of the *población*: shop
> workers, manual workers, and not a few who are out of work.

> ... We go to a meeting of the "ministers of the word." There
> are six men there, chosen from among the elders of the commu-
> nity. They were appointed by the episcopal vicar for the area;
> the local priest laid hands on them at the feast of Pentecost.
> There are ministers for the other sacraments as well. Three
> couples are responsible for preparing ... and administering
> baptism. For first communion, both parents and children must
> attend a meeting once a week for two years under the direction
> of "guides" who have themselves received the same training.
> "It is really a matter of catechism for adults. We try to 'convert'
> them and urge them to join the community."
> Marriages—and there are four a month—are also prepared
> and celebrated by lay ministers: "qualified witnesses" of the
> sacrament. A team of three couples gathers the prospective
> marriage partners together and, over the course of six evenings,
> speaks with them about sexual relations, the Christian meaning
> of marriage, a budget, relations between parents and children,
> and the like. The priest is called in only when there are canon-
> ical problems.
> Lay persons are also responsible for youth activities, the
> aged, visiting the sick, conducting funerals, preparing candi-
> dates for confirmation, and similar functions.

> ... We are in Nicaragua, a few months after the victory of the
> Sandinista revolution, among *campesinos* ("peasants") who for
> the most part own minuscule plots of land on which, with a
> machete, they cultivate corn and kidney beans.
> We begin by singing. ... Then Gerardo Guevara, minister of
> the word, reads the passage in St. Luke on the "useless ser-
> vants" (Luke 17:10). ... They speak of the humility of Christ,
> and they also speak of the revolution.
> "Warfare is not the only kind of revolution. You know what
> war is, with the dead and wounded and destruction every-

311

*Liberation
Theology:
The Voice of
the Church
and the Poor*

where! The revolution that Christ wants is a revolution of peace and love, a revolution of humility and patience. . . ."

. . . On this night twenty-three of these ministers of the word are preparing themselves to participate in a week-long seminar on the theme "Christian faith and the revolution in Nicaragua."

. . . I asked one of them to define for me his role. "It is to assemble the community, proclaim the word of God, and conscientize the Christians."

. . . In his homily Fr. Benito spoke about agrarian reform and the national literacy campaign. He said, "The church must take its part in the revolution. We must combat illiteracy with the resources of our faith." The presence or absence of dedicated and well-trained Christians will determine what Nicaragua looks like tomorrow.[20]

To become self-reliant, the poor must become conscious of their position and power; to become conscious they must be educated; to become educated in their social aspirations they must become involved in action. The clergy and the various surrogates of the church in forming ecclesial communities provide the missing link between consciousness and action as the one reinforces and strengthens the other. There are over 4 million Brazilians who participate in the more than 50,000 Christian "base ecclesiastical communities." The church followers who comprise these base communities represent such societal segments as "labor unions," "Indian groups," "slum organizations," "militant feminist groups," and "peasant movements." They discuss the Bible and apply its religious teachings to everyday political life. In this sense the meaning of praxis appears clearer. It is action within historical circumstances informed by history *and* the gospel in order to transform them.

The base ecclesiastical communities today consist of a large network of communities comprising millions, headed by ordained or newly trained priests or lay surrogates, providing and giving awareness to many not only of the Word but of the need of social and political action. They are the new ministers of God whose function, however, is to make the many and the poor conscious of their predicament and their power. Their function is no longer to proselytize and evangelize but to "conscientize": to make conscious, educate, and create a new dimension of personal and social awareness.

In this manner in the last twenty years the conservative concept of evangelization (limited to preaching the gospel and converting agnostics or pagans) has given way to mass social and political education and social activism.

．

20. From Michel Bavarel, *New Communities, New Ministers: The Church Resurgent in Africa, Asia and Latin America.* Maryknoll, N.Y.: Orbis Books, 1983, pp. 50–55.

312

*Old Voices and
New:
Nationalism, The
Third World,
Feminism,
Liberation
Theology, and
Revolution*

Henri Motte painted "Christ at a Banquet" in 1908. "He who has two coats let him share with him who has none; and he who has food, let him do likewise." (Luke 3:7) *(Photo: Roger-Viollet)*

An Evaluation

Launched by papal encyclicals, solicited by the urgent needs of the poor in different communities, buttressed by a sophisticated body of analysis, part of which is borrowed from Marx, orchestrated by thousands of new specially trained "priests" operating in base ecclesiastical communities, sharing the lives of the poor and the peasantry with a strong anticapitalist posture, seeking alliances with various national liberation and protest movements including guerrillas, liberation theology has gained momentum in Latin America, and elsewhere too as a political movement. In Latin America it is supported by many bishops, especially in Brazil; in Nicaragua and El Salvador priests have assumed leadership positions in revolutionary governments (four priests, for instance, have defied the instructions of their superiors and remain members of the Nicaraguan Sandinista cabinet); in Peru virtually the majority of the bishops seem to favor it. Millions of "poor"—the countryside, the urban proletariat, Indians, the marginals—support it as they are gradually gaining consciousness of their numbers. A new ideology that combines the Word and the Deed is mobilizing the masses in the name of the Bible, socialism, and popular participation. In evaluating its actual and potential strength we must try to answer a number of questions:

1. Is the preferential option demanded for the poor compatible with the gospel? There is hardly any doubt that the answer is affirmative—provided it is understood that the church, as a church, cannot prefer *only* the poor to the exclusion of others. In other words, the proponents of

313

*Liberation
Theology:
The Voice of
the Church
and the Poor*

liberation theology should not opt for one particular category of people on the basis of their predicament and exclude others. Both Christian love and the prospect of salvation should remain open to all. In setting up the poor as a "class," liberation theology is at odds with traditional theology. But in claiming that special and even preferential attention should be given to them it is in line with accepted doctrine.

2. Relatedly, the notion of class struggle between "the poor" and their oppressors may assume a political and confrontational posture not in line with religious doctrine. A class struggle even in the name of justice may lead to violence and civil war—a posture not compatible with Christianity. It may in effect justify violence. The pope and many bishops have rejected the notion of "class struggle" while some liberation theologians consider it an "objective reality" and therefore inevitable.

3. Notwithstanding the many concerns of the Vatican and the hierarchy, the adoption of Marxist analysis can be seriously entertained as long as liberation theologians do not accept the consequences of the Marxist theory. What causes uneasiness in the Vatican is the association of *theology* of liberation with the *politics* of liberation and revolution. In many popular and guerrilla movements led by professed Marxists the theologians of liberation become unwittingly their "objective allies" and the "base Christian communities" provide support and active help. In the process, the fear of the Vatican that what happened to the worker-priests may happen to many of the Catholic priests (ordained or their surrogates) is a genuine one. Both the sacraments and evangelization may be set aside in favor of political action and conflict in the name of class struggle and justice. The priests may become activists; some already are. It will not be a case where the guerillas become the "Jesuits of the revolution" in the words of Che Guevara; it will be the priests themselves, Jesuits or not, who become the leaders of and for the revolution. This is precisely what Pope John Paul II had in mind when he said on one of his most recent trips to Latin America that some "disfigure the Gospel message, using it at the service of political ideologies and strategies in search of an illusory earthly liberation."[21]

4. Over and above the possible deviation of the priests from their religious role, there is the tactical problem of the relationship between them and the secular revolutionary movements and leaders. Who will be the stronger of the two and dominate the other? Liberation theologians, and priests put their faith in the spontaneous activity of the poor, but they promote their organizations in base communities and by so doing become activists. The secular revolutionaries, on the other hand, very much in line with Leninism, believe primarily in organization, leadership, and discipline. They consider the Communist party an avant garde to organize the masses. For the liberation theologians the task ahead is that of political education within the context of freedom and free dialogue. For the Marxist, it is the workers and the party and not the poor who will gain the upper hand and establish a dictatorship.

---

21. Quoted in the *Boston Globe*, Feb. 27, 1985.

314

*Old Voices and
New:
Nationalism, The
Third World,
Feminism,
Liberation
Theology, and
Revolution*

5. Equally important in the eyes of the church hierarchy (especially the Catholic church) is the relationship of the clergy to their national bishops; for the Vatican it is the relationship between the national bishops and cardinals with the Holy See and the pope. Two possible conflicts can be envisaged. One is reminiscent of the Reformation — when the national bishops defied Rome in the name of national imperatives. Without going so far as yet, some Peruvian and Brazilian bishops consider liberation theology to be a national ecclesiastical movement and have defended it even against the pope. The other conflict pits the various local and community churches and their priests against their own bishops. The thesis presented by Friar Boff of Brazil (see inset on page 299) portrays the power structure of the church in class terms and attributes to the higher echelons a bourgeois mentality and orientation as opposed to the democratic grass roots organizations. A struggle within the church is therefore possible; it will split the hierarchy from the priests and decentralize the church.

6. An outstanding question for the future success of liberation theology movement is the accuracy with which it analyzes society — how it reads the "signs of the times"? Among the many Catholics who have studied liberation theology, Michael Novak is particularly concerned about this. In his book, *The Spirit of Democratic Capitalism,* and some recent articles, Dr. Novak argues that the liberation theology "offers, in practice, not so much a cure as a predict-able decline, both in economic development and in personal and social liberty." "Nothing is said [in liberation theology]," he points out, "about creating new wealth, about invention, about entrepreneurship." The "simplistic" remedy sought by liberation theology is to "expropriate the expropriators," because "they" were the ones who are considered responsible for poverty.

Little attention has been paid to the economic policies that the liberation theologians plan to implement "after their revolution." Will there be a continuation of the trend of Latin American societies in the direction of authoritarianism — this time to the left, as opposed to the historical, domination by the conservatives? How will liberation theology safeguard human rights?[22]

The Position of the Vatican

The potential political power of the "base Christian communities" and the extremist overtones of liberation theology in its advocacy of class struggle and revolutionary action against the established order, have become a matter of deep concern to the high clergy: the bishops, the pope, and the Vatican. Liberation theology came came under investigaion by the Sacred Congregation for the Doctrine of the Faith, an office operating directly

---

22. Michael Novak's position is succinctly stated in "The Case Against Liberation Theology," *New York Times Sunday Magazine,* Oct. 21, 1984.

under the pope, responsible for doctrinal clarity and agreement. In the summer of 1984 the Sacred Congregation under Cardinal Ratzinger undertook a thorough review of liberal theology doctrine, as it applied to Latin America, and questioned some of its founders, notably Friar Boff of Brazil. On September 4, 1984, it issued an authoritative statement that was critical of liberation theology but did not explicitly condemn the doctrine or its advocates. But the office of the Vatican took exception to (1) the perversion of the role of the church and the priests; (2) the direct link between liberation theology and Marxism; (3) the dangers of substituting for the word of the gospel secular ideologies that may in the name of liberation bring about an enslavement of the poor that may even be worse than the one experienced now. It is worth noting that at no time did the church reject its special and even preferential care for the poor.

The Sacred Congregation reiterated the classic notion of evangelization: "The church, guided by the Gospel of mercy . . . hears the cry for justice and intends to respond to it . . . with boldness and courage, with farsightedness and prudence, with zeal and strength of spirit, with love for the poor which demands sacrifice. . . . Pastors will consider the response to this call a matter of the highest priority." It agreed that the theology of liberation puts a special emphasis on the poor, the "victims of oppression," and considers it natural that the poor should feel a "supreme reliance" on God's loving Providence. But at the same time, the statement reiterated the doctrine according to which the suffering of the poor is akin to the suffering of Christ and "poverty for the sake of the kingdom" is praised. Cardinal Ratzinger singled out the "evil transformation" of the real gospel for an "earthly Gospel"; the urge for the quick attainment of the earthly goals and the remaking of history. Theology was not to be reduced to the Marxist analysis of the "class struggle" as the way to solve problems of human injustice because, among many doctrinal reasons, the consequences of revolutionary Marxist politics would lead to the subordination of individual rights and freedoms to a secular state.

The manner in which liberation theology treats Christ and the scriptures also came under severe criticism. It is in the scriptures that liberation theologians find the justification for revolutionary praxis. The role of Christ is seen as that of "temporal messianism": to liberate people here on earth rather than to eradicate sin and ultimately lead to salvation. Warning against false secular ideologies, the statement asserts that pastoral praxis, not revolutionary praxis, within and under the church is the road to true liberation. In fact, the poor are warned that:

> The class struggle as a road toward a classless society is a myth which slows reform and aggravates poverty and injustice . . . the overthrow by means of revolutionary violence of structures which generate violence is not *ipso facto* the beginning of a just regime.[23]

23. "Instruction on Certain Aspects of the Theology of Liberation." Issued by the Sacred Congregation for the Doctrine of the Faith, The Vatican, Sept. 4, 1984.

In March 1985 the Congregation for the Doctrine of the Faith publicized a critique of Friar Leonardo Boff's book, *Church: Charisma and Power: A Study of Militant Ecclesiology*. It did not condemn the book but took particular exception to the freedom of every priest and every member to criticize the doctrine. Criticism cannot come from everywhere and anywhere. It must come from authoritative spokesmen of the church, i.e., the hierarchy. The Vatican seemed particularly concerned with the spread of base ecclesiastical communities detached from the hierarchy, free to develop their missions as they chose fit. It is a trend that may lead to the disintegration of the organization of the church. Boff's positions "endanger the sound doctrine of the faith which the congregation must promote and protect." Friar Boff responded that he would continue his work. But significantly enough he added: "I prefer to walk with the Church rather than stand alone with my theology."

Boff was requested by the Vatican to remain silent for a year, but the imposition of silence was lifted in April 1986. This action was coupled, however, with a new statement from the Vatican on liberation theology, "Instruction on Christian Freedom and Liberation."[24] The church appeared increasingly concerned, for reasons already mentioned, with the linkage of revolutionary social activism with Catholicism among the lower clergy and the laity. It expressed its disquiet—indeed its grave concern—with the development of base ecclesiastical communities devoted to social activism rather than the propagation of faith and religious values.

In sum, the church is faced with a difficult compromise between its compassion for the poor, even the preferential option for the poor, and its aversion to Marxism. Both are emphasized. At times the pope continues to assert the liberation of the poor in the most unequivocal terms and does not hesitate to condemn monopolies and capitalist international oligarchies; at other times, however, he emphasizes Christian truth based on love and solidarity beyond and above all "passing ideologies."

In the instruction on Christian Freedom and Liberation there are important qualifications to the spirit of Vatican II, Pueblo, and Medellin. Warnings against Marxism are more explicit; the rejection by the church of all forms of collectivism is more pronounced; the disavowal of conservative and military forces is less overt; the primary duties of Christians to live their faith and abide by the spiritual values are given priority over social and political action.

Conclusion

To the ever-shifting winds of change so much in evidence throughout the Third World, in the name of nationalism, independence, economic equality, Marxism and socialism, a new ideology, liberation theology, has been added. Many of the Latin American bishops are uncertain about its scope and its Christian credentials; others espouse it. The Vatican itself seems

24. The Sacred Congregation for the Doctrine of the Faith, The Vatican, 1986.

317

*Liberation
Theology:
The Voice of
the Church
and the Poor*

deeply concerned about the adoption of Marxist analysis by some of the leading liberation theologians and the political activism of many priests. In the meantime the grassroots ecclesiastical communities are gaining momentum, and the priests or their delegates have become the prime movers in arousing the poor and giving them the social education (the consciousness) without which they are destined to continue living in a state of servitude and misery that has been their most steadfast companion for centuries. Two of the most powerful ideologies—the Christian aspiration for social justice through love, equality, and brotherhood and the Marxist promise of equality and abundance through revolution and violence—may join forces and bring about a vast upheaval in the whole of Latin America.

But it is very doubtful that Christianity and Marxism can result in a lasting synthesis in which secular revolutionary political movements (often led by self-professed communists) will be tempered by the freedoms that Christian liberation theologians espouse or in which the grass roots movements of the base Christian communities will become a powerful democratic force to neutralize the political organization, discipline and ultimately the imposition of a dictatorship of communist revolutionaries. Whatever cooperation there is today between Marxist forces and liberation theology movements derives from a convergence of immediate goals—it is tactical. It is only in the course of praxis that the critical examination of the forces at work will inform the theologians (through critical reflection) about their communist revolutionary allies and will in turn enlighten the secular revolutionary leaders in Nicaragua, El Salvador, Peru, Guatemala, Brazil, and elsewhere about the positions of the Christian activists. Very much in the mind of the Vatican is the impact liberation theology is having upon both the national churches of Latin America and on many of its priests. Will the national churches in Latin America remain united? Will they remain sisters under the Holy Father or will they, as some European Catholic churches did, proclaim their reformation and independence? How far can the church go in the direction of social activism without distorting its spiritual role? The temporal world with all its problems beckons the priests as they search for solutions to alleviate misery, hunger, and oppression. But so does the word of the Spirit enshrined in the doctrine of the church.

Bibliography

Abbot, Walter M. *The Documents of Vatican II.* New York: Herder & Herder, 1966.

Arias, Ester and Mortimer. *The Cry of My People: Out of Captivity in Latin America.* New York: Friendship Press, 1980.

Berryman, Philip. *Liberation Theology.* New York: Pantheon, 1987.

Boff, Leonardo. *Liberating Grace.* Maryknoll, N.Y.: Orbis Books, 1981. An authoritative compendium advocating the rights of all Latin American people to achieve the freedoms inherent to them as human beings: life, liberty, and grace.

——. "Theological Characteristics of a Grassroots Church," in Sergio Torres and John Eagleson (eds.), *Theology in the Americas.* Maryknoll, N.Y.: Orbis Books, 1976, pp. 124-144.

——. *Jesus Christ, Liberator.* Maryknoll, N.Y.: Orbis Books, 1978.

——. "Christ's Liberation via Oppression: An Attempt at Theological Construction from the Standpoint of Latin America," In Rosino Gibellini (ed.), *Frontiers in Theology in Latin America.* Maryknoll, N.Y.: Orbis Books, 1979a, pp. 100–132.

—— and Clodovis Boff. *Salvation and Liberation.* Maryknoll, N.Y.: Orbis Books, 1984.

——. *Church: Charisma and Power.* New York: Crossroads, 1985.

——. *Ecclesiogenesis.* Maryknoll, N.Y.: Orbis Books, 1986.

Cardoso, F. H., and Faletto, E. *Dependency and Development in Latin America.* Berkeley: University of California Press, 1975.

Dussel, Enrique. *History and the Theology of Liberation: A Latin American Perspective.* Translated by John Drury. Maryknoll, N.Y.: Orbis Books, 1976.

Gibellini, Rosino (ed.). *Frontiers of Theology in Latin America.* Translated by John Drury. Maryknoll, N.Y.: Orbis Books, 1975.

Goulet, Denis. *A New Moral Order: Studies in Development Ethics and Liberation Theology.* Maryknoll, N.Y.: Orbis Books, 1979.

Gutierrez, Gustavo. *The Power of the Poor in History.* Maryknoll, N.Y.: Orbis Books, 1983.

Hanson, Eric. *The Catholic Church in World Politics.* Princeton, N.J.: Princeton U.P., 1987.

Hennelly, Alfred T. *Theologies in Conflict: The Challenge of Juan Luis Segundo.* Maryknoll, N.Y.: Orbis Books, 1979.

Kung, Hans, Congar, Yves, and O'Hanlon, Daniel. *Council Speeches of Vatican II.* New York: Paulist Press, 1964.

Medellin Conference Final Documents. *The Church in the Present-day Transformation of Latin America in the Light of the Council.* (Vol. II). Bogota, Colombia: CELAM, 1968.

Novak, Michael. *Freedom with Justice: Catholic Social Thought and Liberal Institutions.* New York: Harper & Row, 1984.

——. (ed.). *Liberation North, Liberation South.* Washington, D.C.: American Enterprise Institute for Public Policy Research, 1981.

——. *The Spirit of Democratic Capitalism.* New York: Simon and Schuster, 1982.

——. "The Case Against Liberation Theology." *The New York Times Magazine,* October 21, 1984, p. 50.

——. *A Theology for Radical Politics.* New York: Herter & Herter, 1969.

O'Brien, David J. *The Renewal of American Catholicism.* New York: Oxford U.P., 1972.

——, and Shannon, Thomas (eds.). *Renewing The Earth: Catholic Documents on Peace, Justice and Liberation.* Garden City, N.Y.: Image Books, 1977.

Pawley, Bernard C. (ed.). *The Second Vatican Council: Studies by Eight Anglican Observers.* London: Oxford U.P., 1967.

Peruvian Bishops' *Commission for Social Action, Between Honesty and Hope: Documents from and about the Church.* Maryknoll, New York: Maryknoll Publications, 1970.

Quade, Quentin (ed.). *The Pope and Revolution.* Washington, D.C.: Ethics and Public Policy Center, 1982.

Ratzinger, Joseph Cardinal, Prefect. Ordinary Meeting of the Sacred Doctrine of the Faith, Vatican Statement (Rome, Italy, September 3, 1984). The official declaration criticizing liberation theology.

319

*Liberation
Theology:
The Voice of
the Church
and the Poor*

Rynne, Xavier. *Vatican Council II*. New York: Farrar, Straus and Giroux, 1964.

Sacred Congregation for the Doctrine of the Faith. "Instruction on Certain Aspects of the 'Theology of Liberation.'" Boston: Daughters of St. Paul, 1984 and 1986.

——. "Instruction on Christian Freedom and Liberation." Boston: Daughters of St. Paul, 1986.

Segundo, Juan Luis. *The Hidden Motives of Pastoral Action: Latin American Reflections*. Maryknoll, N.Y.: Orbis Books, 1972.

Smith, Donald E. *Religion, Politics and Social Change in the Third World*. New York: Free Press, 1971.

14 | *Ideologies of Revolution*

If men cannot refer to a common value, recognized by all as existing in each one, then man is incomprehensible to man. The rebel demands that this value should be clearly recognized in himself because he knows or suspects, that without this principle, crime and disorder would reign throughout the world.

ALBERT CAMUS   The Rebel

I am nothing and I should be everything.

KARL MARX   Critique of Hegel's Philosophy

Most people have romantic notions about revolutions — the mob storming the Bastille, the tea thrown into the Boston Harbor, the Bolsheviks storming the Winter Palace, Gandhi and his followers lying on the railroad tracks in a movement of civil disobedience that paralyzed the British rule in India. Heroic statements come to our minds: "Give me liberty, or give me death"; "the despotism of liberty against tyranny"; "workers of the world arise: you have nothing to lose but your chains."

The conventional wisdom suggests that the poor and the downtrodden will rebel, that poverty will beget revolutionary movements. But it is hardly so. As Leon Trotsky, a foremost practitioner of the art of revolution observed, if poverty was the cause of revolutions, we would all be sitting on an exploding powder keg! Similarly, George Orwell, in his book *1984*, raises the possibility of revolution against the established powerholders, Big Brother, the Inner Brotherhood, and the Party, who have a tight grip over the "proles" — the poor, wretched, and disregarded masses that account for the vast majority of the population in his imaginary state. They could destroy those who have enslaved them. If they could become conscious of their own strength they would rise up "and shake them like a horse shaking off flies." But Orwell quickly stifles all hope . . . "Until [the proles] become conscious, they will never rebel, and until after they have

320

rebelled, they cannot become conscious." The poor, the underprivileged, the slaves, and the wretched of the earth seem to be in a box!

The Nature of Revolution

There is much more than rhetoric and romantic imagery to a revolution and it takes much more than poverty or moral indignation to make it. A revolution is an act of organized violence to bring about radical changes in the economic, social, and political relations within a given system. It uses force to destroy (sometimes physically) and replace those who hold power.

Protests, civil disobedience, turmoil, demonstrations, and acts of violence are not revolutions, as such, though they may precede them. All depends on the degree of mobilization and organization and on the ideas people share when they commit acts of violence.

Gandhi's disobedience in India was aimed at driving out the British and replacing colonial rule with an Indian government—it was a revolutionary movement. Martin Luther King, on the other hand, simply wanted to force concessions that would allow the blacks to participate (as they were entitled to do) in the American system. In the past, periodic peasants' rebellions in Germany, France, Italy, and eastern Europe aimed to reclaim the land from the nobility. These rebellions did not have broad political goals such as changing the political regime.

Major revolutions have been asssociated with: (1) a national or a colonial independence movement against a foreign occupying power—a phenomenon common in Europe in the nineteenth century and throughout most of the colonial world in the twentieth century; (2) separatist movements mobilizing ethnic or religious groups to secede from the state in which they live; (3) a movement organized by some social groups or classes against those that hold power within a given regime. The French Revolution, the Bolshevik Revolution in 1917, and the Chinese Communist Revolution in 1949 are the archetypal cases. But the national independence movements in the nineteenth century, and the guerrilla warfare in Vietnam, Algeria, and elsewhere only a decade or so ago, and in some of the Latin American countries today, are also revolutions.

The Role of Ideology

People do not revolt unless they first get the idea that the use of organized force is a remedy for their situation. Some philosophers have suggested that conflict and revolutions lie in the interstices of the historical process—and we have noted that both Hegel and Marx assumed that a dialectic process (involving conflict between opposing forces) was historically inevitable. According to this notion, history itself is what counts—the actors, individuals, and groups act in accord with "its laws." Conflict and revolutions are, in a sense, predetermined; and so are the ideologies related to them.

322

*Old Voices and
New:
Nationalism, The
Third World,
Feminism,
Liberation
Theology, and
Revolution*

Marx developed the most complete ideology *of* a revolution and *for* a revolution. It is the material conditions that by and large shape ideology. The ruling class—the bourgeoisie—tries to impose its ideology upon all others. But the workers, though not immune to it, ultimately reject it in order to develop a revolutionary ideology—a "counterideology." We saw that Lenin claimed that only a small elite could act for the workers in leading them against their masters.

If circumstances (the material conditions) shape ideologies, what role do ideologies play in shaping circumstances? It is an endless argument. Determinists tend to look primarily at the circumstances and claim that ideologies cannot arise or function independently. Marxists, as we have seen, perform a balancing act between the two—there is interplay between *both* the circumstances *and* the ideology. Other revolutionaries tend to emphasize *will* and *ideas*—so much as to attribute to them an independent role. For these revolutionaries ideology is primary. It is what Marx called the "theory that becomes a material force when it grips the masses."

As for the substance of a revolutionary ideology, a number of elements shape it. A distinction is often made by some between an "inherent" and a "derived" ideology. The first is another name for the culture of a people—the sum total of their experiences and customs, their oral traditions, their habits, and their common memories of past rights, privileges, and claims. The inherent ideology usually provides the context for the development of a revolutionary consciousness, but this is not enough. What is needed is a theory—a derived ideology—that will spell out, in a structured and organized manner, the reasons why force is necessary and will outline the goals that force will realize.

Derived ideologies come from political theorists such as Marx, Rousseau, and Tom Paine. The transmission belt between "derived" and "inherent" consists of the intellectuals. They blend theory, popular culture, and traditions in order to shape a revolutionary ideology and a revolutionary movement. Theory will provide the vocabulary of the revolution, leaving it to the organizers to do the spelling.

The Italian communist theoretician, Antonio Gramsci, emphasized, as we noted, the creative role of ideology. There are many areas of indeterminacy in the society; there are many groups that do not belong either to the bourgeoisie or to the proletariat. They float in limbo. Ideology, he claimed, if it blended theory and popular culture and was developed and propagated by the intellectuals and organizers—the "organic intellectuals" as he called them—would sufficiently mobilize and organize these groups. The intellectuals distill the new ideology drop by drop to conquer the masses slowly and to build ideological pockets and bastions that become immune to the prevailing ideology. It is not an exaggeration to say that the revolution was, for Gramsci, primarily a vast educational and organizational effort that did not necessarily need to rely on the use of force (though never excluding it) against the ruling class. Force would come in handy, but only to enhance the ideological awareness and preparedness of the masses. Revolution was a matter of the mind—the transformation of the ideology held by the people.

When does the "theory ... grip the masses" become a revolutionary movement? Crane Brinton, after a survey of the major revolutions (the Puritan Revolution, the French Revolution, the Bolshevik Revolution, and the American Revolution), found some common structural characteristics.[1] They are the following:

1. The political societies in which revolutions occurred were "on the whole on the upgrade economically before the revolution." In most cases they were revolutions of hope and not despair; the actors were not downtrodden, starving, poor, or slaves. The ideology they shared was one of optimism. There was an expectation of better opportunities. . . .

2. In all cases, although perhaps less so with the American Revolution, there were strong class antagonisms. But revolutions cannot be explained in terms of one class fighting against another. In fact, revolutions occur when social classes come closer together, so that the privileges and power of some appears intolerable. As de Tocqueville had noted, people resent inequalities only when they become a little more equal! Untouchables and slaves rarely revolt. The idea of revolution comes in the minds of men and women who become relatively better-off, whose wants and expectations are on the rise.

3. Another phenomenon associated with revolution is the "desertion of the intellectuals"—of those who write and preach, of the "clerks" and the teachers. They shift their allegiance from the regime in search of alternatives. By doing so, they sap its strength. Revolution, then, "begins" in the minds of the intellectuals, those we called "ideologues" in our first chapter. They think and germinate the thoughts of revolution long before these thoughts trickle down to the hovel of the peasant or the artisan's basement or the slums or the workshops.

4. Before a revolution there is a breakdown in the efficiency and performance of the government. This is due to the fact that economic changes occur, such as industrialization with new technological innovations. The government is unable to take these economic changes into account, to respond to new needs and demands, and to adjust to them. The government officials lose faith in their ability to control events and to govern. Relatedly, the finances and the administration of the government suffer. The "organized discontented groups" press their demands at this juncture and the governmental apparatus is unable to react. In almost all cases, the government and the regime are in a state of virtual collapse *before* the revolution succeeds. A crucial factor in a revolution is the weakness shown at the top of the existing structure and not only the strength mustered at the bottom.

Is it possible, then, to say that a revolution as a process seems to start at the top? That there are structural societal factors that can best explain it? All one can say is that they play a very important role. Marx was clearly

---

1. Crane Brinton, *The Anatomy of Revolution.*

324

*Old Voices and
New:
Nationalism, The
Third World,
Feminism,
Liberation
Theology, and
Revolution*

aware of it because the timing of the workers' revolution was related to major structural changes in the capitalistic economy and the political regime that reflected it. This was not so for Lenin and many of his followers who emphasized will and leadership.

The Individual: Subjective Factors

Even if revolution is a mass organized movement, it is the individual who must be mobilized. Nobody will leave home and family, job, or farm unless prompted by powerful reasons to do so. Only a handful of individuals are "born radicals"; personality propels them to radical action to change things. Most people, however, venture into the unknown world of revolution and violence only because they feel, or are made to feel, that their lives are at stake.

The feeling of threat, particularly the threat of deprivation, is the most common psychological motivation for a revolution. The most common threat is to one's livelihood, one's expectations, and one's position in society — his or her status. Rising material opportunities provide for the hope of more, and when for one reason or another opportunities do not materialize, people become apprehensive. Even more, *they feel deprived* in two ways: (1) their expectations of what they believe they are worth — of what they should be getting — do not materialize; (2) their standard of living falls behind others. This is often referred to as "relative deprivation." The threat to status is generally shared more or less among well-established groups that find their position, income, and importance in the society threatened by other groups. Revolutions motivated by a threat to status have been common among middle-class and lower-middle class groups and are considered, as we have seen, the major reasons for fascism and nazism. Direct deprivation of one's livelihood and expectations is commonly associated with revolutions by peasantry, working classes, and often lower-middle-class groups.

Will and Revolution: The Meaning of Praxis

Historical, economic, psychological, and structural conditions and circumstances prepare men and women for a revolution; they do not make it! Will, leadership, organization, mass involvement and support, or even acquiescence are needed. Revolutionaries emphasize will; they stress the voluntaristic, organizational, and elitist nature of a revolution. They want "praxis" — they want action! Praxis is an act in a play. There are so many acts in a play — three, or four, or five — and we must see them all before we know what the players will do and what will be done to them. A praxis is therefore a time category within which planned actions take place. It combines revolutionary theory and action.

Proponents of praxis, however, put action first. There are two reasons: first, revolutionary action trains, educates, prepares, and above all, mobilizes groups such as students and the intelligentsia into a revolutionary formation that propagates its own ideology—a counterideology; second, praxis, the action of the revolution, appeals to what we called the "inherent ideology"—to all the discontents and the claims inherited by the culture, the history, and the traditions of a society. Through praxis, the discontent of the farmers may blend with the frustration of the unemployed and the resentment of ethnic or racial minority groups. In this manner, the counterideology gradually gains momentum and the official ideology, along with the State and its various institutions, are rendered impotent. The important thing is to begin—to move into action. "We engage the enemy and then we shall see." Both Napoleon, a great general, and Lenin, a great revolutionary, were fond of this expression.

Praxis, then, is the starting point of a revolution to reshape society. But it is also a vast effort consisting of a series of multiple acts of violence and defiance that may stretch over a long period of time, to create the conditions for a revolution—to shape the counterideology. Praxis, gradually and cumulatively, prepares the society for a new way of life with new institutions in accord with the counterideology that is gaining roots. However, both as a frontal revolutionary act and as a gradual process to develop a new revolutionary consciousness, praxis displays the same characteristics: emphasis on political will and leadership and the importance it gives to ideology. Praxis gives a lot of room to "subjective" as opposed to "objective" factors.

In contrast to liberalism and Marxism—both of them powerful revolutionary ideologies—the revolutionary ideologies to be discussed in this chapter and many nationalist ideologies, old and new, have been intensive and unstructured ideological movements. Not only do they appeal to powerful ethical imperatives but they pay little attention to history and circumstances in order to develop a coherent body of theory and to suggest tactics. They seem to have these things in common: to change by an effort of will and organization what has been deeply traced over many centuries, to reshape social, economic, and political life, and to refashion even human nature. Like the Commissar in Orwell's *1984*, many of the contemporary revolutionaries would say, "Forget all these notions about human nature; WE make human nature." All of them are committed to action—revolutionary action—even when the theory behind it is uncertain and the goals unclear. Action by itself and in itself will provide the experience that will guide the revolutionary leaders to reform and change. The revolutionary is expected to learn from the revolution. As with the anarchists, contemporary revolutionaries put the accent on will and action.

Anarchism

As with the terrorists today, anarchists stalked the earth in the latter part of the nineteenth century and continued until the 1930s. Of all revolutionaries they have been and are the most committed to direct action—to praxis.

326

*Old Voices and
New:
Nationalism, The
Third World,
Feminism,
Liberation
Theology, and
Revolution*

Anarchism as a doctrine was inspired by some of the greatest philosophers and was steeped profoundly in moral idealism. A number of powerful intellectual forces have shaped the doctrine of anarchism: Christianity, liberalism, socialism, and idealism were among the most important.

The many intellectual roots of anarchism account for the fragmentation of the movement that began at the First International in 1864. Some anarchists became fully committed to socialism, to the collective ownership of the means of production, while others insisted that some degree of private property should be permitted. Those who argued for collectivization, however, were opposed to State ownership. Indeed, Bakunin and his followers were in favor of the destruction of the State. They had no patience with bureaucracy even if it were to be controlled by the workers as the Marxists favored. The collective property would be handled by associations formed on a voluntary basis. In contrast to the Marxists, they favored direct workers' action — what became known as anarchosyndicalism. The workers by their own efforts, not through political and party action, would undertake to destroy the dominant position of the capitalists and emancipate themselves.

Finally, some anarchists became committed to personal direct action, including assassination, against all agents of authority. In the reaffirmation of their moral autonomy they became known as nihilist — accepting nothing and committed to the rejection of everything.

Violence and Terrorism

Unable to organize a movement, fragmented into many sects, and often propelled by sheer individual determination, the anarchists began to rely more and more on what we might call individual praxis — individual acts of violence to undermine authority, to disrupt order, and even to physically exterminate the "enemy." Assassinations and bombings became widespread. Terrorism was often directed against persons in authority irrespective of any consideration of responsibility or guilt. The more innocent and the more respected the victim and the more senseless the crime, the greater was the damage to the legal order. Random acts of terror such as theft, fire, bombings, and assassination became ennobling in themselves. Destruction wrought for its own sake — the rejection of anything and everything — became the political credo and practice of anarchists according to the *Catechism of an Anarchist,* attributed to Bakunin. The tsar of Russia and some of his ministers, the emperor of Germany, the president of the French Republic and the king of Italy, received special attention, which often resulted in their assassination. In 1893 a bomb, with hundreds of nails, exploded in the French Parliament. In 1901 President McKinley was assassinated by anarchists who had moved to the United States. As with terrorism today, the anarchist impulse was not without appeal. To the romantics and the discontented, many of the anarchists became heroes before they were sentenced to death and after they were executed. In some cases their burial places became places of pilgrimages. "What a magnificent gesture," said a French poet in commenting on the explosion of the bomb in the French Parliament. "Who cares about the victims!"

Ever since the 1960s there has been a return to terrorism that resembles the anarchist actions of the past. Small bands in Germany, France, Italy, and Spain have been responsible for the daily commission of crimes: the Red Brigade in Italy, Direct Action in France, the Baader-Meinhof band in Germany, the Weathermen and the Symbionese Liberation Army in the United States, and others in Japan, Holland, and of course the Middle East. Heads of state, prime ministers, army officials, judges, police officers, and ambassadors have been assassinated. Often there are identifiable political motives and reasons. Acts of violence are committed in the name of separatism, as in Spain or Corsica, and in the name of national identification and autonomy, as among the Palestinians. But generally the philosophy today is not very different from what it was in the past — to discredit the established order and to prepare for a revolutionary change whose goals are unclear.

The New Left

The term "new left," or "radical left," is used to describe the general movement of agitation, protest, and revolt organized and led, in great part, by young people and university students in the 1960s. The system under

The new left in America. Confrontation with the National Guard, Chicago, 1968. *(Photo: UPI)*

328

*Old Voices and
New:
Nationalism, The
Third World,
Feminism,
Liberation
Theology, and
Revolution*

attack was, and continues to be, that of the modern industrialized societies — democratic or not. As seen by its opponents, the system's major characteristics are repressiveness and comprehensiveness; it is bureaucratic,
impersonal, and authoritarian. Everything is subordinated to management, thanks to the advances of technology; production is geared to material
gain and profit; and standards of measurement and evaluation become exclusively quantitative. The State, hand in hand with the huge industrial organizations, socializes people to accept the values the system manufactures —
the ideology of consumerism, wasteful production, and the inculcation of
work discipline. The individual becomes an empty shell, losing all capacity for
pleasure, joy, and fulfillment. He or she becomes "dehumanized." This is the
system the new left paints in order to call for its destruction.

One of the high points of the new left movement was the uprising of
May and June 1968 in Paris and many other French cities. The students led
the way by striking, occupying the universities, throwing out their professors, deriding the meaning and validity of what they were being taught,
and asking for a new university — the "antiuniversity." The revolt spread
to workers, public servants, and salaried personnel. Public buildings were
occupied, TV and radio stations taken over, barricades built, battles with
the "forces of order" fought, and the students seemed on the verge of
taking power. In an unprecedented show of spontaneity, and against the
instructions of their trade union and political leaders, the French workers
began to join. They went on strike, occupied factories, and brought the
whole economy to a standstill. One firm after another, one organization
after another, one administration after another, and one service after another, were taken over by those who worked in them. Theaters, newspapers, the opera, the ballet, and even soccer teams were taken over by actors,
reporters, singers, dancers, and players. The only organization not taken
over was the Paris Stock Exchange — it was set on fire!

Another high point in the political and revolutionary activity of the
new left took place in the United States at the Democratic party convention
held in Chicago at the end of August 1968. Demonstrations against the war
in Vietnam had already reached a peak, forcing Lyndon Johnson to an-
nounce that he would not seek renomination. A number of students and
leftist organizations decided to demonstrate at the Chicago convention
and to force a peace candidate upon the Democratic party. But their demands were broader, and the participants ranged from those who favored
peace and were against the military draft to genuine revolutionaries who
were driven by the vision of a new society. The National Mobilization
Committee to End the War in Vietnam (a loose organization which appealed to all people who were against the war) played an important role.
In addition, there were the Committee for an Open Convention, seeking the
nomination of Eugene McCarthy; the Students for Democratic Society; and
the Youth International Party (Yippies), advocates of the "counterculture."

The new left and the student uprisings should be put in their proper
historical and intellectual context. Like anarchism, the new left represented
the longstanding grievances against industrialization and the impersonality

and coerciveness of modern society with its complexity—all of which were seen to distort human nature and account for "alienation." Even though the movement subsided in the 1980s—especially among the young who spearheaded it—its message of protest and rejection is by no means forgotten.

Alienation

Use of the term "alienation" to describe the state of mind of the people living in an industrialized society appears more often in the literature of the new left than the word "spirit" in the Bible. To be alienated is to be a stranger (alien); in French, the word means insane (*aliené*). In Roman law the term applied to those who could not legally make decisions: the *alieni juris* (women, slaves, minors) were under the jurisdiction of somebody else who made decisions for them and about them. Another word for alienation is "estrangement"—being or feeling like a stranger. Its opposite is "integration" or "participation," wherein an individual feels like part of a whole—whether family, neighborhood, university, factory, city, State, and so on. How to make individuals feel part of the whole, how to make them into social beings without depriving them of their freedoms, individuality, and spontaneity, and how to reconcile the "natural" person with the "social" being has been one of the major and most difficult problems in political philosophy.

No matter how you look at it, alienation, with its consequences, is very serious. To be a stranger in your own home, village, town, or factory is not only to be alone but also to be without means to reach out into the world and to the people surrounding you, and to be unable to communicate with them. Even worse, it is a state of mind that makes it difficult for the alienated individual to receive messages and communications from others. He or she shuts them off: the individual is literally "spaced out." The more the society develops new and rapid mechanisms of communication, the more individual loneliness becomes unbearable. There is boredom at first, then frustration, and then sheer anger. The individual searches for an outlet to find togetherness, love, and fellowship, but in vain. Most other individuals are in the same state of mind, and whatever communication there is among them is superficial—skin deep. All share the same feeling of estrangement. The mass society is a state of "collective loneliness"—a lonely crowd[2]—as anybody who walks the streets of a big city or drives a car during the rush hour can tell. The social person has devoured the individual. Spontaneity, creativity, desire, pleasure are gone. What has brought this situation about? The answer is clear: the modern industrialized society—capitalist or not!

2. The term is the title of David Reisman's path-breaking book, *The Lonely Crowd*. New Haven, Conn.: Yale U.P., 1950.

330

*Old Voices and
New:
Nationalism, The
Third World,
Feminism,
Liberation
Theology, and
Revolution*

"Under the cobblestones, the beach!" This is a street scene from the 1968
student uprising in Paris. (*Photo: Wide World Photos*)

The individual entrepreneur was replaced by the big corporation;
concentration led to the increase of power and decision making for some,
while producing a large number of salaried without power. Big firms began
to dominate the economy. At the same time, advanced technology spread not
only to production but to all forms of social life. Big organizations and new
organizational techniques of management created new forms of control that
subordinated the individual. Mechanization became the rule. Mario Savio,
one of the leaders of the new left in the United States, wrote:

There is a time when the operation of the machine becomes so odious, makes you so sick at heart that you can't take part; you can't even tacitly take part, and you've got to put your bodies upon the levers, upon all the apparatus and you've got to make it stop.[3]

The demand for efficiency and profit develops its own logic, which leads to the production of goods as an end in itself without reference to social goals. Herbert Marcuse, philosopher of the new left, claims that in advanced industrialized societies

the technical apparatus of production and distribution (with an increased sector of automation) functions not as the sum total of mere instruments which can be isolated from their social and political effects, but rather as a system that determines . . . the product of the apparatus as well as the operations of servicing and extending it. . . . The productive apparatus tends *to become totalitarian to the extent to which it determines not only the socially needed occupations and skills and attitudes but also individual needs and aspirations.*[4]

To put this idea quite simply: Society as a whole is supposed to be run by a managerial and technologic elite which, in the name of efficiency and profit, develops methods of organization and coordination that propagate a conformist ideology to its methods and goals. All individuals are required to "march in step." Production is geared to those needs that will keep the industrial apparatus working, even if production is not geared to real needs. Ideology, however, will be used to make the objects produced *seem* desirable and "real." The individual is made to conform to the needs of management, organization, and technology. Thus, the social man leaves behind him the inner man and his own freedom to choose and decide. The technological rationality of the industrialized society

reveals its political character as it becomes the great vehicle of better domination, creating a truly totalitarian universe in which society and nature, mind and body, are kept in a permanent state of mobilization for the defense of their universe.[5]

There can be no better definition of the Nazi principle of "synchronization" which we discussed earlier.

The Role of Ideology

The absorption of the individual into the system of the advanced industrialized societies is a gradual process, and ideology plays the crucial role. It rationalizes and legitimizes production and efficiency; socializes the

3. Massimo Teodori (ed.), *The New Left: A Documentary History*, p. 156.
4. Marcuse, *One Dimensional Man*, p. xv.
5. Marcuse, op. cit.

332

*Old Voices and
New:
Nationalism, The
Third World,
Feminism,
Liberation
Theology, and
Revolution*

young people in the school and the university to accept them; and sets the tone for their preparation to play special roles within the system. It is primarily in the ideology of production that consumerism and material satisfactions predominate. Modernization and growth are viewed exclusively in quantitative terms. It is a materialist ethic that gradually invades our lives until we can no longer refute or avoid it. It affects our moral judgments, our tastes, our pleasures, and our leisure time. Political and ethical considerations are subordinated to it. Education, performance, and lifestyles are reduced to pure material considerations that can be checked, double-checked, and tabulated.

The student will notice here the sharp departure of the new left from the classic Marxist critique. The argument against capitalism is not that it fails to produce enough but that it produces a great deal! The indictment made by the new left is that capitalism has created abundance and continues to be capable of producing an ever-growing variety of material goods. It has become dangerous to all of us precisely because of its efficiency and its ability to give us a relative degree of well-being. It is because of this efficiency that democratic capitalism has managed to integrate everybody, or virtually everybody, within its own logic and ideology. Its tentacles have spread into every home, and into every social, economic, political, or religious group. It is a threat to all of us because it has proven so successful.

The Explosion

The uprising against the industrial society of our times can come only in the form of a moral outburst. It will stem from moral indignation, and its objective will be moral rehabilitation. It will not spring from deprivation, nor will it come from the workers. It will come from all those who have maintained their inner self intact from the ideological contamination the advanced industrial societies spread. It will come from the men and women who have somehow managed to maintain their true consciousness and who will defy the society that tries to mold and shape them.

But defiance is not an explosion. An explosion suggests destruction, not simply a change in the management or leadership of society, nor just the replacement of one class by another as in Marxism. An explosion is the destruction of the dominant ideology, the fundamental values of society, and of the social relations and working practices that its ideology legitimizes.

What are they to be replaced with? Although the new left makes a number of suggestions, there is no blueprint; many among its supporters would argue that none is needed. A prisoner, they would say, must escape from the jail first before he begins to think of where he will go.

Revolutions follow careful guidelines, which revolutionaries provide. They spell out organization, discipline, leadership, and specific procedures. The new left has produced virtually no such guidelines. By appealing directly to the individual conscience they neglect the requirements of common organized effort. In fact, they seem to rely to a great degree on anarchy as the only creative response to organization and totalitarian control. But even so, an explosion requires, as any student of physics or chemistry knows, the bringing together of some ingredients, substances, or chemicals. The explosion of society also requires some such social and human ingredients. What are they?

The three essential elements are *imagination, action,* and *rejection.* All three are linked together in terms of a deeply moral disavowal, almost religious in its fervor, of the ways of life of our contemporary industrialized societies.

Imagination. The French sociologist Alain Touraine points out that the revolution of the students and the new left in general was "the revolution of the imagination" and that, perhaps because of it, it turned out to be "an imaginary revolution."[6] "Be realistic; think of the impossible"; "Under the cobblestones, the beach" — these were two recurring slogans of the French students during their uprising in 1968. Imagination is clearly seen as the outlet for the enslaved self. It is the vision of a new world, without police officers, coercion, rules, roles, and duties; where time will not be measured by minutes and hours; material needs will no longer weigh on our minds; desires will be fulfilled almost instantly; where intuition will provide for truth that can be "understood" and not measured and verified; where there will be no masters, no bosses, no hierarchies; where struggle, domestic and international, will give place to peace; where, finally, everything that separates us from each other — walls, rooms, offices, blocks, and national boundaries — will be erased. There will be no "No Trespass" signs anywhere: this will be the world of the "real self," of the natural self — spontaneous, creative, intuitive, and almost instinctual. It is the exact opposite of the alienated self. It is the real "I," not the fabricated and collective "we."

Action. Imagination must be coupled with action. To be "engaged" is essential not only to promote one's ends but to understand them better. "Being" should not be, and cannot be, separated from "doing." Theory must lead to action and action will refine theory. For it is only in action, and only by acting, that an individual can "enter into the essence of things" and understand them fully. The new left discards objectivity and the separation between the actor and the object. The actor must "enter into" the object. To think of something in a detached way is meaningless, but to think of something and to do it is the essence of comprehension. The new left is therefore activist, but action is not an instrument to attain predetermined objectives. It is, rather, essential to the understanding and the refining of objectives. We learn while we act, and we act in order to learn! Praxis becomes all-important.

Rejection. Imagination and action, however, must both be inspired by a powerful personal and moral rejection of the existing order of things. In the philosophy of the new left there are many powerful negations — as many as in the totalitarian movements we discussed earlier. The new left is

6. Touraine, *The May Movement.*

distinctly anti-State, antinationalist, antiauthoritarian, antiliberal, antiintellectual, and against democratic and parliamentary institutions.

The Counterculture

What will the world be like after the explosion? The revolution of the imagination will result in a utopia. Even if there is no comprehensive blueprint, and even if the new left assumes that once the revolution is started it will gain momentum and shape as the people gain knowledge from the revolutionary experience, there are enough bits and pieces that we can put together. What emerges from them, as Theodore Roszak points out, is a "vision."[7]

In the vision of the future new society three elements predominate: *anarchism, participation,* and the *quality of life.*

Anarchism   The proponents of the new left echo some of the same anarchist themes: rejection of bigness, destruction of authority and political and economic organizational hierarchies and, of course, elimination of the State. They emphasize working and living in small groups—communes and associations through which individuals control their environment, organize their work, and take charge of their own affairs. The new left shares with the anarchists the same quest for individualization, for spontaneity and creativity, and for free play. They too reject private property in favor of communal or associational collectivism. They also believe in the use of force and direct action and share the anarchists' outright moral rejections of existing society. A small number of activists among the new left have joined conspiratorial and terrorist organizations bent upon destruction and political assassination.

Participation   For the new left, participation of all in the management of common affairs is one of the most potent instruments for putting an end to alienation. Limited forms of participation, especially of the workers in industrial firms, have been practiced in many countries. They involve consultations, profit-sharing, and the autonomy of the workers to determine their working conditions. They do not question, however, the basic rules of the capitalistic economy with regard to property ownership and the managerial and hierarchical organization of the firms.

The demands of the new left are far more comprehensive. First, they apply not only to industrial firms and economic activities, but to all others, political, social, and cultural; all those involved in a given activity and in any organization that makes decisions that affect them should participate in making them. Second, the new left has specific notions about organizational structures, advocating their reduction in size and complexity. Finally, it proposes the socialization of all economic units that are privately owned. Participation is, in effect, equivalent to socialism plus internal democracy.

7. Theodore Roszak, *The Making of a Counter-Culture.*

The Quality of Life   One of the recurrent themes of the new left and the many environmentalist groups it has spawned is the degradation (past, present, and future) of the quality of our lives in the industrially advanced societies. Our environment has been used and abused for the sake of immediate benefits and profits. Our forests have been spoiled, lakes and rivers polluted, neighborhoods uprooted in the name of urban renewal, mountains deformed by ugly mining scars, and millions of Americans (and even larger numbers of Europeans) live in areas where the air is fast becoming unbreathable. Cities themselves grow, as population growth continues unchecked, without any consideration to health and beauty and without the realization that cities are for people to live together. High structures have replaced neighborhoods, and neighborly amenities have given place to supermarkets, superhospitals, and multi-universities. Every effort should be made to put an end to the defilement of our natural environment and to restore it to its original purity.

This, then, is the new world the new left painted in the sixties and seventies, when the movement began to subside. For collectivity, read individualism; for bigness, smallness; for complexity, simplicity; for imposition, self-government; for coercion, freedom; for hierarchy, equality; for private property, socialism; for profit, social need; for materialism, spirituality; for war, peace; for competition, cooperation; for science and technology, intuition and spontaneity; for knowledge, experience; for reason, feeling. It is a different, new, and shiny world. One of its advocates stated that the first step of the revolution will be "to proclaim a new heaven and a new earth so vast, so marvelous that the inordinate claims of technical expertise must of necessity withdraw in the presence of such a splendor to a subordinate and marginal status in the lives of men."[8] It was and it remains a call for religious and moral reawakening.

Revolutionary Guerrillas

Guerrilla warfare has been one of the major instruments of revolutions in much of the colonial world. These revolutions have been directed against a colonial power and against the native rulers, landowners, or a bourgeoisie that act on behalf of the interests or in a manner congruent with the interests of a colonial power (and, as in the case of Latin America, of a dominant, even if not a formally colonial power). The themes invariably are: national independence and the radical overhaul of social and economic relations in the direction of socialism. El Salvador, Guatemala, Nicaragua, Colombia (and possibly other countries of Central and South America) appear to be following in the steps of Algeria, China, Vietnam, and many of the former African and Asian colonies.

8. Roszak, op. cit., p. 240.

336

*Old Voices and
New:
Nationalism, The
Third World,
Feminism,
Liberation
Theology, and
Revolution*

Today, Latin America is one of the last remaining areas of the world where guerrilla revolutions are taking place to undermine the dominant elites and their major arsenal of support—the United States. They all are inspired, informed, and, as some point out with considerable justice, are supported by the Cuban revolutionary experience of the 1950s and by direct Cuban military, financial, and technical support. Cuba has become a model for Latin America revolutionaries as the Soviet Union was for European communists after 1917. The ideology of the various guerrilla movements remains in name "Marxism-Leninism."

Guerrilla revolutionary warfare depends, above all, on the organization of a small avant-garde that will lead the masses, mostly the peasantry, into an insurrectional struggle. It is synonymous with praxis. There is a great deal of discussion about the existing conditions—are they "ripe" for a revolution or not? But many believe that even if they are not, the proper action—military and political—will create these conditions. Ché Guevara, considered one of the foremost theoreticians of guerrilla warfare for Latin America, wrote the catechism, or at least what has been taken as such in Latin America, for guerrilla revolutionary warfare.[9] There are three basic precepts and three phases to a successful guerrilla revolution.

The three precepts are:

1. Popular forces can win a war against an army.
2. It is not always necessary to wait until the conditions for making revolution exist; the "insurrectional focus" can create them.
3. In underdeveloped America, the countryside is the basic area for the armed fighting.

The three phases correspond to:

1. The establishment and the consolidation of the "insurrectional focus"
2. Guerrilla warfare against the armed forces of the enemy and the gradual conquest of the hearts and minds of the people, particularly the peasantry
3. The weakening of the governmental forces and, with it, the final assault on them and the takeover of political and economic power by the leadership of guerrilla forces.

In a guerrilla warfare there are many ups and downs. What counts above all is the development of an awareness on the part of the people that their deliverance is possible. A guerrilla war may fail, but the awareness will remain to spark future guerrilla warlike efforts. Praxis shapes the revolutionary even if the revolution fails.

According to Ché Guevara, the starting point in the guerrilla revolutionary war is the establishment of what has been called an "insurrectional focus" ("foco" in Spanish means a hearth, a home, a base in broad terms). It is where the guerrillas find shelter, rest, food, and ammunitions, and

9. Ché Guevara, *Guerrilla Warfare.*

Moving in small groups amidst friendly peasants, the guerrillas gradually undermine the will and organization of the government and its armed force. (*Photo: Wide World Photos*)

where they plan their moves. The "home," in order to be secure, must be located in a hospitable environment — among friendly peasants — and ideally should be immune from enemy detection and direct threats. The establishment of such an insurrectional base is the first step in a long political and military struggle, but it is an irreversible step as it commits the leadership to the revolution.

In the strategy of guerrilla warfare the proper balance between military and political organization remains uncertain. Many claimed that Ché, and also Regis Debray, a French intellectual and activist who spent many years among Latin American guerrillas and in Latin American jails, unduly stressed military action without the proper political preparation. By excluding the towns from the revolutionary effort, they disassociated the guerrillas from the urban proletariat which in some Latin American countries, Bolivia, Peru, Chile, Venezuela, and so on, is strong and can develop a revolutionary consciousness. Also, by insisting on will and organization they underestimated the significance of the specific circumstances, history, culture, and the political situation that distinguish one Latin American country from another.[10]

10. Generally most Latin American communist parties disassociated themselves from Castro and Ché Guevara. They stressed a "nonviolent" revolutionary strategy asserting that conditions for a revolutionary takeover were not ripe.

Some pertinent questions have also been raised about the emphasis placed on the "insurrectional focus." Even if it is not a military basis, it has been thought of in military terms. The "focus" may prove vulnerable unless it finds itself in a particularly hospitable terrain. This requires advance political preparation long before the insurrection. The inhabitants of the area in which it is situated must become friendly and supportive.

Ché, more than twenty years ago, with a small band of twenty revolutionaries undertook to establish an "insurrectional focus" in Bolivia in order to make a revolution in Bolivia and to ignite it throughout the whole of Latin America. He failed. The peasantry, mostly Indians, was not ready; the revolutionary ideology he attempted to spread fell upon deaf ears. The president of Bolivia, at the time, was an active and popular man who had undertaken many liberal and even socialist reforms including land reform. Ché and his band, after some successful skirmishes with the governmental forces, found themselves isolated like fish out of water. They were destroyed, but they also created a legend for themselves and for the revolution.

Today, in many parts of Central America, guerrilla warfare and insurrectional uprisings are ever-present. A committed avant-garde continues to seek the support of the peasantry, the poor, and the underprivileged in order to oust from power the political and economic elites that have dominated them for so long. What accounts for the revolutionary efforts and their successes, against governments supported by the United States, is that the people have been mobilized by the will and the organization of a few, in terms of an ideology that promises so much to the many. Guerrillas, in the words of Ché Guevara, are "the Jesuits of the revolution" committed to spreading the revolutionary faith far and wide.

Bibliography

Albright, David E. (ed.). *Communism in Africa.* Bloomington: Indiana U.P., 1980.

Aron, Raymond. *The Elusive Revolution.* London: Pall Mall, 1969.

Bakunin, M. A. *The Political Philosophy of Bakunin.* Edited and compiled by G. P. Maximoff. New York: Free Press, 1953.

Bouchier, David. *Ideal and Revolution: New Ideologies of Liberation in Britain and the United States.* London: Edward Arnold, 1978.

Brinton, Crane. *Anatomy of Revolution.* Englewood Cliffs, N.J.: Prentice-Hall, 1939.

Brown, Bernard E. *Protest in Paris: Anatomy of a Revolt.* Morristown, N.J.: General Learning Press, 1974.

Carmichael, Stokely, and Hamilton, Charles V. *Black Power: The Politics of Liberation in America.* New York: Vintage Books, 1967.

Carr, E. H. *Michael Bakunin.* New York: Vintage, 1937.

Carter, A. *The Political Theory of Anarchism.* New York: Harper & Row, 1971.

Chaliand, Gerard. *Revolution in the Third World.* Harmondsworth, England: Penguin, 1978.

Cleaver, Eldridge. *Soul on Ice.* New York: Dell, 1965.

Cohn-Bendit, Daniel and Gabriel. *Obsolete Communism: The Left-Wing Alternative.* London: André Deutsch, 1968.

Davies, James C. (ed.). *When Men Revolt and Why*. New York: Free Press, 1971.

Desfosses, Helen, and Levesque, Jacques (eds.). *Socialism in the Third World*. New York: Praeger, 1975.

Draper, Hal. *Berkeley: The New Student Revolt*. New York: Grove Press, 1965.

Ellis, John. *A Short History of Guerrilla Warfare*. London: Ian Allan, 1975.

Erikson, Erik H. (ed.). *The Challenge of Youth*. New York: Anchor, 1965.

Fanon, Frantz. *The Wretched of the Earth*. Trans. Constance Farrington. New York: Grove Press, 1963.

Gerassi, John (ed.). *Venceremos! The Speeches and Writings of Ernesto Ché Guevara*. New York: Simon & Schuster, 1968.

Giap, Vo Nguyen. *The Military Art of People's War: Selected Writings*. New York: Monthly Review Press, 1970.

Goldthorpe, J. E. *The Sociology of the Third World: Disparity and Involvement*. Cambridge, England: Cambridge U.P., 1975.

Guevara, Ché. *Guerrilla Warfare*. New York: MR Press, 1961.

Gurr, Ted Robert. *Why Men Rebel*. Princeton, N.J.: Princeton U.P., 1970.

Gusfield, Joseph R. *Protest, Reform and Revolt: A Reader in Social Movements*. New York: Wiley, 1970.

Hoffman, Abbie (pseud. Free). *Revolution for the Hell of It*. New York: Dial Press, 1968.

Jacobs, Paul, and Landau, Saul. *The New Radicals*. New York: Vintage, 1966.

Kanter, Rosabeth Moss. *Commitment and Community: Communes and Utopias in Sociological Perspective*. Cambridge, Mass.: Harvard U.P., 1972.

Kaplan, Lawrence. *Revolutions: A Comparative Study from Cromwell to Castro*. New York: Vintage, 1973.

Keniston, Kenneth. *Young Radicals: Notes on Committed Youth*. New York: Harcourt Brace Jovanovich, 1968.

Kerouac, Jack. *On the Road*. New York: New American Library, 1957.

Lamb, Robert, et al. *Political Alienation*. New York: St. Martin's Press, 1975.

Laqueur, Walter. *A Guerrilla Reader: A Historical Anthology*. New York: Meridian, 1977.

Lipset, Seymour Martin, and Altbach, Philip G. (eds.). *Students in Revolt*. Boston: Houghton Mifflin, 1969.

Long, Priscilla (ed.). *The New Left: A Collection of Essays*. Boston: Porter Sargent, 1970.

Mao Tse-tung. *On Guerrilla Warfare*. New York: Praeger, 1961.

Marcuse, Herbert. *One-Dimensional Man*. Boston: Beacon Press, 1968.

Miles, Michael W. *The Radical Probe: The Logic of Student Rebellion*. New York: Athenaeum, 1973.

Nasser, Gamal Abdel. *The Philosophy of the Revolution*. Buffalo, N.Y.: Smith, Keynes & Marshall, 1959.

Olman, B. *Alienation*. New York: Cambridge U.P., 1977.

Orwell, George. *1984*. New York: New American Library, 1949.

Reich, Charles. *The Greening of America*. New York: Bantam, 1971.

Roszak, Theodore. *The Making of a Counter-Culture*. New York: Doubleday, 1969.

Rudi, George. *Ideology and Popular Protest*. New York: Pantheon Books, 1980.

Sale, Kirkpatrick. *SDS*. New York: Vintage, 1973.

Sargent, Lyman T. *The Ideology of the New Left*. Homewood, Ill.: Dorsey, 1972.

Sargent Lyman Tower. *New Left Thought: An Introduction*. Homewood, Ill.: Dorsey Press, 1972.

Teodori, Massimo (ed.). *The New Left: A Documentary History*. New York: Bobbs-Merrill, 1969.

Touraine, Alain. *The May Movement*. New York: Random House, 1971.

340

*Old Voices and
New:
Nationalism, The
Third World,
Feminism,
Liberation
Theology, and
Revolution*

Trotsky, Leon. *Terrorism and Communism: A Reply to Karl Kautsky.* Ann Arbor: University of Michigan Press, 1965.

Ulam, Adam. *The Unfinished Revolution.* (Rev. ed.) Boulder, Colo.: Westview Press, 1979.

Vickers, George R. *The Formation of the New Left: The Early Years.* Lexington, Mass.: Lexington Books, 1975.

von der Mehden, Fred R. *Comparative Political Violence.* Englewood Cliffs, N.J.: Prentice-Hall, 1973.

Wolf, Eric. *Peasant Wars in the Twentieth Century.* New York: Harper & Row, 1965.

Wood, James L. *The New Left Ideology: Its Dimensions and Development.* Beverly Hills: Sage Publications, 1975.

Yablonsky, Lewis. *The Hippie Trip.* New York: Pegasus, 1968.

Index

343

explosion of, 332–334
ideology of, 331–332
principle of participation, 334
Nicaragua, 261, 310, 312, 335
Nietzsche, Friedrich, 183, 188
Nigeria, 247
Nihilism, 326
1984 (Orwell), 108, 320, 325
Norway, 48
Novak, Michael, 314
Nyere, Julius Kambarage, 270

Objective economic conditions, 122
O'Connor, Feargus, 53
Oliver, Sydney, 52
On Liberty (Mill), 31, 38
Organization of Afro-American
    Unity, 250
Orthopraxis, 304
Orwell, George, 108, 320–321, 325
Ottoman Empire, 242
Our Political Tasks (Trotsky), 129
Owen, Robert, 57

Paine, Tom, 322
Pankhurst, Christian, 276
Paternalism, 92
Paul, St., 291
Pauperization, law of, 116–118
Peaceful coexistence, 152, 155
Peasantry
    liberation theology and, 307, 312
    Maoism and, 172–173
Perestroika, 153–154
Pericles, 19–20
Perkins, Frances, 280
Personality theory of
    totalitarianism, 222–223
Personal liberty, 24
Peru, 292, 312, 317, 337
Pervasiveness, as criterion, 14
Philippines, the, 254, 261, 265
Philips, Howard, 102
Philosophy, defined, 3
Place, Francis, 53
Plato, 3, 5, 7, 109, 274, 284
Pluralism, 6, 41–42
Poland, 46, 48, 157, 180
Political action, 11–12
Political authority, 7
Political core of liberalism, 32–38
Political ideology
    criteria of choice and, 14–16
    major themes, 4–8
    types of, 12–14
    uses of, 8–12

Political nations, 239
Political parties, 47
    Nazism and, 203
Popular sovereignty, 36–38
Populism, 230
Populorum Progressio, 296, 298
Portugal, 45, 46
Positive state, 20–21
Praxis (action), 235
    liberation theology, 304, 307–311
    revolution and, 324–325
Propaganda, 202
Property, and equality, 7–8
Protestantism, 209
Protocols of the Elders of Zion, The,
    204, 226–227
Psychological interpretations of
    totalitarianism, 220–221

Qaddafi, Muammar al-, 267, 268,
    269
Quadregissimo Anno, 77
Quality of life, 335

Race
    nationalism and, 205–206, 240,
    259
    Nazism and, 204
Radical democracy, 52–56
Radical feminism, 282–284, 287
Radical ideology, 13–14
Radical Left. *See* New Left
Ratzinger, Joseph Cardinal, 299,
    315
Reagan, Ronald, 98, 102, 229
Red Brigade, 71, 327
Reformist ideology, 13–14
Rejection, 333–334
Religion. *See also* Catholic Church:
    Christianity; Liberation
    theology
    conservatism and, 99–102
    Father Coughlin and, 226
    Ku Klux Klan and, 225, 226
    nationalism and, 240
    Nazism and, 209
Religious toleration, 45
Renan, Joseph Ernest, 241
Representation, 32–35, 46–47
Republic, The (Plato), 5, 109
Rerum Novarum, 76
Revisionism, 61–63, 126–127
Revolution, 320–338
    anarchism and, 325–327
    Eurocommunism and, 179
    guerrilla warfare and, 335–338

Lenin and, 130, 134–135
Marx and, 118–125, 321, 322,
    323–324
nature of, 321–325
New Left and, 327–335
Revolutionary Command Council,
    269
Revolutionary ideology, 13–14
Rightist paramilitary groups,
    229–230
Robertson, Pat, 100, 102
Robespierre, Maximilien, 244
Rockwell, Lincoln, 230
Roe v. Wade, 280, 285
Rome, March on, 218
Roosevelt, Eleanor, 280
Roszak, Theodore, 334
Rousseau, Jean Jacques, 20, 36–38,
    56–57, 242, 243, 322
Russia, 45, 46, 139, 242. *See also*
    Soviet communism; Soviet
    Union
Russian Social-Democratic
    Workers' Congress (1903),
    133

SA (Brownshirts), 200
Sandinistas, 312
Sartre, Jean-Paul, 143, 254
Savio, Mario, 330–331
Second General Council of the
    Latin American Episcopate
    (Medellin – 1968), 299–301
Second Vatican Council, 292,
    293–297, 300, 302, 309
Segundo, Juan Luis, 293
Self-determination, 48, 241–242
Self-management, 165–166
Self-regarding acts, 39–41
Senghor, Leopold, 257, 265
Separatism, 248–252
Shaw, George Bernard, 58–59
Sheffield Female Political
    Association, 275
Shelley, Percy Bysshe, 56
Sin, collective, 306–307
Slavery, 45
Smith, Adam, 20, 26–28, 48, 54, 55,
    112
Social Contract (Rousseau), 20
Social criticism, 11
Social Darwinism, 190–191
Social Democratic Party
    (Germany), 71, 72, 126, 205
Social liberty, 25
Social Security, 65